74

RESEARCH IN
RELIGIOUS BEHAVIOR:
SELECTED READINGS

RESEARCH IN RELIGIOUS BEHAVIOR: SELECTED READINGS

Edited by

BENJAMIN BEIT-HALLAHMI

The University of Michigan

BROOKS/COLE PUBLISHING COMPANY
MONTEREY, CALIFORNIA

A Division of Wadsworth Publishing Company, Inc.

ISBN: 0-8185-0091-3

L. C. Catalog Card No: 72-95822

Printed in the United States of America

1 2 3 4 5 6 7 8 9 10---77 76 75 74 73

PREFACE

The idea that religious behavior is a legitimate subject for empirical research still surprises
some people, including some behavioral scientists.
Religion has been called a "taboo topic" in psychology and has been described as a neglected area in
sociology. After a golden age of theory and research on religion around the turn of the century,
interest in this area has almost vanished from the
social-science scene. The past decade has seen a
renewal of interest and research on religion as a
variable in social and private behavior. The increase has been not only in volume but also in
quality. The aim of this volume is to present a
selection of empirical studies dealing with several
dimensions and correlates of religious behavior.
No attempt to suggest or imply a unified, encompass-
ing approach is made. The intent is to select representative research based on several and varied
approaches.

Studies of religious behavior are often saddled
with unstated and nebulous assumptions and suggestions. A statement of the editor's own assumptions
(and biases) seems essential to the understanding of
this project. Religious behavior is regarded as the
proper study of the social sciences. Only the special postulates that are needed when analyzing other
kinds of human activity are needed for the analysis
of religion. The terms to be used in an analysis of
religious behavior should be the same ones used in

any discussion of learned social behavior, such as
attitudes, norms, expectations, and needs. Religion
is defined here as a system of beliefs and practices
that refers to a sacred, "supernatural" domain,
deities, or "supreme beings." The research presented
here deals with Western religion, and the limits of
its generalizability should be noted. Most of the
studies deal with specific situations in the United
States. A final basic assumption that should be
stated is implicit in the selection of interdisciplinary material: such a complex phenomenon as religion cannot be explained by a single research
discipline.

The term "behavior" in the title of this volume
is not meant to drive away those who are interested
in religious beliefs and practices. It was chosen as
a common denominator covering beliefs, practices, reported and observed experiences, and all their correlates. The choice of the term "behavior" also under-
lines a deliberate interest in both observation and
interpretation. As to methods of measurement, none
was banished, including anthropological field observations, questionnaires, surveys, and psychological
tests. Belief in the legitimacy and usefulness of
various observation and measurement approaches has
been the guideline in selecting the articles included.
Each one of them is intended to illustrate an issue,
a methodology, and an implication for the understanding of religious behavior. Each selection should
introduce the reader to additional sources, through
a review of the relevant literature and additional
references.

This book is an introduction to the research
literature on religious behavior. By presenting a
cross-section of significant research, it will guide
the reader to further interest and involvement. The
book is intended primarily for students in courses
on the psychology of religion, sociology of religion,
social psychology, and developmental psychology.
Because of its interdisciplinary approach, it can
be used as instructional material by psychologists,
sociologists, and political scientists. It is hoped
that the book will be of use to any social scientist

working in the field of religious behavior and also
to educated laymen in other fields.
  Since this is a collection of previously published articles, my major debt of gratitude is to
the various publishers and authors who have given
their permission to use the materials. From many
of the contributors I have received not only permission and cooperation but also interest and en-
couragement. For these I am doubly grateful. I
would also like to thank reviewers Benton Johnson
of the University of Oregon and David Wulff of
Wheaton College.

                                    Benjamin Beit-Hallahmi

CONTENTS

PART ONE
RELIGIOUS SOCIALIZATION

PIAGET'S SEMI-CLINICAL INTERVIEW AND THE STUDY OF SPONTANEOUS RELIGION

DAVID ELKIND

Editor's introduction. Most religious people
acquire their faith not by choice but through
the destiny (or accident) of being born into
a certain family. As they grow up, they gradually learn more about the family's belief
system, and, in most cases, are expected to
follow it. Whether they do or not may depend
on the particular techniques of religious socialization in their family. We still know
very little about these socialization processes
and children's reactions to them. The fact
that most people learn their religious beliefs
within their families of origin is so obvious
that it tends to be overlooked. With the exception of a few observational reports, systematic research on this early learning process
is scant. Consequently, we encounter statements regarding the "child's conception of God"
based more often on theology than on psychology.
  Elkind is one of the few psychologists who
have listened to what children say about religious concepts, and in this article he describes
his method. His approach is cognitive. He is
not interested in whether or not the child's

From *Journal for the Scientific Study of Religion,*
1964, 4, 40-47. Reprinted with permission.

conception of religion is related to his conceptions of his parents, or whether it correlates with any other aspect of the child's
behavior. Religion, according to Elkind, is
first and foremost a group of concepts that
has to be grasped cognitively by the child.
Elkind is interested in the *spontaneous expressions* of religious ideas, reflecting the
child's understanding of religious concepts
at various stages of development. The term
"spontaneous" was borrowed from Piaget, together with the cognitive-stage approach and
the semi-clinical interview method. The use
of the word "spontaneous" in the title may
seem misleading without a full understanding
of its connotation. Its meaning here becomes
clear in the context of Piaget's definition of
"spontaneous convictions," which are expressed
when the child responds "quickly, without reflection, because he has already formulated the
solution or because it was latently formulated."
  Elkind used the semi-clinical interview in
three studies to investigate the development
of religious identity in Jewish, Catholic, and
Congregational Protestant children. The richness of findings seems to justify the use of
this technique. The possibilities inherent in
it seem unlimited: by devising new interview
procedures the investigator can cover most
aspects of religious socialization. The article
focuses on the method used and summarizes some
important findings. The only criticism I have
of Elkind's study has to do with his starting
point. The question is whether a cognitive
approach alone is sufficient or whether it
should be balanced by other views. Such other
viewpoints, covering parental roles, personality development, and non-religious thinking,
are presented in this volume.

For research purposes it is convenient to
distinguish between the spontaneous and the acquired religion of the child. The child's spontaneous religion consists of all those ideas and
beliefs that he has constructed in his attempts
to interpret religious terms and practices that
are beyond his level of comprehension. For example,
upon hearing that God was everywhere, a boy refused
to occupy his favorite chair for fear of "sitting
on God" and thus revealed his spontaneous conception of God's omnipresence. In contrast to these
spontaneous mental constructions there are many
religious ideas and beliefs that the child acquires
directly from adults either through imitation or
through instruction. A child's recitation of the
standard definition of theological terms or of
particular prayers would thus reflect acquired rather than spontaneous religion.

It is fair to say that by far the majority of
research on religious development has concerned itself with acquired rather than with spontaneous
religion. For example, in many of the studies dealing with the God conception (Barnes, 1892; Tanner,
1906; Bose, 1929; MacLean, 1930; Mathias, 1943)
questionnaires were employed which either asked
children to choose among standard conceptions of the
Deity or required them to complete sentences which
strongly suggested the standard conceptions (e. g.,
"God, where is he?"). While such studies of acquired religion are of value for assessing the degree to which children profit from religious
education, they do not reveal the full nature of
religious development. Indeed, they can be misleading! In all of the studies mentioned above none of
the investigators noted any marked age differences
in the God concept even when a considerable age span
(4-14) was sampled in the study. Yet, developmental
psychology has repeatedly shown (Reichard et. al.,
1944; Welch & Long, 1940, a, b, c; Piaget, 1928,
1929, 1930, 1952) that children's spontaneous conceptions follow a regular sequence from concrete to
abstract conceptualization between early (4-6) and
late childhood (10-12).

This is not to say that results from the traditional questionnaire studies of religious development are wrong but only that the acquired religion
revealed by these results does not follow the same
developmental course as spontaneous religion. Since
even the young child can memorize definitions of
religious terms, it is not surprising that when
children are tested on these definitions the young
children do about as well as the older children.
If, on the other hand, the *understanding* of these
definitions were to be evaluated, it is likely that
significant age differences would be found because
the understandings would reflect the child's spontaneous and not his acquired ideas. Only the child's
spontaneous ideas follow the sequence from the concrete to the abstract that we have come to expect in
developmental studies of concept formation.

As yet, however, we have little information
about the spontaneous religion of the child, and the
purpose of the present paper is to describe and
illustrate (by means of a completed investigation) a
method for exploring the child's own interpretations
of religious terms and practices. The method to be
described is the semi-clinical interview devised by
the Swiss psychologist, Jean Piaget.

THE SEMI-CLINICAL INTERVIEW

Background of the method. Piaget was one of
the first investigators to realize that the child's
spontaneous remarks were more than amusing errors
and that they reflected forms of thought that were
different from those used by adults. In order to
investigate children's spontaneous thought Piaget
was forced to devise his own method inasmuch as
this aspect of thought had not been previously recognized, much less explored. The specifications for
such a method, however, were exceedingly stringent
and apparently contradictory. For what Piaget required was a method with sufficient flexibility to
enable him to follow the meandering stream of any
particular child's thought and yet with sufficient

standardization to enable him to reach the same
destination with many different children at different age levels.

The only method which met the first of these
specifications was the psychiatric interview, while
the only method which met the second specification
was the mental test. This being the case, Piaget
combined the standard questions of the mental test
with the free inquiry of the psychiatric interview
and labeled the result the semi-clinical interview.
The union of standard question and free inquiry was
a happy one and led to the now classic findings concerning children's conceptions of physical causality
(1930) of the world (1929) and of judgment and
reasoning (1928).

Despite the proven fruitfulness of the semi-
clinical interview, however, it has seldom been employed by American psychologists and with one
exception (Elkind, 1961, 1962, 1963) has never been
brought to bear on the study of religious development.
The reasons for this neglect of Piaget's method are
several, including the amount of time and skill required of the examiner and the difficulty involved
in interpreting the obtained data. While these objections are well taken, they do not outweigh the
potential value of the method for exploring spontaneous religion.

In the first place, although the interview is
more time consuming than the questionnaire, the obtained data will be much more complete and therefore
more revealing than that obtained by more rapid
group testing procedures. In the second place, while
skill in conversing with children is required, most
investigators dealing with children have the basic
requirements for a good interviewer: a liking for
children, a respect for their individuality, and
patience. As for the difficulty in interpreting responses, this is present no matter what method is
used and, in fact, Piaget has given particular attention to this problem and has worked out techniques
and criteria for discriminating between the significant and the trivial in children's verbalizations.
So, on this point the Piaget method is actually
superior to the questionnaire wherein no such

discriminations can be made. There are then no
really good reasons for not using the interview
techniques in studying religious growth.

Construction of Interview Questions

Since the construction of appropriate questions
is one of the most difficult features of the semi-
clinical interview, an illustration of how the author
proceeds in formulating such questions might be helpful to prospective investigators. In general one
begins with a remark that suggests the presence of a
spontaneous conceptualization. For example, after
the tragic death of President Kennedy the author
heard a child say, "Are they going to shoot God too?"
This remark suggested that the child identified God
with famous persons in high offices and opened up a
whole new path of inquiry. If we desire to follow
this lead we might begin formulating some questions
about God and high offices. For example we might
ask, "Can God be president of the United States?
Why or why not?" Furthermore we might ask about how
God obtained his position. For example one might
ask, "Who chooses the president? Who chooses God,
or how did God become God?"
If this line of inquiry proved unfruitful we
might go back to the original remark and note that
it also suggests that God is conceived as a person.
This notion leads to quite another line of questioning (Can God dance, talk French? etc.). Should
this line of inquiry prove barren we might approach
the problem from the fact that the term "God" is a
name and ask such things as "How did God get his
name? Does God have a first name?" etc. The only
requirement in formulating questions is that they
be so absurd, to the adult way of thought, that one
can be reasonably certain children have not been
trained one way or the other regarding them. Trial
and error with various questions proposed to one's
own or to neighbor children will soon reveal which
questions are the most productive of unstereotyped,
spontaneous replies.

Interview technique. Once a group of related
questions about a given topic has been gathered,
the actual interviewing can begin. The child should
be seen in a quiet place where there are few distrac-
tions and at a time when he does not desire to be
somewhere else. As soon as the examiner has won
rapport with the child--most easily accomplished by
asking the youngster a few questions about himself--
he can begin putting his interview questions. After
the child has replied, it is usually necessary to
ask additional questions to clarify the meaning of
the response. It is in this free inquiry part of
the interview that the most skill is required because the examiner must direct the child's thought
without, at the same time, suggesting an appropriate
answer. There is no better preparation for this
part of the examination than a course in Rorschach
testing because in the Rorschach examination non-
suggestive questioning is developed to a fine art.

Interpretation of results: validity. Both
during the examination and afterwards, in analyzing
the data, the most important question is to what
extent the child's response truly reflects his own
mental constructions. To this end Piaget has described five types of response that need to be distinguished in any examination of the child. When
the child is not at all interested in the question
and is bored or tired, he may simply answer with
anything that comes into his head just to be relieved
of the burden of having to answer. Piaget speaks of
such responses as *answers at random.* When a child
fabricates or invents an answer, without really reflecting about the question, Piaget speaks of
romancing. On the other hand, when the child does
attend to the question but his answer is determined
by a desire to please the examiner or is suggested
by the question, Piaget speaks of *suggested conviction.*
In contrast to the three foregoing types of reply, which are of little value to the investigator,
the following two types are of very great significance. When the child reflects about a question
which is new to him and answers it from the reser-
voirs of his own thought, Piaget calls this a

liberated conviction. And when the child answers
quickly, without reflection, because he has already
formulated the solution or because it was latently
formulated, it is called by Piaget *a spontaneous conviction.*

Since the investigator is primarily interested
in the liberated and the spontaneous conviction, it
is important to have ways of separating them from
answers at random, romancing and suggested convictions.
This can be done at two points in the investigation,
one during and the other following the interview. If,
during the interview itself, the examiner suspects
that a reply is other than a spontaneous or a liberated conviction, he can check this in several ways.
First, he can offer counter suggestions to determine
how firmly rooted the idea is ın the child's thought.
A true liberated or spontaneous conviction will withstand counter suggestion whereas romancing, suggested
convictions and answers at random are easily changed
by counter suggestions. Secondly, he can ask about
related issues. If the idea is truly a conviction
of the child's, it will fit a pattern or system of
ideas that follow a general principle or rule which
Piaget calls a *schema.* If the child's response fits
the general trend or schema of his thought, this is
a good indication that it is either a spontaneous
or liberated conviction.

The second point at which one can determine
whether or not replies obtained in the interview
represent genuine convictions occurs after the data
have been collected and age trends can be examined.
First of all, if the majority of children at the
same age level give similar replies, this is evidence
that the responses reflect a form of thought characteristic of that age. If the answers were random,
suggested or romancing, there would be no reason to
expect such uniformity. Secondly, if the responses
show a gradual evolution with age in the direction
of a closer approximation to the adult conception,
this is another evidence that the replies reflect
a true developmental trend. Finally, a valid developmental sequence must give signs of continuity
in the sense that traces of concrete ideas held at
early age levels (adherences) are present among the

abstract conceptions of older children and in the
sense that foreshadowing of abstract ideas typical
of older children (anticipations) are present among
the concrete expressions of the young children.

The use of counter suggestion and varied questioning during the interviewing of individual children and of the three group criteria during the
analysis of the data from all children provides a
good basis for determining whether the obtained responses are indeed liberated or spontaneous convictions. Piaget has thus provided several means
for checking the validity of the data obtained by
his semi-clinical interview.

Interpretation of results: reliability. Although Piaget has always been concerned about the
validity of his observations he has almost ignored
the question of their reliability i. e., their re-
peatability. A possible reason for this neglect is
that Piaget's training in biological science has led
him to assume that a characteristic found in the
individual can automatically be taken as characteristic of the species. Such a position is less de-
fensible for the complex human species than it is
for lesser organisms, however, and reliability
measures probably should be made when using the
Piaget method. Two such measures are needed. One
is a measure of the consistency with which individual
children respond to interview questions at different
times. This measure can be obtained by retesting
each of the subjects, preferably not before a month
and not later than six months after the original
examination. The correlation of initial and retest
responses will provide an index of response reliability.

The second index of reliability that should be
obtained relates to the categorization of responses
into stages or sequences of development. That is
to say, it is necessary to determine whether the
responses are sufficiently distinctive that independent workers will classify them in similar ways.
If several persons independently categorize the responses and a measure of their agreement is determined,
this measure will serve as an index of the reliability

of the categorization. These steps to insure the
reliability of response, together with the fulfillment of Piaget's criteria for determining validity, should suffice to ensure that investigations
employing the semi-clinical interview will be acceptable to even the most hard-headed experimentalist.
        To make the use of the semi-clinical interview
concrete, a study in which the method was applied to
the development of religious identity will be briefly
described and summarized.

THE DEVELOPMENT OF RELIGIOUS IDENTITY

        Religious identity can be defined in terms of
the spontaneous meanings children attach to their
religious denomination. A developmental study of
these meanings was undertaken by the writer who investigated the growth of religious identity among
Jewish (Elkind, 1961), Catholic (Elkind, 1962), and
Congregational Protestant (Elkind, 1963) children.
        In these studies the children were individually
interviewed and asked six novel questions about
their denomination. The questions were, with the
appropriate denominational term inserted: a) Is
your family . . .? Are you . . .? Are all boys and
girls in the world . . .? b) Can a dog or cat be
. . .? c) How do you become a . . .? d) What is
a . . .? e) How can you tell a person is . . .?
f) Can you be . . . and American at the same time?
In order to clarify the meaning of the child's responses and to insure that these were firmly rooted
in his thought, additional questions, following no
set pattern, were asked.
        These questions had their origin in a child's
spontaneous question which the author happened to
overhear. The child asked whether a dog that ate
kosher food became Jewish. From this remark it
was clear that the child did not really understand
the word "Jewish" in the adult sense but had his own
spontaneous conception, namely, that you became
Jewish by eating kosher foods. It seemed to the
author that such spontaneous religious conceptions
were probably not unique to this child and that an

exploration of age changes in the child's spontaneous conceptions of his denomination might reveal
material of interest to the developmental psychology
of religion. Since a denominational term is basically
a class concept, it seemed reasonable to frame questions which would tap various aspects of this class
notion but in ways novel to the majority of children.
Accordingly, questions a, b, and e get at the child's
understanding of the extension of the concept, i. e.,
the groups to which it is appropriately applied and
the external signs by which group membership can be
recognized. Questions c and d, on the other hand,
tap the child's grasp of the intension of the concept, i. e., the property or properties that distinguish members belonging to a particular group. Finally, question f was designed to test the child's
conception of multiple group membership.

     In each denominational group at least 30 chil-
dren at each age level from 5 to 11 (among the Jewish children) and 6 to 12 (among the Protestant and
Catholic children) were interviewed so that more than
700 children were examined. No attempt was made to
control for liberal/conservative status, church
attendance, etc. in the belief that uniformities
which appeared despite a great deal of uncontrolled
variation would be further support for the view
that maturation as well as experience plays a part
in religious development.

     Piaget's (1929) criteria for interpreting chil-
dren's responses as liberated or spontaneous convictions were applied to the interview materials.
The results met all three criteria and there was:
a) uniformity of ideas at a given age level which
often extended over several year levels; b) an increasing correctness (conformance with adult conceptions) of children's ideas with increasing age;
c) adherences of ideas from an earlier year level as
part of, or added to, the more advanced ideas given
at a later age level and also anticipations of later
conceptions in the remarks of younger children. Analysis of the age changes in response made it possible
to distinguish three well-marked stages in the attainment of religious identity which held true of Jewish,
Protestant, and Catholic children.

At the first stage (usually ages 5-7) the child had only a global, undifferentiated conception of his denomination as a kind of proper name. Although he acknowledged being a Jew, Protestant, or Catholic, he confused these names with the terms for race and nationality, for example:

Sid (6-3) What is a Jew? "A person." How is a Jewish person different from a Catholic? "Cause some people have black hair and some people have blond."

Mel (5-9) What is a Jew? "A man." How is a Jewish person different from a Catholic? ..."He comes from a different country." Which one? "Israel." Furthermore, at this stage the child regarded having a denominational name as incompatible with possessing a racial or national designation. For example, it was common for the child at this stage to reply, in answer to the question about being an American and a Jew (Protestant, Catholic) at the same time that, "You can't have two." That is to say, because you can't have two names.

Children at the second stage (usually ages 7-9) had a concretely differentiated conception of their denomination. Their conception was concrete in the sense that they used observable features or actions to define their denomination, and their conception was differentiated because they discriminated among different behaviors in order to distinguish persons belonging to different denominations. For example:

Mae (7-9) What is a Jew? "A person who goes to Temple or Hebrew school."

Bill (8-10) What is a Catholic? "He goes to mass every Sunday and goes to Catholic school."

Ron (7-9) Can you be a Catholic and a Protestant at the same time? "No." Why not? "Cause you couldn't go to two churches."

Unlike the first stage children, young people at the second stage said they could be an American and their denomination at the same time. The reasons given in explanation were concrete and personal to the effect that "You can live in America and go to church" or "I'm an American and I'm a Protestant."

Third stage children (usually ages 10-12) demonstrated an abstract, differentiated conception of

their denomination. It was an abstract conception
in the sense that these children no longer defined
their denomination by mentioning names or observable
activities but rather by mentioning non-observable
mental attributes such as belief and understanding.
For example:

Bi (12-0) What is a Catholic? "A person who
believes in the truths of the Roman Catholic Church."
Can a dog or a cat be Catholic? "No, because they
don't have a brain or intellect."

Sed (11-10) What is a Jew? "A person who believes in one God and doesn't believe in the New
Testament."

When third stage children were asked the question
as to whether they could be American and their denomination at the same time, they replied that one was
a nationality and the other was a religion and that
they were two different things.

In summary, the results of this study dealing
with children's conceptions of their religious
identity have shown that identity is at first vague
and undifferentiated and has no more significance
than a proper name. Gradually the child comes to
think of his religious identity in terms of certain
religious practices and sacred objects, and since
these differ from religion to religion, he now has
a means for discriminating between children of different religions. It is only at the age of 11 or
12, however, that a majority of children come to
think of their religious identity in terms of particular beliefs for it is only at this age that the child
can reflect on his own thought. To the writer it
seems that these interesting findings regarding the
development of religious identity would not have been
found if a pencil and paper technique had been used.

POTENTIAL APPLICATIONS

The foregoing sections have described a method
for exploring the spontaneous religion of children
and the results of a study in which this method was
applied to the problem of religious identity. In
this concluding section it remains to suggest the

range of problems to which the method might be
applied and also to suggest the importance of the
findings which could result.

With regards to the problems to which the semi-
clinical interview could be appropriately applied,
they are the traditional ones of the developmental
psychology of religion. Conceptions of God, of
belief, of prayer, of sin, of morality and many
others all deserve to be looked at from the point
of view of spontaneous religion. It would be fas-
cinating too, if someone were to undertake a study
of children's theologies and cosmologies; of children's confusions between magic and ritual and of
children's attempts at integrating moral and religious ideas. For the study of these issues and
of many more like them, the semi-clinical interview is a necessary starting point.

The results to be obtained from the study of
such issues will be of more than theoretical interest and will pertain directly to religious education. A knowledge, for example, of the erroneous
interpretations children are likely to attach to religious conceptions at different age levels would
suggest ways of teaching these concepts so that they
would not be misunderstood. More importantly, perhaps, the educator's awareness of the ideas children
inevitably associate with religious terms and practices will change his orientation. The awareness
of spontaneous religion carries with it the implication that teaching must be more than writing on a
tabula rasa; and that it must be instead the re-
placement of the correct for the incorrect, the substitution of the proportionate for the exaggerated
and the inculcation of the essential in lieu of
the trivial. To attain this orientation the religious educator must be conversant with the spontaneous thought of the child.

There are then potent reasons for exploring the
spontaneous religion of children and hence for the
use of the semi-clinical interview in the study of
religious development.

REFERENCES

Barnes, E. Theological life of a California child.
   Pedagog. Semin., 1892, 2, 442-448.

Bose, R. S. Religious concepts of children. *Relig.*
   Educ., 1929, 24, 831-837.

Elkind, D. The child's conception of his religious
   denomination I: The Jewish child. *J. genet.*
   Psychol., 1961, 99, 209-225.

Elkind, D. The child's conception of his religious
   denomination II: The Catholic child. *J. genet.*
   Psychol., 1962, 101, 185-193.

Elkind, D. The child's conception of his religious
   denomination III: The Protestant child. *J.*
   genet. Psychol., 1963, 103, 291-304.

MacLean, A. H. *The idea of God in Protestant reli-*
   gious education. New York: Teachers College,
   Columbia University Press, 1930.

Mathias, W. D. *Ideas of God and conduct.* New York:
   Teachers College, Columbia University Press,
   1943.

Piaget, J. *Judgment and reasoning in the child.*
   London: Routledge & Kegan Paul, 1928.

Piaget, J. *The child's conception of the world.*
   London: Routledge & Kegan Paul, 1929.

Piaget, J. *The child's conception of physical*
   causality. Routledge & Kegan Paul, 1930.

Piaget, J. *The child's conception of number.*
   Routledge & Kegan Paul, 1952.

Reichard, S., Schneider, M., and Rapaport, D.
   The development of concept formation in
   children. *Am. J. Orthopsychiat.*, 1944, 14,
   156-162.

Tanner, A. E., Children's religious ideas. *Pedagog. Semin.*, 1906, 13, 511-513.

Welch, L. & Long, L.   The higher structural phases of concept formation in children.   *J. Psychol.*, 1940, 9, 59-95 (a).

Welch, L. & Long, L.   A further investigation of the higher structural phases of concept formation.   *J. Psychol.*, 1940, 10, 211-220 (b).

Welch, L. & Long, L.   The genetic development of the associational structures of abstract thinking.   *J. Genet. Psychol.*, 1940, 56, 175-206 (c).

CHILD-CONTROL THROUGH A "COALITION WITH GOD"

CLYDE Z. NUNN

Editor's introduction. B. F. Skinner (1971)
suggested that the concept of an "all-seeing
God," a concept promoted by many religious systems, makes punitive measures most effective,
since escape from the punisher is impossible.
This latter-day insight was well-known to religious parents long before Skinner appeared
on the scene. The idea of an all-seeing, all-
knowing deity and threats of divine punishment
are indeed parts of the method through which
many children still acquire their first religious concepts. This child-rearing technique
touches on several crucial issues. One is the
process of internalization and the formation
of a conscience, which may be described in
Skinnerian terms as a portable punisher. The
place of God in this portable system of rewards
and punishments has been a major concern of religious literature.

[1]I am indebted to Drs. John W. Thibaut and
Ernest Q. Campbell for their suggestions and en-
couragement in the writing of this paper.

From *Child Development*, 1964, 35, 417-432. ©
Society for Research in Child Development, Inc.,
1964. Reprinted by permission.

Another major psychological question regards
the relationship, in the child's perceptions,
between the earthly parents and the divine father. We may suspect that this relationship,
in the child's mind, is the cornerstone of belief in divine authority and religious morality.
For the adult believer, the fusion of parental
and religious guidance may still be the source
of serious conflicts. Since religious instruction comes primarily from the parents and is
fused with moral prescriptions and proscriptions,
rejection of parental beliefs becomes a painful
process, or may never occur. The enormous power
of religious beliefs acquired early in life can
be understood when we realize that the combination of parental authority, the child's love and
helplessness, and the first rebellions and moral
conflicts all become fused with the early conceptions of deity. The Freudian idea of the
deity as a parental projection can be well ap-
preciated in this context.

The third issue is that of the psychological
consequences and correlates of the use of
threats of divine punishment as a method of child
control. How are children's notions of the world
and themselves affected by this disciplinary technique? What kind of person will the child grow
up to be when his parents claim authority on the
basis of their relationship with an invisible,
omniscient authority?

The analysis in Nunn's article is social-
psychological. He ignores most of the issues
presented above and instead concentrates on the
family interaction. Thus the issue Nunn deals
with is style of parental discipline, not just
religious training. The question is: Why do
certain parents need an external agent to bol-
ster their discipline? When, and why would
parents, confronted with what they see as a
discipline problem, use a "coalition with God"
as a solution? Introducing the idea of an all-
seeing God is not only a function of the family
within the society but is also a way of maintaining the family system itself. Nunn's major

finding is that parents who use this control technique with their children appear to be "limited, powerless, and ineffectual parents who have certain characteristics suggestive of authoritarian personalities." Nunn finds some effects of this control technique on the children involved, but his methodology is unclear, and the results are not statistically significant.

Questions for additional research on the phenomenon of "coalition with God" are numerous and intriguing. We could consider investigating the phenomenon in other parts of the United States and across denominational groups. We could also consider investigating more thoroughly the child's side of the story. Elkind's use of Piaget's semi-clinical interview seems especially appropriate for learning more about children's perceptions of divine power and authority and their relationship to parental authority. A follow-up study of children from "coalition with God" families to assess their later religious beliefs also seems worthwhile.

Reference

Skinner, B. F. *Beyond Freedom and Dignity*. New York: Knopf, 1971.

One of the most salient problems for any family is that of controlling the conduct of its members. Since most societies have specified the problem of child-control as the responsibility of the family, every parent faces the task of developing control over neophyte members of the family. The initially complete dependence of the child on the parents facilitates their performance of this task. However, as the child matures, this complete *dependence* of the child gradually becomes converted to some degree of *interdependence*. Using terminology employed by Thibaut and Kelley (8), we can say that the child

who was under the fate control of his parents has
now come under their implicitly converted fate control.[2] Ultimately some degree of *independence*
between child and parents evolves gradually out of
the direct, personal control by parents that initially characterizes the parent-child relationship.
     From the parental standpoint, a converse pro-
cess takes place. As the child reaches the independent stage of development, the parents necessarily
must reciprocate some dependence on the child,
since the child can now affect the parents' outcomes. While not precisely comparable to the child's
initial total dependence on the parents, the system-
movement is nevertheless in the direction of dependency by parents on child, as Glasser and Glasser
(4) have noted.
     Throughout this developmental process there is
the paramount problem of control. While the parents
can use direct and personal means of control during
the first stage of the parent-child relationship,
this direct control is later impossible and the
parents necessarily must call upon more indirect
techniques. Realizing the loss of the constant
associations of the child and the consequent gap in
their direct control, the parents, still sensitive
to their responsibilities for the child, search
consciously or unconsciously for some means of ex-
tending their control when they are not present with
the child, hoping ultimately for the child's self-
control. How, then, does the parent go about establishing this indirect control of the child? Various
means are used for this purpose. Some parents,
striving for more internalized norms, attempt to
help the child understand and value the stated rules.
Other parents expect only some measure of conformity
from the child, with little realistic hope that the

[2]Fate control is defined as "A's" ability to
vary his behavior in such a manner as to affect "B's"
outcomes regardless of what "B" does; fate control
is implicitly converted, however, when "B" can learn
to affect his own outcomes by matching appropriate
behavior with "A's."

rules will ever be internalized. We might expect that
the latter type of parents would resort to the most
expedient means of achieving their goal of indirect
control. One expedient technique, we might expect,
would be to call upon an external agent to act in
behalf of the parent, as in the case of the Trobriand
Islanders using the uncle to discipline the child.
More specifically, however, we refer to the instances
in which parents call upon or form a "coalition with
God" in order to indirectly control their children,
that is, the parents tell the child that God will
punish him if he misbehaves. This is a frequently
used technique that has some efficacy, as the
following interview with a mother in a study by Sears,
Maccoby, and Levin (7, p. 380) would indicate:

> I.   What do you do about it if she denies
> something you are sure she has done?
> M.   She may deny it at first, but she'll
> usually tell me. She's deathly afraid of
> being punished--not by me--but we've always
> told her that any little girl who tells a lie,
> God always does something terrible to them,
> and she's deathly afraid of that. Like, for
> instance, up the street a little boy was hit
> by an automobile, and Cathy was quite sure it
> was because he did something wrong at some
> time and God punished him. Maybe it's not the
> right thing, but we let her believe it.

This is an ingenious technique to some parents, and
for the social scientist it suggests several intriguing questions regarding such parents and their
more general relationship with their children. We
come now to the central focus of the present investigation.

STATEMENT OF THE PROBLEM

Thibaut and Kelley (8) have stated that a
person who wants to get another person to perform
a specific behavior (a norm) must fulfill (or have
fulfilled) three different kinds of activities: (a)
stating a rule, (b) maintaining surveillance, and

(c) applying sanctions. Parents, then, must fulfill
these three activities in the process of converting
their fate control in order to get their child to perform according to their expectations, even without the
parents' immediate personal surveillance. According
to Thibaut and Kelley, the above three activities do
not necessarily have to be performed by the parent.
Instead, an external agent can be called upon to perform at least some of the functions such as monitoring and applying sanctions. This is, of course, the
point at which the parents may call upon God to perform some of the necessary activities in child-control.
     Using these suggestions from Thibaut and Kelley
as our point of departure, the major problem in the
present investigation is to attempt to understand and
explain why some parents use an external agent such as
God as a means to some control of their children. We
propose to do this by looking, first, at some parental
background factors such as family income, working
mothers, and religious orientations. Secondly, we will
seek support for an explanation of why some parents
form a "coalition with God" by investigating the manner
in which these parents relate to their children, pay-
ing special attention to such factors as parental authority roles and parental affection. Finally, having
looked at some of the familial dynamics and having
suggested an interpretation, we will look at the effect
that these parents have on the self-blame and some
attitudes of their children.

METHODOLOGY

Data Collection[3]

     The data were obtained in Nashville (Davidson
County), Tennessee, in the spring of 1957, for purposes not directly related to the present analysis.

[3]These data were gathered by the late Andrew F.
Henry, Vanderbilt University, under grant M-1294,
National Institute of Mental Health. I am indebted
to Ernest Q. Campbell, University of North Carolina,
and James H. Williams, Florida State University, for

Brief background questionnaires were administered initially to approximately 18,000 sixth to
twelfth grade students. From these, families meeting the following criteria were selected: two and
only two children; both children living at home;
both natural parents living at home; no other adults
resident in the home; no twins. All families were
white.

The original 18,000 yielded approximately 440
appropriate families. An attempt was made to secure
staff-administered questionnaires from all four members of these families. This was accomplished in
367 instances, and the present analysis employs data
from these 367 families. In most cases, the questions asked of the four family members were comparable. For example, all members would be asked this
same question regarding other family members, "What
if 'A' did get mad at 'B,' would you blame 'A'?"
Of course, in the actual questionnaire, family
members' names were used rather than letters. From
this we see that, if you are "A" and are the one
who is reporting, you would be reporting your own
self-blame. If you were reporting and "A" was father and "B" was mother, you would be reporting
blame directed to father.

Definitions

Financial status. The income levels of the
families refer to the total family income and are
defined as follows:

Low: Family income less than $400 per month.
Middle: Family income is $400 to $600 per month.
High: Family income is $600 or more per month.

Family control types. We have delineated four
family control types on the bases of parental responses to the question: "Do you tell your child
that God will punish him if he is bad?" We would

permitting their use. Additional assistance was also
provided under the auspices of the Organization Research Group of the Institute for Research in Social
Science. The O.R.G. is supported by the Office of
Naval Research, Nonr-885(04).

expect that in those families in which both parents
form such a coalition with God, the effects on the
children would be greater than in those families in
which only one or neither parent utilizes this technique in child-control. Proceeding from this expectation, we have ordered the family types, ranging from
the family type in which both parents form a coalition
with God to the type in which neither parent forms a
coalition with God. We have further differentiated
those families in which only one parent forms a
coalition with God into family types in which mother
only or father only tells the children that God punishes them when they are bad. We have made this distinction merely on a hunch and without any rationale
for doing so. Our family control types are indicated
as follows and will be referred to in the remainder
of the paper according to their Roman numerals:

Type I: Both parents tell their children that
             God punishes them if they are bad.
Type II: Mother only tells the children that
             God punishes them if they are bad.
Type III: Father only tells the children that
             God punishes them if they are bad.
Type IV: Neither parent tells the children
             that God punishes them if they are
             bad.

As support for the validity of our ordering of
the four family types, we have cross-tabulated these
family types with responses of the children to the
question: "Do you believe God punishes you when you
get angry?" If our expectations are correct and our
ordering is valid, we would expect the childrens'
responses to fit a continuum between the two extreme
family types.
Relevant data are presented in Table I. The
expected relation generally holds true, but with
little difference observed between types I and II.
This holds true for both the older and the younger
child of the family. The fact that in all family
types the majority of both older and younger children affirm this belief is evidence that forces
other than parents (e.g., fundamentalist Protestant

TABLE I

"Do You Believe God Punishes You When You Get Angry?" by Family Type,
Separately for Older and Younger Child

| Family Type | PER CENT SAYING YES | | (N†) |
	Older	Younger	
I	73.0	84.0	(100)
II	76.2	83.3	(42)
III	62.9	69.5	(105)
IV	53.3	61.7	(120)
	$p<.001, df=3$	$p<.001, df=3$	

† N refers to families rather than respondents, e.g., there are 100 older children *and*
100 younger children in Family Type I.

religious systems) in the child's world propagate
such beliefs; nevertheless, the expected trend, most
notably the greater impact of type I than of type
IV and of mother than of father, is corroborated.
While it appears that logically we should have combined types I and II because they appear to have
similar effects, we chose to keep them separate in
the analysis because we were principally interested
in the comparison between the two family types in
which both parents adhered to the same policy regarding a coalition with God.

FINDINGS

We look first at some of the familial dynamics
related to our various family types. In doing so,
we have found it necessary to combine types II and
III in most tabular presentations due to the small
number of families which qualified as type II families. While this restricts our analysis in regard
to differences between maternal and paternal roles,
it does not limit our attention to the two essential
and contrasting types I and IV, i.e., those families in which both parents tell and in which neither parent tells their children that God punishes
for misbehavior.

Parental Background Factors

What is the life situation of these parents? Table 2 presents data regarding the income levels of the family types. The association between income level and family type is clearly indicated, with type I families being associated with the lower level of the income hierarchy, while type IV families are associated with the highest level of income. Types II and III are intermediate on the income continuum. Table 2 suggests that those families in which the parents tell their children that God punishes them for misbehavior are more likely to exist in life situations in which they have a lessened economic power with its accompanying limitations.

TABLE 2

Family Income, by Family Type

Family Type	FAMILY INCOME PER MONTH†			Total
	$400 *or Less*	$400–$600	$600 *or More*	
I	37.0	41.0	22.0	100% (100)
II	26.2	40.5	33.3	100% (42)
III	23.8	36.2	40.0	100% (105)
IV	14.2	32.5	53.3	100% (120)

† $p < .01, df = 6$.

In our theoretical framework, we have noted that an external agent such as God could be used to assume some of the norm-maintenance functions such as keeping surveillance and applying sanctions. If this is true, and if in fact the parents in our sample are at a developmental stage in which indirect control has a greater salience to them, we could hypothesize that mothers who are employed outside the home would have a greater necessity for some indirect control than would be true of nonworking mothers, who would have more time at home. Accordingly, we may expect that the incidence of working mothers is relatively low in type IV, since we have assumed that parents who form a coalition with God do so as a means of indirect control over their children.

TABLE 3

Mother's Employment Status, by Income and Family Type

Family Type	EMPLOYMENT STATUS			Total
	Full-Time	Part-Time	None	
Low Income Level				
I	40.5	10.8	48.6	100% (37)
II & III	24.3	5.4	70.3	100% (37)
IV	29.4	5.9	64.7	100% (17)
	ns†			
Middle Income Level				
I	34.1	17.1	48.8	100% (41)
II & III	25.9	20.4	53.7	100% (54)
IV	32.5	25.0	42.5	100% (40)
	ns†			
High Income Level				
I	59.1	4.5	36.4	100% (23)
II & III	51.8	19.6	28.6	100% (56)
IV	25.4	15.9	58.7	100% (63)
Between Full-Time & None $p<.01$, $df=2$.				

† *ns* = not significant at .05 or less.

Table 3 presents appropriate data. Generally, the evidence supports the hypothesis, with the exception of the middle income families; type I mothers are definitely more likely to be full-time employees than are type IV mothers. Generally, it could be reasonably argued from the evidence presented in Table 3 that, in light of the working mother's reduced direct control of her children, she has a greater need for indirect means of controlling her children and thereby is more likely to form a coalition with God.

Another background factor examined is the religious orientation of the parents. The type of church one attends, as well as beliefs that are held about God, are revealing aspects of the personality. Consonant with our finding that those parents who tell their children that God punishes for deviant behavior tend to be financially limited, we expect that type I parents are similarly powerless and limited in their religious orientations, i.e., that they participate in religious systems that especially

TABLE 4

Religious Preference of Mother, by Income and Family Type

Family Type	Sect	RELIGIOUS TYPE Transitional	Denominational
Low Income Level			
I	17.4	13.1	4.1
II & III	21.7	12.0	6.2
IV	8.7	6.0	2.9
ns			
Middle Income Level			
I	13.0	16.4	5.5
II & III	4.3	14.8	16.6
IV	4.3	9.3	15.9
$p < .001, df = 2$			
High Income Level			
I	8.9	8.2	2.8
II & III	17.4	12.0	18.6
IV	4.3	8.2	27.6
$p < .001, df = 2$			
	100% (23)	100% (183)	100% (145)

deny the competence of the actor and exalt the direct control of man's affairs by God.

Table 4 and 5 present the data. Table 4, which indicates the religious preference of the mother, suggests that those parents who tell their children that God punishes for bad behavior tend to prefer sect and transitional type churches and those parents who do not form a coalition with God are more likely to prefer denominational type churches, with the exception of the low income level parents. Our classification of religions while following others (6,9) is somewhat arbitrary because we have classified Church of Christ and Southern Baptists as transitional rather than as sect or denominational types. Sect type religions include Jehovah Witness, Baptist sects, and other sects. Denominational type religions include Methodists, Presbyterians, and other Protestants. The number of Jewish, Catholic, and those without a preference was too small to consider in the analysis.

The fathers' preferences were similar to the mothers;
therefore the data are not presented.

It has been previously stated (5) that sectarians are persons who find themselves threatened by
and disassociated from the secular world. Unlike
denominational type participants who are accommodating and adaptable to the secular world, the
sectarians are powerless and ineffectual. Applying
this interpretation to our sample of parents, we
would conclude that our initial expectations are confirmed and further support is added to the hypothesized limited power of those parents who use God as
a coalition partner in child-control.

TABLE 5

"Would God Love You More If You Obeyed His Laws than If You Disobeyed
Them?" by Income and Family Type, Separately for Mother and Father

| | PER CENT SAYING YES | | |
Family Type	Mother	Father	(N)
Low Income Level			
I	100.0	97.3	(37)
II & III	75.7	89.2	(37)
IV	76.5	82.4	(17)
	$p < .01, df = 2$	*ns*	
Middle Income Level			
I	92.7	95.1	(41)
II & III	66.7	92.6	(54)
IV	67.5	75.0	(40)
	$p < .01, df = 2$	$p < .01, df = 2$	
High Income Level			
I	100.0	90.9	(22)
II & III	64.3	87.5	(56)
IV	49.2	68.3	(63)
	$p < .001, df = 2$	$p < .001, df = 2$	

Table 5 reports more specifically the belief
that parents have with respect to God. When asked
a question regarding the conditional nature of God's
love, type I parents are considerably more likely
to view God as One whose love is contingent upon
their own behavior. Withdrawal of God's love is to
be expected by type I parents if the appropriate behavioral item is not produced to deter it. Type IV

parents, both father and mother, are less likely to perceive their relationship to God in these terms. This we would interpret as additional support that type I parents are threatened, not only by others but by God also.

Parental Authority Role

Turning to the relationship between parent and child, we look first at the parents' expectations of their children's conformity to parental authority and to general societal expectations. What kind of response to their authority do type I parents expect? In Table 6 there is a clear-cut answer to this question. Type I and IV parents, both mother and father,

TABLE 6

"A Child Should Obey His Parents without Question," by Income and Family Type, Separately for Mother and Father

| | PER CENT AGREEING | | |
Family Type	Mother	Father	(N)
Low Income Level			
I	78.4	86.5	(37)
II & III	59.5	75.1	(37)
IV	64.7	64.7	(17)
	ns	*ns*	
Middle Income Level			
I	58.5	56.1	(41)
II & III	64.8	61.1	(54)
IV	20.0	47.5	(40)
	$p<.001, df=2$	*ns*	
High Income Level			
I	63.6	36.4	(23)
II & III	30.4	53.6	(56)
IV	28.6	30.2	(63)
	$p<.01, df=2$	$p<.05, df=2$	

are clearly contrasted in the extent to which they expect conformity to their unquestioned authority. The contrast between types I and IV is always in the expected direction; however, for middle and high income fathers the greatest contrast is between types II and III and type IV. The development of unquestioning obedience in their children is essential for type I parents if the full effect of their coalition with God is to be realized. The power in the coalition with God is directly dependent upon the extent to which the children will believe that God will punish them for misbehavior. If, therefore, this belief goes without question from the children, the obvious result is increased potency of the parental power in the coalition with God.

If parents expect their children to obey without question, we should expect also that they would allow very little deviation of their children from what is expected generally of most children. Data in Table 7 support this expectation, although the

TABLE 7

"If a Child Is Unusual in Any Way, His Parents Should Get Him to Be Like Other Children," by Income and Family Type, Separately for Mother and Father

	PER CENT AGREEING		
Family Type	*Mother*	*Father*	*(N)*
Low Income Level			
I	64.9	81.1	(37)
II & III	62.2	78.4	(37)
IV	58.8	82.4	(17)
	ns	*ns*	
Middle Income Level			
I	78.0	65.9	(41)
II & III	64.8	66.7	(54)
IV	52.5	42.5	(40)
	$p<.05, df=2$	$p<.05, df=2$	
High Income Level			
I	45.5	72.7	(22)
II & III	55.4	71.4	(56)
IV	36.5	44.4	(63)
	$p<.01, df=2$	$p<.01, df=2$	

differences are small for mothers and nonexistent for fathers at low income levels. Generally, there is an association between family types and the extent to which the parent agrees with the statement: "If a child is unusual in any way, his parents should get him to be more like other children."

The analytical picture that emerges of parents who tell their children that God punishes them for bad behavior is one of limited, powerless, and ineffectual persons who have certain characteristics suggestive of authoritarian personalities (1).

Parental Affection

As the emerging picture of "coalition" parents suggests, we are dealing with limited and ineffectual persons whom we might also expect to be characteristically less affectionate than their spouses who do not resort to a coalition with God. Therefore, when the parents are compared by the child in terms of affection, we hypothesize that the parent who does not tell the children that God punishes is more frequently chosen as the one showing him most affection. This hypothesis is corroborated to some extent in the data presented in Table 8. Comparing family types III and IV, the proportion of children that chose the father and the proportion that

TABLE 8

"Which Parent Shows You Most Affection?" by Family Type, Separately for Older and Younger Child's Report

Family Type	OLDER'S REPORT Mother	Father		YOUNGER'S REPORT Mother	Father		(N)
II	69.0	31.0	100%	66.7	33.3	100%	(100)
III	81.9	18.1	100%	78.1	21.9	100%	(42)
IV	78.3	21.7	100%	77.5	22.5	100%	(120)

ns

chose the mother are virtually identical. However, comparing types II and III, the father is more likely to be chosen as most affectionate when he does not form a coalition but mother does. Conversely, mother is most likely to be chosen as most affectionate when she is not the coalition parent in the family. This holds true for both the younger and older child. The implication in these data for our analysis is that the parent appears to resort to a coalition with God under conditions in which he or she is less affectionate or is personally less effective with the child.

Effects on the Children

Having delineated our four family types and
compared them in terms of parental background factors and some familial dynamics, we can now ask what
effects can be noted on the children of these families. What effects do the family types have on the
self-blame of the children? What effects do they
have on the attitudes of these children? If a coalition with God is formed for purposes of indirect
child-control, we can expect that, when the child
against whom the coalition is directed becomes angry
or fails to comply with one of the family member's
requests, he will experience some internal discontent
that will lead to the administration of a measure of
self-punitiveness or self-blame. This should be particularly characteristic of those children who profess a belief in the punishment by God, if Thibaut
and Kelley are correct in stating that the effectiveness of these outside agents is dependent upon the
acceptance of the agent's power and action by in-
group members (8). This should also hold true for
the effect on the child's attitudes.

From inspection of Table 9, our expectations
appear to be fulfilled, except for those type II
children who do not believe God punishes. The fact
that the proportions in these particular categories for both older and younger child are not consistent with the over-all pattern is probably due
to the extremely small number of cases in these
categories. The child who believes that God punishes when a bad act is committed is more likely to
feel high self-blame for actions of anger or non-
compliance with other family members. For the older
child, the proportion of "believers" who feel high
self-blame decreases slightly, though consistently,
from type I to type IV families. We infer from this
that some self-control is indicated when the child
believes God punishes him for deviant behavior,
particularly if both parents verbalize such beliefs
in the presence of the child. This self-control,
or indirect control from the parent's point of view,

TABLE 9

Self-Blame† of Older and Younger Child, by Family Type and Child's
Belief in God's Punishment

| Child Believes God Punishes | PER CENT HIGH SELF-BLAME | | | |
	Older	(N)	Younger	(N)
Family Type I				
Yes	36.9	(73)	34.5	(84)
No	18.5	(27)	12.5	(16)
Family Type II				
Yes	34.4	(32)	34.3	(35)
No	40.0	(10)	57.1	(7)
Family Type III				
Yes	33.4	(66)	35.6	(73)
No	18.0	(39)	31.3	(32)
Family Type IV				
Yes	31.2	(64)	32.4	(74)
No	21.4	(56)	21.7	(46)
	ns		*ns*	

† This is a summary of the self-blame felt by the child when he became angry and did not comply with other family members. Of the range of 0 to 6 possible positive replies to self-blame, 4 to 6 such replies were defined as High Self-Blame.

is the goal of those parents who would form a coalition with God, as we have attempted to demonstrate.

Data in Table 10 concern the effects of the family types on the attitudes of the children. Here again, when we control for the child's belief in God's punishment for deviant behavior, we find results similar to those in Table 9. The child's belief in the idea of God's punishment does effect whether he agrees that a child should obey his parents without question. In every family type, excepting only type III for younger children and the two "nonbeliever" categories with small *N*s of 7 and 10, the children who believe that God punishes are more likely than the nonbelievers to agree with the statement. Also for both younger and older children who are "believers" there is a steady decrease in the proportion of agreements from type I to type IV, indicating some structural effect of family types. This seemingly is an example of authoritarian personalities producing reciprocal attitudes in their children.

TABLE 10

"A Child Should Obey His Parents without Question," by Family Type and
Child's Belief in God's Punishment, Separately for Older and Younger Child

Child Believes God Punishes	PER CENT AGREEING			
	Older	(N)	Younger	(N)
Family Type I				
Yes	68.5	(73)	90.5	(84)
No	37.0	(27)	75.0	(16)
Family Type II				
Yes	65.6	(32)	80.0	(35)
No	80.0	(10)	100.0	(7)
Family Type III				
Yes	62.1	(66)	87.7	(73)
No	51.3	(39)	87.5	(32)
Family Type IV				
Yes	53.1	(64)	74.3	(74)
No	42.9	(56)	52.2	(46)
For younger, between family types, $p < .05$, $df = 3$ (No's excluded)				

DISCUSSION

We have attempted to demonstrate that certain
ineffectual, limited, and somewhat powerless parents
are likely to be the ones who would form a coalition
with God in order to gain some degree of indirect
control over their children, especially when direct
surveillance by the parents is minimized. Through
the coalition, God begins to take over some of the
norm-maintenance functions for the parents. Consequently, some variations are found to be evident in
the attitudinal and belief systems of the children.

Certain implications emerge pertaining to both
the parents and the children. For the parents who
utilize the technique, the coalition with God has a
power-enhancing function. Shown to be limited and
powerless in several respects, the coalition parents
employ an external agent (God) that is both convenient and efficacious in remedying their own in-
effectiveness with the children. From the parents'
point of view, if God serves as an effective coalition partner the parents gain some advantage in

child-control, but, if by some process the parent-
God coalition fails to enhance the controlling power
of the parents, very little is lost in the attempted
power strategy, as we will point out more explicitly
below. From the Thibaut and Kelley (8) frame of reference, this power strategy would gain its potency
from the ability of the agent to increase the costs
of punishments of the children. This sort of power
strategy, however, would be applicable only in nonvoluntary situations.[4]

In addition to its function as a power strategy,
a coalition with God has implications for the legitimization of parents' authority. Attempting to control their children, parents have the problem of
establishing the legitimacy of their authority in a
situation of intimacy where fallibility is evident.
This is particularly acute at the stage of development in which the children, striving for some independence, are questioning or rebelling against the
rules of parents. Bossard (3) has suggested that
the respected guest in the home who agrees with the
parents' values and rules creates a situation in
which the children's confidence in the legitimacy of
their parents' authority is increased. Support from
the "authoritative outsider" who agrees with the
parent contributes toward the children's acceptance
of the parents' rules and authority. If this holds
true for the respected person outside the immediate
family, why not for God? If God is seen as an external set of values supporting those of the parents,
we should expect the same effect, the legitimization
of parental authority, indicated by Bossard.

Even if the coalition with God does not always
produce the desired effect and the children deviate
from the expected norms, all is not lost in the
effort. By introducing the external agent (God)
into the parent-child relationship, the limited and
ineffectual parents can reduce some of the costs of

[4]The reader is referred to chapter 10 in Thibaut
and Kelley, *The Social Psychology of Groups*, for
explication of the notion of nonvoluntary situations.

anxieties and uncertainties accruing from their in-
effectiveness with their children, for they are in
effect delegating some of the responsibilities for
the children's behavior to the external agent. The
child, on the other hand, is not defying the parents
so much as God when he acts "bad." Thus the coalition parent need not feel a complete responsibility
for the child's misbehaviors.

We may mention also the child's tendency to
blame himself for deviant behavior when he is told
and believes that God will punish him. Normally,
the child should feel some hostility toward the one
who punishes him, but the sacred character of God
would seemingly deter such aggressions. In this
case, it would seem likely that the aggressions
would often be turned upon the child himself. This
in turn has a significant effect for the cohesion
of the family unit. If the third person is introduced into the parent-child relationship, this has
the effect of avoiding the polarization of conflict
within the parent-child relationship and, in doing
so, avoids the loss of cohesion within the family
unit. Blood (2) cites the same function of religion
in regard to husband-wife relationships. Because
the external agent is God, the child's aggressions
are turned upon himself, and the cohesion of the
family is even better conserved in this instance
than when the external agent is not of such sacred
significance. For the ineffectual and powerless
parent, then, the coalition with God has not only
power and authority enhancing functions but also
may possibly serve to reduce some costs to the parent
in the childrearing process, even to increase the
cohesion of the family.

The discussion of the child's self-blame suggests a question worth further consideration.
Does the child's feeling of self-blame under the
conditions of the parent-God coalition indicate
that a norm has been internalized? We have suggested
at various points that the coalition with God tends
to produce compliance rather than internalization.
Yet we have shown that the children who believe in
God's punitive involvement are more likely to express
a high degree of self-blame, which is often said to

be a manifestation of an internalized norm. These
findings seemingly are self-contradictory. Again,
Thibaut and Kelley (8) provide the theoretical under-
pinning to bridge this dilemma. Compliance is the
type of conforming behavior that exists when the critical antecedents, surveillance and negative sanction-
ing power, are operative. Specifically, B is said to
be in a state of compliance with A when A has the
power to reduce B's outcomes and has B under surveillance. We would conclude that the coalition with God,
meeting the specified criteria as it does, would be
an instance of compliance. Thus we would qualify the
common tendency to link the idea of God to those of
conscience, superego, etc. We would say that the use
of God as a threatening surveillance force is a technique not well calculated to result in the internalization of a given norm. The coalition with God,
as we have used it, does not appear to be an effort
at developing internalized values in the children,
but rather an effort to get compliance to the norm,
or in Sears' terms, merely to extend the parents'
external control over the children (7).

While we have suggested that God and conscience
development do not seem to be associated in the sense
in which we have defined God's role in the child-
control process, this does not disassociate the two
completely. For instance, there is the possibility
that there is a benevolent coalition with God. In
such case, the parent might emphasize God's rewards
to the child when the child acts in the appropriate
manner. This type of relationship of parent-God-
child would appear to fit the criteria for the social
influence process of identification as defined by
Thibaut and Kelley (8). Identification is evident
when A's (God's) enforcement of the norm rests primarily on augmentations (increased rewards or reduced
costs) which are given dependably when B (child)
conforms.[5] After a period of time, not only do

[5]For substantiation of this assertion, see
Kenneth Ring and Harold H. Kelley, "A Comparison of
Augmentation and Reduction as Modes of Influence,"
J. abnorm. soc. Psychol., 1963, 66, 95-102.

augmentations take on value, but God himself begins
to have value to B. It can be seen that the association of God in relation to conscience might develop in such a case. However, the type of social
influence defined as internalization would fit the
association even better.

In the process of internalization, the child
has learned and accepted as his own the norms and
values of another agent. The agent who serves as
the source of values is involved in the process only
indirectly as a credible intermediary between the
child and the task at hand. Rewards and costs
(punishments) derive from the task at hand and not
from the source of values. The agent provides the
means to the child's acquiring right, true, valid,
or meaningful outcomes from the task. The coalition
with God as we have stated it would not fit the
criterion of internalization--it involves both surveillance and negative sanctions. Therefore, the
high self-blame exhibited by the children of coalition parents could not be considered a manifestation
of internalized norms. However, God could be associated with conscience development or internalization under different conditions. God could be
viewed by the child as a source of stable values in
the absence of well defined or acceptable values
from the parents, or in conjunction with the values
of parents or significant others. In such case,
God would be a credible intermediary by being a
means to rather than a source of meaningful outcomes. In this sense, God's relation to the development of conscience or internalized values is, of
course, significant.

REFERENCES

1. Adorno, T. W., et al. *The authoritarian person-
    ality.* Harper, 1950.

2. Blood, R. O. *Marriage.* Free Press, 1962.

3. Bossard, J. H. S. *The sociology of child
    development.* Harper, 1954.

4. Glasser, P. H., & Glasser, L. N. Role reversal
    and conflict between aged parents and their
    children. *Marriage Fam. Living,* 1962, 24,
    46-51.

5. Pfoutz, H. W. The sociology of secularization:
    religious groups. *Amer. J. Sociol.,* 1955, 61,
    121-128.

6. Pope, L. *Millhands and Preachers.* Yale Univer.
    Press, 1942.

7. Sears, R. R., Maccoby, E. E., & Levin, H.
    Patterns of child rearing. Row, Peterson, 1947.

8. Thibaut, J. W., & Kelley, H. H. *The social
    psychology of groups.* Wiley, 1959.

9. Yinger, J. M. *Religion, society and the
    individual.* Macmillan, 1957.

THE SOCIAL DESIRABILITY RESPONSES OF CHILDREN OF FOUR RELIGIOUS-CULTURAL GROUPS*

VIRGINIA C. CRANDALL
JOAV GOZALI

Editor's introduction. To look further at the
effects of religious training in childhood, we
may wish to explore how such training affects
the way an individual sees himself and also how
he presents himself to others. Using psychodynamic terms, we may wish to examine the relationship between religious socialization and
the development of defense mechanisms. Crandall
and Gozali tested the tendency of children
coming from religious backgrounds to present
themselves in a culturally favorable light. The
instrument used, a Social Desirability scale,
presents the child with situations of "right"
and "wrong" behaviors, where the socially desirable choice is well-known. As the authors
state, "The items are worded in such a way that

*This study was primarily supported by grant
MH-02238 from the National Institute of Mental
Health and partially supported by NIH grant FR-
00222 and general research support grant FR-05537.

From *Child Development*, 1969, 40, 751-762. ©
Society for Research in Child Development, Inc.,
1969. Reprinted by permission.

the socially desirable response is behaviorally improbable...." A child scoring high on this scale presents himself as an exemplary "good kid" who "does everything right." Since perfect compliance with social norms is behaviorally rare, we have to assume that this kind of self-presentation reflects a strong need to appear obedient and well behaved and to deny any possible transgressions.

To measure the effects of religious upbringing on Social Desirability responses, a group of 735 U. S. non-Catholic public school children (considered the least influenced by religious teachings) was compared to three groups of children who came from religious environments: a group of 426 Catholic parochial school children in the United States, a group of 154 Norwegian children from a Lutheran church background, and a group of 159 Norwegian children from a fundamentalist Lutheran sect. Thus, four levels of exposure to religious education were represented.

The results indicate clearly that children of greater religiosity (Catholic parochial school children and fundamentalist Lutheran) had significantly higher Social Desirability scores than did children of lesser religiosity. This means that children from more religious backgrounds showed a significantly greater tendency to present themselves in a more favorable light, even when it meant reporting things that were likely to be untrue.

The authors' interpretation is that since Social Desirability scores measure defensiveness and distortion of actual behavior, they may be related to the more frequent use of denial and repression as defense mechanisms. They also suggest that the rigorous religious training and harsher parental discipline found in some religious groups may be the antecedents of the kind of defensiveness measured by the Social Desirability Scale in both children and adults. Thus, results of this study relate to the effects of religion on character structure in adults. The correlation between religiosity and social desirability set has been reported in studies with adults (Dittes, 1969).

An aspect that the study by Crandall and Gozali illuminates is the role of religious socialization as a predecessor of adult social conformity. Thus, we can agree with Wright (1971) that a fairly strict religious upbringing will produce an increased sensitivity to moral reputation and a greater sense of shame in response to transgression.

References

Dittes, J. E. Psychology of religion. In Lindzey, G., & Aronson, E. (Eds.), *Handbook of Social Psychology*. (2nd ed.) Vol. 5. Reading, Mass.: Addison-Wesley, 1969.

Wright, D. *The Psychology of Moral Behavior*, Harmondsworth, England: Penguin, 1971.

Since the late 1950s there have been many demonstrations of the usefulness of social desirability (SD) measures as predictors of individual differences in behavior in both laboratory and natural social settings (e.g., Allison & Hunt 1959; Brown 1960; Crandall 1966; Crowne & Marlowe 1964; Epstein 1964; Fishman 1965). Little research attention has yet been given to the antecedent process by which these tendencies are developed. One way of generating hypotheses concerning antecedent processes is to determine the demographic characteristics associated with individual differences in social desirability response tendencies. Once such demographic correlates are established, they may suggest hypotheses about the psychologically relevant processes that may have accounted for the differential development

of the response in the several demographic groups.
For example, Crandall, Crandall and Katkovsky (1965)
found that higher SD scores were attained by girls
than by boys, by younger than by older children, by
Negroes than by whites, and by duller than by brighter
children.   These and similar findings may help to
focus future research attention on the particular
socialization processes which occur differentially
to, or influence differentially, the two sexes, the
two races, children of various ages, and those who
are more or less intellectually capable.

This is another such study of group differences.
It is concerned with four groups of children who live
in the United States and Norway.   One of the dimensions on which the groups varied was that of religiosity, and we have designated them according to
their country and their religious group membership.
The focal groups may well have differed on other
important factors which preliminary findings had
suggested might contribute to differences in SD
scores, but it was not possible to obtain systematic
observations on these related factors for these four
groups.   Despite the undetermined influence of those
other factors, the following SD data are presented
in the hope that they will provide leads for better
controlled investigations of the psychologically
relevant processes which may determine SD responding.

The measure of social desirability response
tendencies presented in Crandall et al. (1965) and
used in the present study is the Children's Social
Desirability (CSD) questionnaire.   A cross-cultural
comparison of some unpublished CSD data, gathered
from two samples of Israeli children (ages 12 and
14) with those of the southwestern Ohio children used
in the 1965 study, revealed that both age groups of
Israeli children responded significantly more often
in the socially desirable direction than their
American counterparts.   These results were not unexpected since Israeli children are regimented in
youth organizations at an early age and are strongly
indoctrinated with the idea that the welfare of the
social group has precedence over that of the individual.

Second, some additional unpublished data, from a
small sample of 6—12-year-old children and their mothers

in the Fels Institute longitudinal study, again
demonstrated that girls in that sample had higher
CSD scores than boys. From birth to age 6, the
mothers of the girls, as compared with mothers of
boys, had been somewhat less affectionate, more
critical, less protective, less nurturant, more
coercive, more punitive, and more restrictive.
Furthermore, among the boys, maternal criticality,
restrictiveness, coerciveness, and punitiveness
were positively and significantly related to their
CSD scores. Partially based on these two sets of
data, it was reasoned that socially desirable responding might also be more frequent among children
whose socialization experiences had in other respects been harsher, more demanding of morally and
socially righteous attitudes and behaviors, and
less tolerant of personal gratifications and need
fulfillment. It was thought that perhaps there
would be more frequent attempts to appear socially
desirable among children from communities where
religious training was rigorous and doctrinaire,
imposed or threatened severe penalties for defiant
behavior, demanded adherence to an orthodox and incontestable set of tenets, and trained for obedience
and submission to authority. In addition, it was
felt that the more pervasive and consistent such
training was throughout the child's church, home,
school, and community life, the more difficult it
would be for him to admit that he deviated from
such universally held standards, that is, to give
the non-SD response.

It was thought that Catholic parochial schoolchildren might represent one such group available
to us. Boehm (1962) maintains that the Catholic
church exerts more authority over its members than
other churches. She also states that its authority
figures, the parish religious, are awe inspiring to
children, that they keep regular surveillance over
deviant attitudes and behaviors, and that this is
especially true for children who are in their constant charge in parochial schools. In addition,
she contends that the parents of Catholic parochial
schoolchildren also constitute models who are, themselves, submissive to church authority, highly

religious, and likely to reinforce the teaching of church and school.

That Boehm's observations were correct is substantiated by Lenski (1961) in a study of a probability sample of 656 Protestants, Catholics, and Jews. Catholic parents who had themselves attended parochial schools were significantly more likely to send their children to parochial schools, to attend mass more often, to pray more often, to be more doctrinally orthodox, to limit their social contacts to others within a Catholic sub-community, and to believe that they should form close friendships only with other Catholics. He also demonstrated that Catholic parents, as compared with Protestant parents, did not as often believe it was important that the child "think for himself," valued obedience more strongly, and used more physical punishment. It seemed reasonable, then, to anticipate that Catholic parochial schoolchildren might score higher on the CSD than did the public schoolchildren described in Crandall et al. (1965), who were generally Protestant or not affiliated with any church. To distinguish the Crandall et al. (1965) sample from the Catholic parochial school sample, the former will be referred to subsequently in this report as the U. S. non-Catholic sample.

We were also fortunate to have CSD data available to us from children of two Norwegian communities which varied from one another on a dimension of religiosity.[1] One group consisted of children in the village of Tarsand which is located quite close to the city of Oslo and has much interchange with it. The religious affiliation of the townspeople of Tarsand is with the regular Lutheran denomination, the state church of Norway. The other sample was composed of children of Lillesand, a village on the "Black Coastline" of Norway. The term "Black Coastline" is applied to this region because of the strict and dour sect of strong fundamentalist

[1]These data were collected for us by Mr. R. Kristiansen and Mr. J. Steensen. We wish to express our gratitude for their kind assistance.

Lutherans who live there in relative isolation. Although they, too, ostensibly belong to the state
church, they consider its doctrines and practices
too secular and liberal. They have had periodic
conflicts with the state church and have incorpora-
ted a set of more orthodox and fundamentalist tenets
into their religious creed and services. Strong
moralistic judgments and rigid definitions of right
and wrong prevail in respect to a vast array of behaviors, values, and attitudes. Numerous regular
church affairs are supplemented by many religious
functions in the community. For example, "Thurs-
day meetings," held in the community center, are
attended by the whole village, both adults and
children, and consist of public confession, con-
demnation, and pleas for salvation. The Old
Testament is read and laymen preach in revivalist
fashion, emphasizing sin, fear of the devil, and
eternal damnation. Although we have no information
on the child-rearing practices of parents in this
community, it seems likely that they would be more
severe than those of the parents of Tarsand.

It was anticipated that children from the more
religious communities in both countries (U. S.
Catholic parochial and Norwegian fundamentalist)
would score higher on the CSD than those from the
less religious groups (U. S. non-Catholic and
Norwegian State Luthern), and that this difference
would also occur between the two differing religious
groups *within* each of the two countries.

METHOD

The Measure of Social Desirability

The CSD scale presents the subject with 48
statements representing culturally sanctioned attitudes and behaviors. The items are worded in such
a way that the socially desirable response is behaviorally improbable; for example, "When I make a
mistake, I always admit I am wrong" (T), "I sometimes feel angry when I don't get my way" (F), "I
never forget to say 'please' and 'thank you'" (T),

"Sometimes I do things I've been told not to do" (F).
To answer in the socially desirable direction the
subject must maintain that he has attitudes and behaviors entirely and consistently consonant with the
cultural dictum stated in the item. The development
of this scale, its methods of administration, descriptive statistics, split-half and test-retest reliabilities, as well as the demographic correlates
previously mentioned, are described in Crandall et
al. (1965).

For administration to the Norwegian samples,
the scale was translated into Norwegian and five
Norwegian judges were asked to answer the items in
the direction which would be socially desirable for
children of that country.[2] There was complete agreement of these judgments with the direction in which
the items are keyed for American samples. (This is
not so surprising when it is remembered that socially
desirable attitudes and behaviors in both Norway and
in this country are an outgrowth of a general Western Judeo-Christian value system. Lovaas (1958) had
earlier reported that Norwegian judges' social desirability ratings of the items in the Edwards Personal
Preference Schedule correlated .78 with judgments of
those items made by American judges; Lovaas's method
of judging required finer discriminations than the
simple dichotomous judgment required for each CSD
item.)

Test-retest reliability (1-month interval) for
the Norwegian language version of the CSD was established on an independent sample of fourth-and tenth-
grade Norwegian children.[3] The product moment correlation was .81.

[2]We wish to express our gratitude to Mr. Trygve
Lie and members of the Educational Psychology Department, University of Oslo, for their cooperation.
[3]We wish to express our most sincere gratitude
to Mr. and Mrs. Trygve Lie whose assistance made the
Norwegian phase of the investigation possible.

Samples

   U. S. non-Catholic.--The study by Crandall et
al. (1965) employed 956 children from five public
schools in southwestern Ohio. Those subjects were
in grades 3, 4, 5, 6, 8, 10, and 12. A measure of
their socioeconomic status was normally distributed
and slightly higher than that of the general American
population. This sample was 89.5 percent white and
had a mean IQ of 103 (SD = 13). A more complete
description of the sample will be found in Crandall
et al. (1965).
   In the analyses for the present study, the CSD
scores of 735 children from this sample were used.
These were all the subjects in grades 4, 6, 8, 10,
and 12, since those were the grades for which we had
comparison data in the other religious-cultural
samples. At the time these normative data were collected, the religious affiliation of the subjects
and their families was not obtained. However, all
children came from various school systems in Greene
County, Ohio, and Catholic residents of the county
constitute only 7.3 percent of its population. Of
this small percentage, a number of Catholic children
are sent to a parochial school outside the county,
leaving some unknown, but even smaller percentage
of Catholic children in these public school samples.
Thus, perhaps it is safe to describe this group as
primarily non-Catholic.
   U. S. Catholic parochial.--The CSD was administered to 426 Catholic children in grades 4, 6, 8,
10, and 12 enrolled in parochial schools in the New
York and New Haven areas. The schools served
middle-class neighborhoods containing single-family
homes. All children were white. Since children of
less than 75 IQ were in special education classes
and were not used for this study, it may be presumed that the samples used here were of normal
intelligence.
   Norwegian State Lutheran.--The Norwegian version of the CSD was administered to all 154 children enrolled in grades 6, 8, and 10 in Tarsand,
the village near Oslo. These children represent the
full social class distribution of the village in

which they live. The state provides special educational facilities for slow learners and such children were not enrolled in the regular elementary school and *Gymnasium* from which the data were obtained. Thus, all students in the present sample may be presumed to be of average intelligence or above.

    Norwegian fundamentalist Lutheran.--This sample was composed of 159 sixth-, eighth- and tenth-grade children from the village of Lillesand. These children, too, came from the regular elementary school and *Gymnasium* in Lillesand, and were, in social class and intelligence, like the children from Tarsand.

    RESULTS

    Table 1 contains the means and standard deviations of CSD scores for each sex, at each of the grade levels tested in all four religious-cultural samples. These data were analyzed with a 4 (religious-cultural groups) X 3 (grade levels 6, 8, and 12) X 2 (sexes) analysis of variance for unequal cell frequencies using an unweighted means analysis (Winer 1962). The additional data for grades 4 and 12 from the U. S. Catholic and non-Catholic samples were omitted from the analysis of variance because Norwegian data were not available for these grade levels. A summary of this analysis appears in table 2. All tests of significance in this analysis and the subsequent t tests are two-tailed.

    As may be seen in table 2, the main effect for religious-cultural difference is significant at the .001 level. In order to determine whether those children of greater religiosity (regardless of country) had higher CSD scores than those of less religiosity, a test of difference was computed between the sample of U. S. non-Catholic and Norwegian State Lutheran children's CSD scores combined (M = 16.90, SD = 8.43) and the scores of the combined sample of the U. S. Catholic and Norwegian fundamentalist Lutheran children (M = 18.90, SD = 8.31). The resulting t was 3.80, $p <$ .001. Within the

TABLE 1

CSD Means and Standard Deviations by Religious-Cultural
Group, Grade Level, and Sex

	U.S. Non-Catholic		U.S. Catholic Parochial		Norwegian State Lutheran		Norwegian Fundamentalist Lutheran	
Grade	M	F	M	F	M	F	M	F
4th:								
M......	18.71	25.76	27.17	29.14	...	...	...	...
SD......	10.88	9.68	7.21	9.65	...	...	...	...
N.......	66	49	29	29	...	...	...	...
6th:								
M......	17.68	22.12	20.43	21.19	16.35	20.94	21.56	25.72
SD......	8.33	8.82	7.92	7.13	7.47	7.14	8.64	10.00
N.......	93	73	28	31	20	31	25	32
8th:								
M......	15.98	17.53	19.46	20.06	17.13	19.79	19.03	19.05
SD......	9.09	8.63	7.69	8.88	9.45	7.05	7.69	9.14
N.......	69	93	28	32	31	28	32	19
10th:								
M......	13.07	14.55	14.12	16.82	13.58	18.15	16.10	22.40
SD......	6.40	7.30	7.41	6.12	7.89	4.62	6.12	8.92
N.......	90	93	64	66	31	13	31	20
12th:								
M......	10.67	14.47	12.70	16.02	...	...	...	...
SD......	6.80	7.83	5.40	6.55	...	...	...	...
N.......	52	57	60	59	...	...	...	...
				Total Sample				
	M = 15.44		*M* = 17.09		*M* = 17.65		*M* = 20.63	
	SD = 8.84		SD = 8.49		SD = 7.98		SD = 8.91	
	N = 735		*N* = 426		*N* = 154		*N* = 159	

United States sample, the less religious children
(non-Catholic) had a mean CSD score of 16.67 (SD =
8.56), Catholic children had a mean of 17.79 (SD =
7.73), yielding a *t* of 1.81. This difference was
only significant at the .07 level. It will be remembered, however, that CSD data were also available
for non-Catholic and Catholic children in grades 4
and 12 (see table 1). When these data were added
to those from the sixth-, eighth-, and tenth-grade
children of each sample, the mean for the non-
Catholic children was 15.44 (SD = 8.84); that for
the Catholic sample was 17.09 (SD = 8.49). The *t*
between these means for the total samples of Catholic and non-Catholic children was 2.21, $p < .05$.
In the Norwegian samples, the mean of the State
Lutheran children (17.65, SD = 7.98) differed from

that of the fundamentalist Lutheran children (20.63, SD = 8.91) with a t of 3.13, $p < .01$. Thus, considering all four groups in the study, those children from the two groups of greater religiosity showed significantly stronger tendencies to respond in the socially desirable direction than did those from the two less religious groups, and as predicted, these differences were also significant within each country.

TABLE 2

SUMMARY OF ANALYSIS OF VARIANCE OF *CSD* SCORES BY
RELIGIOUS-CULTURAL GROUP, GRADE LEVEL, AND SEX

	SS	df	MS	F	p
Religious-cultural group (A)	1600.65	3	533.55	8.45	.001
Grade level (B)	2834.66	2	1417.33	22.46	.001
Sex (C)	1566.10	1	1566.10	24.66	.001
A × B	630.65	6	105.11	1.67	ns
A × C	194.89	3	64.96	1.03	ns
B × C	257.12	2	128.56	2.04	ns
A × B × C	255.17	6	42.53	0.67	ns
Error	66138.25	1048	63.11	...	...

It might be asked whether all Norwegian children had higher or lower CSD scores than all American children, if religion were collapsed for each country. Such an analysis yielded a t of 3.72, $p < .001$ (U. S. $M = 17.04$, SD = 8.32; Norwegian $M = 19.16$, SD = 8.57), indicating that the Norwegian children did demonstrate stronger social desirability response tendencies than the American children. However, it should be remembered that the fundamentalist children from Lillesand represent slightly over half of our total Norwegian sample, yet the "Black Coastline" region of Norway contains only an extremely small proportion of the population of that country. It may be, then, that the overall American-Norwegian difference found here was produced almost entirely by the scores of this unusual Norwegian group. To examine this possibility, each of the two Norwegian samples was tested separately against the combined sample of American children. The t comparing the State Lutheran children with all American children was 0.86, $p > .50$; that of the fundamentalist Lutheran children versus all American children was 4.67, $p < .001$. Thus, the

overall difference found between children of the two
countries does, in fact, come from the unusually
high scores of the Norwegian fundamentalist group.
It would not be safe to conclude that Norwegian
children have stronger desirability response tendencies than American children, unless this were
demonstrated with a more representative sample of
Norwegian children.

The strong main effects for grade level ($F =$
22.46, $p < .001$) and for sex ($F = 24.66$, $p < .001$)
and the lack of any significant interactions with
religious-cultural group indicate that CSD scores
generally drop with age in these three additional
religious-cultural samples, and that girls in these
samples also have higher scores than boys. These
results are consistent with those previously reported in Crandall et al. (1965) for the sample of
southwestern Ohio children who are here designated
as the U. S. non-Catholic group.

DISCUSSION

It will be remembered that the wording of the
CSD items makes it highly improbable that the child
can give a veridical report of his experiences when
he makes an SD response. Why was it, then, that the
influence of the harsher socialization of the more
religious groups was not counteracted by another aspect of their rigorous Christian training: the
strong inculcation of the importance of being truth-
ful? It would seem that a likely possibility is
that SD responses are not always made with *awareness*
of the distortions they require, that they are, instead, often the result of repression or denial of
actual, but unacceptable, thoughts or behaviors.
Ford (1964a) has, in fact, even suggested that SD
scales may be used as measures of defensive denial
and he and his colleagues (Ford 1964b; Ford &
Hersen 1967; Jacobson & Ford 1966) have demonstrated
that other behaviors indicative of denial are also
associated with high SD responding. Crowne and
Marlowe (1964), too, have summarized a number of

studies indicating that high SD individuals evidence
more defensive behaviors.

Since the groups of greater religiosity gave
more SD responses, is there any evidence that they
might also be more prone to use denial or repression?
The literature is very sparse on this issue. Our
search for studies directly linking religious group
membership with use of defense mechanisms succeeded
in locating only one such study: Lesser (1959) demonstrated that Catholic boys were more prone than
Protestant and Jewish boys to inhibit or avoid expression of aggression in fantasy after provocation
to aggression. Nevertheless, there is some additional indirect evidence that this might be the case.
As previously mentioned, child-rearing practices
have been found to be more severe among Catholic
parents than among Protestant and Jewish parents
(Lenski 1961). Furthermore, Miller and Swanson
(1960) found that mothers who make more arbitrary
demands for obedience, use more severe and less flexible disciplinary techniques, and give fewer rewards,
are more likely to have sons who make greater use of
denial. Ruebush, Byrum, and Farnham (1963) also report that highly defensive boys have mothers who are
less warm, supportive, and encouraging, and hold in-
flexible expectations for their sons' performance.
It will also be remembered that our preliminary data
on the Fels Institute longitudinal study children
and their mothers demonstrated that high SD responding was associated with earlier maternal punitiveness,
restrictiveness, coerciveness, and criticality. Thus,
although there is little research yet reported to
establish the direct link between particular religious training and the denial or repression which
may underlie SD responding, the same child-rearing
antecedents which have been associated with these
defenses are also associated with high SD tendencies
and are most often used by Catholic parents. Obviously, such evidence is only suggestive rather than
conclusive. But it does seem reasonable that strict,
rigid, punitive socializing techniques may make the
child less able to allow into consciousness the recognition that he has deviated from demanding standards of conduct.

There remains the possibility that the higher
SD scores of Catholic children were not caused by
greater use of denial of their own unacceptable behaviors, but that their behavior was so consistently
and undeviatingly consonant with the SD response
that neither dissembling nor denying was necessary.
That is, perhaps these children were so well socialized that they could report with honesty and full
awareness that they *always* admitted wrongdoing,
never felt angry when they didn't get their way, *always* did exactly what they had been told to do, etc.
It is possible that high SD responders had, for example, fewer hostile feelings and had less often
overtly aggressed against others. (Approximately
one-fourth of the items on the CSD deal with hostility or verbal or physical aggression.) Or put
the other way around, since giving a non-SD response
is essentially like "fessing up," perhaps those
children who "fess up" more readily on the instrument
have more to confess. A study by Lefkowitz, Walder,
and Eron (1963) on confession and aggression, however, provides contrary evidence. These investigators found that there were significant *negative*
relationships between sociometric ratings of aggression and children's use of confession. Those who
aggressed most, confessed least. Furthermore, the
value of those negative relationships increased with
increasing use of physical punishment by the parent.
It seems that punitiveness may constitute a threat
which makes for greater denial and less ability to
confess. High SD responding is also associated with
more defensive denial and with harsher parental treatment, the kind of parental discipline Lenski (1961)
found more prevalent among Catholic parents. For
these reasons, it seems likely that the higher CSD
scores attained by the more religious groups are not
the product of intentional deception, but that these
children may more readily repress or deny unacceptable
thoughts and behaviors which must be at the level of
awareness in order to give non-SD response.
It must be pointed out, however, that the samples used in this study did not differ only on a
single religious dimension. Whether the higher CSD
scores of the Catholic and fundamentalist children

result from the particular tenets of their faiths,
the rigor of their religious training, the greater
penalties imposed or threatened for deviance, or
from their relatively greater isolation from other
social groups, and/or the harsher child-rearing
practices used by their parents, cannot be dis-
entangled. These are merely suggested here as some
of the possible antecedents of social desirability
responding which might be pursued with controlled
research designs.

REFERENCES

Allison, J., & Hunt, D. Social desirability and the
    expression of aggression under varying condi-
    tions of frustration. *Journal of Consulting
    Psychology,* 1959, 23, 528-532.

Boehm, L. The development of conscience: A com-
    parison of students in Catholic parochial
    schools and in public schools. *Child Develop-
    ment,* 1962, 33, 591-602.

Brown, P. The social desirability variable on verbal
    learning performance. *Journal of Educational
    Psychology,* 1960, 51, 52-59.

Crandall, V. C. Personality characteristics and
    social and achievement behaviors associated
    with children's social desirability response
    tendencies. *Journal of Personality and Social
    Psychology,* 1966, 4, 477-486.

Crandall, V. C., Crandall, V. J., & Katkovsky, W.
    A children's social desirability questionnaire.
    Journal of Consulting Psychology, 1965, 29,
    27-36.

Crowne, D., & Marlowe, D. *The approval motive:
    studies in evaluative dependence.* New York:
    Wiley, 1964.

Epstein, R.   Need for approval and the conditioning
     of verbal hostility in asthmatic children.
     Journal of Abnormal and Social Psychology, 1964,
     69, 105-109.

Fishman, C.   Need for approval and the expression
     of aggression under varying conditions of
     frustration.   *Journal of Personality and Social
     Psychology,* 1965, 2, 809-816.

Ford, L. H., Jr.   A forced-choice, acquiescence-free,
     social desirability (defensiveness) scale.
     Journal of Consulting Psychology, 1964, 28,
     475.   (a)

Ford, L. H., Jr.   Social desirability, defensive
     denial, and expectancy for success.   Paper
     presented at the annual meeting of the Mid-
     western Psychological Association, St. Louis,
     May 1964.   (b)

Ford, L. H., Jr., & Hersen, M.   Need approval, de-
     fensive denial, and direction of aggression in
     a failure-frustration situation.   *Journal of
     Personality and Social Psychology,* 1967, 6,
     228-232.

Jacobson, L., & Ford, L. H., Jr.   Need for approval,
     defensive denial, and sensitivity to cultural
     stereotypes.   *Journal of Personality,* 1966, 34,
     596-609.

Lefkowitz, M., Walder, L., & Eron, L.   Punishment,
     identification and aggression.   *Merrill-Palmer
     Quarterly,* 1963, 9, 159-174.

Lenski, G.   *The religious factor.*   Garden City, N. Y.:
     Doubleday, 1961.

Lesser, G.   Religion and the defensive responses in
     children's fantasy.   *Journal of Projective
     Techniques,* 1959, 23, 64-68.

Lovaas, O. I. Social desirability ratings of
    personality variables by Norwegian and
    American college students. *Journal of Ab-
    normal and Social Psychology,* 1958, 57, 124-
    125.

Miller, D., & Swanson, G. *Inner conflict and de-
    fense.* New York: Holt, 1960.

Ruebush, B., Byrum, M., & Farnham, L. Problem
    solving as a function of children's defensive-
    ness and parental behavior. *Journal of Ab-
    normal and Social Psychology,* 1963, 67, 355-
    362.

Winer, B. *Statistical principles in experimental
    design.* New York: McGraw-Hill, 1962.

THE EFFECT OF RELIGION UPON CHILDREN'S RESPONSES TO QUESTIONS INVOLVING PHYSICAL CAUSALITY

MELVIN EZER

Editor's introduction. The early effects of
religious socialization on non-religious
thinking of children are examined in the following article by Ezer. Direct effects of
religious training can be measured through the
study of either "acquired" or "spontaneous"
religious concepts, to use Elkind's terms; but
if religious training is effective, it could
produce differences in non-religious behaviors.
One way of conceptualizing Ezer's question is
in terms of religious thinking and language.
How does religious training color perceptions
of physical and interpersonal events in this
world?

Ezer hypothesized that children who come from
religious homes are exposed to ideas that are
animistic (attributing conscious life to nature
or natural objects) and anthropomorphic (as-
cribing human form or human attributes to non-
human things) and that they will use such ideas
to explain cause-and-effect relationships in

the physical world. Ezer, just like Elkind,
starts with Piaget's developmental theory,
but Ezer's study is intended to challenge the
theory rather than support it. Ezer's theoretical thrust is to show that the stages described by Piaget are not universal and uniform,
and are influenced by environmental factors,
such as religiosity. The results essentially
prove Ezer's hypothesis. Children exposed to
more religious training, either in the more
devout families or in religious schools, responded with animistic and anthropomorphic
explanations. An important result is the lack
of differences among religious denominations:
children coming from Jewish, Protestant, and
Catholic families showed similar responses,
given the same level of family devoutness.

The topic of animistic, non-scientific
thinking in childhood as a result of religious
training has two important implications, which
can be stated as questions:

1. How does religious training affect cause-
and-effect thinking in later years?

2. Since the animistic and anthropomorphic
modes of thinking connected with religious
training are non-scientific, how does religious training affect scientific creativity
and productivity?

Shaw's study on "Religion and conceptual
models of behavior," reprinted in this volume,
deals with the first question as it applies to
the area of human behavior. While it is clear
that holding religious beliefs does not pre-
clude scientific thinking and scientific
achievement, studies of prominent scientists
have shown that they are much less religious
than the general population (Roe, 1953). In
terms of religious backgrounds they come from,
eminent American scientists are far from being
a representative sample of the general population. Considering their rates in the
population, Catholics and fundamentalist Protestants are under-represented among eminent
scientists, while liberal Protestants and Jews
are over-represented. This phenomenon has

been explained in terms of specific values
associated with particular religious traditions
(for example, Judaism), which are conducive
to scientific achievement. Datta (1967) tried
to determine if an association between scientific achievement and religious background
appeared among adolescents participating in
the Westinghouse Science Talent Search. Her
results were clear only in regard to the
Jewish group, which was higher on creativity
ratings compared to all other groups. Datta's
(1967) article is recommended as an introduction to other aspects of the relationship
between religion and scientific achievement.

References

Datta, L. E. Family religious background and
early scientific creativity. *American Sociological Review,* 1967, 32, 626-635.

Roe, A. *The making of a scientist.* New York:
Dodd, Mead & Co., 1953.

INTRODUCTION

The purpose of this investigation was to study
the effects of religion upon children's explanations
of cause-effect relationships. The focal point for
the study was the work of Jean Piaget (1928a; 1928b;
1930) who concluded from his investigations that
there are definite steps or stages of thought processes through which children characteristically pass
in their mental development, and that these stages
are, in turn, accompanied by scientific patterns of
causal thinking.

The focus of Piaget's work had been on studying
children's explanations of causal events solely in
relation to the subjects' chronological age with
little systematic investigation of the possible role

of other factors. Piaget asserted that children between the ages of six and eight predominantly explain cause and effect relationships of physical
phenomena in animistic and/or anthropomorphic terms.
He further stated that animistic and anthropomorphic
explanations are spontaneous and impulsive, since
the child is egocentric and prelogical in his thinking. However, a survey of the literature in this
area shows that animism and anthropomorphism are not
always the prevalent mode of response for children
before eight years; instead, children often respond
with objective explanations of physical causality.

Since the publication of Piaget's work, many
experiments and investigations have attempted to
validate his conclusions. The studies to date present conflicting evidence in their support or refu-
tation of Piaget's theory concerning causal thinking. Thompson (1941), Grigsby (1932), Nagy (1948),
Dennis (1940), and Sarvis (1939) are among the investigators whose studies claim to substantiate all
or part of Piaget's conclusions, while the work of
Isaacs (1930), Hazlitt (1930), Deutsche (1943),
Oakes (1947), and Huang (1943) presents evidence
which appears to refute Piaget's findings.

The influence of variables other than age on
the development of causal thinking has also been
investigated. To date the findings of studies involving sex (Deutsche, 1943; McAndrew, 1943),
socio-economic status (Deutsche, 1943; Huang, 1943),
and race or ethnicity (Dennis, 1940; Huang, 1943;
Jones & Arrington, 1945; Menon, 1944) suggest that
these variables do not significantly influence the
level of children's causal thinking. No conclusive
evidence concerning the role of intelligence
(Deutsche, 1943; Granich, 1940; Grigsby, 1932; Huang,
1943; Isaacs, 1930; McAndrew, 1943; Sarvis, 1939)
and question wording (Granich, 1940) has yet been
found. But the amount of experience with the phenomena involved (Granich, 1940; Grigsby, 1932;
McAndrew, 1943; Sarvis, 1939; Werner and Carrison,
1944) has been shown definitely to affect the responses of children to questions involving physical
causality. The variable of religion, which was the
focal point of this study, has not yet been explored.

The author hypothesized that since the three
major contemporary religions in the United States
(Protestantism, Catholicism, and Judaism) have both
animistic and anthropomorphic concepts within their
tenets, the children who have had a greater amount
of formal religious training or who come from in-
tensely religious homes would be more likely to
answer questions involving physical causality with
animistic and/or anthropomorphic responses than
would children who have had a lesser amount of religious training or who come from less devout homes.

PROCEDURE

To test these hypotheses, 153 boys, aged 6-8
and in grades one and two were employed as subjects.
If within a limited age span wide differences among
subjects in causal concepts are found, doubt would
be cast on the validity of Piaget's contention that
causal concepts vary mainly with age.
The sample was composed of 47 Protestant children, 54 Jewish children, and 52 Catholic children.
Of the 47 Protestant children, 22 attended public
school, and 25 attended all-day Episcopal or Lutheran
religious schools; of the 54 Jewish children, 28
attended public school, and 26 attended all-day religious schools (Yeshivas); of the 52 Catholic children, 25 attended public school, and 27 attended
all-day parochial school.
The sample was restricted to emotionally adjusted white males of average intelligence (I. Q.
90-110) whose fathers were classified as non-pro-
fessional "white-collar" workers, e.g. clerks,
salesmen, and minor business executives.
Although, as previously mentioned, the findings of other investigators involving the sex, socio-
economic status, and race of the child suggest that
these variables do not significantly influence causal
thinking, these variables as well as age were held
constant as a precaution. Since no conclusive evidence one way or another concerning the role of
intelligence and its effect upon causal thinking
has been found, this variable also was held constant.

Four measures involving physical causality were constructed by the author with the exception of Test IV, question 1, which was taken from Dennis (1953). In their final form (i.e., subsequent to pretest) the author administered the items individually to the subjects and recorded the children's responses verbatim. The four instruments were as follows:

Test I

Test I consisted of three problem-solving situations which were presented as follows: "I am going to read some stories to you. These stories are about boys just like you who had something happen to them. I want you to listen very carefully to the story because I want you to answer a question at the end of each story."

Question 1. Once a boy, Paul, lived at the beach during the summer. He found an empty rowboat on the beach one day. Paul climbed into the boat and rowed away from shore toward the ocean. When he was quite far out in the water, the boat began to leak. There was no one around Paul in the water or on the beach to whom he could call for help. If he tried to row the boat back to shore, it would sink before he reached shore. Paul could not swim to shore because he did not know how to swim. Now, if you were Paul, what would you do?

Question 2. One day a boy, Jack, was coming home after doing an errand for his mother. He took a short cut along some railroad tracks. Jack had been warned not to walk along the tracks because it was very dangerous. As he walked along the tracks, his foot somehow got caught beneath the track, and he could not pull it out. He knew a train was due to come along the track, and, sure enough, he thought he saw the engine's smoke off in the distance. Jack hollered for help, but he was in a lonely place, and there was no one there to help him. Now, if you were Jack, what would you do?

Question 3. Jim had gone on a hike in the desert all by himself and became lost. When he started out he had taken some food and water with

him, but somehow he had lost the food and water and
could not find them. As Jim wandered about the desert, he became weaker and weaker from thirst and
hunger. There were no people, no roads, and no
houses for many, many miles, so that his chance of
being found was not good. Also, he had not told
anyone that he was going for a hike, so that there
probably would not be anyone looking for him. Now,
if you were Jim, what would you do?

Some actual responses of the different types to
Test I, Q. 1 (the sinking-boat situation) were:

    (a)   animistic: "The ocean would know I am in
           trouble and send a big wave to push me to
           shore."

    (b)   anthropomorphic: "I would pray to God to
           save me."

    (c)   scientific: "I would stop up the hole with
           my finger, and throw the water out with my
           other hand."

Test II

Test II contained three pictures which were
presented to the children. The experimenter said:
"I am going to show you some pictures and ask you
some questions about them. When you answer the
questions, tell me what you really think."

Picture 1. A picture of a zebra grazing was
shown to the subjects and then they were asked:
"How does the zebra get his stripes? What causes
the zebra's stripes?"

Picture 2. A field of multicolored flowers
was shown to the children, and they were asked:
"How do the flowers get their different colors?
What causes the flowers' different colors?"

Picture 3. A picture of a bolt of lightning
was shown to the children and they were asked:
"How does a bolt of lightning form? What causes a
bolt of lightning?"

Typical examples of the various types of response to Test II, Picture 1 (the zebra) were:

    (a)   animistic: "The zebra paints on the
           stripes himself."

(b)   anthropomorphic: "God puts the stripes
      on the zebra."
(c)   scientific: "He is born that way because
      his father and mother are like that."

Test III

Test III was made up of three multiple-choice
questions. The directions were: "I am going to
ask you questions as to why certain things happen.
Then I am going to give you some answers to these
questions. I want you to listen carefully and pick
out the answer you think is most correct. I will
read everything twice, so listen carefully and choose
the answer you think is right. Don't tell me the
answer until I ask for it."

Question 1. Growing flowers sometimes die because:
(1)   the flowers have eaten some poisonous food.
(2)   the flowers kill themselves.
(3)   the flowers do not get enough sun and
      water.
(4)   God wants the flowers to die.

Question 2. Water flows in a river because:
(1)   it goes from a high place to a low place.
(2)   it is pulled along the river by the ocean.
(3)   God makes the water flow along by pushing
      it.
(4)   the water knows where to go, so it flows
      there by itself.

Question 3. Night comes because:
(1)   God wants night to come so he covers up
      the sun.
(2)   the sun wants to hide from the earth.
(3)   the fire in the sun goes out.
(4)   the earth turns away from the sun.

Test IV

Test IV contained three multiple-choice questions which were designed only to get at animism.
The directions to the children were the same as

those for Test III except that the first sentence
read, "I am going to read you some questions about
certain things," and the later phrasing requested
the "best" instead of the "right" answer.

Question 1. Many ships sink and are lost at
the bottom of the ocean. Nobody can find them. Do
you think that the ocean itself knows where the ships
are?

    (1)   Yes, because the water in the ocean rubs
          over the ships and knows that they are
          there.
    (2)   Probably not, because the ocean is so
          big and has so much water that it could
          not have any feelings.
    (3)   No, there are so many ships sunk in the
          ocean that the ocean could not know about
          them all.
    (4)   No, the ocean can't know anything.

Question 2. When you blow up a balloon and
blow so much air into it that it bursts, does the
balloon feel it?

    (1)   No, a balloon can't feel a thing.
    (2)   No, once a balloon bursts, it is too
          dead to feel.
    (3)   Probably not, because the rubber in the
          balloon had been dead a long time, since
          the rubber was once a rubber tree.
    (4)   Yes, the balloon can feel the pushing on
          its sides as you blow it up, and it can
          feel the tearing of its skin.

Question 3. When you throw a stone into the
air and it falls and hits the ground, does the stone
feel it?

    (1)   Probably not, because the stone is so old
          that it has been dead a long time.
    (2)   No, a stone can't feel anything.
    (3)   No, when the stone hits the ground, it is
          probably knocked unconscious and can't
          feel anything.
    (4)   Yes, there is a noise when the stone hits
          the ground, so that the stone can feel it
          and knows that it is hurt.

Since it was not possible to ask children questions dealing with religion in the school situation,

a questionnaire asking the parents about their religious behavior, beliefs, and attitudes was constructed in order to ascertain to what degree
religion in the home might influence the children's
causal thinking. To a large extent the questions
sought to ascertain the degree of "fundamentalism"
or literal belief in the scriptures. The questionnaires were mailed to the mothers and returned to
the investigator.

Following the collection of the data, each parental questionnaire was categorized independently
by three judges into three categories: very devout,
moderately devout, and not devout. There was complete agreement among the three judges in 82.7% of
the cases and agreement between two in all the other
cases.

The responses of the children to the test items
were recorded and classified by the author into the
following categories: animistic, anthropomorphic,
and scientific. If two of the three questions, answered by the child on any one test, were anthropomorphic, and the third was answered scientifically,
the subject was classified as anthropomorphic-
scientific. If two of the questions were answered
scientifically, and the third was answered animisti-
cally, the subject was classified as scientific-
animistic, etc. This procedure was followed on all
four tests.

The categories of children's responses were
then related to the religious devoutness in the home
(i.e. to the parent questionnaire) and to the formal religious training of the children as evidenced
by enrollment in public schools or all-day religious
schools.

RESULTS

Chi square analysis was employed to test the
probability that the results are due to random
error. The probabilities given are based on two-
tail tests.

Hypothesis I

Children who come from very devout homes will
offer more animistic and/or anthropomorphic explanations to problems involving physical causality
than will children who come from less devout
(moderately devout and not devout) homes.

	CHI SQUARE	DEGREES OF FREEDOM	LEVEL OF SIGNIFICANCE
Test I	24.575	5	< .001
Test II	12.322	4	< .02
Test III	17.028	5	< .01
Test IV	15.125	3	< .01

Hypothesis II

Children who have had a greater amount of formal religious instruction, i.e., who attend all-day
religious schools, will offer more animistic and/or
anthropomorphic explanations to problems involving
physical causality than will children who have had
a lesser amount of formal religious instruction,
i.e., who attend public schools.

	CHI SQUARE	DEGREES OF FREEDOM	LEVEL OF SIGNIFICANCE
Test I	16.643	5	< .01
Test II	13.032	4	< .02
Test III	20.767	5	< .001
Test IV	14.431	3	< .01

Without commenting on certain nuances of the
data that the specialist who wishes to follow up
this investigation will discern in Tables I through
VIII, the overall direction of the results is clear:
the tendency to give relatively unscientific answers
is associated with the devoutness of the home and
with attendance at a religious rather than public
school. The direction of the former relationship is
especially evident in Tables I, III, and IV if one

contrasts the proportions of very devout and less devout children who gave scientific or partly scientific answers with the proportions who gave wholly animistic or anthropomorphic replies. In the case of religious schooling versus public schooling (Tables V-VIII), the clearest contrast is that between the predominantly scientific answers (e.g., scientific-anthropomorphic) and the predominantly non-scientific (e.g., anthropomorphic-scientific).

TABLE 1 / DISTRIBUTION OF CHILDREN'S RESPONSES TO TEST I AS RELATED TO RELIGIOUS DEVOUTNESS IN THE HOME.

RESPONSES OF 153 CHILDREN

RELIGIOUS DEVOUTNESS IN THE HOME	SCIENTIFIC	SCIENTIFIC-ANTHROPO.	ANTHROPO-MORPHIC-SCIENTIFIC	ANIMISTIC-SCIENTIFIC	ANTHROPO-MORPHIC	ANIMISTIC
Very devout	23	1	11	8	23	7
Moderately devout	19	11	11	7	8	0
Not devout	6	4	4	5	5	0

TABLE 2 / DISTRIBUTION OF CHILDREN'S RESPONSES TO TEST II AS RELATED TO RELIGIOUS DEVOUTNESS IN THE HOME.

RESPONSES OF 153 CHILDREN

RELIGIOUS DEVOUTNESS IN THE HOME	SCIENTIFIC	SCIENTIFIC-ANTHROPO.	SCIENTIFIC-ANIMISTIC	ANTHROPO-MORPHIC	ANIMISTIC
Very devout	27	13	0	21	12
Moderately devout	19	10	8	12	7
Not devout	12	4	2	1	5

TABLE 3 / DISTRIBUTION OF CHILDREN'S RESPONSES TO TEST III AS RELATED TO RELIGIOUS DEVOUTNESS IN THE HOME.

RESPONSES OF 153 CHILDREN

RELIGIOUS DEVOUTNESS IN THE HOME	SCIENTIFIC	SCIENTIFIC-ANTHROPO.	ANTHROPO-MORPHIC-SCIENTIFIC	ANIMISTIC-SCIENTIFIC	ANTHROPO-MORPHIC	ANIMISTIC
Very devout	12	11	4	5	24	17
Moderately devout	12	10	11	7	14	2
Not devout	6	9	0	1	7	1

The implication for the theoretical position championed by Piaget over the years seems unambiguous. Children's conceptual development, at least as represented in their explanations of physical causality, is not a solely maturational phenomenon unaffected by training. If it were, it should have been unaffected by religious influences.

Another noteworthy aspect of these data is the fact that so many children gave partly or wholly scientific responses and not just the animistic-anthropomorphic replies that some of Piaget's writings would forecast for this age group.

An additional analysis was made by comparing children of the three religious affiliations represented in this study, i.e., Protestant, Catholic,

TABLE 4 / DISTRIBUTION OF CHILDREN'S RESPONSES TO TEST IV AS RELATED TO RELIGIOUS DEVOUTNESS IN THE HOME.

RESPONSES OF 153 CHILDREN

RELIGIOUS DEVOUTNESS IN THE HOME	SCIENTIFIC	SCIENTIFIC-ANIMISTIC	ANIMISTIC-SCIENTIFIC	ANIMISTIC
Very devout	21	10	16	26
Moderately devout	24	17	10	5
Not devout	12	4	3	5

TABLE 5 / DISTRIBUTION OF CHILDREN'S RESPONSES TO TEST I AS RELATED TO SCHOOLS ATTENDED.

RESPONSES OF 153 CHILDREN

SCHOOLS ATTENDED	SCIENTIFIC	SCIENTIFIC-ANTHROPO.	ANTHROPO-MORPHIC-SCIENTIFIC	ANIMISTIC-SCIENTIFIC	ANTHROPO-MORPHIC	ANIMISTIC
Religious school children	18	4	17	15	19	5
Public school children	30	12	9	5	17	2

TABLE 6 / DISTRIBUTION OF CHILDREN'S RESPONSES TO TEST II AS RELATED TO SCHOOLS ATTENDED.

RESPONSES OF 153 CHILDREN

SCHOOLS ATTENDED	SCIENTIFIC	SCIENTIFIC-ANTHROPO.	SCIENTIFIC ANIMISTIC-	ANTHROPO-MORPHIC	ANIMISTIC
Religious school children	30	9	2	25	12
Public school children	28	15	8	9	15

TABLE 7 / DISTRIBUTION OF CHILDREN'S RESPONSES TO TEST III AS RELATED TO SCHOOLS ATTENDED.

RESPONSES OF 153 CHILDREN

SCHOOLS ATTENDED	SCIENTIFIC	SCIENTIFIC-ANTHROPO.	ANTHROPO-MORPHIC-SCIENTIFIC	ANIMISTIC-SCIENTIFIC	ANTHROPO-MORPHIC	ANIMISTIC
Religious school children	11	10	12	5	24	16
Public school children	19	20	3	8	21	4

TABLE 8 / DISTRIBUTION OF CHILDREN'S RESPONSES TO TEST IV AS RELATED TO SCHOOLS ATTENDED.

RESPONSES OF 153 CHILDREN

SCHOOLS ATTENDED	SCIENTIFIC	SCIENTIFIC-ANIMISTIC	ANIMISTIC-SCIENTIFIC	ANIMISTIC
Religious school children	25	9	20	24
Public school children	32	22	9	12

and Jewish. The animistic, anthropomorphic, and scientific responses of the children from each faith were related to religious devoutness in the home and to their formal religious instruction, i.e., school attended. The results (the actual data are given in Ezer's 1961 report) indicate that there is greater similarity in responses among the three religious denominations than within a religious denomination. That is, children who come from very devout homes, or who attend all-day religious schools, offer similar proportions of animistic/ anthropomorphic, and scientific responses regardless of their religious denomination. Correspondingly, children who attend public schools or who come from less devout homes offer similar proportions of animistic/anthropomorphic, and scientific responses, regardless of their religious denomination. It appears to be degree of devoutness or of religious exposure rather than content of the beliefs that makes the difference.

The following objection may be raised regarding the meaning of anthropomorphic answers. When a student in a religious school attributes causation to God, he may be mentioning what is salient to him in that setting--or may be stating what he feels is expected of him, rather than candidly exposing his cognitive processes. Possibly this objection is valid, but to account for animistic answers on the same basis, one must assume that devout parents and religious educators expect or encourage such answers from children as old as first and second graders. This seems implausible, and the conclusion appears justified that even if the more devout and the religiously trained children are not perhaps "really" more anthropomorphic than their less religious peers, they do seem likely to be more animistic!

Some readers may draw an unwarranted conclusion upon first seeing these data. It is easy to assume that religious training somehow impedes the ability of certain children to grasp scientific explanations. Although this may be true, the evidence of the present study does not justify this conclusion. Another explanation could be that the motivation rather than the capacity of seeking or learning scientific explanations is lessened when religious answers have been mastered and have quelled the child's curiosity.

What are the educational implications of this investigation? There is wide recognition that

tomorrow's citizens must comprehend the general
nature of science and technology more than most do
today, and that increasing numbers must become ex-
pert in such fields. This study has not provided
evidence on the question of whether devout religious
belief and religious instruction tend to be necessarily incompatible with scientific understanding.
(Obviously, they are not incompatible in all cases
since some of the "devout" children gave purely scientific answers.) Perhaps there are ways in which
those who seek to teach children particular religious views could make their pupils more aware of
an additional order of explanation, the scientific.
Would children who were taught both explanations
give scientific responses if called for? An experi-
ment could be conducted to find the answer to this
question.

SUMMARY AND CONCLUSIONS

A study was made of the effects of religion on
children's explanations of cause-effect relationships. Religiosity was determined in two ways: (1)
by the child's attendance at religious school vs.
public school, and (2) by questionnaires filled out
by parents which were assigned ratings as to the
degree of religious devoutness in the home. Sex,
race, intelligence, and socioeconomic status were
controlled. Four tests of cause-effect relations
were administered to 153 white boys aged 6 to 8
divided among the three major religions and distinguished by public school or religious school attendance. Responses were scored as animistic, anthropomorphic, or scientific.
The results show: (1) Animistic and/or anthropomorphic responses were found more frequently
among children from the more devout homes (as
assessed from the parental questionnaires). These
findings were significant beyond the .02 level for
all four tests. (2) Animistic and/or anthropomorphic responses were more frequent among students
attending religious schools. Again each of four
tests yielded results significant beyond the .02

level. (3) There are no differences among the
various religions (Protestant, Catholic, and Jewish)
with respect to these relations.

These data fail to support the views suggested
by Piaget's writings that (a) children's causal explanations are a function of maturation and are not
controllable by training, (b) development of causal
thinking follows a similar pattern for all individuals, (c) scientific explanations of events are not
present in the earliest school years.

REFERENCES

Dennis, W. Piaget's questions applied to Zuni and
Navaho children. *Psychol. Bull.*, 1940, 38, 520.

Dennis, W. Animistic thinking among college students. *Scientific Monthly*, 1953, 76 (4),
247-249.

Deutsche, Jean M. The development of children's
concepts of causal relations. In R. G.
Barker, J. S. Kounin, and H. F. Wright (Eds.),
Child behavior and development. New York:
McGraw-Hill, 1943. Pp. 129-145.

Ezer, M. The effect of religion upon children's
responses to questions involving physical
causality. Unpublished doctoral dissertation,
Harvard Univer., 1961.

Granich, L. A qualitative analysis of concepts in
mentally deficient boys. *Arch. of Psychol.*,
N. Y., 1940, No. 251.

Grigsby, Olive J. An experimental study of the development of concepts of relationships in pre-
school children as evidenced by their expressive
ability. *J. exp. Educ.*, 1932, 1, 144-162.

Hazlitt, Victoria. Children's thinking. *Brit. J.
Psychol.*, 1930, 20, 354-361.

Huang, I. Children's conception of physical causal-
    ity: a critical summary. *J. genet. Psychol.*,
    1943, 63, 71-121.

Isaacs, Susan. *Intellectual growth in young chil-
    dren.* New York: Harcourt, Brace, 1930.

Jones, F. N., and Arrington, M. G. The explanation
    of physical phenomena given by white and Negro
    children. *Comp. Psychol. Monogr.*, 1945, 18 (5).

McAndrew, M. B. An experimental investigation of
    young children's ideas of causality. *Stud.
    Psychol. and Psychiat.*, 1943, 6, No. 2.

Menon, T. K. N. Growth of relativity of ideas and
    notions and reasoning of children. *Indian J.
    Psychol.*, 1944, 19, 86-91.

Nagy, Maria. The child's theories concerning death.
    Pedag. seminary and genet. Psychol., 1948, 73.

Nass, M. L. The effects of three variables upon
    children's concepts of physical causality.
    Unpublished doctoral dissertation, New York
    Univer., 1954.

Oakes, M. E. Children's explanations of natural
    phenomena. *Teach. Coll. Contr. Educ.*, 1947,
    No. 926.

Piaget, J. *Judgment and reasoning in the child.*
    New York: Harcourt, Brace, 1928. (a)

Piaget, J. *The child's conception of the world.*
    New York: Harcourt, Brace, 1928. (b)

Piaget, J. The child's conception of physical
    causality. New York: Harcourt, Brace, 1930.

Sarvis, B. C. A study of the development aspects
    of child thought by a clinical method. *Psychol.
    Bull.*, 1939, 36.

Thompson, Jane. The ability of children of differ-
    ent grade levels to generalize on sorting
    tests. *J. Psychol.*, 1941, 11, 119-126.

Werner, H., and Carrison, D.   Animistic thinking in
    brain injured, mentally retarded children. *J.
    abnorm. soc. Psychol.*, 1944, 39.

SELECTED ADDITIONAL READINGS ON
RELIGIOUS SOCIALIZATION

Boehm, L. The development of conscience: A com-
    parison of students in Catholic parochial
    schools and in public schools. *Child Devel-
    opment,* 1962, 33, 591-602.

Boehm, L. The development of conscience: A com-
    parison of upper-middle class academically
    gifted children attending Catholic and Jewish
    parochial schools. *Journal of Social Psy-
    chology,* 1963, 59, 101-110.

Datta, L. E. Family religious background and early
    scientific creativity. *American Sociological
    Review,* 1967, 32, 626-635.

Elkind, D. The child's conception of his religious
    denomination I: The Jewish Child. *Journal of
    Genetic Psychology,* 1961, 99, 209-225.

Elkind, D. The child's conception of his religious
    denomination II: The Catholic Child. *Journal
    of Genetic Psychology,* 1962, 101, 185-195.

Elkind, D. The child's conception of his religious
    denomination III: The Protestant child.
    Journal of Genetic Psychology, 1963, 103,
    291-304.

Elkind, D.   The development psychology of religion.
    In A. H. Kidd & J. I. Rivoire (Eds.), *Per-
    ceptual Development in Children*. New York:
    International Universities Press, 1966.

Elkind, D., & Elkind, S.   Varieties of religious
    experiences in young adolescents. *Journal for
    the Scientific Study of Religion,* 1962, 2,
    102-112.

Hess, R. D., & Torney, J. V.   Religion, age, and sex
    in children's perceptions of family authority.
    Child Development, 1962, 33, 781-789.

Kahana, B.   Stages of the dream concept among
    Hasidic children. *Journal of Genetic Psy-
    chology,* 1970, 116, 3-9.

Long, D., Elkind, D., & Spilka, B.   The child's
    conception of prayer. *Journal for the Scien-
    tific Study of Religion,* 1967, 6, 101-109.

Nelson, M. O.   The concept of God and feelings to-
    ward parents. *Journal of Individual Psychology,*
    1971, 27, 46-49.

Pilkington, G. W., Poppleton, P. K., & Robertshaw,
    G.   Changes in religious attitudes and practices
    among students during university degree courses.
    British Journal of Educational Psychology, 1965,
    35, 150-157.

Quin, P. V.   Critical thinking and openmindedness
    in pupils from public and Catholic secondary
    schools. *Journal of Social Psychology,* 1965,
    66, 23-30.

Stark, R.   On the incompatibility of religion and
    science: A survey of American graduate students.
    Journal for the Scientific Study of Religion,
    1963, 3, 3-21. (Reprinted in C. Y. Glock & R.
    Stark, *Religion and Society in Tension*.   Chicago:
    Rand McNally, 1965.)

Vergote, A., Tamayo, A., Pasquali, L., Bonami, M.,
    Pattyn, M., & Custers, A. Concept of God and
    parental images. *Journal for the Scientific
    Study of Religion,* 1969, 8, 79-87.

Wright, D., & Cox, E. A study of the relationship
    between moral judgment and religious belief
    in a sample of British adolescents. *Journal
    of Social Psychology,* 1967, 72, 135-144.

Wright, D., & Cox, E. Changes in moral belief
    among sixth-form boys and girls over a seven-
    year period in relation to religious belief,
    age and sex difference. *British Journal of
    Social and Clinical Psychology,* 1971, 10,
    332-341.

PART TWO
RELIGIOUS BELIEFS, VALUES, AND ATTITUDES

THE RELIGIOUS CONTEXT
OF PREJUDICE

GORDON W. ALLPORT

Editor's introduction. The relationship between religious belief systems and systems of
values and attitudes that guide individual
behavior has often been the most salient aspect of religion. Moral decisions and choices
have always been the expressed concern of religious institutions and individuals and have
been the basis of religion's claim for unique-
ness and authority. But what about the religious man-on-the-street, the average churchgoer and believer? How concerned is he with
moral questions and his relations with fellow
humans? In social-psychological terms, the
issue is that of locating and correlating the
religious and non-religious values within the
universe of values and attitudes related to
life with others. The advent of attitude
measurement in social psychology and the social
changes and upheavals of the last few decades
gave psychologists an opportunity to look at
this issue. One major outcome has been the
emergence of the research theme of religion

From *Journal for the Scientific Study of Religion,* 1966, 5, 447-457. Reprinted with permission.

and prejudice, undoubtedly the most controversial and the most studied in the social psychology of religion.

The positive correlation between religiosity and prejudice has been called a "paradox," but after numerous empirical confirmations it is no longer a paradox; it is merely a consistent finding. That this finding has caused discomfort is obvious; it is probably very distressing to those who value religion as a social institution and who look to religion for a betterment of the human condition. A related phenomenon, which must be disturbing to politically and religiously liberal social scientists, is the religiosity of the constituency of extremely conservative groups. While we cannot suggest that all religious Americans are conservative, it is safe to assume that most conservative Americans are religious. Members, and leaders, of the Ku Klux Klan, John Birch Society, and similar groups often proclaim Christianity as their major motivation and inspiration. Public pronouncements of religiosity on the part of bigoted, racist individuals should be disturbing to those who consider religion to be an inspiration for brotherhood and equality.

The findings indicating a positive relationship between religiosity and prejudice should not be distressing at all if one is either anti-religious (that is, believes that religion has no positive value) or extremely conservative. For the anti-religious, this finding supplies considerable ammunition for pointing out the negative consequences of religious beliefs. For the conservative, prejudiced person, the findings may provide comfort, since they show religion supporting the "right" kind of social attitudes. Since most of the social scientists who have researched this question are neither anti-religious nor conservative, their reaction has been one of discomfort. Being political and religious liberals, they looked for a formulation that would reflect their positive view of the potential for change in both liberal religion and society.

Gordon W. Allport was one of the psychologists who were troubled by the religion-prejudice correlation, and he suggested an explanation of its nature, which is described in the following article. He theorized that there are two kinds of religious orientation: the intrinsic, genuine one of the person who applies religion to every aspect of his life, and the extrinsic one of the person who is religious by appearance only. Allport hypothesized that people with an extrinsic religious orientation would be more prejudiced than those with an intrinsic orientation.

Allport's explanation for the religion-prejudice relationship is cast in terms of the individual personality. He suggests that "... a large number of people, by virtue of their psychological makeup, require for their economy of living both prejudice and religion." A contrasting view, cast in social-learning terms, has been offered by Glock and Stark (1966). They seem to imply that both religion and prejudice are learned in a specific social context and that the individual acquires both his religious beliefs and prejudices, which are sometimes related through their specific content (for example, anti-Jewish prejudice may be related to Christian mythology).

Allport's article is important for three reasons: first, it is clear and eloquent and presents significant formulations on the psychological meanings of religion; second, it has been influencial in generating research; and third, its major thesis has been tested empirically, as shown in a study presented in the article by Allport and Ross.

Reference

Glock, C. Y., & Stark, R. *Christian Beliefs and Anti-Semitism.* New York: Harper & Row, 1966.

Two contrary sets of threads are woven into
the fabric of all religion--the warp of brotherhood and the woof of bigotry. I am not speaking
of religion in any ideal sense, but, rather, of
religion-in-the-round as it actually exists historically, culturally, and in the lives of individual
men and women, the great majority of whom (in our
land) profess some religious affiliation and belief.
Taken in-the-round, there is something about religion that makes for prejudice, and something about
it that unmakes prejudice. It is this paradoxical
situation that I wish to explore here.

It is a well-established fact in social science
that, on the average, churchgoers in our country
harbor more racial, ethnic, and religious prejudice
than do nonchurchgoers. Needless to say, this fact
is both surprising and distressing to thoughtful
religionists. Many public opinion surveys, as well
as intensive investigations establish this finding.[1]
The finding is always the same: it is secularism
and not religion that is interwoven with tolerance.
In S. A. Stouffer's words, "More churchgoers are
intolerant of ...nonconformity...than nonchurchgoers." And this relationship holds when "education,
age, region, and type of community also are taken
into account."[2]

Although we do not know whether this correlation
holds for other lands, or for past centuries, we can
assume that it does. At least we know that most
persecutions and inquisitions of the past, especially
the vicious and shameful, have occurred within religious contexts.

One can become immediately defensive and argue
that today, as in the past, many (perhaps most)
battlers for civil rights, for social justice, for
tolerance and equi-mindedness--in short, for brother-
hood--have been religiously motivated and fortified
by religious doctrine. The array of such spiritual
heroes is long; it would include Christ himself and
many followers: Tertullian, Pope Gelasius the First,
Raymond Lully, who dared oppose both the Crusades
and the rising Inquisition, Cardinal Cusa, Sebastian
Castellio, Schwenkfeld and the Irenicists; and, in
this country, Roger Williams, John Woolman, and

modern figures such as Father John La Farge, Martin
Luther King, and an expanding army of religiously
motivated workers for civil rights. Gandhi, a non-
Christian, was also religiously motivated. It is
further possible to point to recent pronouncements
from nearly every major religious body stating in
golden words its stand for racial justice and
brotherhood.

All this evidence is convincing; but it does
not cancel the fact that members of Christian
churches in this country are, on the average, more
bigoted than nonchurchgoers. Since the evidence on
both sides is incontestable, we are surely confronted with a paradoxical situation which requires
careful analysis in order to unravel the contrary
sets of threads.

The needed analysis can follow three lines of
inspection, corresponding to the three religious
contexts which seem to me to contain the seeds of
bigotry:

1. The theological context
2. The sociocultural context
3. The personal-psychological context

WHAT IS PREJUDICE?

Before entering upon our analysis it is well
to pause for a moment to ask what we mean by prejudice. At what point do our justifiable predi-
lections, beliefs, and convictions spill over into
prejudice?

The clearest answer, I think, comes from
Thomistic philosophy which defines prejudice very
simply as "thinking ill of others without sufficient
warrant." Such is a definition of "prejudice
against," what Spinoza calls "hate prejudice."
There is, of course, a condition of "thinking *well*
of others without sufficient warrant" (as we sometimes do concerning our own children)--Spinoza's
"love prejudice."

By this definition of hate prejudice (the type
that concerns us here), we identify two ingredients:
a negative feeling or attitude, and a failure of

rationality. A particularly ugly example is the
illogic of the Ku Klux Klan rabble rouser who
justified the killing of Negro children in Birmingham on the grounds that if one kills rattlesnakes
one doesn't care whether they are old rattlers or
young. Or take a person who was once cheated by a
Jew and thereupon turns anti-Semite. Here, also,
is a clear case of "insufficient warrant." Sometimes the situation is subtler, as with the rabbi
who had vigorously fought against the McCarthy concept of guilt by association, but who judged
Kennedy unfit to be President on the basis of a
medieval papal encyclical.

Here we should recall that in many regions of
human life we learn through harsh experience not to
think or act without sufficient warrant. Our scientific work, our family budgets, our jobs, our health
require a measured calculation of warranted cause-
and-effect relationships. But in other regions of
our life there is little if any objective monitoring
of our activities or beliefs. Religion is one such
region; our view of our fellow man is another. Both
of these contexts of living are particularly prone
to unwarranted assumptions.

A more recent attempt to define prejudice proceeds in a different way. It takes off from certain
ideal values affirmed by our democratic society. It
declares that prejudice is a departure from three
different sets of ideal norms. Since prejudice is
ordinarily a matter of gross and unwarranted overgeneralization, it departs from the norm of *rationality* (just as the Thomistic definition says). Since
prejudice often leads to segregation, discrimination,
and denial of rights, it is a departure from the
norm of *justice*. And, finally, since it entails contempt, rejection, or condescension, it is a departure
from the norm of *human-heartedness*.[3] This three-
fold definition somewhat amplifies the Thomistic,
but is not inconsistent with it.

I am not saying that it is always possible to
ticket a given state of mind as clearly prejudiced
or unprejudiced. As in all of our mental life,
there are borderline conditions. My argument is
simply that there are attitudes that are unwarranted,

unjust, and insensitive; and that these attitudes
may all be, in varying degrees and for varying
reasons, interlocked with their possessor's religious life.

THE THEOLOGICAL CONTEXT

We now come to the theological context of prejudice. Although I have little competence in the
field I venture to suggest that, while plentiful
supports for brotherhood are found in nearly all
systems of theology, these systems also contain
three invitations to bigotry. In the past all three
have led to prejudice, injustice, outrage, and inquisition. Even today the peril exists, although
it is greatly lessened.

First, the doctrine of *revelation* has led, and
can still lead, a religion to claim exclusive possession of final truth concerning the destiny and
end of man, as well as sole authority and means for
interpreting that end. Held rigidly, this position
regards the teaching of other religious and philosophical formulations as a threat to human salvation.
Saint Augustine declared that where truth is known
men have not the right to err. Within the Protestant tradition heresy was for a long time a capital
crime. Menno Simons, the Anabaptist, reinterpreted
Saint Paul's injunction to "judge nothing before the
time, until the Lord shall come." It meant, he said,
"none may judge unless he have the Judging Word on
his side."[4]

The General Court of Massachusetts decreed in
1647 that "No Jesuit or spiritual or ecclesiastical
person (as they are termed), ordained by a pope of
the see of Rome, shall henceforth come into Massachusetts. Any person not freeing himself of suspicion shall be jailed, then banished. If taken a
second time he shall be put to death." If the law
has not been repealed, 3,200 Catholic clergy in
Massachusetts are there illegally.[5]

Most theologians today, of course, take a far
softer position, agreeing in effect with Bishop
Lesslie Newbigin, who writes, "We must claim

absoluteness and finality for Christ and His finished work; but that very claim forbids us to claim
absoluteness and finality for our understanding of
it."[6] Firm faith in revelation is not incompatible
with tentativeness and tolerance in our attempts to
interpret this faith to mankind. From the practical
point of view, this leniency is not different from
the "fallibilism" of Charles Peirce and John Dewey,
who held that the best society is one that remains
open and encourages all men to search with equal
freedom for satisfying truths.

Whatever the reasons may be, persecutions de-
riving from rigid interpretations of divine revelation have largely vanished. Today's religious
wars--and we still have them--between Moslem and
Hindu, between Buddhist and Catholic, are largely
due to traditional economic and ethnic hostilities
wearing convenient religious tags.

The second theological goad to bigotry (likewise more common in the past than in the present) is
the doctrine of *election*. The frenzied battle cry
of the Crusades, *Deus vult,* the more recent *Gott
mit uns,* the very concepts of God's chosen people,
of God's country, have all conferred sanctions for
persecution and cruelty. The infidel is accurst;
so, too, the black children of Ham. In speaking to
the Jews, Saint Chrysostom said, "God hates you."
The doctrine of election divides the ins from the
outs with surgical precision. Since God is for the
ins, the outs must be excluded from privileges, and,
in extreme cases, eliminated by sword or by fire.

Such divinely sanctioned ethnocentrism is de-
creasing; ecumenism, its polar opposite, is in as-
cendance. It seems that the principal active residue
of prejudice based on the doctrine of election is
the racial bigotry of South Africa and our own South,
where we find lingering doctrinal justification for
keeping the decendants of Ham in the position of
drawers of water and hewers of wood.

The third and last theological peril has by
now virtually disappeared. I speak of *theocracy*--
the view that a monarch rules by divine right, that
the Church is a legitimate guide for civil government; or that a legal code (perhaps based, as in

early New England, on the Ten Commandments), being divinely ordained, is inviolable on the pain of
fierce punishment or death. No theological idea has
caused so much persecution and suffering in both the
Old World and the New as have the various versions
of theocracy. By virtue of its control over civil
government, ecclesiastical whims based on doctrines
of revelation and election could be translated into
immediate and cruel sanctions.

Theocracy, we now know, disappeared soon after
this country adopted the First Amendment to its
Constitution, guaranteeing religious liberty and
the separation of church and state. Historians have
claimed that this achievement is America's principal
contribution to civilization.[7]

What I have been saying is that, for all its
stress on compassion, theology itself has been far
from blameless. It has encouraged bigotry in
thought, in word, and in deed. At the same time
this particular context of prejudice, prominent in
the past, has undergone marked relaxation, and may
be destined to vanish.

THE SOCIOCULTURAL CONTEXT

Since the average churchgoer has only vague
intimations of theology, it seems farfetched to
search for the roots of his prejudices in their
theological context--especially since, as we have
seen, the pathogenic elements in theology are dis-
appearing. But if theological influences in daily
life are diminishing, sociocultural influences in
religion are increasing. What are the sociocultural
factors in religion that predispose the churchgoer to prejudice?

If we stand off and look at our contemporary
social edifice, we note that without doubt religion
is one of its pillars; but, also, that a parallel
pillar is built of the cliches of secular prejudice. Where would our social structure be if most
people didn't believe in "my country right or wrong,"
in the superiority of Western culture, in the prevailing social stratification and earmarks of status,

in the moral superiority of people with ambition
over people without ambition--which means, in effect,
in the moral superiority of privileged over unpriv-
ileged classes--in the evils of miscegenation, in
the backwardness of immigrants, and in the un-
desirability of deviants? Secular prejudice is a
pillar of a functioning society.

    Now, pillars must be well matched. Religion,
therefore, finds itself peculiarly tailored to the
nationalistic, class, and ethnic cleavages and outlooks that sustain the prevailing social order. It
is a conservative agent, rather than an agent of
change. A striking instance is the extent to which
German Catholicism capitulated to the political and
cultural demands of Nazi pressure.[8]

    The phenomenon is also clearly visible at the
parish level. By and large every congregation is
an assemblage of like-minded people, each congregation representing the ethnic, class, and racial
cleavages of society, over and above denominational
cleavages. Churches exclude Jews, and synagogues
exclude Christians. Protestants and Catholics keep
apart in their religious subcommunities. Negro
churches are peculiarly isolated in tradition and in
function.[9] Sects affirm values held by the less-
educated working classes; churches foster congenial
middle-class values. The fact that many parishioners
leave their group when Negroes or other deviants
are admitted shows that, for them, ethnic and class
values hold priority over religious values. Church
membership for them is primarily a sociocultural
significance, a matter of class and caste--a support
for their own ethnocentrism.

    Here we find a key to our riddle. The reason
churchgoers on the average are more prejudiced than
nonchurchgoers is not because religion instills
prejudice. It is rather that a large number of people, by virtue of their psychological makeup, require for their economy of living both prejudice and
religion. Some, for example, are tormented by self-
doubt and insecurity. Prejudice enhances their
self-esteem; religion provides them a tailored security. Others are guilt-ridden; prejudice provides
a scapegoat, and religion, relief. Still others live

in fear of failure. Prejudice provides an explanation in terms of menacing out-groups; religion
promises a heavenly, if not terrestrial, reward.
Thus, for many individuals, the functional significance of prejudice and religion is identical. One
does not cause the other; rather, both satisfy the
same psychological needs. Multitudes of churchgoers, perhaps especially in times of social anomie
and crisis, embrace both supports.

According to this line of reasoning, we assume
that nonchurchgoers, on the whole, have less psychological need for prejudice and for religion.
Their philosophy of life, whatever it is, seems
self-contained, requiring no direct reliance on
these two common social supports.

Here, then, in broadest outline, is an explanation for the troublesome correlation we find between churchgoing and bigotry. We need, however,
to look much more closely at both data and theory
in order to sharpen our understanding of the religious context of prejudice.

First, we must remind ourselves that there are
churchgoers *and* churchgoers. Today 63 per cent of
the population claims formal religious affiliation,
a figure far larger than in earlier decades. Also,
we recall the common poll finding that as many as
96 per cent of the American people say they believe
in God. Religion seems to be neither dead nor
dying.

But here we need to draw an immediate distinction between two polar types of religious affiliation, as Will Herberg and Gerhard Lenski have done.[10]
Some religious groups and many individuals stress
the sociocultural factor in membership. The result
is a "communal" type of affiliation. For example,
many Jewish congregations and Negro Protestant
groups provide an important communal service quite
apart from their specifically religious functions.
Herberg and Lenski both argue that Americans are
turning increasingly to their religious groups for
the satisfaction of the communal identification and
need to belong. Paradoxically, it can be said that
Americans are becoming more religious while at the
same time they are becoming more secular.

In *all* religious groups we find parishioners
whose interests are primarily communal. Affiliation
is in fashion; it provides status for some, a gossip
center for others, a meeting place for the lonely,
entertainment for the disengaged, and even a good
way to sell insurance. One study reports that 80
per cent of members indicated they are more concerned about a comfortable life on earth than about
other-worldly considerations, and 54 per cent admit
that their religious beliefs do not have any effect
on the way they conduct their daily affairs.[11]

The type opposite to "communal" is "associational" which includes those members whose involvement is primarily for purposes of religious fellowship. Comparing these types revealing differences
emerge. To give one example: Lenski finds that
among Detroit Catholics whose communal involvement
is high and whose associational involvement low, 59
per cent favor segregated schools; whereas among
Catholics whose associational involvement is high
and whose communal involvement low, only 27 per cent
favor segregated schools--a difference of thirty-two
percentage points between the religiously oriented
and the communally oriented churchgoers. A significant trend in the same direction is found also among
Detroit Protestants.[12]

Thus, we see that one type of churchgoer tends
to be prejudiced; another type relatively unprejudiced. To my mind, it is precisely here that we
find the analytic tool we need to solve our problem.
Soon I shall return to this mode of analysis and to
several relevant supporting researches.

Meanwhile, let me say that a sociological or
historical scholar could point to many additional
relationships between religion as a cultural institution and prejudice. For one thing, almost every
religious group has been a target for hostility.
The fierce anti-Catholicism in the United States
during the nineteenth century was certainly in large
part a mask for the workingman's resentments against
the flood of immigration from Ireland, and later
from Italy and other Catholic countries. Not only
was there vague uneasiness about the curious folk-
ways of these foreigners, there was growing fear of

the power of the cities where they settled. Rural
nativism focused upon ecclesiastical visibility as
a target, likewise upon the Jew who was also an
identifiable foreigner.

A different line of sociological interest
deals with the ideological differences among Protestant, Catholic, and Jew; and sometimes between Negro
and white churches. Lenski, for example, argues
that the communications networks, being relatively
limited to the adherents of the same faith, facilitate the development and transmission of distinctive
political and economic norms and outlooks.[13] In
short, religious groups favor provincialism and a
compartmentalization of living. Since immigration
has virtually ceased, the socioreligious community
is becoming a substitute for ethnic groupings, and
we must accordingly expect many of the prejudices
formerly supported in ethnic terms to be sustained
in socioreligious communities. The drift he sees
is toward a more compartmentalized society where
the heightened sense of religious group loyalty will
lead to a lessened sense of responsibility toward
those outside. Lenski's research establishes the
fact that there are appreciable differences (independent of social class) that mark the political
and social attitudes of the major religious groups
and affect their images of one another. The Jews,
for example, turn out to be the least critical of
other groups, but at the same time to suffer the
severest criticism from them.

Virtually all of the studies of religion and
social conflict are focused on the demographic
level. That is to say, trends are found to be true
of certain groups taken as a whole. The spirit of
capitalism, says Max Weber, is built into Protestantism and not into Catholicism. Negro religion
is, by and large, a religion of protection and protest; Jews, having most to lose through violations
of the First Amendment, are its strongest support-
ers. Churches guard middle-class values; sects,
working-class values.[14]

All such analyses are, of course, useful as
background to the study of the religious context of
prejudice. And, yet, I feel that they fail to reach

the heart of the matter. They focus upon religion
as a sociocultural phenomenon, that is to say in
its communal aspects, and overlook its place in the
personal life. Both religion and prejudice are in-
tensely personal states of mind. To understand their
inherent relationships (whether positive or negative)
we have to examine the psychological composition of
individual people.

The Personal-Psychological Context

There are, as we have observed, churchgoers
and churchgoers. Now what is the simplest possible
distinction between them? Well, some attend frequently and regularly, some only on occasion or
rarely. Offhand, this distinction may seem to be
purely demographic--the "regulars" versus the "ir-
regulars." But, in reality, the process of forming
the habit of regular attendance, or the state of
mind that lets weather, circumstance, and mood determine attendance clearly depends on personal motives
and attitudes. True, there is a tendency for Protestants to attend less regularly than Catholics, although much more regularly than Jews. In Detroit
among self-styled Protestants, 30 per cent go to
church every Sunday, 20 per cent between one and
three times a month, 30 per cent only occasionally,
14 never.[15] But, for our purposes, the important
consideration is that each major religious group
has its nuclear and its marginal members in terms of
attendance. The outer fringe of the marginal groups
consists of those who attend exceedingly rarely--as
someone has said, only thrice in a lifetime; once
when they were hatched; again when matched; and,
finally, when dispatched.

Now, many investigations have shown that regular
and frequent church attenders harbor, by and large,
less ethnic and racial hostility than do members who
are casual about their attendance. An illustrative
study is one made by E. L. Streuning whose data come
from nearly 900 faculty members in a large Midwestern university.[16] Besides obtaining scores on
a prejudice scale, he learned what their habits were

regarding church attendance.   Almost a third never
attended church at all, and they had a low prejudice score (14.7).   Many attended once a month,
and, for these, the average prejudice score nearly
doubled (25).   This finding immediately confirms
our earlier statement that nonchurchgoers are less
prejudiced than churchgoers--or at least than casual
churchgoers.   The prejudice scores of those attending once, twice, or three times a month were also
high.   For weekly attenders, the score fell, and it
continued to fall rapidly for those whose attendance
ranged from five to eleven or more times a month.
For the last group (eleven or more a month), the
average score of 11.7 was significantly lower even
than for the nonattenders.   In these data we clearly
perceive what is called a curvilinear relation: nonattenders and frequent attenders having low prejudice
scores; intermediate attenders, high.

The evidence fits well with Lenski's distinction between communal and associational religion.
Frequent attendance is not required to maintain nominal membership or to derive the benefits of communal contact.   On the other hand, a religiously
motivated person who seeks spiritual association is
drawn with greater regularity and frequency to the
church's fellowship.   An imposing array of studies
supports this finding and interpretation.[17]

The lives of many marginal attenders, it seems,
are regulated in a fitful way by what we may call
"religious tokenism."   A token of churchmanship is
all they need--an occasional anchorage against the
gusts of fate.   Tokenism, while superficial, may be
fiercely important.   Its devotees may incline to
see in the Supreme Court ruling against prescribed
prayers in public schools a menacing threat.   Religion resides in a symbol.   One Southern politician
complained that while the Supreme Court ushered
Negroes into the public schools it ushered God out--
as though God dwells in a token.

While the data on frequency of church attendance and its relation to prejudice are revealing,
they do not tell us directly about the nature of the
personal religious sentiment that provides the context for prejudice, nor about the nature of the

contrary sentiment that engenders tolerance, fair play, and humane regard.

To take this additional step, we borrow from axiology the concepts of *extrinsic* value and *intrinsic* value. The distinction helps us to separate churchgoers whose communal type of membership supports and serves other (nonreligious) ends from those for whom religion is an end in itself--a final, not instrumental, good.

The distinction clearly overlaps with that drawn by Father Joseph Fichter in his study of the urban Catholic parish.[18] What he calls the "marginal" and "modal" parishioner corresponds fairly well to our extrinsic type. What he calls the "nuclear" parishioner--who orients his life wholly by the full doctrine of the Church--is essentially our intrinsic type. For our purposes, it is important to note that Father Fichter assigns only 10 per cent to the intrinsic or nuclear group. Unless I am mistaken, the ratio is roughly what we would find in the average congregation of any Christian (and perhaps Jewish) parish.

Every minister knows and laments the preponderance of the extrinsic type. Some such parishioners find self-expression in managing investments, arranging flowers, running bazaars, in simply avoiding loneliness. They have no true association with the religious function of the Church. Others do, to varying degrees, accept the spiritual ministry, but remain dabblers because their connections are determined exclusively by mood or by crisis. Many extrinsics do, of course, have religious needs, but they feel no obligation to attend church regularly nor to integrate religion into their way of life. Lenski, we have seen, regards compartmentalization as the chief mark of religion today. It is something for an occasional Sunday morning, for High Holy Days, or for moments of crisis. Since its function is to serve other needs, we call it an extrinsic value in the personal life.

While most extrinsics are casual and peripheral churchgoers, a few are ideological extremists. With equal fervor, they embrace some political nostrum along with the tenets of some religious (usually

fundamentalist) sect. In such cases religious ex-
tremism is found to be ancillary to a prejudiced
philosophy of life. I am thinking here of the right-
wing groups whose ardent desire is to escape from
the complexities of modern life. They do not seek
so much to preserve the *status quo* as to return to
a former, simple small-town or agrarian way of life
where individual achievement and responsibility are
the only virtues. God has an important role in
this ideology as a dispenser of rewards for individual achievement. Modern life threatens this idyll;
immigrants threaten it; Negroes, Jews, Catholics
are seen as menacing. Extreme right ideology invariably harbors this sort of bigotry; and its supporting religion justifies and rationalizes the prejudice, often through the selection of congenial
scriptural passages.

The same phenomenon is seen, though less often,
in ideologies of the extreme left. Ralph Roy has
pointed to cases of clergy who justify hatred of the
wealthy, expropriation, and extreme left-wing poli-
cies by one-sided scriptural interpretations.[19]

Thus, while there are several varieties of
extrinsic religious orientation, we may say they all
point to a type of religion that is strictly utilitarian: useful for the self in granting safety,
social standing, solace, and endorsement for one's
chosen way of life. As such, it provides a congenial soil for all forms of prejudice, whether
racial, national, political, or religious. Since
extrinsic religion predominates among churchgoers
we have an explanation for our riddle.

By contrast, the intrinsic form of the religious
sentiment regards faith as a supreme value in its
own right. It is oriented toward a unification of
being, takes seriously the commandment of brotherhood, and strives to transcent all self-centered
needs. Dogma is tempered with humility, and in
keeping with the Biblical injunction the possessor
withholds judgment until the day of the harvest. A
religious sentiment of this sort floods the whole
life with motivation and meaning. Religion is no
longer limited to single segments of self-interest.[20]

While many of the intrinsically religious are
pietists and express their religion chiefly by be-

ing good neighbors, others are of a militant stripe.
Were not Saint Francis, John Wesley, Mahatma Gandhi--
was not Christ himself--intrinsically religious; and
were they not all zealous beyond the bounds of moder-
ation? Yes, there are intrinsic as well as extrinsic
zealots. We can usually distinguish between them:
the latter group having ulterior motives of personal
or political advantage; the former being fired only
by a conviction that the kingdom of God should be
realized on earth.

AN EMPIRICAL APPROACH

Up to now we have been speaking chiefly in
theoretical terms concerning the religious context
of prejudice. And I have been moving the argument
closer and closer toward a psychological analysis
of the situation, with the claim that in the last
analysis both prejudice and religion are subjective
formations within the personal life. One of these
formations of religion (the extrinsic) is entirely
compatible with prejudice; the other (the intrinsic)
rules out enmity, contempt, and bigotry.
      With the proposition stated in this way, an
empiricist will ask, "Can we not test it? After all,
you have simply stated an hypothesis at the specula-
tive level. Do not all hypotheses need empirical
verification before they can be accepted?"
      In a series of investigations, my students and
I have undertaken this very task. There is not time
to describe the studies in detail. Essentially,
they consist of using two questionnaires with assort-
ed groups of churchgoers. One undertakes--and I
apologize for the audacity--to determine to what extent a given parishioner holds an extrinsic or an
intrinsic view of his religion. As an example, a
person who agrees with the following propositions
would receive scores indicating an *extrinsic* orientation:

      The purpose of prayer is to secure a happy
      and peaceful life.

The Church is most important as a place to
formulate good social relationships.

A person would be credited with an *intrinsic*
orientation if he subscribed to such statements as
the following:

I try hard to carry my religion over into
all my other dealings in life.
Quite often I have been keenly aware of the
presence of God or the Divine Being.

There are twenty-one items in the scale, which
enables us to locate each subject on a continuum
from consistently extrinsic to consistently intrinsic. There are also a number of subjects who
are inconsistent in the sense that they endorse any
and all propositions favorable to religion, even
though these propositions are contradictory to one
another.

A second questionnaire consists of a valid measure of prejudice.[21] It deals primarily with the
extent to which the subject favors discriminatory
practices and segregation.

In brief, the findings support the hypothesis
that the extrinsic religious orientation in personality is indeed the context of prejudice. The intrinsic orientation is the matrix of tolerance. An
additional interesting finding is that those subjects who are inconsistent--who grasp at any and
all statements favorable to religion, regardless of
their logical consistency, are the most prejudiced
of all. Thus, it seems that the religious context
for bigotry lies both in the extrinsic and in the
muddle-headed types of religious sentiment. Only
the consistent intrinsic type (a small minority)
escapes.[22]

It is clear that these investigations tend to
confirm demographic and sociological studies that
we have also reviewed. Further, I believe, they
are compatible with our theological analysis, since
it is clear that communal and extrinsic religion
can draw strong support from the doctrines of revelation, election, and theocracy, which, as we have

seen, provide the theological context of prejudice, so far as such exists.

We can hope that this convergence of theological, sociological, and psychological analysis will lead to a further cooperation between behavioral and religious disciplines. We can also hope that our findings, when understood by clergy and laity, may lead to a decrease in bigotry and to an enhancement of charity in modern religious life.

If I were asked what practical applications ensue from this analysis, I would, of course, say that to reduce prejudice we need to enlarge the population of intrinsically religious people. There is no simple formula, for each personality is unique and is stubbornly resistant to change. Yet, precisely here lies the pastor's task, his opportunity, and his challenge.

NOTES

1. T. W. Adorno *et al.*, *The Authoritarian Personality*, New York: Harper and Bros., 1950; M. Rokeach, *The Open and Closed Mind*, New York: Basic Books, 1960; G. W. Allport and B. M. Kramer, "Some Roots of Prejudice," *Journal of Psychology*, 1946, 22, 9-39; R. M. Williams, Jr., *Strangers Next Door*, Englewood Cliffs, N. J.: Prentice-Hall, 1964; S. A. Stouffer, *Communism, Conformity and Civil Liberties*, Garden City, L. I., N. Y.: Doubleday, 1955.

2. Stouffer, *op. cit.*, p. 147.

3. Cf. Howard Schuman, "Sympathetic Identification with the Underdog," *Public Opinion Quarterly*, 1963, 27, 230-41. Additional reports in preparation.

4. Menno Simons, "A Foundation and Plain Instruction of the Saving Doctrine of Christ," *On the Ean: Questions and Answers, 1550*, trans. I. D. Rupp, Lancaster, Pa.; Elias Barr, 1863.

5. This and similar instances of theologically
    induced intolerance are presented in G. W.
    Allport, "Religion and Prejudice," *The Crane
    Review*, 1959, 2, 1-10. See also Gustavus
    Myers, *History of Bigotry in the United States*,
    New York, Random House, 1943.

6. Lesslie Newbigin, "The Quest for Unity Through
    Religion," *Journal of Religion*, 1955, 35, 17-33.

7. Leo Pfeffer, "Freedom and Separation: America's
    Contribution to Civilization," *Journal of Church
    and State*, 1960, 2, 100-111.

8. See Gunter Lewy, *The Catholic Church and Nazi
    Germany*, New York: McGraw-Hill, 1964. Also,
    Gordon C. Zahn, *German Catholics and Hitler's
    Wars*, New York: Sheed and Ward, 1962.

9. J. R. Washington, *Black Religion*, Boston:
    Beacon Press, 1964.

10. Will Herberg, *Protestant, Catholic, Jew*,
    Garden City, L. I., N. Y.: Doubleday, 1955;
    Gerhard E. Lenski, *The Religious Factor*, Garden
    City, L. I., N. Y.: Doubleday, 1961.

11. Earl Raab (ed.), *Religious Conflicts in America*,
    Garden City, L. I., N. Y.: Doubleday Anchor
    Books, 1964, p. 15.

12. Lenski, *op. cit.*, p. 173.

13. *Ibid.*, p. 303.

14. Analyses at this demographic level are plenti-
    ful. See, *e.g.*, Robert Lee and Martin E. Marty
    (eds.), *Religion and Social Conflict*, New York:
    Oxford University Press, 1964.

15. Lenski, *op. cit.*, p. 35.

16.   E. L. Streuning, *The Dimensions, Distributions
      and Correlates of Authoritarianism in a Mid-
      western University Faculty Population*, unpub-
      lished Ph.D. dissertation, Purdue University,
      1957.

17.   W. H. Holtzman, "Attitudes of College Men to-
      ward Nonsegregation in Texas Schools," *Public
      Opinion Quarterly*, 1956, 2, 559-69; J. G. Kelly,
      J. E. Ferson, and W. H. Holtzman, "The Measure-
      ment of Attitudes toward the Negro in the South,"
      Journal of Social Psychology, 1958, 48, 305-317;
      R. W. Friedrichs, "Christians and Residential
      Exclusion: An Empirical Study of a Northern
      Dilemma," *Journal of Social Issues*, 1959, 15,
      14-23; Melvin M. Tumin, *Desegregation*, Prince-
      ton, N. J.: Princeton University Press, 1958;
      R. M. Williams, Jr., *Strangers Next Door*,
      Englewood Cliffs, N. J.: Prentice-Hall, 1964.

18.   J. H. Fichter, S. J., *Social Relations in the
      Urban Parish*, Chicago: University of Chicago
      Press, 1954.

19.   R. L. Roy, "Conflict from the Communist Left
      and the Radical Right," *Religion and Social
      Conflict*, pp. 55-68.

20.   For further discussion of the extrinsic and
      intrinsic types see G. W. Allport, "Behavioral
      Science, Religion, and Mental Health," *Journal
      of Religion and Health*, 1963, 2, 187-97; also,
      Personality and Social Encounter, Boston:
      Beacon Press, 1960, Chapter 16; also, *The Na-
      ture of Prejudice*, Reading, Mass.: Addison-
      Wesley, 1954, Chapter 23.

21.   Devised by J. S. Harding and Howard Schuman.

22.   G. W. Allport and J. M. Ross, "Personal Reli-
      gious Orientation and Prejudice," *Journal of
      Personality and Social Psychology*, 1967, 5,
      432-443. (Reprinted next in this volume.)

PERSONAL RELIGIOUS ORIENTATION AND PREJUDICE

GORDON W. ALLPORT
J. MICHAEL ROSS

Editor's introduction. This article reports
the empirical test of Allport's hypothesis
on extrinsic-intrinsic differences in prejudice. We have the opportunity of seeing how
an attractive, lucid theoretical formulation
runs the gauntlet of empirical validation and
emerges wounded, modified, and reformed. Allport and Ross are painfully honest in reporting their modifications, limitations, and
disappointments. The study can be easily criticized on many grounds. The nature of the
sample is poorly specified. We know very little
about the subjects, except that the whole sample is unrepresentative. There are also several
technical questions regarding the instruments
used. Nevertheless, the study is important just
because of its negative results and modifications.
The major revision of the hypothesis came
about because a significant minority of the subjects turned out to be neither extrinsic nor intrinsic in their religious orientations. Rather,

From *Journal of Personality and Social Psychology*, 1967, 5, 432-443. Copyright 1967 by the
American Psychological Association, and reproduced
by permission.

they were "indiscriminately proreligious," and
they were also more prejudiced than either one
of the other groups. Thus, it becomes clear
that the extrinsic-intrinsic dimension is not
sufficient for identifying religious orientation.

The major question regarding the implications
of this study should bring us back to the original issue of religion-prejudice relationships.
It is clear that the study did not succeed in
explaining away, or even explaining, the basic
relationship. If we assume that "intrinsic"
churchgoers are less prejudiced than "extrinsic"
churchgoers, we have to look at their proportion among church attenders. In this sample
(which, as stated above, was unrepresentative),
the majority of subjects turned out to be non-
intrinsic in their orientations. Only 35%
were consistently intrinsic, 34.5% were extrinsic, and 30.7% were "indiscriminately proreligious." Thus, the findings bring us back to
the starting point: some churchgoers are more
prejudiced than others, and some are not prejudiced at all. Still, the majority of church
attenders, most of whom are non-intrinsic in
their religious orientations, are likely to be
more prejudiced than non-attenders.

Previous psychological and survey research has
established three important facts regarding the
relationship between prejudiced attitudes and the
personal practice of religion.

1. On the average, church attenders are more
    prejudiced than nonattenders.
2. This overall finding, if taken only by it-
    self, obscures a curvilinear relationship.
    While it is true that most attenders are
    more prejudiced than nonattenders, a
    significant minority of them are *less*
    prejudiced.

3. It is the casual, irregular fringe members who are high in prejudice, their religious motivation is of the *extrinsic* order. It is the constant, devout, internalized members who are low in prejudice; their religious motivation is of the *intrinsic* order.

The present paper will establish a fourth important finding--although it may properly be regarded as an amplification of the third. *The finding is that a certain cognitive style permeates the thinking of many people in such a way that they are indiscriminately pro-religious and, at the same time, highly prejudiced.*

But first let us make clear the types of evidence upon which the first three propositions are based and examine their theoretical significance.

CHURCHGOERS ARE MORE PREJUDICED

Beginning the long parade of findings demonstrating that churchgoers are more intolerant of ethnic minorities than nonattenders is a study by Allport and Kramer (1946). These authors discovered that students who claimed no religious affiliation were less likely to be anti-Negro than those who declared themselves to be Protestant or Catholic. Furthermore, students reporting a strong religious influence at home were higher in ethnic prejudice than students reporting only slight or no religious influence. Rosenblith (1949) discovered the same trend among students in South Dakota. *The Authoritarian Personality* (Adorno, Frenkel-Brunswik, Levinson, & Sanford, 1950, p. 212) stated that scores on ethocentricism (as well as on authoritarianism) are significantly higher among church attenders than among nonattenders. Gough's (1951) findings were similar. Kirkpatrick (1949) found religious people in general to be slightly less humanitarian than nonreligious people. For example, they had more punitive attitudes toward criminals, delinquents, prostitutes, homosexuals, and those in need of psychiatric treatment. Working with a student

population Rokeach (1960) discovered nonbelievers
to be consistently less dogmatic, less authoritarian, and less ethnocentric than believers. Pub-
lic-opinion polls (as summarized by Stember, 1961)
revealed confirmatory evidence across the board.

Going beyond ethnic prejudice, Stouffer (1955)
demonstrated that among a representative sample of
American church members those who had attended
church within the past month were more intolerant
of nonconformists (such as socialists, atheists,
or communists) than those who had not attended. It
seems that on the average religious people show
more intolerance in general--not only toward ethnic
but also toward ideological groups.

Is this persistent relationship in any way
spurious? Can it be due, for example, to the factor of educational level? Many studies show that
people with high education tend to be appreciably
less prejudiced than people with low education.
Perhaps it is the former group that less often goes
to church. The reasoning is false. Sociological
evidence has shown conclusively that frequent
church attendance is associated with high socio-
economic status and with college education (Demerath, 1965). Furthermore, Stouffer's study found
that the intolerant tendency among churchgoers existed only when educational level was held constant.
Struening (1963), using as subjects only faculty
members of a large state university (all highly
educated), discovered that nonattenders were on the
average less prejudiced than attenders. These studies assure us that the association between churchgoing and prejudice is not merely a spurious product
of low education.

Turning to the theoretical implications of these
findings, shall we say that religion in and of itself
makes for prejudice and intolerance? There are some
arguments in favor of such a conclusion, especially
when we recall that certain powerful *theological*
positions--those emphasizing revelation, election
(chosen people), and theocracy (Allport, 1959, 1966)--
have throughout history turned one religion against
another. And among *sociological* factors in religion
we find many that make for bigotry. One thinks of the

narrow composition of many religious groups in terms
of ethnic and class membership, of their pressure
toward conformity, and of the competition between
them (see Demerath, 1965; Lenski, 1961). It does
seem that religion as such makes for prejudice.

    And yet it is here that we encounter the grand
paradox. One may not overlook the teachings of
equality and brotherhood, of compassion and human-
heartedness, that mark all the great world religions.
Nor may one overlook the precept and example of great
figures whose labors in behalf of tolerance were and
are religiously motivated--such as Christ himself,
Tertullian, Pope Gelasius I, St. Ambrose, Cardinal
Cusa, Sebastian Castellio, Schwenkfeld, Roger
Williams, Mahatma Gandhi, Martin Luther King, and
many others, including the recently martyred clergy
in our own South. These lives, along with the work
of many religious bodies, councils, and service organizations would seem to indicate that religion as
such *unmakes prejudice*. A paradox indeed.

THE CURVILINEAR RELATIONSHIP

    If religion as such made *only* for prejudice, we
would expect that churchgoers who expose themselves
most constantly to its influence would, as a result,
be more prejudiced than those who seldom attend.
Such is not the case.

    Many studies show that frequent attenders are
less prejudiced than infrequent attenders and often
less prejudiced even than nonattenders. Let us cite
one illustrative study by Struening (1963). The
curvilinear trend is immediately apparent in Table 1.
In this particular study nonattenders had lower prejudice scores than any group, save only those devotees
who managed to attend 11 or more times a month. Without employing such fine time intervals other studies
have shown the same curvilinear trend. Thus, in *The
Authoritarian Personality* (p. 212) we learned that
in 12 out of 15 groups "regular" attenders (like nonattenders) were less prejudiced than "seldom" or
"often" attenders. Employing a 26-item Desegregation
Scale in three separate studies, Holtzman (1956)

found the same trend as shown in Table 2. If more
evidence for the curvilinear relationship is needed,
it will be found in community studies made in New
Jersey (Friedrichs, 1959), North Carolina (Tumin,
1958), New England (Pettigrew, 1959), and Ohio and
California (Pinkney, 1961). One could almost say

TABLE 1

**CHURCH ATTENDANCE AND PREJUDICE AMONG
FACULTY MEMBERS OF A MIDWESTERN
UNIVERSITY**

Frequency of attendance (times per mo.)	N	Prejudice score
0	261	14.7
1	143	25.0
2	103	26.0
3	84	23.8
4	157	22.0
5–7	94	19.9
8–10	26	16.3
11 or more	21	11.7

Note.–From Struening (1957).

there is a unanimity of findings on this matter.
The trend holds regardless of religion, denomination,
or target of prejudice (although the case seems less
clear for anti-Semitism than for prejudice against
other ethnic groups).

TABLE 2

**CHURCH ATTENDANCE AND PREJUDICE AMONG STUDENTS
IN THE BORDER STATES**

	1956 study % intolerant	Mean score on D scale	
		1958 study	1960 study
Nonattenders	37	41.3	38.1
Once a mo.	66	48.5	51.4
Twice a mo.	67	50.6	48.4
Once a wk. or oftener	49	44.5	44.3

Note.–Adapted from Holtzman (1956), Kelley, Ferson, and Holtzman
(1958), Young, Benson, and Holtzman (1960).

What are the theoretical implications? To find
that prejudice is related to frequency of church
attendance is scarcely explanatory, since it may reflect only formal behavior, not involvement or commitment to religious values. And yet it seems obvious that the regular attenders who go to church once
a week or oftener (and several studies indicate that
oftener than once a week is especially significant)
are people who receive something of special ideological and experiential meaning. Irregular, casual
fringe members, on the other hand, regard their religious contacts as less binding, less absorbing,
less integral with their personal lives.
    At this point, therefore, we must pass from ex-
ternal behavior evidence into the realm of experience
and motivation. Unless we do so we cannot hope to
understand the curvilinear relationship that has
been so clearly established.

EXTRINSIC VERSUS INTRINSIC MOTIVATION

    Perhaps the briefest way to characterize the
two poles of subjective religion is to say that the
extrinsically motivated person *uses* his religion,
whereas the intrinsically motivated *lives* his religion. As we shall see later, most people, if they
profess religion at all, fall upon a continuum between these two poles. Seldom, if ever, does one
encounter a "pure" case. And yet to clarify the
dimension it is helpful to characterize it in terms
of the two ideal types.

Extrinsic Orientation

    Persons with this orientation are disposed to
use religion for their own ends. The term is borrowed from axiology, to designate an interest that
is held because it serves other, more ultimate interests. Extrinsic values are always instrumental
and utilitarian. Persons with this orientation may
find religion useful in a variety of ways--to provide security and solace, sociability and distraction,

status and self-justification. The embraced creed
is lightly held or else selectively shaped to fit
more primary needs. In theological terms the extrinsic type turns to God, but without turning
away from self.

Intrinsic Orientation

Persons with this orientation find their master
motive in religion. Other needs, strong as they may
be, are regarded as of less ultimate significance,
and they are, insofar as possible, brought into
harmony with the religious beliefs and prescriptions.
Having embraced a creed the individual endeavors to
internalize it and follow it fully. It is in this
sense that he *lives* his religion.

A clergyman was making the same distinction
when he said,

> Some people come to church to thank God, to
> acknowledge His glory, and to ask His guidance
> ...Others come for what they can get. Their
> interest in the church is to run it or exploit
> it rather than to serve it.

Approximate parallels to these psychological
types have been proposed by the sociologists Fichter
(1954) and Lenski (1961). The former, in studying
Catholic parishioners, classified them into four
groups: the dormant, the marginal, the modal, and
the nuclear. Omitting the dormant, Fichter esti-
mated in terms of numbers that 20 per cent are
marginal, 70 per cent modal, and less than 10 per
cent nuclear. It is, of course, the latter group
that would most closely correspond to our conception
of the "intrinsic." Lenski distinguished between
church members whose involvement is "communal" (for
the purpose of sociability and status) and those who
are "associational" (seeking the deeper values of
their faith).

These authors see the significance of their
classifications for the study of prejudice. Fichter
has found less prejudice among devout (nuclear)

Catholics than among others (see Allport, 1954, p. 421). Lenski (1961, p. 173) reported that among Detroit Catholics 59 per cent of those with a predominantly "communal" involvement favored segregated schools, whereas among those with predominantly an "associational" involvement only 27 per cent favored segregation. The same trend held for Detroit Protestants.

The first published study relating the extrinsic-intrinsic dimension directly to ethnic prejudice was that of Wilson (1960). Limiting himself to a 15-item scale measuring an extrinsic (utilitarian-institutional) orientation, Wilson found in 10 religious groups a median correlation of .65 between his scale and anti-Semitism. In general these correlations were higher than he obtained between anti-Semitism and the Religious-Conventionalism Scale (Levinson, 1954). From this finding Wilson concluded that orthodoxy or fundamentalism is a less important factor than extrinsicness of orientation.

Certain weaknesses may be pointed out in this pioneer study. Wilson did not attempt to measure intrinsicness of orientation, but assumed without warrant that it was equivalent to a low score on the extrinsic measures. Further, since the items were worded in a unidirectional way there may be an error of response set. Again, Wilson dealt only with Jews as a target of prejudice, and so the generality of his finding is not known.

Finally, the factor of educational level plays a part. Wilson used the California anti-Semitism scale, and we know that high scores on this scale go with low education (Christie, 1954; Pettigrew, 1959; Titus & Hollander, 1957; Williams, 1964). Further, in our own study the extrinsic subscale is negatively correlated with degree of education ($r = -.32$). To an appreciable extent, therefore, Wilson's high correlations may be "ascribed" to educational level.

At this point, however, an important theoretical observation must be made. Low education may indeed predispose a person toward an exclusionist, self-centered, extrinsic, religious orientation and may dispose him to a stereotyped, fearful image

of Jews. This fact does not in the least affect
the functional relationship between the religious
and the prejudiced outlooks. It is a common error
for investigators to "control for" demographic
factors without considering the danger involved in
doing so. In so doing they are often obscuring and
not illuminating the functional (i.e., psychological)
relationships that obtain (see Allport, 1950).

Following Wilson the task of direct measurement
was taken up by Feagin (1964) who used a more developed scale--one designed to measure not only extrinsic orientation but also the intrinsic. His scales
are essentially the same as those discussed in a
later section of this paper. In his study of Southern Baptists Feagin reached four conclusions: (a)
Contrary to expectation, extrinsic and intrinsic
items did not fall on a unidimensional scale but
represented two independent dimensions; (b) only the
extrinsic orientation was related to intolerance toward Negroes; (c) orthodoxy as such was not related
to the extrinsic or intrinsic orientation; (d) greater orthodoxy (fundamentalism of belief) did, however,
relate positively to prejudice.

Taking all these studies together we are justified in assuming that the inner experience of religion (what it means to the individual) is an important causal factor in developing a tolerant or a
prejudiced outlook on life.

Yet, additional evidence is always in place,
and new insights can be gained by a closer inspection of the rather coarse relationships that have
been established up to now.

THE PRESENT STUDY

We wished to employ an improved and broader
measure of prejudice than had previously been used.
And since direct measures of prejudice (naming the
target groups) have become too sensitive for wide
use, we wished to try some abbreviated indirect
measures. Further, we wished to make use of an improved Extrinsic-Intrinsic scale, one that would
give reliable measures of both extrinsic and

intrinsic tendencies in a person's religious life.
For these reasons the following instruments were
adopted.

Social Problems Questionnaire

This scale, devised by Harding and Schuman
(unpublished;[1] see also Schuman & Harding, 1963,
1964), is a subtly worded instrument containing 12
anti-Negro, 11 anti-Jewish, and 10 anti-other items
(pertaining to Orientals, Mexicans, and Puerto
Ricans). The wording is varied so as to avoid an
agreement response set.

Indirect Prejudice Measures

Six items were taken from Gilbert and Levinson's (1956) Custodial Mental Illness Ideology Scale
(CMI). Example: "We should be sympathetic with
mental patients, but we cannot expect to understand
their odd behavior. a) I definitely disagree. b)
I tend to disagree. c) I tend to agree. d) I definitely agree."
Four items are related to a "jungle" philosophy
of life, suggesting a generalized suspiciousness and
distrust. Example: "The world is a hazardous place
in which men are basically evil and dangerous. a)
I definitely disagree. b) I tend to disagree. c)
I tend to agree. d) I definitely agree."
In all cases the most prejudiced response receives a score of 5 and the least prejudiced response,
1. No response was scored 3.
From Table 3 we see that while the indirect
measures have a positive correlation with each other
and with direct measures the relationship is scarcely
high enough to warrant the substitution of the indirect for the direct. The high correlations between
prejudice for the three ethnic target groups once

[1]J. Harding and H. Schuman, "Social Problems
Questionnaire," Cornell University.

TABLE 3
INTERCORRELATIONS BETWEEN FIVE MEASURES
OF PREJUDICE

	Anti-Jewish	Anti-Other	Jungle	CMI
Anti-Negro	.63	.70	.20	.25
Anti-Jewish		.67	.24	.31
Anti-Other			.33	.36
Jungle				.43

Note.—$N = 309$.

again illustrate the well-established fact that ethnic prejudice tends to be a broadly generalized disposition in personality.

Religious Orientation Measure

The full scale, entitled "Religious Orientation," is available from ADI.[2] It separates the intrinsically worded items from the extrinsic, gives score values for each item, and reports on item reliabilities. In all cases a score of 1 indicates the most intrinsic response, a score of 5, the most extrinsic. While it is possible to use all 20 items as one continuous scale, it will soon become apparent that it is often wise to treat the two subscales separately. A sample item from the extrinsic subscale follows: "What religion offers me most is comfort when sorrows and misfortune strike. a) I definitely disagree, 1. b) I tend to disagree, 2. c) I tend to agree, 4. d) I definitely agree, 5." A sample item from the intrinsic subscale: "My religious

[2]The full Religious Orientation scale has been deposited with the American Documentation Institute. Order Document No. 9268 from ADI Auxiliary Publications Project, Photoduplication Service, Library of Congress, Washington, D. C. 20540. Remit in advance $1.25 for microfilm or $1.25 for photocopies and make checks payable to: Chief, Photoduplication Service, Library of Congress.

beliefs are what really lie behind my whole approach to life. a) this is definitely not so, 5.
b) probably not so, 4. c) probably so, 2. d) definitely so, 1."

SAMPLE

While our sample of six groups of churchgoers
shows some diversity of denomination and region, it
is in no sense representative. Graduate-student
members of a seminar collected the 309 cases from
the following church groups: Group A, 94 Roman Catholic (Massachusetts); Group B, 55 Lutheran (New York
State); Group C, 44 Nazarene (South Carolina); Group
D, 53 Presbyterian (Pennsylvania); Group E, 35 Methodist (Tennessee); Group F, 18 Baptist (Massachusetts).
We labeled the groups alphabetically since such
small subsamples could not possibly lead to valid
generalizations concerning denominations as a whole.
All subjects knew that they were invited to participate as members of a religious group, and this fact
may well have introduced a "proreligious" bias.

GROSS RESULTS

If we pool all our cases for the purpose of
correlating religious orientation with prejudice,
we discover that while the findings are in the expected direction they are much less impressive than
those of previous studies, especially Wilson's.

Correlations with Extrinsic Subscale

Since Wilson employed an extrinsic scale similar to ours, we first present in Table 4 our findings using this subscale and the various measures
of prejudice. Whereas Wilson found a correlation
of .65 between his extrinsic and anti-Semitic measures, our correlation falls to .21. In part the
reason no doubt lies in certain features of Wilson's
method which we have criticized.

TABLE 4
CORRELATIONS BETWEEN EXTRINSIC SUBSCALE
AND PREJUDICE

Anti-Negro	.26
Anti-Jewish	.21
Anti-Other	.32
Jungle	.29
CMI	.44

Note.—$N = 309$.

Correlations with Combined Extrinsic-Intrinsic Scale

From the outset it was our intention to broaden Wilson's unidirectional (extrinsic) measure to see whether our hypothesis might hold for the total scale (combined scores for the 11 extrinsic and 9 intrinsic items). As Table 5 shows, matters do not

TABLE 5
CORRELATIONS BETWEEN TOTAL EXTRINSIC-
INTRINSIC SCALE AND PREJUDICE

Anti-Negro	.26
Anti-Jewish	.18
Anti-Other	.18
Jungle	.21
CMI	.17

Note.—$N = 309$.

improve but seem to worsen. The logic of combining the two subscales is of course to augment the continuum in length and presumably enhance the reliability of the total measure. It soon became apparent, however, that subjects who endorse extrinsically worded items do not necessarily reject those worded intrinsically, or vice versa. It turns out that there is only a very low correlation in the expected direction between the two subscales ($r = .21$). Obviously at this point some reformulation is badly needed.

REFORMULATION OF THE APPROACH

Examination of the data reveals that some subjects are indeed "consistently intrinsic," having a strong tendency to endorse intrinsically worded items and to reject the extrinsically worded. Correspondingly others are "consistently extrinsic." Yet, unfortunately for our neat typology, many subjects are provokingly inconsistent. They persist in endorsing any or all items that to them seem favorable to religion in any sense. Their responses, therefore, are "indiscriminately proreligious."

The problem is essentially the same as that encountered by the many investigators who have attempted to reverse the wording of items comprising the F-scale, in order to escape an unwanted response-set bias. Uniformly the effort has proved to be frustrating, since so many subjects subscribe to both the positive and negative wording of the same question (see Bass, 1955; Chapman & Bock, 1958; Chapman & Campbell, 1959; Christie, 1954; Jackson & Messick, 1957).

An example from our own subscales would be: "My religious beliefs are what really lie behind my whole approach to life" (intrinsic). "Though I believe in my religion, I feel there are many more important things in my life" (extrinsic).

The approach used by Peabody (1961) offers us a model for analyzing our data in a meaningful way. Peabody administered both positive and negative F-scale items to subjects at two different testing sessions. By comparing each individual's responses to the same question stated positively at one time and in reverse at another he was able to separate out those who were consistently pro or anti toward the content of authoritarian items. But he found many who expressed double agreement (or disagreement) with both versions of the same question. Table 6 applies Peabody's paradigm to our data.

In assigning our 309 cases to these categories we employed the following criteria.

Intrinsic type includes individuals who agree with intrinsically worded items on the intrinsic subscale, and who disagree with extrinsically stated

TABLE 6
FOUR PATTERNS OF RELIGIOUS ORIENTATION

	Agrees with intrinsic choice	Disagrees with intrinsic choice
Agrees with extrinsic choice	Indiscriminately proreligious	Consistently extrinsic in type
Disagrees with extrinsic choice	Consistently intrinsic in type	Indiscriminately antireligious or nonreligious[a]

[a] Not found in present sample.

items on the extrinsic subscale. By the scoring method employed these individuals fall below the median scores on both subscales.

Extrinsic type includes individuals who agree with extrinsically stated items on the extrinsic subscale, and who disagree with items on the intrinsic subscale. By our scoring method these individuals all fall above the median scores on both subscales.

Indiscriminately proreligious includes those who on the intrinsic subscale score at least 12 points less than on the extrinsic subscale. (This figure reflects the fact that a subject gives approximately 50 per cent more intrinsic responses on the intrinsic subscale than we should expect from his extrinsic responses to the extrinsic subscale.)

Indiscriminately antireligious or nonreligious includes those who would show a strong tendency to disagree with items on both subscales. Since non-churchgoers are excluded from our samples, such cases are not found. (Some pilot work with markedly liberal groups indicates that this type does exist, however, even among members of "religious" organizations.)

Table 7 gives the percentage of the three types.

RESULTS OF THE REFORMULATION

The five measures of prejudice were analyzed by a 6 (Groups) x 3 (Religious Types) analysis of

variance. Table 8 presents the overall effects for
religious types for each of the five measures of
prejudice. The multivariate analysis of varience

TABLE 7
PERCENTAGE OF EACH RELIGIOUS TYPE IN
EACH SUBSAMPLE

Religious group	N	Consistently intrinsic	Consistently extrinsic	Indiscriminately proreligious
A	(94)	36	34	30
B	(55)	35	36	29
C	(44)	36	39	25
D	(53)	32	30	38
E	(35)	31	29	40
F	(28)	39	39	22

indicates that there is both a significant difference
between the three types of religious orientation and
between the six subsamples in the level of prejudice.[3]
Examination of the means shows two trends: (a) The
extrinsic type is more prejudiced than the intrinsic
type for both direct and indirect measures; (b) the
indiscriminate type of religious orientation is more
prejudiced than either of the two consistent types.
Statistically all these trends are highly significant.

We note especially that the scores of the indiscriminate type are markedly higher on all measures
than the scores of the intrinsic type. Corresponding F ratios for paired comparisons range from 8.4
for the jungle scale to 20.4 for the CMI scale. The
differences between the indiscriminate and extrinsic
types are smaller. For the anti-Jewish and CMI
scales these differences are, however, beyond the

[3]The multivariate F reported here is Wilk's
lambda (Anderson, 1958). Statistical computations
are summarized by Bock (1963) and programmed for
the IBM 7090 by Hall and Cramer (1962). The univariate tests to be reported are adjusted for un-
equal Ns to obtain orthogonal estimates according
to mathematical procedures described in Hall and
Cramer.

TABLE 8
PREJUDICE AND RELIGIOUS ORIENTATION

Target of prejudice	Intrinsic type $N = 108$	Extrinsic type $N = 106$	Incon-sistent type $N = 95$	F ratio
	Mean prejudice score			
Anti-Negro	28.7	33.0	36.0	8.6**
Anti-Jewish	22.6	24.6	28.9	11.1**
Anti-Other	20.4	23.3	26.1	10.9**
Jungle	7.9	8.7	9.6	8.4**
CMI	10.2	11.8	13.4	20.4**

Multivariate analysis of variance

Source of variation	F ratio	df
Religious type (A)	5.96***	10,574
Sample groups (B)	3.19***	25,668
A × B	1.11*	50,1312

*$p > .25$.
**$p > .001$.
***$p > .0005$.

.005 level; for the anti-other and jungle scales, at the .05 level. For the anti-Negro the difference falls below significance.

The relationship between the indiscriminately proreligious orientation and prejudice receives support (see Table 9) when we compare subjects who are

TABLE 9
DEGREES OF INDISCRIMINATENESS AND AVERAGE
PREJUDICE SCORES

Target of prejudice	Moderately indiscriminate $N = 56$	Extremely indiscriminate $N = 39$	F ratio
Anti-Negro	35.4	37.9	.97
Anti-Jewish	28.0	30.1	.90
Anti-Other	24.9	28.2	3.25*
Jungle	9.5	10.2	1.11
CMI	10.2	14.6	3.99*

*$p > .05$.

moderately indiscriminate with those are *extremely*
indiscriminate. (In the first group the scores on
the intrinsic subscale average 16 points lower than
on the extrinsic subscale; whereas the extreme cases
average 23 points less on the intrinsic than on the
extrinsic subscale.)

The discovery that the degree of indiscriminateness tends to relate directly to the degree of
prejudice is an important finding. It can only mean
that some functional relationship obtains between
religious muddleheadedness (for that is what indiscriminate scores imply) and antagonism toward ethnic
groups. We shall return to this interpretation in
the concluding section of this paper.

RESULTS FOR SUBSAMPLES

It would not be correct to assume that the
variance is distributed equally over all the subsamples, for it turns out that the denominational
groups differ appreciably in prejudice scores and
in religious type, as Tables 10 and 11 indicate.

It is true that when we combine subsamples all
the trends are in the expected direction, but
troublesome exceptions occur for single groups as
indicated by the nearly significant interaction
effects. The most troublesome contradictions appear in relation to the anti-Negro measures based
on the Harding-Schuman scale. Table 10 discloses
certain sore points, even though the average trend
over all the subsamples is in the predicted direction.

For Groups A, B, and C we note that the indiscriminate type is slightly less prejudiced than the
extrinsic type, and for Groups D and E the extrinsic
type seems actually less prejudiced than the intrinsic. (Groups D and E are consistently more troublesome than other subsamples, perhaps because of some
salient racial issue in the local community. It will
be noted that both these groups are considerably
more anti-Negro than the other subsamples.)

By way of contrast we present in Table 11 the
results for the short (five-item) CMI scale. With
the exception of the indiscriminate type in Group F,

TABLE 10
ANTI-NEGRO PREJUDICE: MEAN SCORES ON
SOCIAL PROBLEMS SCALE

Religious group	Intrinsic type	Extrinsic type	Indiscriminate type	Group M
A	27.4 (34)	34.8 (32)	32.2 (28)	31.4 (94)
B	27.2 (19)	32.3 (20)	31.9 (16)	30.4 (55)
C	22.4 (16)	36.2 (17)	35.0 (11)	30.9 (44)
D	35.5 (17)	28.7 (16)	42.5 (20)	36.1 (53)
E	40.5 (11)	35.5 (10)	43.0 (14)	40.1 (35)
F	22.6 (11)	27.9 (11)	28.7 (6)	26.0 (28)
Type M	28.7 (108)	33.0 (106)	36.0 (95)	32.5 (309)

Analysis of variance

Source of variation	df	MS	F ratio
Religious type (A)	2	1077.8	8.6**
Religious group (B)	5	952.2	7.6**
A × B	10	251.1	2.0*
Error (w)	291	125.6	

*$p > .10$.
**$p > .001$.

the progression of scores is precisely as expected. Each subsample shows that the intrinsic type is less prejudiced toward the mentally ill than the extrinsic type, and the extrinsic type is less prejudiced than the indiscriminately proreligious.[4]

[4] If we apply a more severe test, asking whether *all* differences between groups are significant, we find the following results. In four of the six groups (in both Tables 10 and 11) the extrinsic type is significantly more prejudiced than the intrinsic. Likewise in four out of six groups (Table 10) and five out of six (Table 11), the indiscriminate type is significantly more prejudiced than the intrinsic. However, in only two of the six groups (in both Tables 10 and 11) is the indiscriminate type significantly more prejudiced than the extrinsic.

TABLE II
INDIRECT (CMI) MEASURE OF PREJUDICE

Religious group	Intrinsic type	Extrinsic type	Indiscriminate type	Group M
A	11.2 (34)	12.4 (32)	13.6 (28)	12.3 (94)
B	10.1 (19)	10.8 (20)	13.4 (16)	11.3 (55)
C	9.5 (16)	12.2 (17)	12.6 (11)	11.3 (44)
D	10.6 (17)	11.4 (16)	14.8 (20)	12.4 (53)
E	8.6 (11)	12.9 (10)	13.6 (14)	11.8 (35)
F	9.2 (11)	10.7 (11)	9.2 (6)	9.8 (28)
Type M	10.2 (108)	11.8 (106)	13.4 (95)	11.9 (309)

Analysis of variance

Source of variation	df	MS	F ratio
Religious type (A)	2	255.0	20.4**
Religious group (B)	5	36.5	2.9*
A × B	10	15.3	1.2
Error (w)	291	12.5	

*$p > .05$.
**$p > .001$.

Returning in a different way to the original question of whether consistent extrinsic and intrinsic orientations make for prejudice and for tolerance, respectively, we shall now examine this matter in each subsample separately. Inspection of the mean scores and variance for the total scale indicates that we are dealing with a relatively narrow range of variation. To minimize the effect of a narrow range of scores and skewed distributions, we used Kendal's (1955) tau as a measure of degree of relationship between prejudice and consistent religious orientation. The results are given in Table 12. While the correlations are not high (14 are significant in the expected direction), only one (in the troublesome Group E) is significant in the reverse direction.

EDUCATIONAL DIFFERENCES

Computing the actual years of schooling for all groups we find that the indiscriminate type has

TABLE 12
CORRELATIONS BETWEEN COMBINED EXTRINSIC-INTRINSIC
RELIGIOUS SCORES (FOR CONSISTENT SUBJECTS) AND
PREJUDICE (KENDAL'S TAU)

Religious group	Anti-Negro	Anti-Jewish	Anti-Other	Jungle	CMI
A	.31***	.26***	.24***	.14*	.19***
B	.19*	.13	.15	−.05	.03
C	.32***	.17*	.35***	.14*	.28***
D	−.12	.05	−.09	.03	.11
E	−.24*	−.11	−.13	.26*	.46***
F	.39***	.13	.25*	−.01	.24*

*p > .10.
**p > .05.
***p > .01.

significantly less formal education than the intrinsic cases ($p > .005$, $F = 18.29$), and somewhat
less than the extrinsic type ($p > .10$, $F = 2.89$).
Comparing extrinsic with intrinsic types we find
that the former has finished fewer years of schooling ($p > .10$, $F = 3.45$). (Oddly enough the groups
with highest average education are D and E, which
also displayed the highest anti-Negro and anti-
Semitic prejudice--perhaps because of particular
local conditions.)

In our survey of earlier studies we saw that
educational level is often a factor in the various
relationships discovered between religion and prejudice. We have also argued that demographic factors
of this sort should not be allowed to obscure the
functional (psychological) analysis that the data
call for. Granted that low education makes for indiscriminate thinking, the mental confusion that
results from low education may have its own peculiar
effects on religious and ethnic attitudes.

SUMMARY AND INTERPRETATIONS

At the outset we stated three propositions that
seem to be firmly established: (a) Churchgoers on
the broad average harbor more ethnic prejudice than
nonchurchgoers; (b) in spite of this broad tendency

a curvilinear relationship in fact exists; (c) the
intrinsically motivated churchgoers are significantly less prejudiced than the extrinsically motivated. Our present research supplies additional
strong support for the second and third of these
propositions.

To these propositions we add a fourth: *churchgoers who are indiscriminately proreligious are more
prejudiced than the consistently extrinsic, and very
much more prejudiced than the consistently intrinsic
types.*

The psychological tie between the intrinsic
orientation and tolerance, and between the extrinsic
orientation and prejudice, has been discussed in a
series of papers by Allport (1959, 1963, 1966). In
brief the argument holds that a person with an extrinsic religious orientation is using his religious
views to provide security, comfort, status, or social support for himself--religion is not a value in
its own right, it serves other needs, and it is a
purely utilitarian formation. Now prejudice too is
a "useful" formation: it too provides security, comfort, status, and social support. A life that is
dependent on the supports of extrinsic religion is
likely to be dependent on the supports of prejudice,
hence our positive correlations between the extrinsic orientation and intolerance. Contrariwise, the
intrinsic religious orientation is not an instrumental device. It is not a mere mode of conformity,
nor a crutch, nor a tranquilizer, nor a bid for status.
All needs are subordinated to an over-arching religious commitment. In internalizing the total creed of
his religion the individual necessarily internalizes
its values of humility, compassion, and love of
neighbor. In such a life (where religion is an intrinsic and dominant value) there is no place for
rejection, contempt, or condescension toward one's
fellow man. Such is our explanation for the relationship between extrinsic religion and prejudice, and
between intrinsic religion and tolerance.

Our present task is to discover, if we can, some
similar functional tie between prejudice (as measured
both directly and indirectly) and the indiscriminately proreligious orientation. The common factor seems

to be a certain cognitive style. Technically it
might be called "undifferentiated thinking," or
excessive "category width," as defined by Pettigrew (1958). Rokeach (1960) notes the inability of
the "dogmatic" mind to perceive differences; thus,
whereas some people distinguish in their thinking
and feeling between Communists and Nazis, the undifferentiated dogmatist has a global reaction
(cognitive and emotional) toward "Communazis."

    We have no right, of course, to expect all our
subjects to make discriminations exactly corresponding to our own logic. Nor should we expect them to
read and respond to every item on the Extrinsic-
Intrinsic scale according to its full meaning as intended by the investigators. Perhaps we should be
gratified that two-thirds of our cases can be safely
classified as "consistent" (i.e., having about the
same strength of disposition toward an extrinsic or
intrinsic orientation across most of the items).
These consistent cases, as we have seen, support the
hypothesis with which we started. It is the remaining (indiscriminate) one-third of the cases which obscure the trend (or diminish its statistical significance).

    In responding to the religious items these indi-
viduals seem to take a superficial or "hit and run"
approach. Their mental set seems to be "all religion
is good." "My religious beliefs are what really lie
behind my whole life"--Yes! "Although I believe in
my religion, I feel there are many more important
things in my life"--Yes! "Religion is especially important to me because it answers many questions about
the meaning of life"--Yes! "The church is most important as a place to formulate good social relationships"--Yes!

    There seems to be one wide category--"religion
is OK." From the way in which the scale is constructed this undifferentiated endorsement can be the product of an agreement response set. Our inconsistently
proreligious may be "yeasayers" (Couch & Keniston,
1960). But if so, we are still dealing with an undifferentiated cognitive disposition. We recall likewise that the inconsistent cases have a lower level
of formal education than the consistent cases. This

factor also is relevant to the formation and holding
of overwide categories.

But why should such a disposition, whatever its
source, be so strongly related to prejudice, in such
a way that the *more* undifferentiated, the *more* preju-
diced--as Table 9 shows?

The answer is that prejudice itself is a matter
of stereotyped overgeneralization, a failure to distinguish members of a minority group as individuals
(Allport, 1954, Chaps. 2, 10). It goes without saying that if categories are overwide the accompanying
feeling tone will be undifferentiated. Thus, religion as a whole is good; a minority group as a whole
is bad.

It seems probable that people with undifferentiated styles of thinking (and feeling) are not entirely secure in a world that for the most part demands fine and accurate distinctions. The resulting
diffuse anxiety may well dispose them to grapple
onto religion and to distrust strange ethnic groups.
The positive correlation between the jungle items
and other prejudice scales (Table 3) is evidence for
this interpretation.

Our line of reasoning, readers will recognize,
is compatible with various contributions to the theory of prejudice. One thinks here of Rokeach's concept of dogmatism; of Schuman and Harding's (1964)
discovery of a "confused" type in their study of
the relation between rational consistency and prejudice; of the same authors' work on sympathetic identification (1963); of studies on the dynamics of
scapegoating, the role in insecurity, of authoritarian submission, of intolerance for ambiguity, and
of related concepts.

All in all, we conclude that prejudice, like
tolerance, is often embedded deeply in personality
structure and is reflected in a consistent cognitive
style. Both states of mind are enmeshed with the
individual's religious orientation. One definable
style marks the individual who is bigoted in ethnic
matters and extrinsic in his religious orientation.
Equally apparent is the style of those who are
bigoted and at the same time indiscriminately pro-
religious. A relatively small number of people

show an equally consistent cognitive style in their
simultaneous commitment to religion as a dominant,
intrinsic value and to ethnic tolerance.

One final word: our research argues strongly
that social scientists who employ the variable "religion" or "religiosity" in the future will do well
to keep in mind the crucial distinction between
religious attitudes that are *intrinsic, extrinsic,*
and *indiscriminately pro.* To know that a person is
in some sense "religious" is not as important as to
know the role religion plays in the economy of his
life. (The categories of *nonreligious* and *indiscriminately antireligious* will also for some purposes be of central significance, although the
present research, confined as it is to churchgoers,
does not employ them.)

REFERENCES

Adorno, T. W., Frenkel-Brunswik, E., Levinson, D. J.,
     & Sanford, R. N., *The authoritarian personality,*
     New York: Harper, 1950.

Allport, G. W., review of S. A. Stouffer, E. A.
     Suchman, L. C. De Vinney, S. A. Star, & R. W.
     Williams, Jr., *The American soldier,* Vol. I,
     Adjustment during Army life. *Journal of Ab-
     normal and Social Psychology,* 1950, 45, 168-173.

_____, *The nature of prejudice,* Reading, Mass.:
     Addison-Wesley, 1954.

_____, "Religion and prejudice," *The Crane Review,*
     1959, 2, 1-10.

_____, "Behavioral science, religion, and mental
     health," *Journal of Religion and Health,* 1963,
     2, 187-197.

_____, "Religious context of prejudice," *Journal
     for the Scientific Study of Religion,* 1966, 5,
     447-457.

_____, & Kramer, B. M., "Some roots of prejudice,"
     Journal of Psychology, 1946, 22, 9-39.

Anderson, T. W., *An introduction to multivariate
     statistical analysis*, New York: Wiley, 1958.

Bass, B. M., "Authoritarianism or acquiescence,"
     Journal of Abnormal and Social Psychology,
     1955, 56, 616-623.

Bock, R. D., "Programming univariate and multivariate
     analysis of variance," *Technometrics*, 1963, 5,
     95-117.

Chapman, L. J., & Bock, R. D., "Components of vari-
     ance due to acquiescence and content in the F-
     scale measure of authoritarianism," *Psycholog-
     ical Bulletin*, 1958, 55, 328-333.

Chapman, L. J., & Campbell, D. T., "The effect of
     acquiescence response-set upon relationships
     among the F-scale, ethnocentrism, and intelli-
     gence," *Sociometry*, 1959, 22, 153-161.

Christie, R. C., "Authoritarianism re-examined," in
     R. C. Christie & M. Jahoda (eds.), *Studies in
     the scope and method of the authoritarian
     personality*, New York: Free Press of Glencoe,
     1954. Pp. 123-196.

Couch, A., & Keniston, K., "Yeasayers and naysayers:
     Agreeing response set as a personality variable,"
     Journal of Abnormal and Social Psychology, 1960,
     60, 151-174.

Demerath, N. J., III, *Social class in American
     Protestantism*, Chicago: Rand McNally, 1965.

Feagin, J. R., "Prejudice and religious types: A
     focused study of southern fundamentalists,"
     Journal for the Scientific Study of Religion,
     1964, 4, 3-13.

Fichter, J. H., *Social relations in the urban parish,* Chicago: University of Chicago Press, 1954.

Friedrichs, R. W., "Christians and residential exclusion: An empirical study of a Northern dilemma," *Journal of Social Issues,* 1959, 15, 14-23.

Gilbert, D. C., & Levinson, D. J., "Ideology, personality, and institutional policy in the mental hospital," *Journal of Abnormal and Social Psychology,* 1956, 53, 263-271.

Gough, H. G., "Studies in social intolerance: IV," *Journal of Social Psychology,* 1951, 33, 263-269.

Hall, C. E., & Cramer, E., *General purpose program to compute multivariate analysis of variance on an IBM 7090,* Washington, D. C.:   George Washington University Biometric Laboratory, 1962.

Holtzman, W. H., "Attitudes of college men toward non-segregation in Texas schools," *Public Opinion Quarterly,* 1956, 20, 559-569.

Jackson, D. H., & Messick, S. J., "A note on ethnocentrism and acquiescence response sets," *Journal of Abnormal and Social Psychology,* 1957, 54, 132-134.

Kelly, J. G., Ferson, J. E., & Holtzman, W. H., "The measurement of attitudes toward the Negro in the South," *Journal of Social Psychology,* 1958, 48, 305-317.

Kendal, M. G., *Rank correlation methods* (2nd ed.), London: Griffin, 1955.

Kirkpatrick, C., "Religion and humanitarianism: A study of institutional implications," *Psychological Monographs,* 1949, 63 (9, Whole No. 304).

Lenski, G., *The religious factor,* Garden City, N. Y.:
    Doubleday, 1961.

Levinson, D. J., "The inter-group workshop: Its
    psychological aims and effects," *Journal of
    Psychology,* 1954, 38, 103-126.

Peabody, D., "Attitude content and agreement set in
    scales of authoritarianism, dogmatism, anti-
    Semitism and economic conservatism," *Journal of
    Abnormal and Social Psychology,* 1961, 63, 1-11.

Pettigrew, T. F., "The measurement and correlates
    of category width as a cognitive variable,"
    Journal of Personality, 1958, 26, 532-544.

_____, "Regional differences in anti-Negro preju-
    dice," *Journal of Abnormal and Social Psychology,*
    1959, 49, 28-36.

Pinkney, A., *The anatomy of prejudice: Majority
    group attitudes toward minorities in selected
    American cities.* Unpublished doctoral disser-
    tation, Cornell University, 1961.

Rokeach, M., *The open and closed mind: Investiga-
    tions into the nature of belief systems and
    personality systems,* New York: Basic Books,
    1960.

Rosenblith, J. F., "A replication of 'Some roots of
    prejudice,'" *Journal of Abnormal and Social
    Psychology,* 1949, 44, 470-489.

Schuman, H., & Harding, J., "Sympathetic identifi-
    cation with the underdog," *Public Opinion
    Quarterly,* 1963, 27, 230-241.

_____, & _____, "Prejudice and the norm of ratio-
    nality," *Sociometry,* 1964, 27, 353-371.

Stember, H. C., *Education and attitude change,* New
    York: Institute of Human Relations Press, 1961.

Stouffer, S. A., *Communism, civil liberties, and conformity,* Garden City, N. Y.: Doubleday, 1955.

Struening, E. L., "Antidemocratic attitudes in a Midwest university," in H. H. Remmers (ed.), *Anti-democratic attitudes in American schools,* Evanston: Northwestern University Press, 1963, Ch. 9.

Titus, H. E., & Hollander, E. P., "The California F scale in psychological research: 1950-1955," *Psychological Bulletin,* 1957, 54, 47-64.

Tumin, M., *Desegregation: Resistance and readiness,* Princeton: Princeton University Press, 1958.

Williams, R. M., *Strangers next door: Ethnic relations in American communities,* Englewood Cliffs, N. J.: Prentice-Hall, 1964.

Wilson, W. C., "Extrinsic religious values and prejudice," *Journal of Abnormal and Social Psychology,* 1960, 60, 286-288.

Young, R. K., Benson, W. M., & Holtzman, W. H., "Changes in attitudes toward the Negro in a Southern university," *Journal of Abnormal and Social Psychology,* 1960, 60, 131-133.

RELIGION, VALUES, AND
SOCIAL COMPASSION

MILTON ROKEACH

Editor's introduction. This two-part contribution by Rokeach is important for several
reasons. First, it presents an innovative
technique for measuring the content of value
structures. Second, it investigates the relationship of values and attitudes; and third,
it introduces an approach to the question of
religion and social attitudes that contrasts
sharply with the one suggested by Allport. On
a social-psychological theoretical level, Rokeach introduces the concept of instrumental
and terminal values. As Rokeach defines them:
"Terminal values refer to preferred end-states
of existence; instrumental values refer to preferred modes of behavior."
    The Rokeach value measure is applied first to
a study of religious differences. The question,
simply put, is whether we can find a distinctly
religious pattern of values in American society.
The answer, given by Rokeach in the first part,
is positive. When religiosity is measured by
nominal religious identification, frequency of

From *Review of Religious Research,* 1969, 11,
3-23. Reprinted with permission.

church attendance, and self-ratings on the
importance of religion in one's life, clear
differences emerge among the religious, less
religious, and the non-religious. Religious
Christians ranked the terminal value *salvation*
higher and the terminal value *pleasure* lower
than those less religious and non-religious.
Religious respondents also ranked the instrumental values *forgiving* and *obedient* higher,
and the instrumental values *independent, intellectual*, and *logical* lower than the less
religious and the non-religious respondents.
Overall, *salvation* and *forgiving* were found to
be the most distinctively Christian values.

Establishing the existence of differences in
values between religious and non-religious respondents is the first part of Rokeach's argument. Since such differences exist, we can
now turn to the second part and look at the related differences in social attitudes. The
attitudes examined by Rokeach pertained to what
he calls "a compassionate social outlook."
This outlook was determined by responses to the
assassination of Dr. Martin Luther King, attitudes toward equal rights for blacks, views
about the poor, opinions on student protest
movements, and attitudes about the church's involvement in social and political affairs. The
results show those who place a high value on
salvation, the most distinctively Christian
value, to be rather low on "social compassion."
They are portrayed by Rokeach as more conservative, anxious to maintain the status quo, and
generally indifferent and unsympathetic to the
plight of the black and the poor. They had
reacted in a more fearful and "calloused" way
to the King assassination, were unsympathetic
to the student protest movement, and were more
opposed to church involvement in social and
political affairs than were the other respondents. The findings for correlates of *forgiving*
(the second most distinctively Christian value)
are similar, but less pronounced. *Forgiving*
was negatively correlated with social compassion,

but to a lesser extent than *salvation*. Rokeach
takes issue with the Allport and Ross assertion,
presented previously, regarding the curvilinear
relationship between church attendance and social compassion. He reports that frequent
churchgoers in his sample were somewhat less
compassionate than infrequent church attenders.

Rokeach's departure from Allport's approach
is clear and strong. Both in findings and
interpretation, he adds to the long list of previous studies that found religious devoutness
to be positively related to "bigotry, authoritarianism, dogmatism, and anti-humanitarianism."
Rokeach is no apologist for religion. He is
ready to take a critical position, indict the
churches for most of what they have been doing,
and suggest some alternative ways of teaching
values. Still, these suggestions show that
Rokeach regards the religious institution in
society as potentially worthy of salvage, if
not salvation. While both Allport and Rokeach
regard the positive relationship between religiosity and prejudice as a social problem, the
solutions they offer are clearly different.
Allport would like to concentrate on changing
individuals, while Rokeach would like to trans-
form institutions. To use Allport's terms, the
problem could be solved if the extrinsics were
converted into intrinsics. According to Rokeach,
however, the churches themselves are extrinsic
and therefore incapable of converting their
members.

On methodological grounds, some psychologists
may want to criticize Rokeach for using the term
"salvation" to differentiate the religious value
system. It is clear that "salvation" may have
different meanings for different religious
groups, but its choice as a discriminating variable was not Rokeach's; it emerged from the
data. If the value of salvation discriminates
between religious and non-religious respondents,
and if, moreover, it correlates with a distinct
value structure, then its choice as a crucial
variable is hard to challenge. Rokeach's sample,

which is the most representative in studies
dealing with religion and social attitudes,
makes the findings more convincing and more
definitive.

PART I: VALUE SYSTEMS IN RELIGION

Regardless of what sociologists, Marxists, or
Freudians may have said about the functions of religion in society, those who are partisan to religion must necessarily be committed to at least the
following two assumptions: first, that religion
teaches man a distinctive system of moral values
that he might not otherwise have and, second, that
such moral values guide man's everyday relations to
his fellowman toward higher, nobler, or more humane levels than might otherwise be the case. Both
of these assumptions are empirically testable; yet,
I know of no studies that systematically attempt to
identify the specific values or value systems of
the religious, the less religious, and nonreligious,
or that attempt to show empirically the relevance of
such specific values for improving everyday life in
a complex society.

This paper concerns the first of religion's
assumptions, namely, that those who are religious do
indeed have a distinctive system of moral values
that sets them apart from others who are less religious. The second assumption is that the moral
values claimed by and for those who are religious
have relevance for life in a modern society, whether
they facilitate or hinder the growth of concern for
the welfare and well-being of other members of the
human species.

I have already suggested elsewhere (Rokeach,
1968a, 1968-69) that there are two major reasons
why we know so little as yet about the nature and
the consequences of human values and value systems.
First, methods for measuring values and value systems are considerably less advanced than methods

for measuring attitudes. A closely related second
reason is that social scientists still have a poor
consensus about the conceptual differences between
values and attitudes and between values and value
systems; more often than not these concepts have
been used synonymously even though values are obviously deeper than attitudes, and value systems
are broader than values. Because these concepts
have been employed interchangeably, data from empirical research on attitudinal differences between
one and another group have often been interpreted
in a general way as representing value differences;
such differences are not directly measured but are
typically inferred from obtained differences in beliefs and attitudes. Because of such vagueness of
conception and associated measurement difficulties,
we have not been able to state with any precision
exactly which value differences underlie differences in religious orientation, or underlie differences in beliefs and attitudes that are associated
with religious differences.[2]

  There are, of course, many empirical studies
that show significant differences in beliefs and
attitudes between groups varying in religion, between Jew, Catholic, and Protestant, and between
various Protestant denominations (Adorno, *et al.*,
1950; Allport, 1954; Allport and Ross, 1967; Glock
and Stark, 1965, 1966; Kirkpatrick, 1949; Lenski,
1961; Rokeach, 1960, 1968b; Young, Benson, and
Holtzman, 1960). Most disturbing are those findings that show religious devoutness to be positively
rather than negatively related to bigotry, authoritarianism, dogmatism, and anti-humanitarianism.
Such findings are disturbing from a religious standpoint because they point to a social institution
that needs to be reformed, and they are also disturbing from an antireligious standpoint because
they point to the existence of a social institution
that deserves to be destroyed. From either viewpoint they suggest the presence of deeper differences
in values that merit further investigation and understanding.

  Other research by social scientists has succeeded in softening the blow of findings such as those

just cited that suggest negative, dehumanizing effects of organized religion. Various suggestions
have been offered to the effect that there are several types of religious devoutness--intrinsic and
extrinsic (Allport, 1959; Wilson, 1960; Feagin,
1964; Allport and Ross, 1967), associational and
communal (Lenski, 1961), experiential, ideological,
ritualistic, intellectual, and consequential (Glock
and Stark, 1965)--that are differentially related to
attitudes concerning civil rights, social welfare,
and so forth. All such findings would also suggest
the presence of underlying value differences. It
would indeed be helpful if methods were available
to identify the values that are implicated in such
differences in religious outlook.

The data on religious values that I will report
here were obtained as part of a broader, ongoing research program on the theory and measurement of
values and value systems, their relation to attitudes
and behavior, the conditions under which change may
be expected in values and value systems, and their
consequences for attitude and behavior change.[3] The
main instrument employed in this research is the
Value Survey, which consists of 18 terminal values
and another 18 instrumental values, as shown in
Tables 1 and 2. Terminal values refer to preferred
end-states of existence; instrumental values refer
to preferred modes of behavior. The respondent's
task is simply to rank each list of 18 values in
order of perceived importance as guiding principles
in his daily life.

I will report here on data now available for
two kinds of samples: a national area probability
sample of about 1,400 Americans over 21, obtained
by the National Opinion Research Center in April,
1968, and a sample of about 300 college students
taking an introductory psychology course at Michigan
State University. Both sets of respondents were
tested with Form D of the Value Survey wherein the
values are presented in alphabetical order, each on
a separate gummed label that can easily be moved
about from one position to another. The respondent
first ranks the 18 gummed labels representing the
terminal values, and then does the same with the 18

labels representing the instrumental values. Other
data obtained from the respondents included information on demographic variables, religious affiliation, frequency of church attendance, and in the
case of the college sample, perceived importance of
religion in one's daily life. The data thus obtained provide us with perhaps the first comprehensive
and representative description of the value systems
in American society as well as in a selected sample
of midwestern college students attending a large
state-supported university.

Value Systems of Groups Nominally Identified with Religion

As a first approximation to the assessment of
value similarities and differences among groups
varying in religion, I first present the findings
obtained for the national sample of respondents who
identify themselves nominally as Protestants, Catholics, Jews, or professing no religion. Table 1
shows the median ranks and the composite rank orders
of these median ranks for each of the terminal
values, and Table 2 shows the same data for the instrumental values. Also shown, for each value considered separately, is whether the difference in
rankings of the four groups is statistically significant, as determined by the nonparametric Median
Test (Siegel, 1956). A glance down the last column
of both sets of data quickly reveals that about half
of the 36 values show significant differences among
the four groups.

Considering first the results shown in Table 1,
it is immediately evident that the largest terminal
value difference is found for *salvation:* Protestants
ranked it fourth on the average, Catholics thirteenth,[4]
and Jews and nonbelievers ranked it last --eighteenth.

The four groups showed other significant terminal value differences that are probably cultural or
socio-economic rather than religious in origin: (1)
Jews ranked *a sense of accomplishment, equality,*
and *pleasure* more highly than Protestants and Catholics, and they ranked *family security, inner harmony,*

and *wisdom* more highly than all three remaining groups. These six terminal values would thus seem to identify, at least in part, the specific values implicated in whatever may be meant by a "Jewish value system." (2) Nonbelievers placed a higher value on *an exciting life, a sense of accomplishment, equality,* and *pleasure* than the remaining groups, and they placed a lower value on *family security* and *national security.* (3) Aside from *salvation,*

TABLE 1

TERMINAL VALUE MEDIANS AND COMPOSITE RANK ORDERS FOR
PROTESTANTS, CATHOLICS, JEWS, AND THOSE PROFESSING NO RELIGION
(N=1391)

	Prot.		Catholic		Jewish		None		Median Test	
N=	996		322		28		45			
	Md.	Rnk.	Md.	Rnk.	Md.	Rnk.	Md.	Rnk.	Chi-Sq.	p=
A comfortable life	8.7	9	9.9	12	8.5	10	9.0	9	3.66	.300
An exciting life	15.5	18	15.3	18	15.8	17	11.1	13	15.88	.001
A sense of accomplishment	9.3	11	8.5	7	7.0	6	6.3	4	12.40	.006
A world at peace	3.3	1	3.2	1	2.9	2	7.0	5	6.17	.103
A world of beauty	13.5	15	13.7	15	14.0	16	11.8	15	5.08	.166
Equality	8.7	8	9.1	8	7.0	5	5.3	2	12.27	.007
Family security	4.0	2	3.2	2	2.3	1	5.6	3	18.36	.001
Freedom	5.6	3	5.7	3	7.0	7	4.0	1	4.89	.180
Happiness	7.7	5	7.1	4	6.8	4	8.9	8	3.63	.304
Inner harmony	10.7	13	9.8	11	8.0	8	10.3	11	10.21	.017
Mature love	12.5	14	12.2	14	12.8	14	10.8	12	2.31	.512
National security	9.8	12	8.5	6	10.5	12	11.6	14	10.54	.015
Pleasure	14.7	17	14.8	17	13.8	15	13.2	16	13.89	.003
Salvation	6.7	4	10.8	13	17.7	18	17.0	18	87.91	.001
Self respect	7.8	7	7.4	5	8.3	9	7.3	6	.80	.850
Social recognition	14.5	16	14.2	16	12.5	13	15.1	17	4.18	.243
True friendship	9.2	10	9.6	10	10.2	11	9.3	10	1.60	.658
Wisdom	7.7	6	9.3	9	6.5	3	7.8	7	11.36	.010

which the Protestants had ranked higher than the remaining groups, we found that Protestants ranked *a sense of accomplishment* lower than the remaining groups. This finding provides little support for the notion that Protestants are more motivated by a Protestant ethic than non-Protestants. (4) Finally, the only distinctive finding for Catholics is that they valued *national security* more and *equality* and *pleasure* less than any of the remaining groups.

Before I discuss the findings concerning instrumental value differences, a few words are in order about moral and nonmoral values. To my mind, the

general concept of value is considerably broader
than the concept of moral value. For one thing,
moral values refer only to modes of behavior, instrumental values, and not to end-states of existence, terminal values. For another, moral values refer mainly to those modes of behavior which,
when violated, arouse pangs of conscience or feelings of guilt or wrongdoing; they have an *interpersonal* focus. Of the 18 instrumental values
shown in Table 2, about half appear to be *moral*
values; the remainder I will call *competence* values. Competence values refer to preferred modes
of behavior which, when violated, lead to shame
about competence rather than to guilt about wrongdoing; their focus is personal rather than interpersonal. The following classification may help
make the distinction clearer:

Moral values:	clean, forgiving, helpful, honest, loving, obedient, polite, responsible, self-controlled.
Competence values:	ambitious, broadminded, capable, imaginative, in-dependent, intellectual, logical.
Indeterminate:	courageous, cheerful.

While I am not at all sure that everyone would
fully agree with this particular classification,[5]
my main reason for drawing attention to it is to
refine the hypothesis about the relation between religion and moral values. There are generally fewer
grounds for anticipating differences between the
religious and the nonreligious on competence values,
and more grounds for expecting such differences on
moral values.
    Turning now to Table 2, it is noted that the
instrumental value *forgiving* showed the sharpest
difference among the four groups. Protestants and
Catholics ranked it fourth on the average, Jews
fifteenth, and nonbelievers sixteenth. *Forgiving*
is clearly a moral value that is central within
Christian theology; the findings confirm that

Christians do indeed place a considerably higher value on it than do non-Christians.

TABLE 2

INSTRUMENTAL VALUE MEDIANS AND COMPOSITE RANK ORDERS FOR
PROTESTANTS, CATHOLICS, JEWS, AND THOSE PROFESSING NO RELIGION
(N=1391)

	Prot.		Catholic		Jewish		None		Median Test	
N=	996		322		28		45			
	Md.	Rnk.	Md.	Rnk.	Md.	Rnk.	Md.	Rnk.	Chi-Sq.	p=
Ambitious	6.5	2	6.0	2	8.0	6	8.0	5	2.21	.531
Broadminded	7.6	5	8.2	6	5.2	2	4.9	2	14.68	.002
Capable	9.8	11	8.9	8	7.0	5	9.4	8	10.45	.015
Cheerful	10.0	12	9.6	10	10.3	10	11.0	13	.95	.814
Clean	8.4	8	9.1	9	10.5	11	12.0	15	9.52	.023
Courageous	7.7	6	8.1	5	8.2	7	8.3	6	1.19	.756
Forgiving	6.8	4	7.7	4	12.2	15	12.1	16	28.06	.001
Helpful	8.0	7	8.6	7	9.5	9	10.3	11	6.00	.112
Honest	3.2	1	3.6	1	4.1	1	4.3	1	7.51	.057
Imaginative	15.7	18	14.8	18	13.8	17	9.4	9	30.02	.001
Independent	10.7	14	10.7	14	6.0	3	6.4	3	18.33	.001
Intellectual	13.2	16	13.5	17	9.0	8	10.3	12	17.89	.001
Logical	14.7	17	13.2	15	10.8	12	12.0	14	23.46	.001
Loving	9.6	10	10.1	11	11.0	14	9.7	10	1.39	.708
Obedient	13.1	15	13.2	16	15.5	18	16.2	18	26.32	.001
Polite	10.7	13	10.6	13	13.8	16	14.1	17	18.08	.001
Responsible	6.6	3	6.8	3	6.5	4	7.4	4	1.09	.780
Self controlled	9.5	9	10.2	12	11.0	13	9.0	7	5.08	.166

Three other moral values besides *forgiving* also distinguished significantly among the four groups; these are *clean, obedient,* and *polite*: Christians ranked these highest, Jews next highest, and non-believers lowest. *Honest* showed a similar pattern but does not reach statistical significance. The remaining values that I have identified as moral--*helpful, loving, responsible,* and *self-controlled*--showed no significant differences among the four groups.

Several competence values also showed significant differences. Non-believers ranked *imaginative* relatively high--ninth--and Jews, Catholics, and Protestants ranked it considerably lower--seventeenth or eighteenth. Jews valued *capable, independent, intellectual,* and *logical* relatively more than the others, and these can therefore also be said to represent Jewish values (along with the terminal values, *a sense of accomplishment, equality, pleasure, family security, inner harmony,* and *wisdom*). As for

the Protestant ethic, there is no suggestion here
that Protestants adhere to values that are more consistent with it than non-Protestants. The four
groups did not differ on *ambitious,* and Protestants
as a group valued *capable* less than any of the remaining three groups.

As already stated, the value differences shown
in Tables 1 and 2 probably reflect not only religious
differences but also cultural and socio-economic
differences. Two values, *salvation* and *forgiving,*
stand out as the most distinctively Christian, since
they distinguished more sharply than any of the remaining values between Protestants and Catholics on
the one hand and Jews and nonbelievers on the other.

Glock and Stark (1966) have shown, however, that
Protestants are far from homogeneous in their religious orientation, that there are often greater differences in belief within Protestant denominations
than between Protestants and Catholics. It is therefore reasonable to expect additional value differences among the various Protestant denominations, although not as many perhaps as have been found when
comparing Christians with Jews and with nonbelievers.
The pertinent results are shown in Tables 3 and 4; a
comparison of the value systems of six major Protestant denominations generally confirm that this is
indeed the case. Now, only nine values instead of
nineteen were found to be significant among the 36
values.

The terminal value that differentiated most
sharply among the Protestant groups was again *salvation:* Baptists ranked it third on the average,
the remaining Protestant groups ranked it anywhere
from ninth on down, Episcopalians ranking it lowest
--fourteenth. Paradoxically, Baptists seem to be
the most deviant Christian group in the sense that
they ranked *salvation* considerably higher than
either Catholics or the other Protestant groups.

Only two other terminal values showed significant differences among the Protestant denominations.
A sense of accomplishment was ranked highest by
Episcopalians and lowest by Baptists. *Mature love*
was also ranked highest by Episcopalians, but this
time it was the Methodists who valued it less than
the remaining groups.

TABLE 3

TERMINAL VALUE MEDIANS AND COMPOSITE RANK ORDERS FOR
VARIOUS PROTESTANT DENOMINATIONS
(N=790)

	Baptist		Method.		Episcop.		Presbyt.		Lutheran		Congreg.			
N=	324		199		39		76		113		39		Median Test	
	Md.	Rnk.	Md.	Rnk.	Md.	Rnk.	Md.	Rnk.	Md.	Rnk.	Md.	Rnk.	Chi-Sq.	p=
A comfortable life	8.3	8	8.1	7	10.1	11	11.2	13	9.1	10	7.4	5	5.88	.318
An exciting life	15.7	18	14.9	18	14.0	16	15.7	18	15.4	18	15.6	18	6.77	.239
A sense of accomplishment	10.4	12	9.3	12	6.4	4	9.1	9	8.4	7	7.6	6	14.72	.012
A world at peace	3.4	1	2.8	1	3.6	2	3.1	2	3.0	1	2.6	1	2.35	.800
A world of beauty	14.1	15	12.9	14	13.3	15	13.6	15	13.5	15	13.0	16	6.66	.247
Equality	8.2	7	8.3	8	10.6	12	8.5	7	10.3	12	11.0	13	5.18	.395
Family security	4.2	2	4.0	2	2.4	1	3.1	1	4.1	2	3.2	2	9.13	.104
Freedom	5.4	4	6.5	3	5.8	3	5.6	3	4.3	3	5.4	3	8.16	.147
Happiness	7.7	6	7.7	4	7.1	6	6.5	4	8.3	6	8.6	8	3.18	.673
Inner harmony	11.2	13	10.6	13	9.7	10	10.3	12	10.8	13	10.4	12	6.35	.274
Mature love	12.6	14	13.6	15	11.2	13	12.0	14	12.7	14	12.0	14	13.49	.019
National security	10.3	11	8.9	11	8.2	7	9.4	10	8.2	5	8.8	9	8.23	.144
Pleasure	14.4	17	14.7	17	15.2	18	14.7	16	15.0	16	15.1	17	1.16	.948
Salvation	4.4	3	8.7	10	13.0	14	10.0	11	8.8	9	9.3	11	29.50	.001
Self respect	7.3	5	7.8	5	8.8	8	8.3	6	8.7	8	8.0	7	8.34	.139
Social recognition	14.2	16	14.4	16	14.4	17	15.4	17	15.3	17	12.7	15	8.06	.153
True friendship	9.7	10	8.6	9	9.6	9	7.9	5	9.4	11	9.0	10	7.01	.220
Wisdom	8.3	9	8.0	6	6.8	5	8.6	8	8.0	4	7.0	4	2.76	.737

Considering next the instrumental values, the
findings (Table 4) show that three moral values--
clean, forgiving, and *obedient*--were ranked higher
and three competence values--*broadminded, capable,*
and *logical*--were ranked lower by the Baptists than

TABLE 4

INSTRUMENTAL VALUE MEDIANS AND COMPOSITE RANK ORDERS FOR
VARIOUS PROTESTANT DENOMINATIONS
(N=790)

	Baptist		Method.		Episcop.		Presbyt.		Lutheran		Congreg.			
N=	324		199		39		76		113		39		Median Test	
	Md.	Rnk.	Md.	Rnk.	Md.	Rnk.	Md.	Rnk.	Md.	Rnk.	Md.	Rnk.	Chi-Sq.	p=
Ambitious	5.7	2	6.5	3	8.0	5	6.8	4	6.1	2	7.3	5	3.57	.612
Broadminded	8.2	7	6.4	2	7.0	3	6.0	3	7.8	5	5.3	2	10.96	.052
Capable	10.5	14	9.3	9	8.3	6	7.8	5	9.8	10	11.0	13	13.41	.020
Cheerful	9.9	11	9.8	10	12.3	16	10.3	11	10.2	12	9.8	11	3.24	.662
Clean	6.6	3	9.1	8	11.3	14	10.5	12	9.5	9	8.3	9	22.63	.001
Courageous	8.2	8	7.0	6	8.3	7	8.1	8	7.8	6	8.1	8	5.20	.393
Forgiving	6.6	4	7.0	5	8.8	8	7.8	6	6.1	3	6.1	3	11.33	.045
Helpful	7.8	6	7.9	7	9.9	11	8.1	7	8.5	7	7.6	6	5.97	.309
Honest	2.9	1	3.2	1	3.3	1	2.5	1	3.7	1	4.3	1	4.55	.473
Imaginative	15.9	18	15.9	18	14.6	17	15.4	18	15.6	18	16.1	18	1.78	.879
Independent	10.4	12	10.6	13	9.0	9	10.0	10	10.8	13	9.4	10	1.15	.950
Intellectual	13.4	16	13.1	16	11.3	13	12.5	15	13.4	16	12.7	15	4.49	.482
Logical	15.4	17	14.6	17	12.0	15	12.8	16	13.4	15	13.3	16	16.51	.006
Loving	9.3	9	11.2	14	9.4	10	9.2	9	9.1	8	8.0	7	8.82	.117
Obedient	12.3	15	12.8	15	15:8	18	15.1	17	13.7	17	13.9	17	23.04	.001
Polite	10.5	13	10.5	12	10.6	12	11.2	14	10.9	14	11.3	14	2.52	.773
Responsible	7.2	5	6.8	4	5.6	2	5.8	2	6.2	4	6.6	4	8.07	.152
Self controlled	9.7	10	10.0	11	7.8	4	10.7	13	9.8	11	10.3	12	3.85	.571

by the remaining Protestant groups. These findings,
when considered alongside the terminal value findings for Baptists (who were high on *salvation* and
low on *a sense of accomplishment*) would seem to describe a fundamentalist value system on one extreme
of the Christian continuum. On the other extreme
are the findings for Episcopalians which seem to
describe a "high church" value system, the main difference being that Episcopalians generally ranked
salvation and the moral values lower and *a sense of
accomplishment* and the competence values higher than
the Baptists.

Values, Religion, and Social Class

The fact that Baptists and Episcopalians, the
nominally religious and nonreligious, Christians and
Jews all differed so markedly from one another on
essentially the same sets of terminal and instrumental values raises the question as to whether the
observed differences could have arisen from differences in social class rather than from differences
in religion. To determine if this is indeed the
case, value data were obtained for respondents of
different income groups on the assumption that income is the best single index of social class. The
results are shown in Tables 5 and 6.
Twenty of the 36 values showed statistically
significant differences related to differences in
income. By inspection of Table 5 it is noted that
the poor valued *salvation* more than the rich and
they also valued *a comfortable life* and *true friendship* more. Conversely, the poor placed a lower value than the rich on *a sense of accomplishment, family
security, inner harmony, mature love,* and *wisdom.*
As for the instrumental values, Table 6 shows
that the poor ranked five values more highly than
the rich and that all of these are moral values;
clean, forgiving, helpful, obedient, and polite. The
only exception is *responsible,* which showed a reverse pattern, the rich valuing it more than the
poor. Furthermore, the poor ranked four values lower than the rich, and all of these turn out to be

competence values: *capable, imaginative, intellectual,*
and *logical.* This pattern of differences distinguish-
ing the poor from the rich is highly similar to the
patterns previously noted that distinguish Baptists
from Episcopalians, the nominally religious from the
non-religious, and Christian from Jew. This rein-
forces the hypothesis that social class may be the
basis of the value differences found between religious
groups. But it hardly seems likely that all the value
differences found between religious groups can be
accounted for in this way. There must surely be some
value differences remaining among the several religious groups even if social class were held constant.

To determine whether this is indeed the case,
the 28 Jews in the national sample--the smallest of
the various subgroups--were matched for income with
28 randomly selected white respondents from each of
the remaining subgroups.[6] These matched groups were
then compared on each of the terminal and instrumental values, as before.

With income and race held constant, four terminal and five instrumental values were found to distinguish among the eight groups at statistically significant levels, as shown in Tables 7 and 8. Considering
the terminal values first, nonbelievers ranked *an
exciting life* considerably higher than the remaining
seven groups. Nonbelievers also ranked *equality*
higher than did the other groups, followed by Jews
and Presbyterians, and it received its lowest group
ranking by Episcopalians. *Pleasure* also was ranked
highest by nonbelievers and then by Jews, with the
Catholics ranking it lower than did the other groups.
But it is *salvation* that emerged most clearly as a
Christian value: the Baptists ranked it first, the
other Christian groups ranked it from eleventh to
fourteenth, and the Jews and nonbelievers ranked it
last.

As for the instrumental values, nonbelievers
ranked *broadminded* highest, followed by the Presbyterians and Jews, and Baptists ranked it lowest. The
rankings of *forgiving* ranged from fourth to fifteenth,
with Lutherans and Baptists ranking it fourth and the
nonbelievers and Jews ranking it fifteenth. *Imaginative* was ranked fourth by nonbelievers and seventeenth

TABLE 5

TERMINAL VALUE MEDIANS AND COMPOSITE RANK ORDERS FOR GROUPS VARYING IN INCOME
(N=1325)

N =	Under $2000		$2000-3999		$4000-5999		$6000-7999		$8000-9999		$10-14999		$15000+		Median Test	
	139		239		217		249		178		208		95			
	Md.	Rnk.	Md.	Rnk.	Md.	Rnk.	Md.	Rnk.	Md.	Rnk.	Md.	Rnk.	Md.	Rnk.	Chi-Sq.	p=
A comfortable life	7.2	6	8.5	7	8.4	7	8.1	6	10.0	11	11.0	13	13.4	15	41.76	.001
An exciting life	15.3	18	15.4	18	15.6	18	15.4	18	15.4	18	15.2	18	14.3	16	4.80	.570
A sense of accomplishment	10.4	12	10.3	12	9.1	9	9.4	10	8.4	8	7.6	6	6.1	5	35.42	.001
A world at peace	2.7	1	3.1	1	3.2	1	3.4	2	3.9	2	3.8	2	3.5	1	9.68	.139
A world of beauty	13.6	14	12.7	14	13.5	15	14.0	15	13.8	15	13.7	15	12.6	13	6.81	.338
Equality	7.0	5	8.5	8	8.3	6	9.0	9	7.8	5	9.7	9	7.5	6	19.65	.003
Family security	5.6	2	4.6	2	3.6	2	3.2	1	3.2	1	3.6	1	4.1	2	33.73	.001
Freedom	6.8	4	5.2	3	5.2	3	5.4	3	5.9	3	5.9	3	5.0	3	8.29	.218
Happiness	7.7	7	8.0	6	7.1	4	6.9	4	7.6	4	8.1	7	9.2	8	9.87	.130
Inner harmony	11.6	13	10.9	13	10.8	13	10.5	13	10.2	13	9.9	11	9.2	9	18.78	.005
Mature love	14.4	17	14.0	16	12.3	14	12.2	14	10.8	14	11.5	14	11.8	12	35.79	.001
National security	8.9	11	9.5	11	9.7	12	9.5	11	9.3	10	9.4	8	11.3	11	5.74	.453
Pleasure	13.6	16	14.5	17	14.7	16	14.7	17	15.1	17	15.0	16	15.2	18	10.68	.099
Salvation	6.6	3	7.3	5	9.4	11	8.4	8	1.6	9	10.1	12	13.3	14	22.51	.001
Self respect	7.9	8	7.2	4	7.6	5	8.4	7	7.9	6	7.2	4	7.8	7	6.59	.361
Social recognition	13.6	15	13.9	15	14.8	17	14.6	16	14.2	16	15.1	17	14.6	17	12.16	.058
True friendship	7.9	9	8.5	10	9.2	10	9.9	12	10.1	12	9.7	10	9.4	10	18.35	.005
Wisdom	8.7	10	8.5	9	8.8	8	7.0	5	8.1	7	7.4	7	5.6	4	20.08	.003

TABLE 6
INSTRUMENTAL VALUE MEDIANS AND COMPOSITE RANK ORDERS FOR GROUPS VARYING IN INCOME
(N=1325)

N=	Under $2000		$2000-3999		$4000-5999		$6000-7999		$8000-9999		$10-14999		$15000+		Median Test	
	139		239		217		249		178		208		95			
	Md.	Rnk.	Md.	Rnk.	Md.	Rnk.	Md.	Rnk.	Md.	Rnk.	Md.	Rnk.	Md.	Rnk.	Chi-Sq.	p=
Ambitious	8.0	6	6.9	3	6.1	2	6.8	3	6.6	3	5.8	2	6.4	3	8.33	.215
Broadminded	8.6	8	7.2	4	8.1	8	8.1	6	7.1	4	6.4	4	7.0	4	11.92	.064
Capable	9.5	10	10.5	14	9.8	11	9.3	11	9.8	11	8.4	7	8.8	8	14.98	.020
Cheerful	9.0	9	8.6	9	10.6	14	10.3	12	10.7	12	10.2	11	11.3	14	16.33	.012
Clean	6.4	2	7.3	5	8.0	7	8.6	8	9.3	10	10.4	12	14.4	17	72.35	.001
Courageous	7.5	5	8.1	8	8.0	5	7.5	5	7.4	6	8.0	5	7.2	5	2.87	.825
Forgiving	6.4	3	6.5	2	7.3	4	6.8	4	7.4	5	8.1	6	10.7	12	20.23	.003
Helpful	7.1	4	7.4	6	8.0	6	8.2	7	8.9	8	9.3	8	9.1	9	17.69	.007
Honest	3.3	1	3.7	1	3.4	1	3.0	1	3.0	1	3.4	1	3.0	1	4.71	.582
Imaginative	15.2	18	15.8	18	15.6	18	15.9	18	15.0	18	14.6	18	11.4	15	29.32	.001
Independent	10.5	14	10.3	12	10.0	12	10.7	14	11.4	13	11.0	13	8.3	6	5.54	.476
Intellectual	13.9	16	13.4	16	13.3	16	13.6	16	13.1	15	12.1	15	8.6	7	25.00	.001
Logical	15.2	17	14.8	17	14.7	17	14.1	17	14.0	16	12.8	16	10.9	13	36.59	.001
Loving	10.0	11	10.3	13	9.5	10	9.1	10	8.8	7	10.2	10	9.8	10	2.47	.872
Obedient	12.0	15	12.4	15	13.3	15	13.2	15	14.2	17	14.3	17	15.3	18	27.06	.001
Polite	10.4	13	10.2	11	10.2	13	10.4	13	11.4	14	11.2	14	13.2	16	26.11	.001
Responsible	8.2	7	7.8	7	7.1	3	5.8	2	6.0	2	6.0	3	5.9	2	33.51	.001
Self controlled	10.2	12	9.9	10	9.2	9	9.0	9	9.0	9	9.7	9	9.9	11	3.21	.782

TABLE 7
TERMINAL VALUE MEDIANS AND COMPOSITE RANK ORDERS FOR RELIGIOUS GROUPS MATCHED ON INCOME AND RACE
(N=224)

N=	Jews		Catholic		None		Baptist		Methodist		Episcop.		Presbyt.		Lutheran		Median Test	
	28		28		28		28		28		28		28		28			
	Md.	Rnk.	Md.	Rnk.	Md.	Rnk.	Md.	Rnk.	Md.	Rnk.	Md.	Rnk.	Md.	Rnk.	Md.	Rnk.	Chi-Sq.	p=
A comfortable life	8.5	10	12.5	13	8.5	8	11.5	13	9.0	9	10.3	11	13.0	15	9.5	10	11.55	.116
An exciting life	15.8	17	14.8	16	10.0	12	15.0	17	15.5	18	13.5	16	15.8	18	15.8	18	17.36	.015
A sense of accomplishment	7.0	6	6.2	5	6.3	4	10.8	11	8.0	6	6.0	4	9.5	9	7.0	4	7.67	.363
A world at peace	2.9	2	4.5	2	7.5	6	5.2	3	2.5	2	4.5	2	4.0	2	2.9	1	10.29	.173
A world of beauty	14.0	16	13.3	15	11.8	14	13.0	15	12.2	14	13.5	15	12.0	14	14.5	16	8.57	.285
Equality	7.0	5	9.5	11	5.2	2	10.2	10	9.5	10	10.8	12	7.0	5	10.3	12	14.79	.039
Family security	2.3	1	4.0	1	5.3	3	3.1	2	3.8	2	2.2	1	3.3	1	5.0	3	7.58	.371
Freedom	7.0	7	5.0	3	4.3	1	6.5	5	6.1	4	5.2	3	5.5	3	3.8	2	8.70	.275
Happiness	6.8	4	7.2	7	9.5	11	6.0	4	5.4	3	6.8	5	8.5	8	8.0	6	5.44	.607
Inner harmony	8.0	8	9.5	10	11.5	13	9.0	8	10.0	12	8.0	8	9.5	10	9.0	9	3.93	.788
Mature love	12.8	14	13.2	14	9.0	9	11.5	12	13.8	15	11.3	13	11.2	12	13.2	14	11.36	.124
National security	10.5	12	9.2	9	12.5	15	11.5	14	8.5	8	8.1	9	11.5	13	8.5	7	7.84	.347
Pleasure	13.8	15	16.0	18	12.8	16	14.0	16	14.8	16	15.2	18	15.0	16	15.3	17	18.05	.012
Salvation	17.7	18	10.5	12	17.3	18	2.5	1	10.3	13	12.5	14	10.0	11	10.0	11	45.84	.001
Self respect	8.3	9	6.9	6	8.5	7	6.7	6	7.8	5	7.5	7	7.8	6	8.8	8	7.26	.402
Social recognition	12.5	13	15.3	17	15.3	17	15.5	18	14.9	17	14.2	17	15.5	17	14.5	15	6.20	.517
True friendship	10.2	11	9.0	8	9.5	10	10.0	9	10.0	11	9.8	10	8.1	7	10.8	13	7.38	.391
Wisdom	6.5	3	5.2	4	6.8	5	8.5	7	8.2	7	7.5	6	6.3	4	8.0	5	9.38	.226

or eighteenth by all the remaining groups. *Independent* was ranked third by Jews, nonbelievers, and Episcopalians and anywhere from twelfth to sixteenth by the remaining groups. Finally, Baptists ranked *obedience* highest, and nonbelievers ranked it lowest.

It is thus seen that value differences remain among the groups varying in religion even after social class and race have been held constant. *Salvation* and *forgiving* once more differentiated most sharply between the Jews and nonbelievers on the one hand and the various Christian groups on the other. The data also show that two moral values, *forgiving* and *obedient*, were generally ranked higher by Christians and three competence values, *broadminded*, *imaginative*, and *independent*, were generally ranked higher by non-Christians. A similar statement can also be made when Episcopalians and Baptists are compared with one another; that is, the former generally ranked the competence values higher, and the latter generally ranked the moral values higher.

Since Jews and Episcopalians showed such similar value patterns, the question may be raised as to whether there are any values that distinguish Jewish from high-church value systems. A direct comparison of these two groups showed only that the Episcopalians ranked *salvation* significantly higher than the Jews, and that the Jews ranked a *world at peace*, *equality*, and *pleasure* significantly higher than the Episcopalians. Inspection of Table 8 also revealed a consistent tendency for the Jews to rank the competence values generally higher and the moral values generally lower than the Episcopalians. All in all, the data suggest the presence of a Jewish value system that differs from a high-church value system in the manner indicated above, despite the fact that the small number of cases involved precluded all these differences from being statistically significant. The analysis of similarities and differences between these two value systems merits further study with larger numbers of cases.

*Value Systems, Religious Involvement, and
Commitment*

The value differences considered thus far can
be said to characterize only those who are nominally
identified with one or another or with no religion.
They are obviously a function of differences in religious upbringing, of socioeconomic status, and,
no doubt, of cultural differences as well. While
all these value differences are interesting in their
own right, they cannot necessarily be taken as descriptive of those varying in commitment to religion.
The search for a distinctive set of religious values
requires the employment of more stringent criteria
of religious involvement or commitment.

1. *Church attendance and value systems.* One
criterion of active religious involvement that has
perhaps been most widely employed in social research
is frequency of church attendance. Tables 9 and 10
show the results relating churchgoing to values.
Considering the terminal value findings first
(Table 9), it is again noted that the largest difference was found for *salvation,* which was ranked third
by those attending church weekly and then decreased
linearly to eighteenth for those never attending.
The remaining four terminal values that showed significant differences were all, in contrast, negatively
related to church attendance: churchgoers placed
lower values than nonchurchgoers on a *comfortable
life, an exciting life, freedom,* and *pleasure.*
The differences between churchgoers and nonchurchgoers on instrumental values followed patterns
similar to those previously noted. Three moral
values--*forgiving, helpful,* and *obedient*--signifi-
cantly distinguished between churchgoers and nonchurchgoers, churchgoers valuing them more highly.
Consistent with earlier findings, the largest of
these differences was again found for *forgiving.*
Three competence values, on the other hand, differentiated significantly in the opposite direction:
nonchurchgoers valued *imaginative, independent,* and
logical more than churchgoers.[7]

TABLE 8

INSTRUMENTAL VALUE MEDIANS AND COMPOSITE RANK ORDERS FOR RELIGIOUS GROUPS MATCHED ON INCOME AND RACE
(N=224)

N=	Jews		Catholic		None		Baptist		Methodist		Episcop.		Presbyt.		Lutheran		Median Test	
	28		28		28		28		28		28		28		28			
	Md.	Rnk.	Md.	Rnk.	Md.	Rnk.	Md.	Rnk.	Md.	Rnk.	Md.	Rnk.	Md.	Rnk.	Md.	Rnk.	Chi-Sq.	p=
Ambitious	8.0	6	10.5	11	8.5	7	5.2	2	6.5	3	8.0	6	9.5	8	5.5	2	10.41	.166
Broadminded	5.2	2	9.5	7	4.8	2	10.8	12	6.5	4	7.5	4	5.0	2	7.9	6	20.83	.004
Capable	7.0	5	7.5	3	9.5	9	9.5	11	9.2	8	8.0	7	7.0	4	10.0	9	4.78	.687
Cheerful	10.3	10	11.0	13	10.0	10	9.3	10	9.5	10	12.5	16	11.9	14	9.8	8	10.56	.159
Clean	10.5	11	10.5	12	13.5	16	8.2	5	9.5	11	10.0	10	12.8	16	10.5	10	10.85	.145
Courageous	8.2	7	7.8	3	8.2	6	8.5	7	7.5	6	7.5	5	7.2	5	7.2	5	1.75	.972
Forgiving	12.2	15	8.5	5	12.5	15	6.5	4	9.0	7	11.0	13	7.5	7	6.0	4	17.56	.014
Helpful	9.5	9	11.2	15	11.0	14	8.5	6	6.5	5	11.0	14	7.5	6	8.0	7	13.03	.071
Honest	4.1	1	4.0	1	3.8	1	1.8	1	3.5	1	3.0	1	4.0	1	3.8	1	5.20	.635
Imaginative	13.8	17	14.5	18	7.5	4	15.9	17	16.2	18	13.3	17	14.5	17	15.3	18	23.17	.002
Independent	6.0	3	11.5	16	6.5	3	11.2	13	10.7	12	7.5	3	12.0	15	11.3	13	26.79	.001
Intellectual	9.0	8	10.0	10	10.3	12	12.8	16	12.5	14	10.5	12	11.8	13	12.8	16	6.41	.493
Logical	10.8	12	10.0	9	10.3	13	16.2	18	15.0	17	11.5	15	10.5	11	12.0	15	13.72	.056
Loving	11.0	14	8.5	6	8.0	5	9.0	9	11.5	13	9.5	9	9.8	9	10.8	11	3.29	.857
Obedient	15.5	18	12.8	17	16.5	18	11.5	15	13.5	16	16.1	18	15.5	18	13.7	17	31.50	.001
Polite	13.8	16	11.2	14	15.0	17	11.3	14	12.8	15	10.2	11	11.8	12	11.5	14	8.90	.260
Responsible	6.5	4	5.5	2	8.8	8	5.8	3	6.2	2	5.0	2	5.8	3	5.8	3	5.59	.588
Self controlled	11.0	13	9.8	8	10.2	11	9.0	8	9.5	9	8.5	8	10.5	10	11.0	12	3.73	.810

TABLE 9

TERMINAL VALUE MEDIANS AND COMPOSITE RANK ORDERS
FOR GROUPS VARYING IN CHURCH ATTENDANCE: NATIONAL SAMPLE
(N = 1406)

N =	Every Wk. 553		Near Ev. Wk. 121		2-3 Mon. 139		Once Mon. 116		Sev. Year 159		1-2 Year 126		Less 1 Yr. 96		Never 96		Median Test	
	Md.	Rnk.	Md.	Rnk.	Md.	Rnk.	Md.	Rnk.	Md.	Rnk.	Md.	Rnk.	Md.	Rnk.	Md.	Rnk.	Chi-Sq.	p =
A comfortable life	10.3	13	9.0	11	7.2	4	9.1	8	7.9	6	7.9	6	7.5	5	8.0	7	22.59	.002
An exciting life	15.7	18	15.4	18	15.5	18	15.7	18	14.7	17	14.6	18	14.5	17	14.1	17	20.29	.005
A sense of accomplishment	9.3	11	8.8	10	9.1	9	9.9	11	8.9	8	8.1	8	8.5	8	8.3	8	6.81	.449
A world at peace	3.3	1	3.0	1	3.4	1	3.4	2	3.0	1	3.8	1	3.7	2	3.5	1	5.37	.615
A world of beauty	13.8	15	13.8	15	13.7	15	13.9	15	13.1	15	13.5	15	13.1	14	11.8	13	11.97	.102
Equality	8.4	8	8.1	7	8.2	7	8.3	6	9.0	10	10.0	10	8.5	9	7.8	6	7.38	.391
Family security	4.0	2	3.4	2	3.5	2	3.2	1	3.5	2	4.0	2	3.6	1	5.2	3	12.21	.094
Freedom	5.9	4	5.3	3	5.0	3	5.1	3	5.4	3	5.5	3	7.0	3	4.4	2	14.33	.046
Happiness	7.9	7	7.3	4	8.0	6	7.7	5	6.8	4	7.4	4	7.2	4	7.0	4	2.20	.048
Inner harmony	10.2	12	10.6	13	10.5	13	11.2	13	10.2	12	11.7	14	10.6	12	9.9	12	8.62	.281
Mature love	12.9	14	13.2	14	12.4	14	11.6	14	12.0	14	11.4	12	11.2	13	12.3	14	8.94	.257
National security	9.3	10	8.6	8	10.0	12	9.2	9	9.7	11	11.2	11	9.2	10	9.4	11	6.47	.486
Pleasure	15.3	17	15.2	17	13.9	16	14.7	17	14.4	16	13.9	16	13.5	16	13.3	15	35.18	.001
Salvation	4.3	3	7.4	5	9.7	10	10.3	12	11.3	13	11.5	13	13.2	15	15.5	18	123.41	.001
Self respect	7.6	6	8.8	9	7.8	5	7.1	4	7.3	5	7.3	5	8.2	7	7.5	5	6.42	.492
Social recognition	14.2	16	14.8	16	14.5	17	14.2	16	15.4	18	14.2	17	15.1	18	13.8	16	12.26	.092
True friendship	9.0	9	10.1	12	9.8	11	9.4	10	9.0	9	8.7	9	9.9	11	9.3	10	11.29	.127
Wisdom	7.6	5	7.8	6	8.8	8	8.5	7	8.2	7	8.0	7	8.0	6	8.9	9	7.13	.415

TABLE 10

INSTRUMENTAL VALUE MEDIANS AND COMPOSITE RANK ORDERS FOR GROUPS VARYING IN CHURCH ATTENDANCE: NATIONAL SAMPLE
(N=1406)

N=	Every Wk. 553		Near Ev. Wk. 121		2-3 Mon. 139		Once Mon. 116		Sev. Year 159		1-2 Year 126		Less 1 Yr. 96		Never 96		Median Test	
	Md.	Rnk.	Md.	Rnk.	Md.	Rnk.	Md.	Rnk.	Md.	Rnk.	Md.	Rnk.	Md.	Rnk.	Md.	Rnk.	Chi-Sq.	p=
Ambitious	6.7	4	6.4	4	5.4	2	6.8	3	6.6	2	5.9	2	6.0	3	8.5	6	3.52	.833
Broadminded	8.0	7	7.7	5	8.1	5	7.3	4	7.8	5	6.6	3	5.3	2	5.5	2	13.53	.060
Capable	9.7	12	9.5	10	9.8	10	9.8	11	9.5	9	9.4	9	8.0	6	9.3	10	2.37	.936
Cheerful	9.6	10	10.6	11	10.3	14	10.7	14	10.2	13	10.0	11	9.5	11	10.0	12	5.50	.600
Clean	8.9	8	9.4	9	9.1	8	7.3	5	8.0	6	8.1	7	9.1	9	8.6	8	2.60	.919
Courageous	7.7	5	7.7	6	9.2	9	8.3	6	7.5	4	7.8	5	7.2	4	8.3	4	8.20	.315
Forgiving	6.1	2	5.9	3	8.1	6	8.6	7	8.3	7	8.1	6	8.1	7	9.6	11	45.72	.001
Helpful	7.7	6	8.1	7	7.7	4	9.4	9	8.5	8	9.1	8	8.5	8	10.5	13	23.72	.001
Honest	3.2	1	3.0	1	3.5	1	3.4	1	3.2	1	3.8	1	3.8	1	3.3	1	4.70	.696
Imaginative	16.0	18	15.8	18	15.5	18	15.8	18	14.9	18	14.3	17	15.0	18	13.5	17	29.17	.001
Independent	11.2	14	11.1	14	8.5	7	10.5	13	9.6	11	10.1	12	9.5	10	8.4	5	16.91	.018
Intellectual	13.6	16	12.8	15	11.4	15	12.2	15	12.4	15	13.3	15	14.0	17	10.5	14	15.65	.028
Logical	14.7	17	13.8	17	14.8	17	14.4	17	13.1	16	13.7	16	13.8	16	12.3	16	15.15	.034
Loving	9.5	9	10.8	12	10.0	11	9.2	8	9.6	10	10.4	13	10.0	13	8.5	7	4.53	.717
Obedient	12.6	15	13.4	16	13.5	16	13.3	16	14.4	17	14.5	18	13.5	15	14.9	18	25.22	.001
Polite	10.9	13	11.0	13	10.2	12	10.1	12	10.8	14	10.9	14	10.3	14	11.8	15	4.24	.752
Responsible	6.5	3	5.5	2	6.7	3	6.8	2	6.9	3	6.7	4	7.6	5	7.6	3	9.42	.224
Self controlled	9.7	11	8.7	8	10.3	13	9.5	10	9.7	12	9.5	10	9.9	12	9.2	9	3.82	.800

Data comparable to those shown in Tables 9 and
10, which had been obtained from the national sample,
were also obtained from the college student sample,
and for the sake of completeness these are presented
in Tables 11 and 12. The results are highly similar.

TABLE 11

TERMINAL VALUE MEDIANS AND COMPOSITE RANK ORDERS
FOR GROUP VARYING IN CHURCH ATTENDANCE: COLLEGE SAMPLE
(N=298)

| | Never | | Rarely | | Monthly | | Weekly | | Kruskal-Wallis | |
| | 29 | | 82 | | 40 | | 147 | | | |
N=	Md.	Rnk.	Md.	Rnk.	Md.	Rnk.	Md.	Rnk.	H=	p=
A comfortable life	12.3	14	11.0	12	8.3	8	13.5	14	16.49	.001
An exciting life	10.8	12	10.5	11	10.5	11	13.6	15	14.58	.002
A sense of accomplishment	7.3	6	6.7	4	7.3	4	8.8	11	6.48	.090
A world at peace	8.8	9	7.3	6	9.2	9	8.6	10	0.46	.927
A world of beauty	9.8	11	14.2	17	14.0	16	14.2	17	13.09	.004
Equality	7.3	7	11.2	13	10.5	13	10.1	12	4.41	.221
Family security	11.3	13	8.5	9	9.2	10	7.2	7	7.61	.055
Freedom	3.7	1	5.0	1	3.5	1	6.2	3	8.62	.035
Happiness	6.7	4	6.0	2	6.0	2	6.3	4	1.20	.753
Inner harmony	8.0	8	8.6	10	10.5	12	7.8	9	3.15	.369
Mature love	7.1	5	8.2	8	6.5	3	7.1	6	1.19	.755
National security	15.3	17	12.8	14	14.7	18	13.4	13	4.02	.259
Pleasure	13.6	15	13.6	16	12.5	15	14.8	18	12.70	.005
Salvation	17.7	18	17.0	18	14.5	17	3.9	1	89.76	.001
Self respect	5.3	2	6.2	3	7.3	5	6.8	5	3.12	.373
Social recognition	15.0	16	13.0	15	12.5	14	14.1	16	7.46	.058
True friendship	9.3	10	7.7	7	7.5	6	7.6	8	3.08	.380
Wisdom	5.4	3	6.8	5	7.7	7	5.9	2	2.23	.525

Those who never or who rarely attend church ranked
salvation last, those who attend monthly ranked it
seventeenth, and those who attend weekly ranked it
first. Both samples showed consistent significant
differences on five terminal values--*a comfortable
life, an exciting life, freedom, pleasure,* and *salvation*--and consistent significant differences on
seven instrumental values--*forgiving, helpful,
imaginative, independent, intellectual, logical,* and
obedient.

The fact that frequency of church attendance
predicted value differences in much the same way as
did income variations suggests that the poor may
attend church more frequently than the rich and
that the differences in value patterns associated
with church attendance may once again be accounted
for by social class. But the data from the national

sample revealed no significant relationship between
income and frequency of church attendance. This
finding is at variance with those reported by Glock
and Stark (1965) and by Lenski (1961), which both
show a somewhat greater frequency of church attendance to be more characteristic of those with higher
social status.

TABLE 12

INSTRUMENTAL VALUE MEDIANS AND COMPOSITE RANK ORDERS
FOR GROUPS VARYING IN CHURCH ATTENDANCE: COLLEGE SAMPLE
(N=298)

	Never		*Rarely*		*Monthly*		*Weekly*		
N=	29		82		40		147		*Kruskal-Wallis*
	Md.	*Rnk.*	*Md.*	*Rnk.*	*Md.*	*Rnk.*	*Md.*	*Rnk.*	*H=*	*p=*
Ambitious	8.6	9	6.6	4	5.5	1	7.9	5	5.01	.171
Broadminded	4.8	1	5.1	1	6.8	5	7.2	4	5.83	.120
Capable	7.4	7	8.3	7	9.5	10	10.4	12	10.97	.012
Cheerful	12.4	15	11.8	14	12.0	14	10.6	13	2.09	.554
Clean	15.6	17	14.8	17	14.0	17	13.8	17	1.80	.616
Courageous	7.3	5	8.8	9	8.5	8	8.4	6	0.88	.831
Forgiving	11.3	13	10.4	13	11.0	12	8.4	7	15.28	.002
Helpful	11.6	14	12.1	15	12.5	15	9.2	8	16.25	.001
Honest	4.8	2	5.3	2	6.0	2	3.3	1	11.06	.011
Imaginative	7.8	8	9.8	12	11.5	13	12.9	16	20.36	.001
Independent	5.4	3	7.1	5	6.5	4	10.2	11	16.01	.001
Intellectual	5.7	4	9.4	11	10.5	11	9.9	10	9.36	.025
Logical	9.3	11	8.1	6	9.5	9	11.6	14	9.22	.027
Loving	11.3	12	9.4	10	7.5	6	5.7	2	12.04	.007
Obedient	16.7	18	16.1	18	16.3	18	14.0	18	25.16	.001
Polite	13.8	16	13.6	16	13.5	16	12.1	15	1.95	.582
Responsible	7.3	6	5.6	3	6.0	3	6.0	3	2.55	.467
Self controlled	9.0	10	8.5	8	8.5	7	9.4	9	0.82	.846

2. *Value differences among frequent churchgoers.* While the main purpose of this paper is to
identify those values that distinguish between the
religious, the less religious, and the nonreligious,
it is also of interest to determine whether there
are value differences among different types of
Christians attending church at least once a week.
It is reasonable to expect that the number of value
differences found between such homogeneous groups
would be fewer than the number found when comparing
the various nominal Christian groups or when comparing churchgoers with nonchurchgoers. This expectation
was confirmed. Only seven value differences, three
terminal and four instrumental, were statistically
significant, as shown in Table 13.[8] These differences were, moreover, generally smaller in magnitude
than those obtained when comparing the various

nominal Christian groups with one another or when comparing Christians with Jews and with nonbelievers.
    The findings for *salvation* and *forgiving* de-
serve some further consideration. Both sets of
findings are highly similar to those previously shown
for nominal Christian groups, except for the fact
that *salvation* was now generally ranked higher by
all Christian groups. The fact that even churchgoing
Catholics and Episcopalians ranked *salvation* relatively low (tenth by churchgoing Catholics, thirteenth by churchgoing Episcopalians) suggests that
there may be other reasons besides religious ones
that prompted them to attend regularly.

TABLE 13

SIGNIFICANT VALUE DIFFERENCES FOR VARIOUS
CHRISTIAN GROUPS REGULARLY ATTENDING CHURCH*

	Baps.	Cath.	Meth.	Episcop.	Presbyt.	Lutheran	Congreg.
Terminal Values:							
Family security	3	2	3	3	1	2	8
Inner harmony	13	11	12	11	8	9	5
Salvation	1	10	2	13	3	3	1
Instrumental Values:							
Cheerful	10	10	9	17	8	10	18
Forgiving	2	4	2	14	4	4	3
Helpful	4	7	7	9	7	8	8
Logical	17	16	17	11	18	16	10

*Significance was determined by the Median Test.

    Paralleling the findings for *salvation,* the
largest instrumental value difference was obtained
for *forgiving,* churchgoing Baptists ranking it
higher than any of the other Protestant groups and
Episcopalians ranking it lowest. But there is
evidently no necessary connection between *salvation*
and *forgiving*. The Baptists ranked both of these
values relatively high and the Episcopalians ranked
them both relatively low. Catholics, however, ranked
salvation relatively low and *forgiving* relatively
high.[9]

    3. *Religious importance and value systems.*
Another index of religious commitment was obtained
only for the college students who responded to the
question, "How important is your religion to you in
your everyday life?" on a 7-point rating scale, with

TABLE 14

TERMINAL VALUE MEDIANS AND COMPOSITE RANK ORDERS
FOR GROUPS VARYING IN PERCEIVED IMPORTANCE OF RELIGION*
(N=298)

	High		Medium		Low		Kruskal-Wallis	
N=	92		131		75			
	Md.	Rnk.	Md.	Rnk.	Md.	Rnk.	H =	p =
A comfortable life	13.7	15	11.1	12	11.3	11	19.31	.001
An exciting life	13.7	14	11.2	13	11.4	12	4.99	.082
A sense of accomplishment	9.5	12	7.6	6	5.8	2	10.36	.006
A world at peace	8.5	10	8.1	9	8.8	8	1.85	.397
A world of beauty	13.3	13	14.4	18	13.4	16	5.06	.080
Equality	9.0	11	11.0	11	11.9	13	3.85	.146
Family security	7.2	7	8.0	8	10.6	10	6.74	.034
Freedom	5.8	3	5.1	1	4.1	1	2.74	.254
Happiness	6.7	4	6.2	2	5.9	4	2.13	.345
Inner harmony	7.6	8	8.8	10	9.4	9	3.74	.154
Mature love	6.7	5	7.1	4	8.0	6	1.79	.409
National security	14.6	16	13.1	15	13.9	17	3.18	.204
Pleasure	14.8	17	14.2	17	13.2	15	13.41	.001
Salvation	2.8	1	14.0	16	17.6	18	68.15	.001
Social recognition	15.1	18	12.8	14	12.8	14	16.37	.001
Self respect	6.9	6	6.9	3	5.9	3	2.35	.309
True friendship	7.6	9	7.7	7	8.1	7	0.76	.683
Wisdom	5.5	2	7.2	5	6.1	5	4.17	.125

*Significance was determined by Kruskal-Wallis one-way analysis of variance.

TABLE 15

INSTRUMENTAL VALUE MEDIANS AND COMPOSITE RANK ORDERS FOR
GROUPS VARYING IN PERCEIVED IMPORTANCE OF RELIGION*
(N=298)

	High		Medium		Low		Kruskal-Wallis	
N=	92		131		75			
	Md.	Rnk.	Md.	Rnk.	Md.	Rnk.	H =	p =
Ambitious	9.5	8	5.5	2	7.1	5	17.05	.001
Broadminded	6.9	4	6.7	4	6.3	4	1.77	.413
Capable	11.0	12	9.2	8	7.3	6	13.56	.001
Cheerful	10.3	10	11.3	14	12.4	14	4.59	.101
Clean	14.4	18	14.0	17	14.6	17	0.03	.985
Courageous	8.3	7	8.6	7	8.2	10	1.06	.588
Forgiving	7.5	6	10.2	12	11.4	13	25.61	.001
Helpful	7.0	5	11.1	13	12.7	15	24.30	.001
Honest	3.3	1	4.6	1	5.1	1	5.99	.050
Imaginative	12.2	16	11.3	15	10.4	11	1.46	.482
Independent	9.8	9	9.6	10	5.6	2	14.69	.001
Intellectual	11.2	13	9.3	9	7.4	7	11.82	.003
Logical	11.8	14	10.0	11	7.7	8	14.15	.001
Loving	4.9	2	7.2	5	11.3	12	29.44	.001
Obedient	14.0	17	15.8	18	15.6	18	9.62	.008
Polite	12.0	15	13.7	16	12.8	16	1.57	.455
Responsible	6.8	3	5.8	3	5.7	3	2.44	.296
Self controlled	10.8	11	8.4	6	8.1	9	4.17	.125

*Significance was determined by Kruskal-Wallis one-way analysis of variance

1 representing "extremely important" and 7 "extremely
unimportant." Tables 14 and 15 show the value data
obtained for those rating religion high (1-2), medium (3-5), and low (6-7) in importance. Sixteen of
the 36 values showed significant differences.

These findings are highly consistent with those
already reported. Those judging religion to be
high, medium, and low in importance ranked *salvation*
first, sixteenth, and eighteenth, respectively.
Other terminal value differences were found to be
highly similar to those previously described. Ten
instrumental values, five of them moral and the
other five competence values, also showed significant differences (Table 15). All five moral values
were ranked more highly by those reporting religion as important, and they ranked all five competence values lower than those who regarded religion
as unimportant.

Discussion

I now return to the main questions posed at the
beginning of this paper: Can a religious person be
said to possess a set of values that are demonstrably
different from those of a less religious or a non-
religious person? And can the values that distinguish
such groups from one another be identified? Adequate answers to these questions depend on how religiousness is defined. Since there is probably no
single criterion of religiousness that is best, my
strategy has been to employ what Campbell and Fiske
(1959) have called convergent validation, using a
variety of criteria of religiousness and considering
the question of value similarities and differences
by employing each criterion in turn. The first
criterion involved nothing more than a comparison
between those nominally identified as Protestant,
Catholic, Jew, or as nonbelievers. The differences
and similarities thus obtained are interesting in
their own right if for no other reason than that they
describe the value systems of representative subsamples of adult Americans differing in religious
outlook. The second and third criteria are more

stringent--frequency of church attendance, and perceived importance of religion in everyday life.

Significant value differences were found between the religious, the less religious, and the
nonreligious, regardless of the criterion employed.
Since the data presented here were obtained within
a predominantly Christian culture, it goes without
saying that "variations in religiousness" refers
primarily to variations within Christendom.

All findings presented here seem to converge.
Religious persons can indeed be characterized as
having value systems that are different from those
of the less religious and the nonreligious, and the
specific values on which they differ can be identified. But since the values so identified will
necessarily vary with the particular criterion of
religiousness employed, it might be helpful to
summarize first the findings obtained with all three
criteria.

Table 16 identified the particular values that
significantly distinguished the religious from the
less religious and nonreligious and shows, further,
whether those who are religious ranked a particular
value "high" or "low" when compared with the less
religious. Most consistent across all three criteria, for the terminal values, are the findings for
salvation and *pleasure*. The religious consistently
ranked *salvation* higher than the less religious who,
in turn, ranked it higher than the nonreligious.
The same is true for *pleasure*, but in the opposite
direction.

In general, more of the instrumental than the
terminal values distinguished among the various
groups. One of the most interesting findings shown
in Table 16 is that the religious, however defined,
consistently ranked the moral instrumental values
higher than the less religious and nonreligious, and,
conversely, that the nonreligious and the less religious typically ranked the competence values higher.
The findings for two moral values, *forgiving* and
obedient, are especially consistent, the religious
ranking them higher in all comparisons. And three
competence values stand out in the same way--*independent, intellectual,* and *logical*--the less religious ranking them higher.

When magnitude of value difference as well as statistical significance is taken into account, one terminal value, *salvation,* and one instrumental value, *forgiving,* emerge as the two values that are the most distinctively Christian.

I am reluctant to conclude this report without also noting that certain values simply do not

TABLE 16
SUMMARY OF SIGNIFICANT DIFFERENCES FOUND FOR NATIONAL AND COLLEGE SAMPLES DIFFERENTIATING RELIGIOUS FROM NONRELIGIOUS

	National Sample		College Sample	
	Prot. Cath. Jew None	*Church Attendance*	*Church Attendance*	*Relig. Importance*
A comfortable life	-	Low	Low	Low
An exciting life	Low	Low	Low	-
A sense of accomplishment	Low	-	-	Low
A world at peace	-	-	-	-
A world of beauty	-	-	High	-
Equality	Low	-	-	-
Family security	High	-	-	High
Freedom	-	Low	Low	-
Happiness	-	-	-	-
Inner harmony	-	-	-	-
Mature love	-	-	-	-
National security	High	-	-	-
Pleasure	Low	Low	Low	Low
Salvation	High	High	High	High
Self-respect	-	-	-	-
Social recognition	-	-	-	Low
True friendship	-	-	-	-
Wisdom	-	-	-	-
Number of significant values	**7**	**5**	**6**	**6**
Ambitious	-	-	-	Low
Broadminded	Low	-	-	-
Capable	Low	-	Low	Low
Cheerful	-	-	-	-
Clean	High	-	-	-
Courageous	-	-	-	-
Forgiving	High	High	High	High
Helpful	-	High	High	High
Honest	-	-	High	High
Imaginative	Low	Low	Low	-
Independent	Low	Low	Low	Low
Intellectual	Low	Low	Low	Low
Logical	Low	Low	Low	Low
Loving	-	-	High	High
Obedient	High	High	High	High
Polite	High	-	-	-
Responsible	-	-	-	-
Self-controlled	-	-	-	-
Number of significant values	**10**	**7**	**10**	**10**

distinguish among the various groups. There are
values that are clearly shared by all groups.
These include at least seven terminal values--a
*world at peace, happiness, inner harmony, mature
love, self-respect, true friendship,* and *wisdom*--
and at least four instrumental values--*cheerful,
courageous, responsible,* and *self-controlled.*
    Returning to the main focus of this report,
the data presented here leave little room for doubt
about the existence of value differences between
the religious, less religious and nonreligious.
The question that may now be asked is whether or
not such value differences make a difference in defining man's everyday relations to man. I propose
to deal with this question in the second part.

PART II: RELIGIOUS VALUES AND SOCIAL COMPASSION

    Values are multi-faceted standards that may
serve a number of purposes. They may guide conduct,
lead us to take a particular position on a specific
social issue, predispose us to favor one or another
political ideology. They are standards employed to
judge, to heap praise or fix blame on ourselves or
others. They are standards that tell us which beliefs, attitudes, and actions of others are worth
arguing about or worth trying to influence. Values
are, moreover, standards that tell us how to go about
rationalizing, in the psychoanalytic sense, beliefs,
attitudes, and actions that would otherwise be
personally and socially unacceptable, so that we
will end up feeling self-righteous or to otherwise
end up with an enhanced ego. An unkind remark made
to a friend, for example, may be rationalized on
the ground that it is honest communication; an inhibited sex life may be rationalized as self-control;
an aggressor nation may be expected to justify its

    From *Review of Religious Research,* 1969, 11,
24-39. Reprinted by permission.

aggression on grounds of self-defense, national
security, or the preservation of freedom.

Empirical findings reported in Part I confirm
that the religious, the less religious, and the non-
religious are characterized by value systems that
are discriminably different from one another. Religiously oriented Christians consistently ranked the
terminal value of *salvation* higher and *pleasure* lower than those less religious and the nonreligious.
The religious, moreover, typically ranked the moral
values *forgiving* and *obedient* higher and the competence values *independent, intellectual,* and *logical*
lower than those who were less religious or non-
religious. When magnitude of value difference was
considered as well as statistical significance of
differences, two values, *salvation* and *forgiving,*
empirically emerged as the most distinctively
Christian values.

Some questions may now be raised about these
two religious values and, by implication, about the
religious institutions that foster them. What kinds
of standards do they serve? Are they more often
employed as standards to guide social action and a
concern for the well-being of others, or are they
more often employed as standards to rationalize
self-preoccupation, withdrawal from worldly concerns,
or indifference to the plight of others? Do religious values serve more as standards to judge ourselves by or to judge others by? Is it possible to
estimate whether religious values and, by implication, the institutions that foster them, are on
balance relevant or irrelevant, facilitating or
hindering, as determinants of man's relation to and
concern for his fellowman?

As pointed out in the first part, it is by
now a well-established fact that there is a positive
rather than a negative relationship between religiousness and bigotry. But a question may be
raised about the validity of the indices of religiousness that have been employed in previous research. Nominal church membership, frequency of
church attendance, perceived importance of religion,
and high scores on a religiosity scale are not

necessarily indications of the truly religious person. The hallmark of a truly religious person is
rather the espousal of a recognizable set of reli-
giously-inspired values that is distinctively different from those espoused by the less religious
and nonreligious.

      The influence of organized religion is readily
apparent in the value findings previously reported.
Individuals who are nominally identified with organized religion, individuals who attend the churches
built and staffed by organized religion, and individuals who report that religion is important in
their everyday life were all found to share a common
set of religious values that set them apart from
those not nominally identified with religion, from
nonchurchgoers, and from those reporting religion
to be unimportant in their everyday life.

      My main purpose in this paper is an empirical
one--to examine the relation between adherence to
distinctively Christian values and position on a
large variety of contemporary social issues. The
Value Survey was given to an area probability sample of about 1,400 adult Americans in April, 1968,
by the National Opinion Research Center. The respondents were also asked to express their opinions
on many salient issues of the day: their reactions
to the assassination of Dr. Martin Luther King that
had occurred earlier that month, their opinions
about equal rights for blacks in housing, education,
and employment, their views about race differences
in intelligence. Moving beyond the race issue the
respondents were also asked to express their feelings about providing the poor with a college education, medical and dental care, and a guaranteed income. They also responded to other questions
designed to elicit their opinions about the student
protest movement currently sweeping across the
college campuses of America. And, finally, they
expressed their opinions about the role that the
churches in general and the National Council of
Churches in particular should play in political
and social affairs. For each of the many questions
put to the respondents those varying in response

were compared for similarities and differences in values; my purpose here is to report the data thus obtained on the relation between religious values and social attitudes. Since *salvation* and *forgiving* were the two values that were found to be most systematically associated with a religious Christian orientation I will, for the sake of simplicity, deal here primarily with these two values.

Religious Values and Reactions to the King Assassination

One of the questions put to the respondents was: "When you heard the news of the assassination of Dr. Martin Luther King, Jr., which one of these things was your strongest reaction: 1. Sadness 2. Anger 3. Shame 4. Fear 5. "He brought it on himself." Table 17 shows the relation between these five responses and religious values.

TABLE 17

COMPOSITE RANK ORDERS FOR SALVATION AND FORGIVING FOR FIVE TYPES OF RESPONDERS TO THE QUESTION:

"When you heard the news of the assassination of Dr. Martin Luther King, Jr., which one of these things was your strongest reaction?"

	Sadness	Anger	Shame	Fear	Brought it on himself	
N =	503	71	205	132	426	p*
Salvation	9	14	9	4	4	.002
Forgiving	2	9	5	4	4	N.S.

*Obtained by Median Test. All significance values shown in succeeding tables are likewise obtained by the Median Test.

The first finding that may be noted is that about one out of every three Americans (32%) reported that Martin Luther King had "brought it on himself," and that an additional one in ten (10%) reported "fear" as their main response. These two subgroups of respondents were found to have value systems that are considerably different from those reacting to the assassination with "sadness," "anger," or "shame." .The value that best

distinguished these subgroups is *equality* (not
shown in Table 1) which was ranked fourth or fifth
by those who reacted with "sadness," "anger," or
"shame," eleventh by those who responded with
"fear," and thirteenth by those who felt he "brought
it on himself." *Salvation* was the value that next
best distinguished among these groups, but in the
opposite direction. Those who felt Dr. King had
"brought it on himself" or who had responded to the
assassination with "fear" ranked *salvation* fourth
on the average, and those who responded with "sadness," "anger," or "shame" cared considerably less
for *salvation*, ranking it anywhere from ninth to
fourteenth. These differences among the five groups
were statistically significant. The findings concerning *forgiving*, however, did not follow any such
pattern and were not statistically significant;
there was simply no relationship between the importance attached to *forgiving* and reactions to the
assassination.

TABLE 18
COMPOSITE RANK ORDERS FOR SALVATION AND FORGIVING FOR
THOSE RESPONDING TO TWO ADDITIONAL QUESTIONS CONCERNING
MARTIN LUTHER KING'S ASSASSINATION

	Felt this very strongly	*Felt this fairly strongly*	*Crossed my mind*	*Never occurred to me*	*p*	*The Question*
Salvation	13	12	4	4	.001	*After Dr. King's death did you feel angry about the murder?*
Forgiving	5	3	4	4	N.S.	
Salvation	13	8	9	4	.002	*After Dr. King's death did you think about the many tragic things that have happened to Negroes and this was just another one of them?*
Forgiving	3	4	4	4	N.S.	

The results concerning two additional questions
dealing with the King assassination are shown in
Table 18. It is evident that those giving the most
uncompassionate response, "never occurred to me,"
placed a significantly higher value on *salvation* than
those giving more compassionate responses. And again,
rankings on *forgiving* showed no significant relationships, those giving the more compassionate responses

valuing *forgiving* no more and no less than those
giving the less compassionate responses.

Religious Values and Position on Civil Rights

Table 19 shows the relationship between position
on thirteen civil rights issues on the one hand and
rankings on the two religious values on the other.
For lack of space I will not discuss all these results in detail but instead content myself to point
out that on all civil rights issues, which concern
open occupancy, fair employment, education, dating,
intermarriage, race difference in intelligence, and
the black struggle for equality, a high value for
salvation was indeed significantly related to civil
rights position but in a negative direction, that
is, those who opposed equal rights for blacks placed
a higher value on *salvation* than those who favored
equal rights.

In contrast, only three of the thirteen civil
rights issues showed significant relationships with
forgiving. The three that did were again negatively
rather than positively related to *forgiving*, those
favoring school segregation, those favoring laws
forbidding interracial marriage, and those generally
disapproving of black activism caring more for being
forgiving.

Religious Values and Attitudes toward the Poor

Table 20 shows the relationship between the two
major Christian values and attitudes toward eleven
issues concerning the poor. These issues cover a
wide range of topics: free college education for
the poor, better housing, guaranteed minimum income, free dental and medical care, increased taxes,
and additional welfare legislation. Seven of the
eleven issues showed significant relationships between ranking of *salvation* and attitudes toward the
poor; in all of them those unsympathetic with the
poor were found to rank *salvation* higher than those
sympathetic. Of particular interest are the findings

TABLE 19
COMPOSITE RANK ORDERS FOR SALVATION AND FORGIVING FOR RESPONDENTS WHO VARY IN THEIR ATTITUDES TOWARD CIVIL RIGHTS

	Strongly agree or favor	Agree or favor	Disagree or oppose somewhat	Strongly disagree or oppose	p	The Question
Salvation	14	8	7	4	.001	Open occupancy laws
Forgiving	4	5	4	5	N.S.	
Salvation	13	4	4	3	.001	Fair employment laws
Forgiving	5	4	5	6	N.S.	
Salvation	5	8	12	14	.024	Negroes shouldn't push themselves where they're not wanted.
Forgiving	4	3	6	5	N.S.	
						White people have a right to keep Negroes out of their neighborhoods if they want to, and Negroes should respect that right.
Salvation	5	6	9	12	.001	
Forgiving	3	4	4	4	N.S.	

	Too much	Too little	Just about what they should	Don't know		
Salvation	6	17	12	3	.001	All in all, do you think Negro groups are asking for:
Forgiving	4	4	4	6	N.S.	

	Desegregate	Segregate	Don't know			
Salvation	11	3	4		.001	School segregation vs. desegregation?
Forgiving	5	3	3		.005	

	Yes	No	Don't know			
Salvation	4	12	3		.001	Laws forbidding interracial marriages?
Forgiving	3	6	2		.001	

	Object Strongly	Object Mildly	Not at all			
Salvation	5	13	18		.001	Interracial dating between teenagers?
Forgiving	4	4	6		N.S.	

	Yes, as intelligent	No, not as intelligent	Don't know			
Salvation	9	4	4		.027	Do you think Negroes are as intelligent as white people—that is, can they learn things just as well if they are given the same education and training?
Forgiving	5	3	2		N.S.	

	Lack of initiative	Restrictions imposed by white society	Don't know			
Salvation	5	12	4		.012	Which factor do you believe accounts most for the failure to achieve equality?
Forgiving	4	3	3		N.S.	

	Yes	No	Don't know			
Salvation	10	5	5		.004	If you were referred to a Negro doctor, would you go to him?
Forgiving	5	3	4		N.S.	

	Generally Approve	Generally Disapprove	Don't know			
Salvation	12	6	14		.001	How do you feel about the actions Negroes have taken to get the things they want?
Forgiving	7	4	8		.028	

	More	Less	Same			
Salvation	10	7	6		.043	In general, would you say you have become more favorable or less favorable toward social integration in recent years?
Forgiving	5	4	3		N.S.	

obtained in response to the question: "Who is more
to blame if a person is poor?" Those answering
that it is "lack of effort" ranked *salvation* fifth
on the average, those answering that it is "circumstances" ranked it eleventh, and those answering
"both" ranked *salvation* eighth.

Again, rankings on *forgiving* were typically not
related to attitudes toward the poor. Significant
findings were obtained on only two of the eleven
issues. A positive relationship was found for the
first time on the minimum income question, those
favoring it ranking *forgiving* higher. But those
favoring a tax increase to pay for free dental care
ranked *forgiving* lower than the others.

Religious Values and Attitudes toward Student Protest

The respondents were asked two questions about
the student protest movement, as shown in Table 21.
These questions avoided the controversial issue of
means versus ends and instead focused on whether or
not the respondent had a basic sympathy with the
student protest movement in general. The pattern of
results is about the same as those previously presented; sympathizers ranked *salvation* significantly
lower than nonsympathizers. Again, *forgiving* was
not significantly related one way or the other to
sympathy with student protests.

Religious Values and Attitude toward Church Involvement in Worldly Affairs

The general picture that emerges from the results presented thus far is that those who place a
high value on *salvation* are conservative, anxious
to maintain the *status quo,* and unsympathetic or
indifferent to the plight of the black and the poor.
They had reacted fearfully or even gleefully to the
news of Martin Luther King's assassination, and they
are unsympathetic with student protests. Value for
forgiving is, however, generally not related one

TABLE 20

COMPOSITE RANK ORDER FOR SALVATION AND FORGIVING FOR
RESPONDENTS WHO VARY IN THEIR ATTITUDES TOWARD THE POOR

	Strongly agree or favor	Agree or favor	Disagree or oppose somewhat	Strongly disagree or oppose	p	The Question
Salvation	10	6	3	7	.002	Every capable person has a right to a college education even if he cannot afford it.
Forgiving	3	4	4	9	N.S.	
Salvation	10	7	4	8	.004	Every person has a right to adequate housing even if he cannot afford it.
Forgiving	5	3	5	7	N.S.	
Salvation	9	5	5	6	N.S.	Every person has a right to a minimum income which would be enough to maintain an adequate standard of living.
Forgiving	2	5	4	9	.006	
Salvation	11	7	4	6	.011	Every person has the right to free dental care if he needs it but cannot afford it.
Forgiving	3	5	4	5	N.S.	
Salvation	9	7	4	12	N.S.	Every person has a right to free medical care if he needs it but cannot afford it.
Forgiving	3	4	4	5	N.S.	
	Yes	No	Don't Know			
Salvation	9	4	12		.030	Should public funds be used to provide dental care?
Forgiving	4	4	5		N.S.	
	Favor	Not Favor	Don't Know Depends			
Salvation	12	5	1		.001	Would you or wouldn't you favor the use of public funds for free dental care even if it meant a tax increase?
Forgiving	5	4	2		.030	
	More Laws	No More Laws	Don't Know			
Salvation	10	7	9		N.S.	Which is more important, to pass more laws to help poor people or to help them without any more laws?
Forgiving	2	4	3		N.S.	
	Lack of effort	Circum- stances	Both			
Salvation	5	11	8		.014	Which is more to blame if a person is poor?
Forgiving	4	3	3		N.S.	
	For	Against	Don't Know			
Salvation	9	6	6		N.S.	Raise local taxes for roads, schools, hospitals.
Forgiving	4	4	2		N.S.	
Salvation	11	4	4		.024	Guaranteed income, or negative income tax or children's allowances.
Forgiving	4	5	4		N.S.	

TABLE 21

COMPOSITE RANK ORDER OF SALVATION AND FORGIVING
FOR RESPONDENTS WHO VARY IN ATTITUDES TOWARD STUDENT PROTEST

	Strongly Agree	Agree	Disagree Somewhat	Strongly Disagree	p	The Question
Salvation	12	13	7	3	.001	*The protests of college students*
Forgiving	5	5	4	3	N.S.	*are a healthy sign for America.*
Salvation	4	9	9	14	.002	*This country would be better*
Forgiving	3	5	4	4	N.S.	*off if there were less protest and dissatisfaction coming from college campuses.*

way or the other to position on these social issues.
Considered all together, the data suggest a portrait
of the religious-minded as a person having a self-
centered preoccupation with saving his own soul, an
other-worldly orientation coupled with an indifference
toward or even a tacit endorsement of a social system
that would perpetuate social inequality and injustice.

This general pattern of findings is supported by
additional findings concerning the relationship between Christian values and attitude toward the church's
involvement in social and political affairs. As shown
in Table 22 those expressing an unfavorable attitude
toward the National Council of Churches and those
opposed to the church's involvement in contemporary
affairs ranked both religious values significantly
higher than those expressing more favorable attitudes.

Relevant here is a study recently completed by
Willis and Goldberg (1969) in which the differences
between black militant and non-militant students in
Atlanta, Georgia, were investigated. Paradoxically,
the question that most sharply distinguished the two
groups from one another was the question asking their
racial identification. The militants typically responded "black," and the non-militants typically
responded "Negro." The variable that next best
discriminated militants from non-militants was the
rankordering of *salvation*. Militants ranked it
fourteenth on the average while non-militants ranked
it third. One possible interpretation of Willis and
Goldberg's data is that a strong belief by black
people in a future world is incompatible with a mil-

itant stance toward the problems facing them in this
world. This finding suggests that a growing militancy on the part of black people may come to the
extent that they are able to free themselves from
their commitments to religious end-goals. One may
well wonder, after seeing these data, whether Marx
was right after all when he suggested that religion
is the opiate of the people. Willis and Goldberg's
data as well as those presented here are at least
consistent with if not confirming of Marx's hypothesis.

TABLE 22
COMPOSITE RANK ORDER OF SALVATION AND FORGIVING FOR RESPONDENTS WHO VARY IN ATTITUDE TOWARD CHURCH INVOLVEMENT IN SOCIAL AND POLITICAL ISSUES

	Favorable	*Unfavorable*	*Don't Know*	*p*	*The Question*
Salvation	11	1	7	.001	*In general, do you have a favor-*
Forgiving	5	2	2	.038	*able or unfavorable impression of what the National Council of Churches is trying to do?*
	Approve	*Disapprove*	*Don't Know*		
Salvation	10	6	4	.018	*In general, do you approve or*
Forgiving	5	4	3	.024	*disapprove of the churches be- coming involved in social and political issues, such as the urban crisis, Vietnam and civil rights?*

Religious Values and Powerlessness

Sociological as well as Marxist theory suggests
that an other-worldly orientation would appeal most
to those who feel powerless, to those who feel that
they exert little or no influence in affecting the
course of political and social events in their society. This feeling of powerlessness, which is a
component of more pervasive feelings of alienation
(Seeman, 1959), was measured in the national sample
with the following question: "Because the experts
have so much power in our society, ordinary people
don't have much of a say in things." The data relating responses to this question to the two religious values are shown in Table 23, and they confirm
this expectation at statistically significant levels.
Those who agreed that they "don't have much of a say
in things" ranked *salvation* higher and *forgiving*

higher than those who disagreed. This greater
feeling of powerlessness on the part of those identified with Christian values is, of course, at variance with Christian doctrine asserting that the individual can be a tremendous force for good in this
world, whether by personal example or by active
involvement, and therefore that he does have "much
of a say in things."

TABLE 23

COMPOSITE RANK ORDER OF SALVATION AND FORGIVING
FOR RESPONDENTS VARYING IN ALIENATION

	Agree strongly	Agree somewhat	Disagree somewhat	Disagree strongly	p	The Question
Salvation	4	8	11	12	.025	Because the experts have so much power in our society, ordinary people don't have much of a say in things.
Forgiving	3	5	5	7	.029	

Church Attendance and Social Compassion

The data considered thus far concern the relation between two major Christian values and various
indices of social compassion. A question may now
be raised whether other indices of religiousness
are also related to social compassion. Most particularly, I have in mind the question as to whether
church attendance is similarly related, particularly
in view of the apparently well-established finding
noted by Allport and Ross (1967) of a curvilinear
relationship between church attendance and bigotry.
Recall Allport and Ross' conclusion following their
review of the relevant studies: churchgoers are
more bigoted than nonchurchgoers, but frequent churchgoers are less bigoted than infrequent churchgoers.
Presumably frequent churchgoers are more intrinsically
oriented, that is, have internalized a religious creed
that they try to follow fully. Frequent churchgoers
should therefore be more compassionate than infrequent
churchgoers who are presumably more extrinsically religious, that is, inclined to use and exploit religion
for their own ends.

But this line of reasoning is not altogether
compatible with the data presented in this and the
preceding report showing that ranking of *salvation*

is linearly related to frequency of church attendance and to social compassion. From Allport and
Ross' data a curvilinear rather than linear relationship may be expected, with those never attending church being the most compassionate, but
with frequent churchgoers being more compassionate
than infrequent churchgoers. From my own data a
linear relationship may be expected, with those
never attending church being the most compassionate
and those most frequently attending being the least
compassionate.

To determine which of the two hypotheses is
the more tenable, church attendance was cross-
tabulated against all the 32 issues previously considered in this report. The findings are summarized
in Table 24 with the issues being presented in the
same order as those previously presented in Tables
17 through 23.

In contrast to 28 of 32 significant relationships previously found with *salvation*, now only 14
of the 32 issues show significant relationships with
church attendance. The relationship between church
attendance and social compassion is generally weaker
than the relationship between value for *salvation*
and social compassion. Nevertheless, the findings
concerning church attendance show systematic trends
that merit closer scrutiny.

1. *Differences between churchgoers and nonchurchgoers.* All the 14 significant differences
were without exception in the same direction: those
who never go to church were found on the average to
be consistently more compassionate than those who do.
If statistical significance is disregarded, it is
noted that on almost all the 32 issues nonchurchgoers were more compassionate than churchgoers.
These findings hold whether those who never attend
are compared with those who attend regularly or with
those who attend to one extent or another.

2. *Differences between frequent and less
frequent churchgoers.* There is no evidence in
Table 24 that suggests a curvilinear relationship
between church attendance and social compassion.

On not one of the issues do frequent churchgoers
show more compassion than infrequent churchgoers.
If anything, those who attend church frequently
were found to be somewhat less compassionate than
those attending infrequently. But I do not wish to
make too much of these findings; the differences between frequent and infrequent churchgoers are slight
and insignificant in the national sample, as they
also seem to be in the studies cited by Allport and
Ross (1967). In any case, there is no evidence from
this representative sample of adult Americans or,
for that matter, from Allport and Ross' study that
would suggest that frequent churchgoers have religious orientations that are more intrinsically
oriented than those of infrequent churchgoers.

Implications

        To describe the differential reactions of the
respondents to the many social issues presented them,
I have deliberately put the matter in terms of social
compassion rather than in terms of liberalism-conservatism. Liberal and conservative political philoso-
phies are alternative conceptions for achieving
human happiness, welfare, and dignity, and many of
the questions put to the national sample of respondents could indeed have been reasonably ordered
along such a continuum. But others cannot. The
reaction to Martin Luther King's murder "He had it
coming to him," for example, is a calloused, uncompassionate response rather than a conservative
response. Similarly, it seems more accurate to say
that it is a lack of compassion rather than political
conservatism that would prompt a person to endorse
the idea that blacks are basically not as intelligent
as whites, to advocate laws forbidding interracial
marriage, to assert that the reason why blacks have
failed to achieve equality is because of lack of
initiative, and to state the poor remain poor because of lack of effort. Virtually all the issues
presented to the respondents elicited reactions that
can reasonably be said to vary along a dimension of
social compassion, and for this reason I do not

TABLE 24
RELATIONSHIP BETWEEN CHURCH ATTENDANCE AND INDICES OF SOCIAL COMPASSION

Percent Responding:	*Every week*	*Nearly every week*	*Seldom*	*Never*	*p*
Reactions following King assassination					
King brought it on himself	30	26	35	26	N.S.
Felt very angry about King murder	29	41	33	45	.02
Felt very strong sympathy for Negroes after King's death	19	21	2?	27	N.S.
Attitudes toward civil rights					
Strongly favor open occupancy laws	16	21	18	30	.01
Strongly favor fair employment laws	42	37	42	56	N.S.
Negroes shouldn't push: agree strongly	49	39	51	41	.05
Keep Negroes out of neighborhood	31	25	33	25	N.S.
Negroes asking too much	69	73	65	56	.05
Favor school integration	69	83	74	85	.01
Laws against racial intermarriage: Yes	58	55	55	46	N.S.
Interracial dating by whites: do not object	5	5	9	21	.001
Negroes as intelligent as whites	76	76	75	90	.05
Negroes lack initiative	61	60	59	40	.01
Would go to Negro doctor	71	71	69	83	N.S.
Approve Negro activism	17	25	23	27	.05
Am now more favorable to integration	43	43	40	37	N.S.
Attitudes toward the poor					
College education for poor: strongly agree	57	60	59	61	N.S.
Adequate housing for poor: strongly agree	35	35	38	38	N.S.
Minimum income for poor: strongly agree	46	43	49	60	N.S.
Dental care for poor: strongly agree	40	38	47	42	N.S.
Medical care for poor: strongly agree	51	53	59	57	N.S.
Favor public funds for dental care	73	74	78	79	N.S.
Favor tax increase to subsidize dental care	74	86	78	81	N.S.
Pass more laws to help poor	23	27	31	33	.02
Poverty caused by lack of effort	44	50	41	30	.05
Raise local taxes	53	60	53	51	N.S.
Favor guaranteed income	59	61	65	70	N.S.
Attitudes toward student protest					
Student protests healthy: agree strongly	10	12	16	29	.001
We need less student protest: strongly disagree	9	6	11	26	.001
Attitudes toward church involvement					
Favorable toward National Council of Churches	65	84	77	76	.01
Approve church involvement in social issues: agree strongly	39	40	38	43	N.S.
Powerlessness					
Ordinary people are powerless: agree strongly	37	35	42	37	N.S.

believe that it would have been accurate to have put the matter in terms of liberalism-conservatism.

The findings presented here strongly suggest a pervasive social outlook among those generally possessing religious values that seems to be

incompatible with and often opposite to the compassion taught in the Sermon on the Mount. If Christian values do indeed serve as standards of conduct,
they seem to be standards more often employed to
guide man's conduct away from rather than toward his
fellowman. Moreover, the results seem compatible
with the hypothesis that religious values serve more
as standards for condemning others or as standards
to guide rationalization than as standards to judge
oneself by or to guide one's own conduct.

If we define hypocrisy as a discrepancy between espoused values and conduct, or as a discrepancy
between espoused values and position on salient contemporary issues, then these data from a representative sample of Americans strongly suggest an hypocrisy
deeply embedded, on the psychological level, within
many religiously-oriented individuals. Assuming
that there is at least some causal connection between religiously-oriented individuals and religious
institutions, the data also suggest a hypocrisy
deeply embedded, on the sociological level, within
organized religion as a social institution.

The data are sufficiently consistent to suggest
the following sociological hypotheses: All advanced
societies require for their perpetuation the formation of some social institution whose major function
is to socialize those within its sphere of influence
to employ mechanisms of self-enhancement regardless
of the amount of compassion felt for or shown toward
one's fellowman. This social institution provides
its members with ready-made value standards to be
employed as bases for rationalization, and as frames
of reference for morally judging or condemning others
on the one hand and for feeling morally superior or
self-righteous on the other. It may be further hypothesized that, in Western societies at least, this
major function has somehow been "assigned" to religious institutions. The data reported here would
seem to be compatible with, or at least not incompatible with, such hypotheses.

The evidence put forward by Allport and Ross
(1967) suggests that only 35% of their churchgoing
subjects were consistently intrinsic, the remainder
being about equally divided between the extrinsically-

oriented (34.5%) and the indiscriminately proreligious (30.7%). While their samples of churchgoers
were by no means representative, their findings
made it possible to estimate tentatively that organized religion is socializing only about one of
three regular churchgoers to become truly religious,
another one of three to become hypocritical, and
the remaining one of three to become something in-
between truly religious and hypocritical.

One source of this hypocrisy may be a religious value system that has all sorts of incongruities built into it. It is reasonable to expect that Americans who place a high value on
salvation would also rank other terminal and instrumental values in certain ways. This is often
the case but not always. In the national sample
442 respondents--about one in three--ranked *salvation* relatively high (from 1 to 6). Of these:

    45.5% also placed a high value on being
        ambitious (ranking it from 1 to 6)
    24.0% also placed a high value on *a com-
        fortable life*
    3.2% also placed a high value on *social
        recognition*
    1.6% also placed a high value on *an excit-
        ing life*
                    while
    53.4% placed a low value on being *obedient*
        (ranking it from 13 to 18)
    36.9% placed a low value on being *polite*
    32.7% placed a low value on *inner harmony*
    30.1% placed a low value on being *loving*
    28.7% placed a low value on *equality*
    28.1% placed a low value on being *clean*
    27.8% placed a low value on being *self-
        controlled*
    24.0% placed a low value on *true friendship*
    23.1% placed a low value on being *broadminded*
    19.7% placed a low value on being *helpful*
    13.6% placed a low value on *self-respect*
    13.3% placed a low value on being *forgiving*
    12.4% placed a low value on being *responsible*
    6.3% placed a low value on *a world at peace*
    2.5% placed a low value on being *honest*

Of course, not all of the above necessarily represent value incongruities. But many of them do, and I am content to let the reader decide for himself which ones do and which ones do not. Nor do value incongruities such as those mentioned above necessarily exist within the same respondents. The frequency of value incongruities implicating religious values would undoubtedly vary from one person to the next, and I would guess that a person would be upset to the extent that he discovers that he has them. I would also hypothesize that one necessary precondition for the removal of hypocrisy is the removal of value incongruity, that is, the reorganization of the value system so that it becomes a more integrated value system. Conversely, it is also possible that it is the other way around, that the removal of hypocrisy would lead to less value incongruity.

It is now necessary to draw attention to an important qualification. When the data for the national sample were analyzed separately for Catholics, Baptists, Methodists, and Lutherans, it was found that the relationship between religious values, especially *salvation*, and social compassion was generally negative, more so for Baptists and somewhat less for Methodists and Lutherans. The findings for Catholics were, however, somewhat better: for them there was typically no relationship rather than a negative relationship between religious values and social compassion. It would thus seem that while the religious values held by Protestant groups (at least the Protestant groups studied here) are negatively related to social compassion, the religious values of Catholics are more or less irrelevant as guides to a compassionate social outlook. I trust that someone more acquainted than I with the history of Christianity will be able to offer some plausible explanation for this difference.

I have focused primarily in this report on *salvation* and *forgiving* as religious values, and I have not said anything about other Christian values, such as being *loving, helpful,* and *obedient*. There are two reasons besides saving space for my

neglect of such moral values. First, they do not
consistently distinguish among Christian groups
varying in religiousness, as do *salvation* and *forgiving.* Second, they typically show only chance
relationships with the various indices of social
compassion considered here.

*   *   *

Very much in the news nowadays are accounts of
efforts by black and white students to radically
change the fundamental structure of educational institutions, on the grounds that they support racism
and the military-industrial complex at home, impe-
rialism and immoral wars abroad. The findings discussed here lead me to suggest that religious institutions are also in need of change. If religious
institutions taken as a whole are indeed, at best,
irrelevant and, at worst, training centers for
hypocrisy, indifference, and callousness, it is unlikely that those who are part of the Religious
Establishment will voluntarily initiate the program
of radical change that seems called for. We are
now witnessing the beginnings of a genuine protest
movement against the Religious Establishment within the Catholic Church and, to a somewhat lesser
extent, within the various Protestant churches. My
guess is that such a movement will escalate in the
months and years ahead, as a protest against the
kind of role that organized religion seems to have
been playing in contemporary society. This role is
not only indicated by the present findings but also
by those others have presented. It is also evidenced by a recent Gallup Poll (Detroit Free Press,
June 1, 1969) reporting that, while 69% of a representative cross-section of adult Americans felt
that religion was increasing its influence on
American life in 1957, only 14% felt the same way
in 1969.

John McKinney, my colleague at Michigan State
University, has recently formulated an important
distinction between proscriptive and prescriptive
learning, that is, learning what not to do and
learning what to do (McKinney, 1969). This

distinction is, of course, parallel to the sociologist's distinction between proscriptive and prescriptive norms. In the religious realm, learning
the "thou shalt nots" of the Ten Commandments would
be proscriptive, while learning the "thou shalts"
of the Sermon on the Mount would be prescriptive.
The data presented here would suggest that Christianity has done a much better job teaching the
former than the latter. It may be hypothesized
that Christianity, by committing itself to the
teaching of religious values to the very young, has
necessarily been forced to teach that salvation is
the reward for obeying the "thou shalt nots" of the
Ten Commandments rather than the "thou shalts" of
the Sermon on the Mount.

It is perhaps this way of teaching religion
that has led Marx to propose--with some justification, as my data suggest--that religion is the
opiate of the people. But religion may not *have* to
be the opiate of the people. If a way can be found
to reverse the emphasis between proscriptive and
prescriptive learning, children can be taught that
salvation is a reward for obeying the "thou shalts"
of the Sermon on the Mount rather than the "thou
shalt nots" of the Ten Commandments. Such a simple
shift of focus, however, would probably require a
profound reorganization of the total social structure of organized Christian religions. And if
such a reorganization turns out to be too difficult
to bring about because of rigidity, dogmatism, or
vested interest, the data presented here lead me to
propose that man's relations to his fellowman will
probably thrive at least a bit more if he altogether forgets or unlearns or ignores what organized religion has tried to teach him about values
and what values are for.

FOOTNOTES

1.   The research reported herein and the prep-
     paration of this paper was supported by a
     grant from the National Science Foundation.

2. Data obtained with such scales as the
    Allport-Vernon Scale typically confirm
    that those having religious commitments
    score higher on religious values than
    those who do not. Such a finding provides
    more information about the measurement de-
    vice than about the respondents.
3. See Rokeach (1968a, 1968b, 1968-69) for
    discussions of the differences between the
    concepts of attitudes and values, between
    instrumental and terminal values, between
    values and value systems, and for a dis-
    cussion of the functional relations con-
    ceived to exist between values, attitudes,
    and behavior.
4. In contrast, Catholic students at Michigan
    State University ranked *salvation* first on
    the average. This difference is surpris-
    ing not so much because of the relatively
    low ranking given *salvation* by the nation-
    al sample of Catholics but because of the
    relatively high ranking obtained for Cath-
    olic college students. I am presently un-
    able to account for this difference.
5. I am uncertain about the classification
    of *courageous* and *cheerful* because they
    may be "moral" under certain conditions
    and "competent" under others. If the val-
    ues of behaving courageously or cheerfully
    are violated under conditions perceived to
    be harmful to others, they would probably
    lead to a feeling of wrong-doing or guilt.
    Otherwise, their violation would probably
    reflect a lack of ability and thus lead to
    shame about incompetence. Also bothersome
    is the classification of *clean* and *self-
    controlled* as moral values: they do not
    seem to have an interpersonal focus. Vio-
    lation of these two values seems to re-
    present what some would consider a sin
    against God rather than man. I would,
    therefore, have to extend the idea of mor-
    al values as interpersonal in focus by

defining interpersonal to include "man's relation to God" as well as "man's relation to man."
The results of several factor analyses empirically confirm the distinction between moral and competence values. The strongest factors are bipolar ones with different combinations of the moral values loading at one pole and different combinations of competence values loading at the other pole.

6. The only group that could not be matched for income with the Jews was the Congregationalists. It was accordingly omitted from the analysis.

7. A statistically significant difference was also found for *intellectual*, but this difference was not linearly related to church attendance.

8. I am ignoring the findings for the Congregationalists since only two of them reported that they attended church once a week or more.

9. Despite all the clusterings noted, the correlations between values are generally low. For the N.O.R.C. sample the most positive correlation in the 36-value matrix is +.35 and the most negative correlation is -.32. (N = 1409). The correlation between the rankings for *salvation* and *forgiving* is only +.28.

REFERENCES

Adorno, T. W., Else Frenkel-Brunswik, D. J.
    Levinson, and R. N. Sanford
    1950   The authoritarian personality. New
    York: Harper.

Allport, G. W.
    1954   The nature of prejudice. Cambridge:
    Addison-Wesley.
    1959   Religion and prejudice. Crane Review
    2:1-10.

Allport, G. W. and J. M. Ross
    1967 Personal religious orientation and prej-
    udice. *Journal of Personality and Social
    Psychology* 5:432-443.

Campbell, D. T. and D. Fiske
    1959 Convergent and discriminant validation
    by the multitrait-multimethod matrix. *Psy-
    chological Bulletin* 56:81-105.

Feagin, J. R.
    1964 Prejudice and religious types: A
    focused study of southern fundamentalists.
    Journal for the Scientific Study of Religion
    4:3-13.

Glock, C. Y. and Rodney Stark
    1965 Religion and society in tension.
    Chicago: Rand McNally.
    1966 Christian beliefs and anti-Semitism.
    New York: Harper and Row.

Kirkpatrick, Clifford
    1949 Religion and humanitarianism: A study
    of institutional implications. *Psychological
    Monographs 63:* Whole No. 304.

Lenski, Gerhard
    1961 The religious factor. Garden City, New
    York: Doubleday.

McKinney, J. P.
    1969 The development of values--proscriptive
    or prescriptive? Unpublished Manuscript.
    Michigan State University.

Rokeach, Milton
    1960 The open and closed mind. New York:
    Basic Books
    1968a A theory of organization and change in
    value-attitude systems. *Journal of Social
    Issues* 24:13-33.
    1968b Beliefs, attitudes, and values. San
    Francisco, Calif.: Jossey-Bass.

1968-69   The role of values in public opinion
research. *Public Opinion Quarterly* 32:547-
559.

Seeman, Melvin
1959   The meaning of alienation. *American
Sociological Review* 24:783-791.

Siegel, Sidney
1956   Nonparametric statistics.   New York:
McGraw-Hill.

Wilson, W. C.
1960   Extrinsic religious values and prejudice. *Journal of Abnormal and Social Psychology* 60:286-288.

Young, R. K., W. M. Benson, and W. H. Holtzman
1960   Change in attitude toward the Negro in
a southern university. *Journal of Abnormal
and Social Psychology* 60:131-133.

SELECTED ADDITIONAL READINGS ON
RELIGIOUS BELIEFS, VALUES, AND ATTITUDES

Allen, R. O., & Spilka, B. Committed and consensual religion: A specification of religion-prejudice relationships. *Journal for the Scientific Study of Religion*, 1967, 6, 191-206.

Bagley, C. Relation of religion and racial prejudice in Europe. *Journal for the Scientific Study of Religion*, 1970, 9, 219-225.

DeJong, G. F. Religious fundamentalism, socio-economic status, and fertility attitudes in the southern Appalachians. *Demography*, 1965, 2, 540-548.

Feagin, J. R. Prejudice and religious types: A focused study of Southern Fundamentalists. *Journal for the Scientific Study of Religion*, 1964, 4, 3-13.

Glock, C. Y., & Siegelman, E. (Eds.), *Prejudice, U. S. A.* New York: Praeger, 1969.

Glock, C. Y., & Stark, R. *Christian Beliefs and Anti-Semitism.* New York: Harper & Row, 1966.

Putney, S., & Middleton, R. Dimensions and correlates of religious ideologies. *Social Forces*, 1961, 39, 385-390.

Rokeach, M. *Beliefs, Attitudes, and Values.* San
    Francisco: Jossey-Bass, 1968.

Weima, J. Authoritarianism, religious conservatism
    and sociocentric attitudes in Roman Catholic
    groups. *Human Relations,* 1965, 18, 231-239.

Wilson, W. C. Extrinsic religious values and prej-
    udice. *Journal of Abnormal and Social Psy-
    chology,* 1960, 60, 286-288.

PART THREE

RELIGIOUS BELIEFS AND PERSONAL ADJUSTMENT

AGE AND FAITH: A CHANGING OUTLOOK OR AN OLD PROCESS?*

RODNEY STARK

Editor's introduction. The specific question
for study in Stark's article is the relationship between age and religiosity. This relationship is commonly assumed to be positive,
and one reason often suggested for it is the
solace given by religion in the face of ever-
nearing death. Indeed, the most prominent
aspect of religious explanations for the human
condition has been the promise of immortality.
It is reasonable to assume that this idea will
be especially attractive to old people, but,
asks Stark, does this make them more religious?
The assumption of increased religiosity with
age has been successfully challenged before
(for example, Orbach, 1961), but Stark, by using the multidimensional definition of religiosity, makes a better case for the challenge.

*This is a publication from the Program in
Religion and Society of the Survey Research Center,
University of California, Berkeley and is identi-
fied as A-65 in the Center's reprint series.

From *Sociological Analysis,* 1968, 29, 1-10.
Reprinted with permission.

His conclusion is that older people do not
become more religious as they grow older; they
merely tend to believe in immortality more
often than younger believers. The belief in
afterlife is unrelated to doctrinal orthodoxy. Older people also tend to pray more
often in private, possibly as a means of
securing the right kind of afterlife, and
possibly because they are more isolated and
lonely (see the article by Lindenthal et al.,
reprinted in this volume). One criticism of
this study may stem from the fact that Stark
did not use any direct measure of the fear
of death. The connection between belief in
immortality and the fear of death is implied
rather than shown directly. The implication
seems reasonable and sound, but a direct measure of attitudes toward death could have made
the connection stronger.

Reference

Orbach, H. L. Aging and religion: A study
of church attendance in the Detroit metropolitan area. *Geriatrics*, 1961, 16, 530-540.

Man's ubiquitous fear of death has long been
judged a mainspring of Christian commitment. From
its earliest days, Christian proselytization has
stressed the promise of life ever-lasting as the
central and glorious message of the New Testament--
"O death, where is thy sting? O grave, where is
thy victory" (I Cor. 15:55 A. V.).
Indeed, for centuries the major spokesmen of
Christianity have deemed it unthinkable that the
faith would have any relevance to the human condition without the promise of immortality. According
to the Apostle Paul, "If in this life only we have
hope in Christ, we are of all men most miserable"

(I Cor. 15:19). As one might expect, Martin Luther
expressed these sentiments in earthier language,
"If you believe in no future life, I would not give
a mushroom for your God."[1]

More recently, Harry Emerson Fosdick wrote
that "The goodness of God is plainly at stake when
one discusses immortality, for if death ends all,
the Creator is building men like sand houses on the
shore, caring not a whit that the fateful waves
will quite obliterate them."[2] In this he echoed
Tennyson's line, "If immortality be not true, then
no God but a mocking fiend created us."[3]

This centrality of the "victory over death"
in Christian teaching is connected with a basic
tenet of conventional wisdom: Men get more pious
as they get older and begin to fear the imminence
of their death. "Beads and prayer-books are the
toys of age" wrote Alexander Pope in *An Essay on
Man*. Of course, as is always the case with conventional wisdom, there is an opposing minority
view that it is the young, not the old, who fear
death most. Indeed, as George Herbert put it,
"Old men *go* to death; death *comes* to young men."[4]
Still, the stereotype of piety in old age seems
very credible, and is continually reinforced by
anecdotes of death-bed conversions.

In this paper I shall take up the question of
whether or not people do become increasingly committed to religion as they get older.

Past research has provided a smattering of
data on the relationship between age and piety.

[1]Quoted in Radoslav A. Tsanoff, *The Problem
of Immortality,* New York: Macmillan, 1924, p.
245.
[2]*The Assurance of Immortality,* New York:
Association Press, 1926, p. 100.
[3]Quoted in A. Seth Pringle-Pattison, *The Idea
of Immortality,* London: Oxford University Press,
1922, p. 184.
[4]*Jacula Prudentum,* 1651. Italics added.

Studies by Fichter,[5] Gorer,[6] Cauter and Downham,[7]
and Glock, Ringer and Babbie,[8] have shown that weekly church attendance is slightly higher among older
people than younger people. In addition Gorer found
slight differences in belief in life after death between older and younger persons.[9] However, all of
these findings are subject to a major problem of interpretation. Each is based on differences between
younger and older persons at a single point in time.
None charted changes in the same persons over time.
Consequently, we cannot say whether these differences represent changes over age or whether they
show instead that recent generations are simply less
religious than earlier ones. This is a most vexing
difficulty. If there is strong reason to predict
increases in religious commitment as persons age,
there are equally persuasive reasons to expect that
secularization has been occurring in modern society
and thus that the young will be less religious.

[5]Joseph H. Fichter, "The Profile of Catholic
Religious Life," *American Journal of Sociology,* 58
(July, 1952), pp. 145-49.
    [6]Geoffrey Gorer, *Exploring English Character,*
London: Cresset, 1955.
    [7]T. Cauter and J. S. Downham, *The Communication
of Ideas,* London: Reader's Digest and Chatto and
Windus, 1954.
    [8]Charles Y. Glock, Benjamin B. Ringer, and
Earl Babbie, *To Comfort and To Challenge: A
Dilemma of the Contemporary Church,* Berkeley: University of California Press, 1967.
    [9]*Op. cit.* In addition, Cavan and his asso-
ciates found slight increases in the proportion
believing in life after death as age increased in
a study, however, restricted to persons over 60.
For lack of denominational controls, and because of
the small and somewhat inconsistent difference, it
is difficult to say what, if anything, these data
mean. R. S. Cavan, et al., *Personal Adjustment in
Old Age,* Chicago: Science Research Associates, 1949.

A second inadequacy of previous research is
that the data have been exceedingly skimpy--handi-
capped by poor samples and few indicators of
religious commitment; indeed nearly all of these
findings are based on nothing more than church
attendance. But, as much recent research has shown,
religious commitment is a complex phenomenon requiring a variety of measurements. Thus, at present
we really know very little about the empirical relationship between age and faith.

In what follows I shall examine this relationship and attempt to resolve the question of whether
differences are attributable to aging or to changes
in the religious commitment of society reflected in
lower religiousness among the younger generations.

The data were collected from a random sample
of the church-member population of four West Coast
counties centered on San Francisco. All Protestant and Catholic congregations in the four counties were included in the sampling frame. Congregations were selected randomly, each having the
number of chances for selection equal to its total
membership. After drawing congregations, random
samples of members were drawn from the church rolls.
Each respondent selected was sent a lengthy mail
questionnaire--approximately 500 items were in-
cluded--and 73 per cent of the Protestants and 54
per cent of the Roman Catholics returned completed
documents.

Telephone interviews were conducted with random samples of both Protestant and Roman Catholic
non-respondents to assess what biases may have
operated in the return rate. These findings indicate that the data were remarkably representative
of the population sampled. With the data finally
gathered, 2,326 Protestants and 545 Roman Catholics
had returned questionnaires.[10]

[10]Full details in sampling and data collection
are reported in Charles Y. Glock and Rodney Stark,
Christian Beliefs and Anti-Semitism, New York:
Harper and Row, 1966.

ORTHODOXY[11]

The argument that secularization is taking
place in America depends upon evidence that the
young are less likely to hold the traditional tenets
of Christian orthodoxy than are the old. But it is
also supposed that persons become more likely to
hold these beliefs as they get older. Yet, these
are not in fact exactly similar predictions, and
the pattern of the data in Table 1 seems to permit
the hypothesis of secularization, but not that of
increasing orthodoxy with age.

If orthodoxy increased with age we would expect this to be a systematically cumulative process.
Thus, we would expect some persons to respond to
this process in their forties, to be joined by more
persons during their fifties, and more again in
their sixties and so on, so that each older group
would show a higher proportion of believers than
would the next younger group. However, a secularization hypothesis need not assume such cumulative
changes. A major change could have occurred at
some point in recent history and all the subsequent
generations show this new lower level of piety without becoming successively less pious. Furthermore,

[11]Four items were scored to create the Orthodoxy Index. These measured firm belief in a personal God, in the divinity of Jesus Christ, in the
authenticity of Biblical miracles, and in the
existence of the Devil. Respondents received one
point for each of these in which they believed without doubt. Respondents who expressed doubt or dis-
belief on an item were scored zero. Persons who
failed to answer any of the four were not scored.
The initial index thus ranged from a high of four
through a low of zero. As used here "high" indicates a score of three or four on the index. A
full account of construction and validation of the
index may be found in Rodney Stark and Charles Y.
Glock, *American Piety*, Berkeley and Los Angeles:
University of California Press, 1968, Ch. 3.

age changes should operate in all Christian groups,
Protestants as well as Catholics, and among liberal
Protestants as well as moderate and conservative
ones. But the data shown in Table 1 indicate that
there seem to be no meaningful differences with age
among the liberal Protestants or among the Roman
Catholics. We shall return to this point in a
moment. Furthermore, age differences among moderate and conservative Protestants are not the cumulative increases over age required by a theory of
belief increasing as people get older. Instead,
the only meaningful shift in orthodoxy with age
occurs between the 40-year-olds and the 50-year-
olds in both the moderate and conservative Protestant groups. Above 50 there are no meaningful
increases, nor are there any meaningful decreases
below 40.

What can we conclude from this? It seems more
than coincidental that the age at which fewer persons adhere to traditional religious beliefs occurs
precisely at the age that separates the pre-World
War II generations from the post-war generations.
Persons who were from 40 to 49 in 1963, at the time
these data were collected, were from 17 to 26 at
the time the war broke out. It is these people,
and those born after them, who have been most shaped
by the emergence of an America of mobile city-
dwellers, inhabiting a fast, technical, mass society.
World War II was a watershed between this new world
and the older America of parochial small town and
rural society. While all of the persons in this
sample today live in this new America, those past 50
did not grow up in it. The data strongly suggest
that in this newer America traditional Christian
orthodoxy is less powerful.

But why do there seem to be no similar shifts
among the liberal Protestants and the Roman Catholics? While it appears in the table as if the
liberal Protestants have been unaffected by recent
social changes, this is in part an artifact produced
because there are very few orthodox believers of any
age in these denominations. Consequently, only very
small differences in the proportions of highly
orthodox persons between the pre-war and post-war

generations *could* have occurred. However, if we
examine instead the proportions who scored zero or
one on Orthodoxy, and thus were the least possible

TABLE 1
AGE AND ORTHODOXY PER CENT HIGH ON ORTHODOXY INDEX

Age:	Liberal Prot.	Moderate Prot.	Conservative Prot.	Roman Catholics
Post War Generations				
Under 20	5	29	•	•
	(19)	(15)	(12)	(9)
20-29	10	26	75	64
	(91)	(95)	89)	(89)
30-39	10	27	79	66
	(243)	(203)	(101)	(141)
40-49	9	28	78	48
	(262)	(244)	(102)	(124)
Pre-War Generations				
50-59	11	40	94	61
	(157)	(134)	(67)	(83)
60-69	14	49	89	73
	(80)	(79)	(43)	(41)
70 and over	27	45	100	64
	(40)	(51)	(19)	(15)

• Too few cases for stable percentages.

orthodox believers, we find that slightly more than
half (52%) of those from post-war generations received such scores, while only 40 per cent of those
in pre-war generations did so. Thus, the younger
generations show an increased tendency to reject
traditional orthodoxy in the liberal denominations
too.
  The resistance of Roman Catholics to the post-
war changes in religious perspectives may be based
on the fact that the new urban America is not so
new for the Catholics. They have historically been
city-dwellers in this country and the great changes
of recent decades only seem to be extreme when
viewed from the perspective of an earlier agrarian

America, not when viewed from the city. For the
cities haven't changed so much, it is rather that
Protestants have moved to town. Thus, Catholicism
perhaps long ago made an adjustment to maintaining
faith in urban society, however, it may also be
that the younger Catholics have undergone changes
in their religious perspective which are simply not
reflected by the tenets making up this measure of
orthodoxy.

Fortunately, data are available to pursue this
possible explanation. As can be seen in Table 2,
the younger generations of Catholics do show a drop

TABLE 2
AGE AND BELIEFS ABOUT BIRTH CONTROL AND PAPAL INFALLIBILITY AMONG ROMAN CATHOLICS

Per cent who thought that "practicing artificial birth control" would "definitely prevent" salvation

Age:	Per Cent	N
Post War Generations		
-20	20	10[*]
20-29	20	88
30-39	23	142
40-49	18	122
Pre-War Generations		
50-59	38	80
60-69	38	39
70 and over	38	16

Per cent who thought it "completely true" that "The Pope is infallible in matters of faith and morals."

Age:	Per Cent	N
Post War Generations		
-20	40	10[*]
20-29	69	91
30-39	69	142
40-49	69	121
Pre-War Generations		
50-59	75	85
60-69	80	44
70 and over	89	18

[*] Too few cases for stable percentages, shown for descriptive interest only.

in commitment to several specifically Catholic beliefs. The first of these, shown in the upper half
of the table, asks about the relevance of practicing artificial birth control for gaining salvation.
While roughly 20 per cent of those Catholics under
50 think this would "definitely prevent" salvation,
38 per cent of those over 50 think this is the case.
Above 50 there are no differences among the age
groups, below 50 there are no significant differences either. These data precisely match the pre-
war/post-war shifts seen among Protestants in
Table 1.

The second specifically Catholic belief shown
concerns the infallibility of the Pope in matters
of faith and morals. Here again the major shift in
the proportions who think it "completely true" that
the Pope is infallible is between the pre-war and
post-war generations. Ignoring data on those under
20 years of age, because the percentage is based
upon too few cases to be trustworthy, there are no
differences in the proportion accepting Papal infallibility among the post-war generations. A
slight increase from one age group to the next is
suggested. However, the main effect seems to be a
slight shift away from this belief by the younger
generation.

These data show that Catholicism has not been
impervious to the secularizing forces of the new
America. However, the impact so far seems to have
been confined to tenets which are exclusively Cath-
olic--beliefs which separate Rome from the rest of
Christianity--while the universal tenets of Christianity seem so far unaffected among Roman Catholics.
These, and all other relationships reported in this
section, proved to be independent of sex or social
class.

Thus, we have seen that commitment to Christian
orthodoxy does not appear to be related to the process of getting old. However, belief in life after
death is not one of the four basic beliefs making
up the Orthodoxy Index. These four are belief in
God, in the Divinity of Jesus, in the authenticity
of Biblical miracles, and in the existence of the

Devil.[12] Even though unwavering commitment to these
tenets does not seem related to aging, it could be
the case that belief in immortality, because of its
special relevance for the elderly, does in fact increase systematically with age. And surprising as
this may seem, Table 3 clearly shows that this is
in fact the case among Protestants.

For example, while only 38 per cent of the
liberal Protestants who are less than 20 years old
felt that the existence of life after death was
"completely true," this proportion rises to 51 per
cent among those in their fifties and on up to 70
per cent of those 70 and over. (The several small
reversals are probably only random fluctuations.)

Among moderate Protestants these proportions
increase from 56 per cent of those less than 20, to
75 per cent of those in their fifties, and 88 per
cent of those 70 and over. Belief in life after
death also increases with age among conservative
Protestants, however, here the extraordinarily
large proportions at all age levels who believe in
immortality make it impossible for very large differences to obtain.

The pattern among Roman Catholics is not altogether clear. For Catholics the data suggest that
belief is high among the very young and slowly falls,
perhaps as younger adults shrug off their childhood
training, and then begins to increase again at about
age 50.

In any event it is clear that although commitment to Christian orthodoxy in general does not increase as people age, belief in survival beyond the
grave *does* increase among Protestants. What are
we to make of this? James B. Pratt anticipated such
an empirical finding in his theological study of the
psychology of religion published in 1920.[13] He
wrote that:

[12]Analysis of the relationship between each of
these items and age showed patterns identical with
that produced by the index.
    [13]*The Religious Consciousness*, New York:
Macmillan, 1920.

As the belief in miracles and special answers
to prayers and in the interference of the supernatural with the natural has gradually disappeared, almost the only pragmatic value of the
supernatural left to religion is the belief in
a personal future life.[14]

TABLE 3
AGE AND BELIEF IN LIFE AFTER DEATH

Per cent who think it "Completely true" that "There is a Life beyond death."

Age:	Lib. Prots.		Mod. Prots.		Cons. Prots.		Roman Cath.	
-20	38%	(21)	56%	(16)	87%	(15)	90%	(10)°
20-29	41	(95)	62	(99)	90	(89)	84	(93)
30-39	47	(249)	65	(205)	92	(105)	78	(145)
40-49	44	(278)	69	(251)	90	(103)	70	(122)
50-59	51	(169)	75	(149)	99	(68)	80	(87)
60-69	75	(91)	86	(92)	96	(45)	81	(47)
70 and over	70	(52)	87	(59)	100	(20)	78	(18)

° Too few cases for a stable percentage, presented for descriptive interest only.

Indeed our data show that elderly liberal
Protestants have overwhelmingly surrendered belief
in the authenticity of miracles, admit considerable
doubt concerning the existence of a personal God,
and the divinity of Jesus, but overwhelmingly retain their firm belief in the promise of the life
everlasting. Corliss Lamont wrote in 1934 concerning this emerging pattern of doubt in all religious
truths except life beyond death that:

> To an increasing number of moderns, God, if he
> is not actually an "unnecessary hypothesis,"
> has become a kind of God Emeritus, retired
> peacefully in his old age to the pleasures of
> professorial contemplation....Thus, in the
> modern world, little else remains for God to
> do but to function as the benevolent purveyor
> of man's immortality.[15]

[14]*Ibid.*, p. 253.
[15]*The Illusion of Immortality*, New York:
Philosophical Library, 1934-1959, pp. 6-7.

Be that as it may, further examination of many other responses to questions on belief contained in the data revealed none on which there were cumulative increases with age. Thus, it is necessary to conclude that changes in the religious perspective of American society are revealed by comparisons between church members of different ages, but that people do not get more orthodox or conservative in their religious beliefs as they get older, *except* that they do increasingly become certain of the existence of life beyond death. In general, then, people do not get more pious with age, insofar as piety means belief in God, the divinity of Jesus, and similar bedrocks of Christian theology. There is, of course, nothing in these tenets that is more relevant to the aged than to the young. However, where Christian belief does assume special relevance for the existential anxieties of aging, in its doctrine of victory over death, the aging process does seem to produce increased belief.

RITUAL PARTICIPATION[16] AND PRIVATE DEVOTIONALISM[17]

If the aged do not express increasing piety in terms of adherence to the theology of Christianity (aside from immortality), perhaps they do show

[16]The Index of Ritual Involvement consists of answers to two questions: 1) the frequency of church attendance and 2) the frequency of saying table grace. Persons who *both* attended church every, or nearly every, week and who said grace at least once a week were classified as high on the index. Persons who did either this frequently were scored as medium. Persons who did neither this often were scored as low. A full account of index construction and validation can be found in Stark and Glock, *op. cit.*, Ch. 4.

[17]The Index of Private Devotionalism was based on the frequency of private prayer and the importance the individual placed upon private prayer.

increasing engrossment in the ritualistic and de-
votional aspects of religious commitment. Table 4
allows a test of this hypothesis.

TABLE 4
PUBLIC RITUAL INVOLVEMENT AND PRIVATE DEVOTIONALISM

	Per cent high on Index of Public Ritual Involvement			
Age:	Lib. Prots.	Mod. Prots.	Cons. Prots.	Roman Cath.
-20	19 (21)	38 (16)	36 (14)•	30 (10)•
20-29	23 (97)	40 (99)	73 (89)	46 (92)
30-39	38 (247)	45 (208)	73 (107)	47 (146)
40-49	28 (282)	46 (258)	75 (104)	46 (129)
50-59	24 (168)	41 (146)	83 (65)	43 (94)
60-69	24 (95)	47 (90)	75 (43)	54 (46)
70 and over	54 (54)	53 (60)	90 (21)	41 (22)

	Per cent high on Index of Private Devotionalism			
Age:	Lib. Prots.	Mod. Prots.	Cons. Prots.	Roman Cath.
-20	37 (19)	29 (14)•	64 (14)•	56 (9)•
20-29	34 (90)	35 (97)	62 (87)	58 (93)
30-39	41 (237)	43 (204)	75 (105)	63 (142)
40-49	35 (268)	46 (246)	79 (104)	62 (125)
50-59	48 (163)	58 (148)	88 (68)	74 (91)
60-69	51 (94)	71 (93)	93 (45)	77 (47)
70 and over	68 (53)	81 (57)	96 (21)	75 (20)

• Too few cases for stable percentages, presented for descriptive purposes only.

The relationship between age and public ritual
participation, as shown in the upper half of the
table, seems very slight. Among Protestants it
appears that persons 70 and over are more inclined
to ritual commitment than those below 70. However,
there are no interpretable differences among the
below 70 age groups, except for the possibility

Scored high were those who said prayer was "extremely" important and who pray privately at least once
a week. Those scored medium met one of these
criteria. Those scored low met neither. A full
account of index construction and validation can be
found in Stark and Glock, *op. cit.*, Ch. 5.

that persons under 20 are a bit less likely to be ritually involved than are those over 20. This difference is uncertain, however, because of the small number of cases on which the percentages are based.

Among Roman Catholics, aside from the possibility that those under 20 are less likely to be ritually involved than the rest, there appears to be no interpretable relationship between age and ritual involvement.

This lack of any important connection between age and ritual involvement may stem from the fact that although older persons do get more engrossed in religion, the difficulties of attending worship services because of ill-health and disability work against any increase in their attendance. However, this would not apply to saying table prayers, or grace, and this item, which is included in the index, shows no connection with age either.

Nevertheless, looking at private devotionalism, shown in the lower half of the table, it is apparent that this aspect of religious commitment increases greatly with age. Among liberal Protestants, while 34 per cent of those in their twenties scored high on private devotionalism, 48 per cent of those in their fifties, and 68 per cent of those 70 and over did so. Among moderate Protestants these same proportions are 35%, 58%, and 81%, and among conservative Protestants 62%, 88%, and 96%. A similar increase can be seen among Roman Catholics, from just more than half scoring high in the younger age groups on up to about three-fourths scoring high in the older groups.

The systematic way in which these proportions increase, while not precluding an explanation based on social change, strongly suggests that it is aging that accounts for them.

Thus, the effect of age seems to be not so much in what one believes, but in what one does about what he believes. The elderly do not shift their image of God from a "higher force" to a kindly man with a white beard, but they begin praying a good deal more to whatever conception of God they do hold.

RELIGIOUS EXPERIENCE[18]

How does aging effect the propensity to have religious experiences? The data shown in Table 5 indicate that the tendency to have religious experiences does not increase with age except among

TABLE 5
AGE AND RELIGIOUS EXPERIENCE

Age:	Per cent high on Index of Religious Experience			
	Lib. Prots.	Mod. Prots.	Cons. Prots.	Roman Cath.
-20	67 (18)	70 (10)°	79 (14)	78 (9)°
20-29	53 (89)	63 (95)	83 (83)	62 (84)
30-39	44 (227)	53 (191)	89 (100)	60 (127)
40-49	39 (231)	51 (218)	89 (84)	48 (99)
50-59	39 (129)	66 (116)	91 (58)	60 (63)
60-69	41 (66)	65 (63)	96 (28)	60 (30)
70 and over	36 (25)	59 (34)	100 (12)	50 (10)°

° Too few cases for stable percentages, presented for descriptive interest only.

the conservative Protestant groups. Indeed, there is some suggestion in the data that in the other Protestant bodies and among Roman Catholics younger persons might be slightly more prone to such experiences than the older. Because of small case bases in the under 20 group, this suggestion must be taken with caution, still it is also supported by contrasts between persons in their twenties and those in their thirties, where the case bases are

[18]Three items constitute the Religious Experience Index: "A sense of being saved in Christ," "A feeling that you were somehow in the presence of God," and "A feeling of being punished by God for something you had done." Those scored high on the index at least thought they had experienced all three. Those scored medium thought they might have had one or two of these experiences. Those scored low were certain they had not had any of these experiences. A full account of index construction and validation can be found in Stark and Glock, *Op. cit.*, Ch. 6.

quite large. It may be that in the moderate and
liberal Protestant bodies where the churches do not
formally attempt to produce such experiences that
they are mainly associated with the impressionabil-
ity of youth--a suggestibility and naivete that is
outgrown (albeit some would wish to call it an inno-
cence that is lost).

However, among conservative Protestants, whose
churches maintain organized social situations aimed
at producing such religious encounters, the proportions who "succeed" in fulfilling this expectation rise with age. While 79 per cent of those
under 20, and 83 per cent of those in their twenties
scored high on the Index of Religious Experience,
96 per cent of those in their sixties, and 100 per
cent of those 70 and over, scored high.

Thus, the effect of age on religious experience depends on the nature of the religious expectations of the denomination to which one belongs.
Where religious experiences are fostered in situations created by the churches, the propensity for
this form of commitment increases with age. Where
it is not greatly or formally encouraged, it seems
to occur more commonly among the very young.

Finally, an examination of the relationship
between age and religious knowledge revealed no
patterns to indicate either social change or a
connection with aging.

These data force the conclusion that the primary outlet provided by religion for the anxieties
and deprivations of old age is in personal devo-
tional activities--that is, the increasing piety of
the elderly is manifested through prayer. While
church members seemingly are more likely to believe
in the doctrine of immortality as they get older,
in no other way does their theological outlook
change or become more conservative. Nor are the
aging more likely to undergo religious experiences
(indeed, the opposite may be the case), nor to take
part in ritual activities, nor to be more informed
about religion.

Thus, the widespread notion that men become increasingly pious as a means to overcome the ravages
of time is true only if piety is carefully defined

as private devotionalism and belief in an immortal
soul.   It is not true if the word piety is used as
a synonym for religious commitment in its other
aspects.

RELIGION AND CONCEPTUAL MODELS OF BEHAVIOUR

BLAIR W. SHAW

Editor's introduction. Ezer, in his study
presented earlier in this volume, showed how
family devoutness affected children's perceptions of physical causality. In the present
study Shaw extends the same basic notion to
assess the impact of devoutness on explanations
for human behavior at a later age. The basic
social-psychological question is that of at-
tribution--explaining changes in human behavior in terms of external or internal forces.
Early religious socialization and continuing
religious commitment should influence our
understanding of life events, such as illness
or deviance. At the same time, the impact of
secularization should lessen the extent to
which people will use religious explanations
for everyday behavior. Shaw constructed a
Beliefs About Behavior Inventory (BABI), which
assesses the relative extent to which a person
uses each of three conceptual models of behavior: a theological model, an illness model,
and a psychological model. These models were
identified as three alternative ways of

From *British Journal of Social and Clinical
Psychology,* 1970, 9, 320-327. Reprinted with
permission.

looking at human behavior. The medical model,
with the disease concept as central, and the
psychological model, using learning concepts,
represent two competing ideologies in contemporary psychiatric and psychological literature.
The theological model incorporates the ideas
of free will, sinful habits, and virtue.

To measure religiosity in his subjects, Shaw
used the Allport and Ross religious orientation
measure, a devoutness scale, and a denominational classification. The results show that
all measures of religiosity were related to
the choice of a conceptual model. Those subjects who were fundamentalist, devout, or indiscriminately proreligious were significantly
lower in their use of psychological approaches
to human behavior. Conversely, those subjects
who were low on the dimensions of religiosity
were more likely to use a psychological approach
and reject a theological conceptualization of
human behavior.

Given the fact that the subjects were all
university students who had had at least an
elementary course in psychology, the results
are indeed striking. They point to a strong
residual influence of religious training in
childhood, despite later secularizing influences. A possible criticism of Shaw's study
may be based on the observation that his Theological Scale on the BABI is indeed another
measure of religiosity, and thus he is only
correlating two measures of the same variable.
At the same time, the results show that a
theological conception of human behavior is
indeed incompatible with psychological notions.
The relationship between the Allport and Ross
intrinsic scale and the BABI Theological Scale
should be noted in this context.

Lenski's (1961) research in the Detroit area
on the significance of religion in social life concluded that religious organizations not only are

remaining vigorous and influential in contemporary
American society, but that there is evidence of an
increase in 'associational' vigour. He interpreted
the evidence as indications that religion acted in
a causal way and was not merely correlated with
certain kinds of behaviours and events. This is
consistent with Brown's (1966) conclusion that religious beliefs are categories by which people explain, interpret and cope with the natural world.

Stark (1963), writing on the incompatibility
of religion and science, suggests that men with
strong religious commitment are seldom scientific
and have not often been major contributors to the
ongoing scientific quest. Roe's (1952) study of
64 selected scientists supports this contention.
Stark explains this in terms of religion's ultimate adherence to a non-empirical system in which
man's reason is held to be subordinate to faith as
a means of truth. Thus, he notes, 'we are concerned with those faiths which posit the existence
of a relevant supernatural being, world, or force,
and generally ignore those which retain only ethi-
cal positions' (Stark, 1963, p. 4).

In the light of these positions, the research
reported in this paper was conducted to investigate further the relationships between a number of
religious variables (specifically, denominational
affiliation, devoutness and 'intrinsicness') and
the ways in which people tend to perceive, think
about and respond to the behaviour of others. The
latter variable was measured by use of the Beliefs
About Behaviour Inventory (BABI), which assesses
the relative extent to which a person uses each of
three 'conceptual models'* of behaviour: theological,

*'Conceptual model' will be used throughout
this paper to describe 'the manner in which a particular thinker (or group of thinkers) describes
and conceptualizes mental phenomena, including the
assumptions implicit in these descriptions' (Simon
& Weiner, 1966, p. 304). This is in contrast to
the use of the term model to mean 'representations
or likenesses of certain aspects of complex events

illness and psychological. These models were selected for measurement because of their significance
historically and in contemporary debates (Sarbin,
1967; Szasz, 1960; Bandura, 1967). Denominational
variations in attitudes and other psychological
variables have been identified by Linsky (1965)
(differences in attitudes towards alcoholism and
its treatment), Larson (1967) (differences in clergymen's attitudes concerning mental health), Ashcraft (1964) (differences in perception of others)
and Webster (1966) (differences in dogmatism and
psychological health).

The three models are not mutually exclusive,
nor are they the only possible models which can be
studied, but they are significant and, for this
study, are briefly defined as follows. Theological
--man's behaviour is partly a function of free will
and harmony with God who can and does intervene in
human affairs. Illness--abnormal behaviour is a
function of illness (including reified psychodynamic
dysfunction) and can be changed through treatment.
Psychological--social learning theory.

METHOD

Subjects. Three hundred and fifty-nine under-
graduate university students at a major Canadian
university completed the Beliefs About Behaviour
Inventory (described below) and 170 of these also
completed Allport & Ross's Religious Orientation
Scale (ROS) and a simple measure of 'devoutness'.
All subjects had at least an elementary study of
psychology in their university programmes.

---

or systems made by using symbols or objects which
in some way resemble the things being modelled'
(Chapanis, 1961, p. 115). The usage of the term
conceptual model in this document is similar to
that used by Brown & Long (1968) in a review of the
'medical model issue', and is consistent with frequent use in the literature.

Analyses of scores on each of the three scales
(T-theological, I-illness and P-psychological) of
the BABI were made for subjects grouped by denomination, religious orientation and devoutness.

Beliefs About Behaviour Inventory (BABI). The
BABI is a measure of the relative extent to which
subjects agree with each of three conceptual models
of behaviour. It consists of 40 items, each item
containing a triad of alternatives to which the
subject responds by allocating three values: 3 to
the one he most agrees with, 2 to his second choice,
and 1 to the one with which he least agrees. The
triads contain one alternative from each of the
three conceptual models, thus providing for 40 items
on each model. Test-retest reliabilities in the
order of 0.75 and stratified split-half reliabilities
in the order of 0.90 have been established with appropriate populations. Validity was established
through: (1) the writing of the items in accord
with the descriptions of the models, (2) the blind-
sort of items by competent judges, who reached perfect agreement, (3) the analysis of the internal
consistency of the scales of the inventory, (4)
through the use of criterion groups for the Theological scale (Christian Fundamentalists at a Bible
camp) and for the Psychological scale (psychologists).

In the theological model, human behaviour is
seen as being, to a considerable degree, a function
of the exercise of free will. Many kinds of undesirable and inappropriate behaviours are caused
by defects of the will and these may be indications
that the person is somewhat out of harmony with the
Divine Will. Prayer, the loving help of God, His
Church and His ministers can be major sources of
aid for people who are using undesirable or failing
to use desirable behaviour. Virtue, goodness and
proper behaviour are all closely related and these
characteristics are the opposites of sinful habits.
The true meaning of man is spiritual and man can
only be fully understood by recognizing this fact.
Learning God's will, developing moral strength and
overcoming the evil tendencies of man are the paths
to proper and successful behaviour. For example,

Card (1960, p. 25), in reference to the Canadian
Prairie Provinces, states that the churches 'were
outposts of civilization as well as religion....
They acted as the West's moral conscience'. He
further notes that 'despite cumulating evidences at
mid-century of increasing secularism, particularly
in the cities, religion as an institutional field
was generally more robust, more fundamental than
liberal, and simply and practically fused with
other aspects of society and culture' (1960, p. 27).
    In the illness model, all behaviour is seen as
ultimately understandable in terms of the physical
organism but abstractions of defective personality
capacities are often useful explanations of the
causes of abnormal or inappropriate behaviour. For
example, 'to summarize the personality-deficit point
of view, Ausubel and Bettelheim assume that the
lower-class Negro emerges out of childhood psychologically incapable of adjusting to *any* type of
organized social environment...' (Katz, 1967, p.
137). The best approach to understanding and cor-
recting behaviour is through diagnosis and treatment, much of which should be carried out in an
adequate clinic or hospital under the supervision of
a properly trained doctor. People displaying abnormal or inappropriate behaviour should be regarded
as being, to some degree at least, sick and in need
of treatment both to cure them and to prevent further development of the illness. Underlying disease
processes exist in cases of disrupted social functioning (Bandura & Walters, 1963, p. 30).
    In contrast to both the theological and illness
models of behaviour, the eclectic psychological
model of Bandura & Walters (1963) utilizes 'a single
set of social-learning principles [to] account for
the development of both prosocial and deviant behavior and for modifications of behavior toward
greater conformity or greater deviation' (1963, p.
32). It is clearly a scientific model which seeks
relationships between variables and does not use
religious notions of free-acting forces and facul-
ties such as will, moral goodness, harmony with the
Divine, or state of grace. It does not seek the
determinants of behaviour in autonomous internal

agents or processes or underlying disease entities
and in these ways radically differs from the illness model. For example, consider the modelling
theory of aggression presented (with the support of
empirical data) by Bandura & Walters (1963, pp. 69-
70).

The psychological (social-learning) model sees
behaviour as learned in the course of the person's
experiences. 'Normal' and 'abnormal', appropriate
and inappropriate behaviours are all learned in the
same way. Prevention of or changes in inappropriate
behaviour are best carried out as a process of re-
learning. The kind of programme or institution
which would best organize such services would be of
an educational nature, and the personnel would be
specialists in human learning. The social-learning
model is not inconsistent with or used without
awareness of the human as a biological entity.
(The significance of the anatomy and physiology of
the organism in relation to conceptual models of behaviour is concisely presented by Bailey (1960).)

The following are representative items from the
BABI: (1) Very frequent indecisiveness is caused
by: (a) weak will; (b) a very minor sort of mental
illness; (c) the person's background of learning.
(2) Being very aggressive and domineering: (a) is
a result of one's life experience; (b) is caused by
a lack of harmony with God's will; sinfulness; (c)
is caused by what could be the beginning of a degree of mental illness. (3) People who are very
suspicious are best regarded as: (a) using ineffective behaviour; (b) somewhat sick; (c) having a
bad, even sinful, habit. (Copies of the complete
instrument are available from the author.)

The conceptual models of behaviour measured by
the BABI constitute sets of beliefs and attitudes
regarding the causes of and methods of changing behaviour and for the selection and development of
personnel and institutions to serve society's needs
in the promoting of certain behaviours and changing of others. The relationships between the
various behaviours used by individuals are differentially viewed and explained, and patterns of appropriate ways of regarding those displaying deviant behaviour are suggested.

Religious Orientation Scale. The Religious Orientation Scale (ROS) is a 20-item scale which measures the extent to which a person's subjective religious orientation is characterized by extrinsic motivation (he 'uses' religion) or by intrinsic motivation (he 'lives' religion) (Allport & Ross, 1967). There are 11 items on the extrinsic scale and nine on the intrinsic scale. A high score on the extrinsic scale indicates high 'extrinsicness' and a low score on the intrinsic scale indicates high 'intrinsicness'. Those subjects who score at least 12 points less on the intrinsic scale than on the extrinsic scale are classed as indiscriminately pro-religious, since they agree with a very high number of pro-religious items from both scales. Those who score at least 12 points higher on the intrinsic scale than on the extrinsic scale are classed as indiscriminately anti- or a-religious since they tend to disagree with the pro-religious items on both scales.

Devoutness. This is a five-item instrument requiring responses which indicate 'the frequency of behaviors directly pertaining to religious practice by the individual respondent and by his family' (Quinn, 1965, p. 37). Reported retest reliabilities (n=117) over a nine-week interval are 0.74 to 0.86, with a mean of 0.80 (Quinn, 1965, p. 107).

Denominational classification. The denominational classification used in his study follows that of Linsky (1965). The Protestant groups, in order of high-to-low secularity are: group 1--Anglican, Presbyterian and Congregationalist; group 2--Lutherans, Methodists, Baptists and Disciples of Christ; group 3--Fundamentalists such as Mennonite, Pentecostal, Christian Reformed, Evangelical, Nazarene, Moravian and Interdenominational. Other groups include (4) no religion, (5) unclassified, (6) Greek Catholic and Greek Orthodox, (7) Roman Catholic and (8) United Church.

RESULTS

Analysis of variance of the eight denominational groups shows significance on the T scale (0.0004),

on the I scale (0.0398) but not on the P scale.
Table I shows the groups ranked on each of the
three scales with a clear trend evidenced for the
Fundamentalist (high on T, low on I and P) and for
the no-religion group (low on T and high on I and
P).

Groups based on the ROS show a clear trend in
that the 'not indiscriminate' subjects are, on all
three scales, in the middle between the 'indiscriminately pro-religious' (high on T, low on P) and
the 'indiscriminately anti-religious' (low on T
and high on P). (See Table 2.) The analysis of
variance shows statistical significance (0.0040)
on the T scale. The Intrinsic scale of the ROS
correlated 0.44 with the T scale, -0.28 with the I
scale and -0.28 with the P scale (all significant).
The Extrinsic scale of the ROS correlated -0.08
with T, 0.10 with I and 0.01 with P (none significant). A very clear pattern of relationship between 'devoutness' and the relative use of each of
the three conceptual models of behaviour is presented in Table 3. Almost without exception, those
subjects high on the T scale were high on devoutness and those high on the P scale were low on
devoutness.

DISCUSSION

The significance of religious beliefs and
practices in the interpersonal perception and relations of large segments of the population is
clearly evidenced by the data analysed in this study.
The subjects were of relatively high and homogeneous
educational status and yet, with some of the subjects, the theological view of behaviour was very
much in competition with a psychological or scientific view.

Almost without exception those in the high-
devout categories were lowest on the psychological
scale and highest on the theological scale. Less
clearly, yet quite distinctly, the high-devout subjects were low on the illness scale. By way of
interpretation we conclude (on the basis of the

content of the BABI items) that these subjects consider the causes, 'cures' and nature of many human
behaviours in terms of 'will', 'sin', 'prayer' and
virtue and that they look to the Church and its
leaders for behavioural guidance. Their use of the
theological model of behaviour is congruent with
Brown's (1966) conclusion that religious beliefs
are categories used to explain, interpret and cope
with the natural world. The 10 behavioural refer-
ents used in the BABI (such as 'being over-critical',
'being over-confident', 'being excessively fearful',
etc.) are very real in the world of commonly observed behaviours. The ways in which people think
about and respond to these behaviours of others is,
apparently, often far from what is considered appropriate and effective by a contemporary science
of behaviour.

The denominational differences are striking,
especially in the clear position of the Fundamentalists on the high end of the theological scale
and on the low end of the illness and psychological
scale. Possibly the low illness scale scores indicate a less 'humanitarian' orientation (for the
origin of the illness model was to rescue the 'mentally ill' from the harsh treatment given them and
to have them benefit from the humanitarian treatment given the sick by treating the former 'as if'
they were sick) (Sarbin, 1967). The devoutness and
denominational relationships with the theological
way of thinking about behaviour are further classified by the strong relationships identified between
religious orientations (Allport & Ross, 1967) and
conceptual models of behaviour.

Those subjects who were 'indiscriminately pro-
religious' were significantly higher (than the indiscriminately anti-religious and the not-indis-
criminate subjects) on the theological scale and
lower on the psychological scale. The predictable
reverse pattern was evidenced by the indiscriminately anti-religious group. Additionally, we have
a high (0.44) and significant correlation between
the Intrinsic scale of the ROS and the theological
model and rather high and negative correlations
between that scale and the illness (-0.28) and the

Table 1. *Ranked means by religious groups on the three scales of the BABI*

	T scale				I scale			P scale	
Rank	Group	n	Mean	Rank	Group	Mean	Rank	Group	Mean
1.	Fundamentalists	31	74·9	1.	No religion	85·4	1.	Gk. Cath. + Orthodox	95·9
2.	Unclassified	14	69·2	2.	United Church	85·2	2.	No religion	95·8
3.	Luth. Meth. Bap. Disp.	28	63·9	3.	Pres. Ang. Cong.	84·1	3.	Unclassified	95·1
4.	Gk. Cath. + Orthodox	22	63·3	4.	Luth. Meth. Bap. Disp.	81·3	4.	Luth. Meth. Bap. Disp.	94·7
5.	Rom. Catholic	59	59·5	5.	Gk. Cath. + Orthodox	80·8	5.	United Church	93·8
6.	United Church	146	59·3	6.	Rom. Catholic	79·2	6.	Pres. Ang. Cong.	93·2
7.	No religion	24	58·8	7.	Fundamentalists	75·8	7.	Fundamentalists	89·3
8.	Pres. Ang. Cong.	35	55·9	8.	Unclassified	75·6	8.	Rom. Catholic	88·7

Table 2. *Ranked means by religious orientation groups on the three scales of the BABI*

	T scale				I scale			P scale	
Rank	Group	n	Mean	Rank	Group	Mean	Rank	Group	Mean
1.	Indiscriminately pro-religious	31	71·0	1.	Indiscriminately anti-religious	81·1	1.	Indiscriminately anti-religious	99·6
2.	Not indiscriminate	121	61·2	2.	Not indiscriminate	80·3	2.	Not indiscriminate	92·4
3.	Indiscriminately anti-religious	18	52·3	3.	Indiscriminately pro-religious	77·5	3.	Indiscriminately pro-religious	91·5

psychological (0.28) scales. People who 'live' their religion tend to be theological, not illness orientated or psychological in their thinking about and responding to the behaviours of others.

Table 3. *Analysis of variance: devoutness groups*

Group	T scale Mean	S.D.	I scale Mean	S.D.	P scale Mean	S.D.
I go to church						
High (n = 10)	73·9	30·9	62·9	23·4	77·2	31·3
Medium (n = 73)	66·5	19·2	76·3	19·9	90·5	20·0
Low (n = 88)	56·4	15·6	84·7	14·7	96·1	15·7
Mother goes to church						
High (n = 12)	71·3	20·5	79·7	15·3	89·1	15·6
Medium (n = 92)	62·0	19·3	78·3	20·1	91·6	21·2
Low (n = 65)	59·4	18·0	82·2	16·3	94·7	17·2
Father goes to church						
High (n = 5)	75·2	20·3	75·6	17·8	89·2	16·5
Medium (n = 81)	64·4	20·3	76·4	20·5	90·0	22·1
Low (n = 77)	59·7	16·4	84·5	13·1	95·8	12·3
Family prays together						
High (n = 51)	67·9	19·1	76·3	18·5	91·0	19·0
Medium (n = 5)	74·2	15·2	82·8	16·8	83·0	8·7
Low (n = 106)	59·3	16·7	83·4	14·9	95·2	15·6
I pray alone						
High (n = 95)	67·9	19·2	77·0	18·6	89·8	18·5
Medium (n = 13)	55·3	9·1	85·2	10·3	99·4	10·7
Low (n = 63)	54·3	17·3	83·1	19·2	94·9	21·1
Totals (n = 836)	62·0	18·7	80·2	17·9	92·8	18·5
	P = 0·000005		P = 0·0002		P = 0·0331	

	M.S.	D.F.	F	M.S.	D.F.	F	M.S.	D.F.	F
Groups	1415·86	14	4·25	920·07	14	2·96	613·21	14	1·81
Error	333·39	821		310·70	821		338·71	821	

In all, we have some definite implications for the consideration of religion in our planning of social and educational institutions. The subjects studied in the analysis reported here had all studied psychology and were well towards the end of a programme of professional education in teaching,

yet their thinking about the behaviour of others
was determined to a very significant degree by
their childhood learning of categories and beliefs
and by their continuing religious orientation. If
we are to look towards the application of a scientific analysis of behaviour in, for instance,
educational institutions, these indications merit
careful consideration in terms of their significance in professional education. Further implications may point to questions about how these
community leaders, because of their ways of thinking about human behaviour, promote or hinder the
utilization of the real benefits of a developing
psychology in the areas of judiciary, community
mental health, penal reform, education and child-
rearing.

REFERENCES

Allport, G. W. & Ross, J. M. (1967). Personal re-
    ligious orientation and prejudice. *J. Person.
    soc. Psychol.* 5, 432-443.

Ashcraft, C. (1964). Relationships between reli-
    gious attitudes and perception of others in
    varied environmental settings. (Unpublished
    address, Southeastern Psychological Associa-
    tion, Gatlinburg, Tennessee.)

Bandura, A. (1967). Behavioral psychotherapy.
    Sci. Am. 216, 78-86.

Bandura, A. & Walters, R. H. (1963). *Social Learn-
    ing and Personality Development.* New York:
    Holt, Rinehart & Winston.

Bailey, P. (1960). Modern attitudes toward the
    relationship of the brain to behavior. *Archs
    gen. Psychiat.* 2, 361-378.

Brown, B. S. & Long, S. E. (1968). Psychology and
    community mental health: the medical muddle.
    Am. Psychol. 23, 335-341.

Brown, L. B. (1966). The structure of religious belief. *J. sci. Study Religion* 5, 259-272.

Card, B. Y. (1960). *The Canadian Prairie Provinces from 1870 to 1950: A Sociological Introduction.* Toronto: Dent.

Chapanis, A. (1961). Men, machines and models. *Am. Psychol.* 16, 113-131.

Katz, I. (1967). The socialization of academic motivation in minority group children. In D. Levine (ed.), *Nebraska Symposium on Motivation.* Lincoln, Nebraska: University of Nebraska Press.

Larson, F. L. (1967). Denominational variations in clergymen's attitudes concerning mental health. *Ment. Hyg.* 51, 185-192.

Lenski, G. (1961). *The Religious Factor: A Sociological Study of Religion's Impact on Politics, Economics and Family.* Garden City, N. Y.: Doubleday.

Linsky, A. S. (1965). Religious differences in lay attitudes and knowledge on alcoholism and its treatment. *J. sci. Study Religion* 5, 41-50.

Quinn, J. W. (1965). An investigation of personality and cognitive correlates of religious devoutness. (Unpublished doctoral dissertation, University of Alberta.)

Roe, A. (1952). *The Making of a Scientist.* New York: Mead.

Sarbin, T. R. (1967). On the futility of the proposition that some people be labeled 'mentally ill'. *J. consult. Psychol.* 31, 447-453.

Simon, B. & Weiner, H. (1966). Models of mind and mental illness in Ancient Greece. *J. Hist. behav. Sci.* 2, 303-314.

Stark, R.   (1963).   On the incompatibility of reli-
    gion and science: a survey of American grad-
    uate students.   *J. sci. Study Religion* 3, 3-20.

Szasz, T. S.   (1960).   The myth of mental illness.
    Am. Psychol. 15, 113-118.

Webster, A. C.   (1966).   Patterns and relations of
    dogmatism, mental health and psychological
    health in selected religious groups.   *Diss.
    Abstr.* 27, 41-42.

CAUSAL LOCUS OF ILLNESS AND ADAPTATION TO FAMILY DISRUPTIONS*

CLYDE Z. NUNN
JOHN KOSA
JOEL J. ALPERT

Editor's introduction. Through explanations
for what is sometimes beyond the individual's
control, religion can alleviate anxieties and
rekindle hope, and in this way fulfill its
"integrative" function. The support, solace,
and optimism of religion in the face of the
trials and tribulations of life have been the
subject of numerous sermons, songs, and testimonials. The hope offered by religious belief
systems in times of crisis is often mentioned
in "pragmatic" discussions of their function.
This study by Nunn, Kosa, and Alpert looks at
the integrative effects of religion at the
family level and relates the effects to concepts of illness causation and to characteristics of family crisis.
   Using the terms suggested by Shaw in the study
on religion and conceptual models of behavior,
we may ask to what extent the theological model

*The authors gratefully acknowledge the help-
fulness of the critical reading of the paper by
Nicholas Babchuk and Harry J. Crockett, Jr.

From *Journal for the Scientific Study of
Religion*, 1968, 7, 210-218. Reprinted with
permission.

of illness causation affects the adaptation of
a family in crisis. Nunn, Kosa, and Alpert go
one step beyond Shaw by looking at real-life
situations dealing with crises caused by physical illness. Their hypothesis was that under
special conditions religious beliefs can function as a stabilizing force on personal and
social systems. Their sample was drawn from
an urban hospital population, using criteria
that produced a largely low-income sample of
mothers. These mothers were asked about their
belief in God as a source of illness, the existence of serious illness in their families,
and their resources for meeting crises.

The results show that under the conditions of
heightened psycho-situational stress and limited resources for adaptation, mothers who
located causality of illness in God, in contrast to those who viewed illness as naturally
determined, were more likely to report a marginal adjustment. Mothers who had given naturalistic explanations for the source of illness
were more likely to report either a difficult
or a smooth adjustment to family disruptions
during illness. The results have to be interpreted in the context of an industrialized,
secularized society, in which religious beliefs
are not the main source of life adaptations.
The authors interpret the results to mean that
non-religious responses to disruptions (whether
the adjustments are smooth *or* difficult) are
more reliable, even under strong situational
pressures. At the same time, the religious adaptation is seen by the authors as undependable
and inadequate. The authors seem to be saying:
"When everything else fails, try religion!"

Nunn, Kosa, and Alpert are aware of the main
limitation of their study, which is its reliance on self-report rather than on actual behavior. The nature of their sample should also
caution us against generalizing the interpretations. It is possible that different patterns of
adaptation might emerge at higher socioeconomic
levels.

The relationship of religion and system stability and integration is the concern of this paper.
Specifically, it will focus on the relationship between beliefs (religious vs. nonreligious) about the
sources of illness and difficulty in adapting to the
disrupting circumstance of serious illness in the
family.
     A number of psychologists, anthropologists, and
sociologists have produced an impressive body of
theory and research evidence that consistently and
substantially supports the contention that religion
is tied intimately with system integration.[1] Though
there are differences, such as those between Malinowski and Radcliffe-Brown who argue over whether
religion helps to stabilize the person or the society, there is little disagreement about the fact
that religion has played an important part in the
integration of man's world, at least in his primitive world. Religious belief and practice, it is
claimed, were well-designed to assist primitive
tribesmen's efforts to grapple with personal anxieties or the problem of social solidarity.

[1]See Bronislaw Malinowski, *Magic, Science and
Religion and Other Essays* (Glencoe, Illinois: The
Free Press, 1948); Alfred R. Radcliffe-Brown, *Reli-
gion and Society* (London: Royal Anthropological
Institute of Great Britain and Ireland, 1945); Paul
Radin, *Primitive Religion: Its Nature and Origin*
(New York: The Viking Press, 1937); Clyde Kluck-
hohn, *Navaho Witchcraft* (Cambridge, Mass.: Peabody
Museum, 1944); Emile Durkheim, *The Elementary Forms
of the Religious Life,* translated by Joseph W.
Swain (London: George Allen and Unwin, Ltd., 1915);
E. Franklin Frazier, *The Negro Church in America*
(New York: Schocken Books, 1963); Gordon W. Allport,
The Individual and His Religion (New York: The
Macmillan Co., 1950); John W. M. Whiting and Irwin L.
Child, *Child Training and Personality* (New Haven:
Yale University Press, 1953); Knight Dunlap, *Reli-
gion: Its Functions in Human Life* (New York:
McGraw-Hill, Inc., 1946).

While the stabilizing function of religion in primitive societies seems well-documented, the existence and nature of such effects in modern industrial societies remains an open question for several reasons. Essentially, the question arises in view of enormously heightened rationality, predictability, and non-religious forms of control and adaptation that the modern society commands.[2]

Curiously we find even within the same contemporary society and within a single individual the co-existence of religious and scientific belief systems, each with a quite distinct epistemological base. Illness, for example, has been attributed to both natural and supernatural sources, particularly, but not exclusively by the less educated.[3] Religion remains a prominent feature of modern life, apparently without major conflict with the pervasive system of science.[4]

The explanation for this curious co-existence apparently lies in the fact that while modern society commands a wide range of non-religious sources of adaptation and stabilization, there often remain significant residues of anxiety and uncertainty in such areas as illness, death, and accidents, leading

[2]Milton Yinger specifies some conditions, most evident in industrial societies, under which the social integrative function of religion should be reduced; in *Religion, Society and the Individual* (New York: The Macmillan Co., 1957), pp. 67-69.

[3]In the sample of low-income, urban mothers to be analyzed in the present study, for instance, nearly a fourth thought that "God's Will" was a source of some illness, even though they included in their answers naturalistic sources as well. But consider also the appeal of Christian Science among middle class persons.

[4]Gerhard Lenski found a relatively small percentage of Jews, Protestants, and Catholics who considered the conflict between science and religion a serious one. *The Religious Factor,* (Garden City, N. Y.: Doubleday and Company, 1961), pp. 280-284.

us to suspect that in those areas religious beliefs
continue to function as system stabilizers, allowing
people to cope with conditions otherwise unmanageable.
      Empirical work on the issue in more modern soci-
eties provides some evidence consistent with conclusions drawn from studies of more primitive societies.
In two independent studies, Babchuk, Crockett, and
Ballweg, and Holt suggested that their data indirectly indicated that religion functioned to enhance familial stability and offset disorganizing effects of
cultural shock.[5] Moberg found, in a more direct test,
that religion was associated with personal adjustment
in old age.[6]
      But rather than just additional evidence that re-
ligion is or is not related with stability, it should
be evident by now that advance in our understanding
of the issue depends on exploration of the nature of
the relationship. Especially the question needs to
be raised: *Under what conditions* might religious belief and practices be associated with adaptation and
stability of personal and social systems? It is this
problem of *conditions* of the association that represents the focus of the present paper.
      Since illness and death remain, even in modern
societies, sources of considerable anxiety and suffering without clearcut meaning, stabilizing effects
of religion in modern societies are most likely to
occur in these anxiety-provoking areas. The present
study will limit its attention to the area of illness.
      In addition, the stabilizing effect of religion
is likely to occur particularly when pressures and
strains reach crisis proportions. Rokeach supports

      [5]Nicholas Babchuk, Harry J. Crockett, Jr.,
and John A. Ballweg, "Change in Religious Affiliation and Family Stability," *Social Forces,* 45
(June, 1967) pp. 551-555; John B. Holt, "Holiness
Religion: Cultural Shock and Social Reorganization," *American Sociological Review* (October, 1940)
pp. 740-747.
      [6]David O. Moberg, "The Christian Religion and
Personal Adjustment in Old Age," *American Sociological Review,* 18 (February, 1953) pp. 87-90.

such a contention in his conclusion that particular belief-disbelief systems are activated only as a result of relevant situational forces.[7] We can expect then that: *The association between religious beliefs and system stability will be most likely to occur under conditions of greatest situational stress.*

Another expectation is based on the supposition that the stabilizing effect of religious beliefs is likely to be residual in nature. That is, religion will tend to function as a stabilizer of personal and social systems when other means have been expended or are not accessible. Both Yinger and Dunlap have arrived at this theoretical position.[8] Yinger makes the point lucidly in his statement that "...religion can be thought of as a kind of residual means of response and adjustment. It is an attempt to explain what cannot otherwise be explained; to achieve power, all other powers having failed us; to establish poise and serenity in the face of evil and suffering that other efforts have failed to eliminate."[9] From these theoretical leads, we predict: *The association between religious beliefs and system stability will be most likely to occur under conditions of limited resources for adaptation.*

PROCEDURE

Sample

The data for the present study came from a larger longitudinal study done in the Boston area,[10] which selected for interview all patient families

[7]Milton Rokeach, *The Open and Closed Mind,* (New York: Basic Books, Inc., 1960), p. 402.
[8]J. Milton Yinger, *op. cit.,* pp. 9-10. Knight Dunlap, *op. cit.,* p. 321.
[9]Yinger, *op. cit.,* p. 10.
[10]This paper was developed in the course of a more extensive research project supported by grants from the Commonwealth Fund and the United States Children's Bureau (Grant No. H-74) to the Medical

coming as new cases to the Emergency Clinic at the
Children's Hospital Medical Center over a period
of twenty-four weeks. From this initial intake
sample of more than 4300, a study sample was composed of those who (a) lived within a radius of
three miles from the hospital, (b) had no family
physician or pediatrician and did not participate
in certain special clinical programs of the hospital, (c) were medically indigent, and (d) intended
to remain in the area for at least three years.
810 were eligible for the sample determined by these
criteria. The data used for the present analysis
came from 540 respondents who had been randomly
assigned to control or experimental groups and had
completed a structured interview containing the information for present analyses.

For purposes here, we made two additional qual-
ifications, namely including: (1) only mothers
(which excluded only eight of the respondents); and,
(2) only those with family incomes of $6,000 or less
(most were definitely less). The remaining 436 made
up our present sample, of which only 20 per cent reported family incomes as high as $4,500-$6,000.

The sample then is one of low-income, and relatively geographically stable respondents who use
emergency clinics.

Major Variables

Belief in God as a source of illness was measured with a question which asked the respondents
to indicate which of several sources they considered
determinants of illness. Two categories were derived; those who included "God's Will" as well as
naturalistic sources and those who indicated only

Care Research Unit, Family Health Care Program,
Harvard Medical School. The authors gratefully
acknowledge the contribution of Robert J. Haggarty,
M. D. (University of Rochester School of Medicine)
in planning and implementing the research.

naturalistic sources, (germs, diet, work, worry, getting tired, draft-chills, and heredity) as the causal locus of illnesses.

Stability, or adaptation, was measured with the following question: "When there is serious illness in the family, how difficult is it for you to take the situation in hand and do what needs to be done?" Five response alternatives were provided. Those who indicated that it was "very difficult" or "somewhat difficult" were combined for our purposes and regarded as reporting "difficult adaptation." Those who indicated that it was "difficult, but I seem to be learning how to handle it," were clas- sified as making a "marginal adaptation." Those who said that it was "not difficult" or "not diffi- cult at all" were combined and classified as "not difficult adaptation." It is assumed that a con- tinuum is indicated by these categories, though it is not necessarily the case that the intervals are equidistant.[11]

[11]There were several reasons for assuming this variable represented a continuum. First, the cate- gories of this question were arranged in the ques- tionnaire, as were many questions preceding it, in a manner intending to represent a continuum to the respondent. While not certain as to how the re- spondent might have interpreted the categories, in- dependent judges who were not informed as to the investigators' interpretation without exception saw the categories as a continuum. Second, in a cross- tabulation of this variable with a separate indi- cator of stability which had categories more clear- ly representing a continuum ("Your marriage has been: very smooth, smooth, frequently upset, al- ways upset."), there was a linear association be- tween the two. Those who had "marginal adaptations" on the first indicator also clustered between the two extremes of the second indicator, suggesting that "marginal adaptation" is properly placed as an in-between category.

Conditions

Psycho-situational stress was measured with
two items:

Existence of serious illness
    Thinking back over the last five years, have
    any of the following problems come up in your
    family?

If the respondent said either "serious illness,"
"long-term hospitalization," or "death," he was
classified as having serious illness in the family.
All those not reporting the presence of these
medically-related problems, even though indicating
other kinds of problems, were classified as not
reporting serious illness.

Perceived amount of family illness relative to others
    When thinking about other families, would you
    say that your family has had more or less
    illness?

Three alternatives were presented: more illness
than others, the same, or less illness than others.
The same three categories were used in the present
analysis.
    Resources that are believed to facilitate or
inhibit the coping process in the family were indicated by the mother's education, acceptance-rejection of the maternal role, and general optimism-
pessimism. The attitude measures relied for the
most part on the summated scale procedure.

Acceptance-Rejection of Maternal Role[12]

(a) Having to be with the children all the
     time gives a woman the feeling her wings
     have been clipped.

[12]This scale was developed and validated by

(b)   Most young mothers are bothered more by
      the feeling of being shut up in the home
      than anything else.
(c)   One of the worst things about taking care
      of a home is a woman feels that she can't
      get out.

Five response categories ranging from "strongly agree" to "strongly disagree" were included for
each item. A summing of the values (1 to 5) of the
categories checked by the respondent indicated her
score. The higher the numerical score on the
summated scale, the greater the acceptance of the
maternal role. Due to the size of the sample, we
dichotomized the distribution on the scale at the
median, calling those with scores of five or more
acceptors of the maternal role and those with scores
less than five as rejectors of the maternal role.

Optimism-Pessimism[13]

(a)   There is no reason to anticipate trouble
      or worry about what may never happen.
(b)   Nothing is impossible to a willing heart.
(c)   It's easy to get what one wants out of
      life.

The same procedures as above were followed in
scoring and dichotomizing.
Neither measure of the stress variable was
found to be associated with any of the limited re-
source indicators, thus, seemingly measuring different phenomena.

Earl S. Schaefer and Richard Q. Bell, "Developing
a Parental Attitude Research Instrument," *Child
Development*, 29 (September, 1958), pp. 339-361.
      [13]Formulated after Henry Murray, *Explorations
in Personality,* (New York: Oxford University Press,
1938), pp. 48-49.

FINDINGS

Relation of Belief and Stability

Previous research and theory suggests that we might find a direct relationship between our measures of religious attribution of illness and of stability. The tendency we found was curvilinear, rather than linear, but the relationship was not statistically significant.
Our analysis turned to the predicted interaction of this relationship with our specified conditions.

Effect of Stress Condition

We expected that the association between causal locus of illness and adaptation should be evident particularly when there are strong psycho-situational forces that would heighten the probability that adaptive problems would be maximized. We find in Table 1 that when a serious illness has been reported in the family in the past five years, the curvilinear relationship between the major variables becomes statistically significant. Among those who consider God a source of illness, 54 per cent, in contrast to 38

TABLE 1

BELIEF IN GOD AS A SOURCE OF ILLNESS AND ADAPTATION TO DISRUPTIONS IN THE FAMILY DURING SERIOUS ILLNESS, BY EXISTENCE OF SERIOUS ILLNESS IN THE FAMILY IN THE PAST FIVE YEARS.

Serious Illness in the Family	God is a Source of Illness	Adaptation to Disruptions			
		Difficult	Marginal	Not Difficult	(N)
Yes	Yes	23%	54%	23%	(44)
	No	19	38	43	(167)
		$X^2 = 6.30$	$p < .05$		
No	Yes	12	37	51	(43)
	No	20	34	46	(181)
		$X^2 = 1.72$	$p < .50$		

per cent of those who do not hold this view, report a "marginal adaptation" ("difficult but seem to be learning to handle it"). Non-believers in God as a source of illness cluster predominantly in the "not

difficult" category. Differences between believers
and non-believers are small but reversed among those
who deem adaptation difficult. For those who report
no serious illness in the family, there is clearly
no association found between causal locus of illness
and adaptation to disruptions, as expected.

A second test of this prediction includes a
more subjective variable, the perceived amount of
illness in the family relative to other families.
We assume that if a mother perceives her family to
be burdened with an inequitable share of illness,
she should feel a heightened sense of urgency and
desire for adaptive mechanisms. Thus, the expected
relationship between causal locus of illness and
adaptation to disruptions should once again be most
observable when the mother perceives her family to
have more illness than other families.

While the number of cases is small among those
mothers who feel their family has more illness than
other families, Table 2 shows significant differences in this group between those who believe God to
be a source of illness and those who do not.

TABLE 2

BELIEF IN GOD AS A SOURCE OF ILLNESS AND ADAPTATION TO DISRUPTIONS IN THE FAMILY DURING
SERIOUS ILLNESS, BY PERCEIVED AMOUNT OF ILLNESS IN FAMILY RELATIVE TO OTHERS.

Relative Amount of Illness	God is a Source of Illness	Adaptation to Disruptions			
		Difficult	Marginal	Not Difficult	(N)
More Illness	Yes	7%	64%	29%	(14)
	No	17	30	52	(46)
		$X^2 = 6.44$	$p < .05$		
About Same	Yes	17	50	33	(46)
	No	20	38	42	(143)
		$X^2 = 1.92$	$p < .40$		
Less Illness	Yes	21	32	46	(28)
	No	20	36	44	(152)
		$X^3 = .12$	$p < .95$		

The curvilinear relationship remains among
those who consider their families have equal amounts
of illness, but it fails to achieve statistical
significance. The association entirely disappears
among those mothers who perceive their families have
the good fortune of having less illness than others.

Effect of Perceived Resources

Education of mother. We predicted that the association between causal locus of illness and adaptation to disruptions will be particularly marked when the mother is limited in resources that would be useful in the coping process. The first of these resources under consideration is the educational attainment of the mother, and these data are presented in Table 3.

TABLE 3

BELIEF IN GOD AS A SOURCE OF ILLNESS AND ADAPTATION TO DISRUPTIONS IN THE FAMILY DURING SERIOUS ILLNESS, BY MOTHER'S EDUCATION.

Mother's Education	God is a Source of Illness	Adaptation to Disruptions			
		Difficult	*Marginal*	*Not Difficult*	*(N)*
Grade School or Less	Yes	7%	73%	20%	(15)
	No	20	44	36	(50)
		$X^2 = 4.60$	$p < .10$		
High School Grad. or Some High School	Yes	18	41	41	(71)
	No	20	35	45	(295)
		$X^2 = 1.23$	$p < .60$		

Again, while the number of cases is relatively small, the curvilinear association is definitely present among poorly educated mothers and fails to materialize when the mothers have more than a grade school education.

Acceptance of maternal role. The second indicator of limited resources for adaptation is the extent to which the mother accepts or rejects her maternal role, assuming that her performance in the role would be markedly enhanced by the acceptance of that role. In Table 4 we find that among those mothers who reject their maternal role, and only among them, the curvilinear pattern is clearly present.

Optimism. Finally, we submit that general pessimism-optimism toward life should be another relevant indicator of resourcefulness among mothers who face the problems inherent in serious illness in the family. Indeed, pessimism-optimism is likely

to be a more inclusive measure of an accumulation
of several resources or the lack of them. We find
in the data of Table 5 that those mothers who express a generally pessimistic view of life and who

TABLE 4

BELIEF IN GOD AS A SOURCE OF ILLNESS AND ADAPTATION TO DISRUPTION IN THE FAMILY DURING
SERIOUS ILLNESS, BY ACCEPTANCE-REJECTION OF MATERNAL ROLE.

Acceptance-Rejection of Maternal Role	God is a Source of Illness	Adaptation to Disruptions			
		Difficult	Marginal	Not Difficult	(N)
Reject	Yes	15%	59%	26%	(34)
	No	20	33	47	(160)
		$X^2 = 9.05$	$p < .01$		
Accept	Yes	17	40	43	(53)
	No	20	38	42	(187)
		$X^2 = .19$	$p < .95$		

believe God to be responsible for illness are more
likely to fall in the intermediate category, whereas those pessimistic mothers who do not hold such
beliefs tend to report adapting to these disruptions without difficulty. Once again the curvilinear pattern persists. Among the more optimistic
mothers, as we expected, the association between
causal locus of illness and adaptation is virtually
non-existent.

TABLE 5

BELIEF IN GOD AS A SOURCE OF ILLNESS AND ADAPTATION TO DISRUPTIONS IN THE FAMILY DURING
SERIOUS ILLNESS, BY OPTIMISM-PESSIMISM.

Optimism-Pessimism	God is a Source of Illness	Adaptation to Disruptions			
		Difficult	Marginal	Not Difficult	(N)
Pessimistic	Yes	20%	51%	29%	(41)
	No	22	31	47	(165)
		$X^2 = 6.98$	$p < .05$		
Optimistic	Yes	13	44	43	(46)
	No	18	40	41	(181)
		$X^2 = 3.17$	$p < .30$		

DISCUSSION

Reviewing our evidence, it is apparent that
in order for a relationship between religious belief and system stability to appear, some specific
conditions need to be present. To say merely that
religious belief is related to system integration
or stabilization in an industrial society over-
simplifies the matter. The evidence in confirming
Yinger and Dunlap's predictions, with some modifications, reveals the nature of religious effect
on stability to be contingent on both residual and
temporal conditions.[14]
We saw in the data the consistency with which
these conditions produced almost no variation in
adaptation response among those who did not believe
God to be a source of illness; while under the predicted conditions, those who did attribute causal
powers to God were significantly more likely to
report "marginal adaptation" rather than "difficult" or "not difficult" adaptation. Does this
unaltered pattern among the non-believers attest
to the reliability of non-religious responses to
disrupting circumstance, even under conditions of
limited resources and pressing situational demands?
It would appear so from our data. On the other
hand, the data on those who located causality in
God convincingly portrayed their mode of adaptation
as something less than a dependable and adequate
recourse to meet episodes without difficulty. In
fact, the evidence suggests that the religious
effect on personal and social stability appears to
be that of encouraging what might be called "religious brinkmanship" in the coping process. That
is, belief in God as a source of illness functions
to assist the person in maintaining a *marginal*

[14]Previous research has also underscored the
residual nature of religious beliefs in power-
enhancing attempts by parents; see Clyde Z. Nunn,
"Child-Control through a 'Coalition with God',"
Child Development, 35 (1964), pp. 417-432.

level of difficulty during especially trying times
rather than some less difficult stability or a
more unmanageable attempt at adaptation.

These findings question the contention that
religious beliefs have a pervasive integrating and
stabilizing effect in the industrial society, at
least as we have measured these variables. Other
measures might not produce similar results, especially (1) measures of adaptation or stability that
depend on other than self-report data (It is conceivable, for instance, that the present results
reflect differential claim at coping, rather than
actual differential ability at coping.); (2) other
and less specific definitions of religious belief;
and (3) measures of stability in a larger social
unit than the family.

Another question that deserves further attention is to what extent the stabilizing effect of
religious beliefs represents only a temporary effect
or can include a more sustained effect as well.
Perhaps the more ephemeral effects are tied to the
more specialized religious belief (such as we have
measured) and the long-term effects more closely
associated with general religious commitments.

Future research might also find our results
instructive in formulating adequate indicators of
the major dependent variable, personal or social
stability. Allowance for an intermediate category,
particularly in view of the results attained,
suggests that use of a dichotomous variable might
not adequately indicate what in fact may be the
most likely religious effect, marginal stability
rather than presence or absence of stability.

MENTAL STATUS AND RELIGIOUS BEHAVIOR

JACOB J. LINDENTHAL
JEROME K. MYERS
MAX P. PEPPER
MAXINE S. STERN

Editor's introduction. The major contribution
of the following study is in showing that religious activities are closely tied to the individual's ability to maintain interpersonal
contact. Since interpersonal contact is a
crucial aspect of institutional religious activity, psychological impairment is likely to
lead to a reduction in "public" religious behavior. At the same time, it is likely to increase "private" religious activity. The
study measured the relationship between impaired psychological functioning and two measures of religious activity. The two measures
were institutional participation and private
prayer, and the sample included 938 urban
adults. The measure of psychopathology (a list
of twenty psychiatric symptoms) was found to be
negatively correlated with church affiliation,

The research upon which this paper is based
was supported by PHS Contract No. 43-67-743 and
Research Grant MH 15522, National Institute of Mental Health, Public Health Service, Department of
Health, Education and Welfare.

From *Journal for the Scientific Study of Religion,* 1970, 9, 143-149. Reprinted with permission.

with church attendance, and with increased
church attendance at times of life crises.
At the same time, the measure of psychopathology was positively correlated with reported
prayer at times of life crisis.
  The differentiation between institutional and
private religious activities is related to differences in the psychological functions of the
activities. Participation in the more "extrinsic," institutional activities satisfies social
needs, in addition to being an expression of
religious beliefs. Prayer can be seen as the
more "intrinsic" form of religious activity and
may express the need for personal support. As
the data here show, psychological impairment is
related to the use of a more personal, internalized kind of religious behavior. Those who
pray in times of crisis are not only the "true
believers" but those most in need of personal
support.

  Introduction. This paper reports on relationships between mental impairment and two aspects of religious behavior--institutional participation and prayer. Most research on the relationship between psychopathology and religious behavior[1]

[1]In a research note, R. Hugh Burns and Aubrey
Daniels, in "Religious Attitudes among Psychiatric
Patients and Normals," *Journal for the Scientific
Study of Religion* 8, no. 1 (Spring 1969): 165,
discussed differences in church attendance and religious outlook between a patient and a nonpatient
population. See also Irving E. Bender, "A Longitudinal Study of Church Attenders and Nonattenders,"
ibid. 7, no. 2 (1968): 230-37; George W. Bohrn-
stedt, Edgar F. Borgatta, et al., "Religious Affiliation, Religiosity and MMPI Scores," ibid.: 255-
58; Richard E. Carney and Wilbert J. McKeachie,
"Religion, Sex, Social Class, Probability of Success
and Student Personality," ibid. 3, no. 1 (1963):

has not made this distinction between the external or social aspects of religious behavior and its internalized dimension. Although these dimensions of religious behavior are not independent, the rewards of institutional religious behavior are probably different from those of prayer. Therefore, persons whose needs are primarily social or external may partake in the institutional aspects of religious life, largely ignoring or only secondarily appreciating the internal aspects of religious belief; and those who look to religion for help in maintaining psychological stability may turn to prayer and other private behavior, but not partake in the organized aspects of the faith.

This study also investigates *changes* in religious behavior in response to crises or life events during the year preceding the interview. Therefore, the data presented in this paper deal with two issues: general institutional aspects of religious behavior[2] and changes in the institutional aspects of religious behavior and prayer at a time of crisis. The specific hypotheses are:

1) The greater the degree of psychological impairment of the respondent, the less likely he will partake in the institutional aspects of religious behavior, as measured by church affiliation and frequency of attendance at religious services.

2) In response to particular life events or crises: (a) The greater the degree of psychological

---

32-42; Andrew M. Greeley, "The Religious Behavior of Graduate Students," ibid. 5, no. 1 (1965): 34-40; Jacob Jay Lindenthal, "The Delayed Decision to Enter the Ministry: A study in Occupational Change" (doctoral diss., Yale University, 1967); Rodney Stark, "On the Incompatibility of Religion and Science: A Survey of American Graduate Students," *Journal for the Scientific Study of Religion* 3, no. 1 (1963): 3-20.
    [2]The respondents were not asked whether they prayed in general, only whether they prayed for help at the time of each crisis.

impairment, the more likely that his church attendance will decrease at the time of crisis; (b) The
greater the degree of psychological impairment, the
more likely that he will pray at the time of crisis.

METHOD

Sample

The data are part of a longitudinal study ex-
amining changes in health status and role performance in reaction to life crises. The sample consisted of one adult (18 years of age or over)
selected at random from each of 938 households in
a systematic sample of a mental health catchment
area (of approximately 72,000 population) in metropolitan New Haven. The area includes a changing
inner city section of 22,000 and a more stable industrial town of 50,000. It represents a cross-
section of the community's population and includes
all ethnic, racial, and socioeconomic groups. Between July 1967 and January 1968, a total of 1,095
individuals were contacted in person. Of these,
11.9 percent refused to be interviewed, 2.5 percent
were never home to be contacted, while 85.7 percent
(938) were interviewed. The sample is being re-
interviewed in 1969-1970, two years after the
original study.

Measures of Psychopathology

Although a comprehensive evaluation of mental
status requires an intensive clinical examination
in which a composite assessment is made of the individual's behavior, thought, and emotional processes, recent studies have demonstrated that short
devices may be employed as an alternative to this
clinical evaluation.[3] The index of mental status

[3]See, e.g., Leo Srole et al., *Mental Health
in the Metropolis* (New York: Mc-Graw-Hill, 1962),

developed by MacMillan[4] and modified by Gurin and
associates[5] utilizes a list of twenty psychiatric
symptoms. It has been found to discriminate between schizophrenics and nonschizophrenics and
between mental patients and persons not in treatment. There are also high correlations between
classification on this index and classification on
the basis of more intensive examination by
clinicians.[6]
Examples of the questions: Do you ever feel
that you are bothered by all sorts of pains or
ailments in different parts of your body? Do you
ever have trouble in getting to sleep or staying
asleep? Are you ever bothered by nervousness
(feeling fidgety, irritable, tense)?
A response of "often" is scored 1; "sometimes,"
2; "hardly ever," 3; "never," 4. Scores range from
20 (maximum impairment) to 80 (total absence of

---

esp. chap. 4 and appendices E and F; Derek L.
Phillips, "The 'True Prevalence' of Mental Illness
in a New England State," *Community Mental Health
Journal* 2 (1966):   35; Lloyd H. Rogler and A. B.
Hollingshead, *Trapped: Families and Schizophrenia*
(New York: Wiley, 1965), pp. 22-27; and Jerome G.
Manis, Milton J. Brawer, Chester L. Hunt, and
Leonard C. Kercher, "Validating a Mental Health
Scale," *American Sociological Review* 28 (1963):
108.
[4]Allister M. MacMillan, "The Health Opinion
Survey: Technique for Estimating Prevalence of
Psychoneurotic and Related Types of Disorder in
Communities," *Psychological Reports* 3 (1957):   325;
and D. C. Leighton et al., *The Character of Danger*
(New York: Basic Books, 1963).
[5]Gerald Gurin, Joseph Veroff, and Sheila Feld,
*Americans View their Mental Health: A Nationwide
Survey* (New York: Basic Books, 1960), pp. 175-205.
[6]See, e.g., Leighton et al., *The Character of
Danger;* Srole et al., *Mental Health;* and Manis et
al., "Validating a Mental Health Scale."

symptoms). Previous research indicates that relatively low scores identify individuals with major
psychological problems, and that the individual
scores may be grouped into larger categories.[7]
Those scoring 66 and lower (18 percent of our sample) are classified as "very impaired psychologically"; those scoring between 67 and 76 (47 percent
of our sample) as "moderately impaired"; and those
scoring 77 and above (35 percent of our sample) as
"unimpaired."

Measures of Institutional Religious Behavior

The institutional aspects of religious behavior
were measured with two questions: Are you affiliated with any church or religious group? About how
often do you usually attend religious services?

Life Events and Measures of Religious Behavior

A crucial aspect of our larger study is an
effort to ascertain the behavioral response of individuals to given crises or life events, that is,
any event which has the potential for disturbing
the individual's social-psychological equilibrium.
Such crises or events include experiences involving a role transformation, change in status or
environment, and/or the imposition of pain. Each
respondent was asked if any of a series of 62
events had happened to him or to anyone within his

---

[7]See, e.g., Srole et al., *Mental Health;* and
Manis et al., "Validating a Mental Health Scale."
Scores of 66 or lower indicate a significant
number of psychiatric symptoms and are considered
to represent "impaired" mental status in our research. This grouping of scores follows the
procedure of Elton F. Jackson, "Status Consistency
and Symptoms of Stress," *American Sociological
Review* 27 (1962): 469-80.

social field during the past year.[8] These events
ranged from a move, a child starting school, marriage, and loss of a job, to divorce, serious illness, and the death of a loved one. Data were
collected regarding changes in many aspects of daily
life in relation to these crises, but in this paper
we will discuss only those associated with religious behavior--any change in his previously reported church attendance and if he turned to prayer
in order to cope with the problem. The exact questions follow: When (specific event) occurred, was
there any change in your church attendance? When
(specific event) occurred, did you pray for help
in meeting crisis?

In the year preceding our interview, 80 percent
(753) of the respondents experienced at least one
life crisis, and many experienced several for a
total of 2,186 events.

RESULTS

*Psychological Impairment and Institutional
Aspects of Religious Behavior*

It is clear that the more severely one is impaired, the *less* likely he is to be affiliated with
a church and to attend church frequently. (See
Table 1.)

The data were further analyzed to determine
whether social class, sex, marital status, age, race,
or religion accounted for the relationship found

[8]This list of events was based upon selected
items developed by Aaron Antonovsky and Rachel Kats,
"The Life Crisis History as a Tool in Epidemiological
Research," *Journal of Health and Social Behavior* 8
(March 1967): 15-21; Richard H. Rahe, M. Meyer, M.
Smith, G. Kjaer, and T. H. Holmes, "Social Stress
and Illness Onset," *Journal of Psychosomatic Research* 8 (1964): 35-48; and an array of other items
developed by ourselves.

between mental status and church participation.
When these cross-controls were applied, the same
basic relationship was found: among the more psychologically impaired, the smaller proportion of
respondents belong to a church and attend regularly.[9]

TABLE 1. Relationships (in Percent) between Psychological Impairment,
Church Affiliation, and Frequent Church Attendance

	Unimpaired	Moderately impaired	Very impaired
Church affiliation	78	70	62
Frequent church attenders (more than once a month)	61	53	37
Affiliated with a church, and attend church frequently	70	65	56
Not affiliated with a church, and attend church frequently	38	30	9

[9]The control factors were divided into the following
categories: *social class:* I-II, III, IV, V; *sex:*
male, female; *marital status:* single, married, separated or divorced, widowed; *age:* less than 30, 30-
39, 40-49, 50-59, 60-69, 70 and over; *race:* Negro,
white; and *religion:* Catholic, Protestant, Jewish.
Within each of the above 21 categories, analyses
were made for the relationship between degree of impairment and both church affiliation and church attendance. In 17 of the 21 categories the relationships
were similar to the ones found before controlling:
the more impaired, the lower the proportion of persons affiliated with a church and attending church
regularly. In one age category, 60-69, essentially
no differences were found between religious behavior
and degree of impairment.
    Among Negroes, Class I-II persons and Jews, as
among all groups, the very impaired were less likely
than the unimpaired to belong to a church and to
attend frequently. However, moderately impaired
Negroes and Class I-II individuals had a higher proportion of church affiliation and attendance than
the unimpaired, while the moderately impaired Jews
had lower proportions than the very impaired.

The relationship between psychological impairment and church affiliation and attendance resembles the relationship between psychological impairment and participation in organized community activities in general. For example, 49 percent of "unimpaired" persons in our study belong to some social organization or club other than a church or church organization, whereas only 34 percent of the "very impaired" had such an affiliation. Thus the greater the degree of psychological impairment, the greater the tendency for the individual to isolate himself from organized social activities of any type, including religious ones.

Changes in Religious Behavior in Response to Life Events

Church attendance. Among the 753 respondents who experienced any one of the 62 life events, changes in church attendance were related significantly to the degree of psychological stability; the more impaired the individual, the more likely he was to attend church even less frequently than before. (See first line of Table 2.) Regardless of the number of events or the type of event experienced by the respondent in the course of the year, this same general relationship held.

TABLE 2. Percentage Who Decreased Church Attendance in Response to Life Events*

	Unimpaired	Moderately impaired	Very impaired
All respondents	4	11	20
Frequent church attenders (more than once a month)	5	16	33
Infrequent church attenders (once a month or less)	3	6	12

*Respondents may have experienced more than one event. But those counted here report at least one decrease in the frequency of church attendance and never an increase.

Reported change in attendance, in response to crisis, was related with initial frequency of

attendance. (Compare second and third lines of
Table 2.) Thus, the pattern noted previously in
Table 1 of infrequent attendance being more common
among the very impaired seemed to be maintained and
exaggerated in time of crisis.

Prayer. A far larger number of people report
prayer in response to at least one event than report
change in church attendance. (See Table 3.) The
greater the impairment, the more likely that the
person prayed in response to that event.

**TABLE 3. Relationships between Psychological Impairment and Prayer
in Response to Types of Events.**

	Unimpaired		Moderately impaired		Very impaired	
	Percent	Number	Percent	Number	Percent	Number
Any event*	31	223	46	352	58	141
Catastrophic	52	81	53	152	64	72
Legal	11	9	33	24	63	27
Financial	28	40	39	101	59	58
Health	42	94	48	179	55	80
Job	20	65	38	146	50	66
Marriage	10	40	32	88	50	40
Interpersonal	23	13	33	30	48	31
Family	21	103	32	163	46	67
Education	14	57	29	107	35	51
Relocation	17	46	19	69	28	32

*Respondents may experience more than one event. They report that they have prayed for help in
meeting at least one event.

Table 3 shows the reported prayer in response
to different categories of events.[10] Mental status

[10]The ten categories and the specific events
within each are as follows: *education-related
events:* started in school, graduated from school,
failed school, changed school, problems in school;
relocation: moved to same type of neighborhood,
moved to better neighborhood, moved to worse neighborhood, built a new house; *marriage related:* engaged, married, divorced, separated, intermarried,
major change in relationship with spouse; *catas-*

was least important in determining the likelihood
of prayer in response to three types of events:
catastrophic, health, and relocation events.
    In the remaining categories of events--marriage,
interpersonal, family, legal, education, and job--
there is generally a direct relationship between psychological impairment and prayer: the greater the
impairment the higher the proportion who pray.

    SUMMARY

    As psychological impairment increases, partic-
ipation in organized religious activity decreases.
In time of crisis the same pattern is found: church
attendance is even less for a larger proportion of

---

trophic: widowed, divorced, separated, serious
physical illness, serious injury or accident, death
of a loved one, detention in jail or other correc-
tional institution; *family:* engaged, married, family member entered armed forces, birth of child,
birth of first child, adoption of child, new persons
moved into household, member of family left home,
change in number of family get-togethers, pregnancy;
interpersonal: major changes in relationship with
friends; *health:* birth of child, birth of first
child, serious physical illness, serious injury or
accident, pregnancy, stillbirth, frequent minor illness, mental illness; *work:* started to work for the
first time, changed to same type job, promoted or
moved to responsible job, demoted or changed to less
responsible job, laid off (temporarily), expanded
business, business failed, trouble with boss, trou-
bles at work, out of work over a month, fired, any
big reorganization at work, retirement, success at
work; *financial:* laid off (temporarily), business
failed, out of work over a month, improvement in
financial status, financial status a lot worse,
foreclosure of mortgage or loan; *legality:* been in
court, detention in jail, being arrested, law suit
or legal action, loss of driver's license.

the "very impaired" than for the "moderately impaired" and the "unimpaired." The mentally impaired
do not seem to use the religious institution to cope
with reality, as commonly believed, nor do they turn
to its organized activities for help in times of
crisis.

In contrast, the degree of psychological impairment is related directly to the more personal
or internalized dimension of religious behavior.
In time of crisis, the more impaired the individual,
the more likely he is to turn to prayer even though
his church attendance becomes less frequent.

The relationship between type of life crisis,
degree of impairment, and prayer support the general
pattern we have found. All persons are more likely
to turn to prayer for events over which they have
little personal control, such as health and catastrophic problems, than for those situations where
there is a greater degree of control. Moreover,
differences in the proportion of persons who pray
by degree of impairment are not as great for these
health and catastrophic events as for most other
types. For those social and environmental situations
over which persons have more control, the increases
in the proportion of persons who pray are substantial
as psychological impairment becomes more severe.
Thus the subjective or internal aspect of religion
does seem to serve a function for the mentally impaired during a time of crisis. When problems arise,
the impaired are more likely to turn inward and seek
help from a divine being through personal prayer.

SELECTED ADDITIONAL READINGS ON RELIGIOUS BELIEFS AND PERSONAL ADJUSTMENT

Amir, M.   Criminality among Jews: An overview.
    Issues in Criminology, 1971, 6, 1-39.

Gannon, T. M.   Religious control and delinquent
    behavior.   In M. Wolfgang (Ed.), *The Sociology
    of Crime and Delinquency.* New York: Wiley,
    1970.

Glenn, N. D., & Hyland, R.   Religious preference and
    worldly success: Some evidence from national
    surveys.   *American Sociological Review,* 1967,
    32, 73-85.

Greeley, A. M.   The influence of the 'religious
    factor' on career plans and occupational val-
    ues of college graduates.   *American Journal of
    Sociology,* 1963, 68, 658-671.

Jackson, E. F., Fox, W. S., & Crockett, H. J.   Reli-
    gion and occupational achievement. *American
    Sociological Review,* 1970, 35, 48-63.

Kosa, J., & Rachiele, L. D.   The spirit of capital-
    ism, traditionalism, and religiousness: A re-
    examination of Weber's concepts.   *Sociological
    Quarterly,* 1963, 4, 243-260.

Knudten, R. D., & Knudten, M. S.   Juvenile delin-
    quency, crime, and religion.   *Review of Reli-
    gious Research,* 1971, 12, 130-152.

Marino, C. Cross-national comparisons of Catholic-Protestant creativity differences. *British Journal of Social and Clinical Psychology,* 1971, 10, 132-137.

Martin, D., & Wrightsman, L. S., Jr. The relationship between religious behavior and concern about death. *Journal of Social Psychology,* 1965, 65, 317-323.

Orbach, H. L. Aging and religion: A study of church attendance in the Detroit metropolitan area. *Geriatrics,* 1961, 16, 530-540.

Rhodes, A. L., & Nam, C. B. The religious context of educational expectations. *American Sociological Review,* 1970, 35, 253-267.

Rhodes, A. L., & Reiss, A. J. Jr. The "religious factor" and delinquent behavior. *Journal of Research in Crime and Delinquency,* 1970, 7, 83-98.

Sanua, V. D. Religion, mental health and personality: A review of empirical studies. *American Journal of Psychiatry,* 1969, 125, 1203-1213.

Skolnik, J. H. Religious affiliation and drinking behavior. *Quarterly Journal of Studies in Alcoholism,* 1958, 19, 452-470.

Slater, M. K. My son the doctor: Aspects of mobility among American Jews. *American Sociological Review,* 1969, 34, 359-373.

Srole, L., & Langner, T. Religious origins. In Srole, L., Langner, T., Michael, S. T., Opler, M. K., & Rennie, T. A. C. *Mental Health in the Metropolis: Midtown Manhattan Study.* Vol. I. New York: McGraw-Hill, 1962.

Stark, R. Psychopathology and religious commitment. *Review of Religious Research,* 1971, 12, 165-176.

Veroff, J., Feld, S., & Gurin, G.   Achievement
    motivation and religious background. *Amer-
    ican Sociological Review,* 1962, 27, 205-217.

Walberg, H. M.   Religious differences in cognitive
    association and self-concept in prospective
    teachers. *Journal of Social Psychology,* 1967,
    73, 89-96.

Williams, R. L., & Cole, S.   Religiosity, gener-
    alized anxiety and apprehension concerning
    death. *Journal of Social Psychology,* 1968, 75,
    111-117.

PART FOUR

INTENSE RELIGIOUS EXPERIENCE

"POSSESSION" IN A REVIVALISTIC NEGRO CHURCH[1]

ALEXANDER ALLAND, JR.

Editor's introduction. Those experiences in
which the individual goes through intense and
sudden changes as a result of, and in the context of, religious motivations have long been
a source of interest and speculation. The
seeming universality of intense states of religious excitement, despite the variety in
their manifestations, is partly responsible
for our fascination with them and our desire to
explore them. Psychologists of religion, ever
since the days of James and Starbuck, have made
the understanding of conversion and mystical
experiences the focal point of their efforts to
study religious behavior. Some of the approaches to the study of intense religious behavior have emphasized the pathological and the

[1]The research on which this paper is based was
carried out in connection with a course in anthropological field methods under Clellan Ford in the
Department of Anthropology in Yale University during
the academic year 1959-60.

From the *Journal for the Scientific Study of
Religion,* 1962, 1, 204-213. Reprinted with
permission.

sensational, reflecting popular conceptions of
"holy rollers."

The articles presented in this section, by
Alland, Hine, and Allison, approach intense
religious behavior in a non-pathological, non-
sensational context. These articles were selected to illustrate the idea that both individual and social determinants play a part in
the formation of intense religious experiences
and that the authentication of any religious
activity, even the most esoteric, is always
social and communal.

The "trance" phenomenon, which includes
"possession" and glossolalia ("speaking in
tongues"), is examined by Alexander Alland.
His analysis, based on anthropological field
observations, focuses on social learning
factors. "Possession" is seen as a learned
pattern of group-centered behavior; it is a
source of acceptance and status in the congregation, and it is undoubtedly a source of
self-esteem for the individual. Alland points
a critical finger at past theorizers, who have
emphasized the pathological nature of trance
behavior, when he writes: "A culture or sub-
culture composed of either hysterics or schizophrenics would be difficult to imagine." He
accepts the notion of individual differences
in susceptibility to trance but insists on seeing this susceptibility only in the context of
group norms. Socio-cultural conditions, necessary for the learning of trance behavior, include the presence of strong models for trance,
lack of rational explanations for "possession,"
and isolation of sect members from the rest of
the community.

Alland's explanation for the existence of the
United House of Prayer for All People, the revivalistic church in which the trance states
are displayed, is in line with what Karl Marx
(in 1844) and Gary Marx (in this volume) have
said about the function of religion among the
oppressed. He directs our attention to the
deprivation and misery of the Negro community,

which produced this church. The activities in
the United House of Prayer are directed away
from misery and toward joy, ecstasy, and salvation. The trance states themselves are seen
as a "...sublimination of a range of frustrated
drives which is patterned as a specific aspect
of a given cultural vocabulary." Alland thus
illustrates the Marxian reference to religious
suffering as an expression of real suffering.
Trance behavior is, for members of this church,
the sanctioned and accepted way of expressing
their very real frustration and suffering.
They are reinforced for expressing these frus-
trations in a sublimated way rather than trying
to react to them directly. Alland also points
to the pacifying effects of involvement in revivalistic church activities. If members of
the United House of Prayer "live clean" (follow
strict church rules), they have few associations outside the church and have little interest in or energy for changing their situations
in the real world.

Trance has an almost world-wide distribution,
particularly if we include as equivalent phenomena
the ecstatic states of the shaman and priest, possession induced by the physiological action of various drugs, and multiple possession at religious
and semi-religious ceremonies.[2]

[2]The occurrence of trance states in religious
ceremonies has been reported from several areas,
among them: Indonesia, Africa, the Caribbean, and
the United States.
    Indonesia:
    Belo, J., *Trance in Bali,* New York: Columbia
University Press, 1960; Bateson, G. and Mead, M.,
Balinese Character: A Photographic Analysis, New
York, New York Academy of Sciences Special Publication II, 1942; Burridge, K., 'Kuda Kepang' in
Batu Pahat, Johore," *Man,* 61 (Feb. 1961), pp. 33-36.

If we exclude chemically induced trance, the other forms may be distinguished on two possible grounds: (1) a suggested, but not proved, physiological and psychological difference between the two states, and (2) the valid sociological distinction that in one case only people occupying particular and limited statuses within a wider group experience trance, and in the other case, the experience is open to all members of a defined group, regardless of status.

The type of trance referred to in this paper is of this latter category and is associated with participation in a religious ceremony during which one or several of the lay or ecclesiastical participants may manifest the behavior patterns to be described below.

Africa:
Herskovits, M. J., *The Myth of the Negro Past*, New York: Harper and Brothers, 1941.
The Caribbean:
Williams, J. J., *Voodoos and Obeahs: Phases of West India Witchcraft*, New York: Dial Press, 1932; Simpson, G., "The Vodun Service in Northern Haiti," *American Anthropologist*, 42 (1940), pp. 236-255; Simpson, G., "The Belief System of the Haitian Vodun," *American Anthropologist*, 47 (1945), pp. 35-59; Mischel, F., "African 'powers' in Trinidad: The Shango Cult," *Anthropological Quarterly*, 30 (1957), pp. 45-59; Mischel, W. and Mischel, F., "Psychological Aspects of Spirit Possession," *American Anthropologist*, 60 (1958), pp. 249-260; Hogg, D., "The Convince Cult in Jamaica," *Yale University Publications in Anthropology*, 58 (1961).
The United States:
Davenport, F. M., *Primitive Traits in Religious Revivals*, New York: Macmillan Co., 1905; Jones, R., "A Comparative Study of Religious Cult Behavior with Special Reference to Emotional Group Conditioning." *Howard University Studies in Social Sciences*, II, No. 2 (1939); Fauset, A. H., *Black Gods of the Metropolis: Negro Religious Cults of the Urban North*, Philadelphia: University of Pennsylvania Press, 1944.

This does not mean that we assume an inherent difference between "types" of trance, but rather that we are primarily involved in the analysis of our own field data and feel that the sociological distinction drawn above will be useful in the following discussion in which we shall attempt to show a connection between group participation and possessive states.

Our analysis centers upon the external (physical and socio-cultural) circumstances and the internal (individual psychological and physiological) states which elicit trance. Our major assumptions are: (1) that individuals acting in social situations are affected by the behavior and attitudes of other individuals with whom they interact, and (2) that social responses can be learned and internalized in sets which may become more or less automatic when triggered by the proper cues. Both of these assumptions have been suggested by such authors as Cooley, Mead, Freud, Parsons, and others, and demonstrated experimentally by countless workers in psychology and social psychology. Their validity is accepted here.

Trance state shall be defined descriptively for the moment as: a configuration of behavior patterns involving (1) mild body convulsions (snapping of the neck, bending of the trunk and/or legs in which the person regains control almost instantly); (2) prolonged dancing, usually to music in what appears to be a semi-stuporous state, and (3) falling to the floor either with body contractions or remaining still as in a faint. The latter two forms of trance may last from less than a minute to (rarely) several hours. This behavior is described by participants as a prolonged or momentary loss of voluntary control over body movements. "You have no power over yourself when the Holy Ghost enters."

DATA

The United House of Prayer for All People was founded by C. E. (Sweet Daddy) Grace, a Portuguese-Negro immigrant from the Cape Verde Islands. Early

in the present century Grace settled in New Bedford,
Mass., a city with a large Portuguese population.
     In 1921 he constructed his first House of Prayer
in Wareham, a suburb of New Bedford. Members were
attracted to the new sect by the story that Grace had
raised his sister from the dead. The sect was relatively ineffective in New England and Grace moved
south where he rapidly obtained a substantial following. As Grace's reputation as a curer and miracle
worker grew, the church gradually spread northward.
This growth was probably facilitated by the great
lower-class Negro migrations during the depression
and the Second World War and the impetus created by
the successful southern crusade.
     Grace opened a church in Brooklyn in 1930 and in
New York City in 1938. The first church in Connect-
icut was built in 1956 in New Haven. Since that
time, branches have been organized in Stamford,
Bridgeport and Hartford--other cities with substantial Negro populations.
     While the national organization is large, the
local chapters in New England are quite small.
Middle-class Negroes do not join this kind of church,
and the religious lower-class Negro divides his alle-
giance among several churches of this type. What
makes this group stand out in the local community is
its substantial building, paid for out of Grace's
accumulated fortune.
     The theology of the United House of Prayer is
similar to that of other eschatological churches with
the emphasis on imminent doom and salvation. Salvation, however, can only be achieved through the
intercession of Daddy Grace who is accepted as God's
last earthly prophet. The church grants the unique
gift of salvation to those members who live according to church doctrine (a strict code: no smoking,
drinking, dancing, or adultery) and who experience
the Holy Ghost. The latter is manifested in a
trance state, the achievement of which is uppermost
in the minds of the membership. Church services
emphasize "joy in the House of the Lord" and there
is the customary shouting and singing. Music is
provided by a jazz band, piano and tambourines.
The trance is spoken of as dancing for God and

completely replaces forbidden social dancing. Members are enjoined to come and enjoy themselves, to "have a good time"; to shout and sing. The emotions of the community are poured into services which are attended by the faithful several times a week and on Sundays. Part of the service on special nights consists of a program in which members perform for one another, singing hymns, reciting prayers or testifying to the power of the church. Sermons follow the free-flowing hell and damnation extemporaneous tradition of the store-front church.

If members "live clean," i.e. follow church rules, they have few, if any, social outlets beyond the church. This isolation is increased by their status within the local community, which is low. Their church is considered an oddity, and on special occasions, such as visits from Daddy Grace or the newly elected Bishop, many local people, white and colored, attend service to watch the spectacle. Unsurprisingly, members are not unaware of this attitude of the community at large and they make frequent mention in testimonials to the attitudes of outsiders which are taken as tests of faith. In-group feeling is strengthened by participation in a range of activities which tend further to isolate members as a separate segment of the Negro subculture: dinners, picnics and cocktail sips (fruit juice). They attempted to run a cafeteria, the latter with little success because it depended upon outside patronage.

The yearly cycle culminates with a traveling convocation and baptism which tours the cities in which there are member churches. Those who can afford it attend the convocation in several cities to enjoy the drama of the church and to be near the leaders who, it is believed, project spiritual powers.

In addition to these activities members are enjoined to purchase a range of Grace products which include soaps, perfumes, pomades and other toilet articles, including bleaching cream. At the height of his entrepreneural career Grace even offered coffee from his plantation in Brazil and eggs from the Grace farm, all of these products believed to be endowed with curative powers.

The activities described above and the consumer
interest aroused by the special curative properties
of Grace products contribute to the isolation of the
church community. The members' lives literally over-
flow with "Grace." The double meaning of this expression has not gone unnoticed within the group and is
used as a main theme in sermons.

THE TRANCE

In this section we shall present a more detailed
description of trance behavior and "seeking," i.e.,
the attempt to achieve the first possessive state.
Trance usually occurs during musical interludes.
These are under the control of the pastor who may
start or stop the band on signal, but band playing
is usually structured into specific parts of the
service. Women are generally the first to go into
trance states, and under most conditions more women
than men have trance in any one evening. There are
definite parts of the service in which trance is
inappropriate. It may occur at these times, however,
if there is some extra cause of excitement such as a
visit from the Bishop or some other charismatic leader in the church. When the trance occurs at an odd
time, and it is a full dance trance, the band is likely to commence playing and continue to do so as more
people go into trance. Mild or momentary trances
occur when people are seated in the pews during less
exciting parts of the service or testifying before
the congregation. These are usually accompanied by
a flinging of the arms and possibly some "speaking
in tongues."

THE DANCE TRANCE

Body: Usually almost erect with little movement although there is some bending forward and, in
some people, varying degrees of pelvic movement.
When a person falls to the floor he or she may writhe
for a few minutes and then lie still, usually on the
side but sometimes on the back. *Feet and legs:* Some
variation on the Lindy step is the most common

movement. This may be done in half time, time, or
double time, to the music. *Head:* The head may be
rocked back and forth or held steady. One or two
people snap their necks rather vigorously. *Face:*
Facial expressions vary from what is best described
as painful to euphoric. *Arms:* May fling freely or
be held up, bent at the elbow. The hands may wave
or may be rubbed over the body, especially over the
hips and stomach in what appear to be erotic movements. *Duration:* The trance usually lasts from 10
to 15 minutes per person, but many have shorter or
longer trances. One female was timed at one and
one-half hours. People may have from zero to five
trances in any one evening. Frequency, duration
and number of trances are higher when the church is
crowded and attended by special personalities.

SEX DIFFERENCES

Men have fewer trances than women. We have observed no instances of males in trance during normal
services except during the music periods. Some wom-
en appear to have trances much more easily than
others. Fewer men fall to the floor than women.
There is less "speaking in tongues" by the men. The
overt intensity of the men's trance may be as strong
as the women's, if not stronger.

SEEKING

Seeking involves the active attempt of a person
who has never experienced the Holy Ghost to achieve
first trance. In this process the person is aided
by the congregation, the band, and the pastor.
Special "Flood Gate" weeks are set aside for those
seeking the Holy Ghost, and traveling evangelists
make the church circuit working with initiates. One
of these, Elder B., is effective in inducing first
trance in seekers.
Seekers fast all day before coming to the "mountain," a raised platform at the front of the church.
There they kneel down and repeat rapidly Daddy Daddy

Daddy, etc. ... The band plays loudly with a highly
repetitive, simple melody and strong beat while
the pastor preaches directly to the person or persons attempting to gain trance.

B. operates differently. A few direct quotes
from the field notes collected during his visit to
the local church will best illustrate his technique.

"Toward the end of the evening Elder H. got up
to deliver the sermon. He then told the congregation
that Elder B. was with them for the week. He explained that Elder B. was the greatest evangelist.
B. is an old but vigorous man of 78 or 79. He has
rather long, white hair, is of medium build, and is
quite short. B. began his sermon by telling a joke
about his daughter, a well-known Negro entertainer.
He then began the usual stomping and shouting sermon... Occasionally he would stop without warning
and shriek "Yeh" at the top of his voice.

"After several minutes B. asked the congregation
if there were any there who were seeking. Four wom-
en eventually went to the 'mountain.' B. told the
congregation that they 'were going to see something.'
He then asked the women to hold up their right hands
and to look at the floor. They did so. B. told
them that the Devil was down there and that no good
came from that direction. Then he told them to look
up at the ceiling. After they did this he told them
that Jesus was up there and that He would come to
them. He lowered his hand in a swift movement and
three of the four women fell to the floor in trance.
This was the signal for several of the other women
to go into trance and with this the band began to
play. The trances were more violent than usual and
several women fell to the floor."

It is important to note that the four women who
came forward in response to Elder B. were not seekers
in the strict sense, that is, they had already had
the Holy Ghost and were highly susceptible to trance.

Working with real seekers B. developed the following pattern: "First B. invited the band to come
down off the podium. He asked them to join hands in
a circle, that is, to form a star with their left
hands, and to raise their right hands. He instructed
all the men to close their eyes, to hold their lips

tight and to think hard of Daddy. Deacon T. was
the first man to go off. He was followed by the
rest of the band except the two youngest boys
(about 10 and 11).

"After his success with the band, B. asked for
young girls who were seeking. He said he did not
want anyone to come up who had had the Holy Ghost.
A group of young girls came up and formed a star.
The band began to play but only one girl went into
trance. She went into violent trance and fell on
the floor, remaining on the floor emitting cries of
gibberish for over one hour. Toward the end of the
evening the women gathered around her and began to
sing and clap their hands. They kept this up until
she came to, but the excitement of the clapping
seemed to put her back in trance for a short time.
Finally a chair was put under her and she calmed
down. After this B., working on various individuals,
tried with limited success to put her back in trance.
He told her that the Holy Ghost was in her mouth,
and also had her hold up her right arm. Finally he
told her that the Holy Ghost was in her right arm.
Her arm began to shake and then as she walked across
the floor she stopped shaking in one arm and picked
it up in the other. B. had little success with the
other young girls, possibly because one of them, who
was a seeker, laughed during the session. (B. tried
very hard to get this girl and another into trance
states.) At the side of the mountain we noticed
a man tarrying, i.e. repeating Daddy, Daddy, over and
over again. He was obviously seeking the Holy Ghost.
The pastor took the microphone and began to sing
over him. Finally after the pastor had worked himself into a state of shouting, the man went into
trance."

It is clear that when working with seekers who
are actual novitiates it is difficult to induce first
trance. B. always has his greatest success with experienced people. These, however, are used by him
to infect seekers with the spirit and there is no
doubt they add to the general excitement and drama
generated by seeking sessions.

There is no doubt that the first trance is the
most difficult. We have no data on a gradient of

receptivity which might occur after first trance
but would certainly predict such a response pattern.
     No interviews were obtained with members who
had recently experienced their first trance. For
this data we must borrow from field data collected
in another church in New Haven which has a similar
belief in the Holy Ghost and possession. While
this material must be accepted with caution, the
experience described is offered here since it is
informative and does not contradict any of the
material collected in the United House of Prayer.
     "...It's a matter of faith, and once your mind
is made up, there shouldn't be a lot of tarrying.
Once your mind is made up that you want the Holy
Ghost, it will come. But you can't doubt it, you
can't doubt the Lord you know. ...Now I'm talking
about the day on which I really got it. Oh, I had
my experiences before ... but I was really determined in my heart I was going to get it. I got
down on my knees and some people came around me
and started tarrying with me ... There I was with
my eyes closed and I was trying to picture Him on
the cross or on the throne or something, just to
get my mind only on Him and to forget all about
everything all around me, and just keep my mind directly on heavenly things you know ... Before you
know it I was speaking tongues ... I forgot about
myself, I forgot about everything, I forgot about
my feet feeling tired, I forgot about my legs, I
forgot about people saying Hallelujah, tarrying,
I forgot everybody around me and I kept my mind on
one thing, that was Jesus and getting the Holy Ghost,
and I was telling the Lord in my mind, 'Lord, you
know my heart, you know, please give me the Holy
Ghost' ... And I was light and nobody was around me,
and it was a good feeling inside, I mean you just
feel clean ... you feel peace and joy right deep in
your heart..."[3]

[3]Sparky Ravenscroft: Personal Communication.

ANALYSIS

Old-line psychoanalysts and psychologists
writing on trance can generally be divided into two
schools: those who favor hysteria in the etiology
of trance and those who favor schizophrenia.
Neither of these theories is acceptable in the
light of the socio-cultural data. In fact it is a
general blindness to the social environment associated with trance which leads to these gross over-
simplifications.

Some of the more recent workers in ego psychology[4] have suggested that trance is a form of
hypnosis and that hypnosis itself is a form of regression in the service of the ego in which a
transference-dependency relationship is set up between the hypnotist and his subject. It is this
sort of analysis which seems most reasonable. We
are not prepared to generalize to a hypothesis
which relates the occurrence of trance to a model
of child training within a specific group. While
we accept the data of Hilgard and Gill and Brenman
that susceptibility to hypnosis depends largely
upon specific types of socialization, our data show
there is actually a wide range of susceptibility
among members of the church. What is interesting
and significant is that a limited but varied range
of personality types can, under the proper conditions, ultimately achieve a possessive state. Thus
the significant variables in what we might call
trance culture are both sociocultural and psychological, with child training perhaps turning out to
be rather insignificant in the overall etiology of
possessive states.

A culture or sub-culture composed of either
hysterics or schizophrenics would be difficult to
imagine. Schizophrenia is a serious illness in
which the affected individual has a great deal of
difficulty communicating, much less adjusting to
the outside world. Members of the United House of
Prayer are not only adjusted to their social

[4]Gill, M. M., and Brenman, M., *Hypnosis and
Related States,* New York: International Universities Press, 1959.

environment but are unlikely to commit anti-social
acts either against the community at large or within their own group. Their behavior is normal in
any sense of the word with the single exception
that they are subject to possessive states in the
context of a particular milieu. Even the so-called
ambulatory schizophrenics are not able to isolate
their problems so well that they manifest them in
only one small segment of behavior, which, while it
is spectacular to outsiders, is by no means unusual
in the context of a specific culture. Certainly
Benedict's formula of normality, i.e. what is normal in one culture may appear abnormal in another,
applies here, even though it has been misapplied to
the behavior of certain disordered personalities in
other cultures. Hysteria fits the picture only
slightly better than schizophrenia. To grant that
this extreme form of neurosis were operational we
should have to assume that trance was an automatic
result of personality disorder rather than a technique learned with a certain amount of difficulty
by participation in a special group.

Hilgard[5] cites several studies which show that
normal subjects are more susceptible to hypnosis
than schizophrenics and suggests that this may also
apply to hysterics, although there is some contradictory evidence in regard to this latter point.

There is no doubt that some people find it
easier than others to have trance. This confirms
the suggestion that the susceptibility to trance
may be, and probably is, related to personality
traits. These may be based on neurotic patterns
emerging from the guilt and anxiety which is known
to be high in the lower class Negro church community. It seems reasonable, however, to regard the
overall phenomenon of religious trance primarily as
a sublimation of a range of frustrated drives which
is patterned as a specific aspect of a given cultural vocabulary. Trance is in one sense a highly
distilled essence of all activities in the United
House of Prayer which are directed toward joy,

[5]Hilgard, E. R., "Lawfullness within Hypnotic
Phenomenon," M. S., 1960.

ecstasy and final salvation, and away from the deprivation and misery of the Negro community.   Attention to the sociological situation highlights
the additional fact that trance fulfills a member's
status rights in the eyes of the congregation.   Repetition of trance acts to reinforce the belief of
performers and spectators alike, proving that the
people involved have not wandered from a state of
grace.

The extreme deprivation of members of this
sect which is economic and psychological is not in
itself a sufficient cause of trance.   There are
other deprived groups which do not experience this
kind of release.   Possession has been borrowed from
other groups.   First cause may possibly be explained
by the existence at one time of one or a few truly
psychotic personalities who acted as models for behavior within the context of some ceremony in the
presence of psychologically receptive normals.   Nonpsychotic shills may then have taken their places in
the ranks of teachers so that the process could continue and be transferred to other exposed groups.

Who joins this particular kind of sect may ultimately be a combination of chance circumstances
in which a receptive person is accidentally exposed
to the available cultural pattern.   Lower-class urban Negroes are more likely to be both receptive
(due to their social status and personality problems flowing from it) and exposed (due to the pro-
liferation of this kind of church in the urban
Negro ghetto).   For recruitment to occur, a particular personality type must intersect with the
proper socio-cultural conditions.

While, as we have suggested above, we agree
with Gill and Brenman that trance is a form of hypnosis we are in no position to prove empirically
that this is actually the case.   We can, however,
offer considerable evidence to show a probable identity between the two phenomena.   The hypnotic process has been described by Gill and Brenman as one
in which: the hypnotist attempts to "impoverish the
subject's inflow of sensory stimuli in his attempt
to further cut down normal guideposts by strictly
limiting the subject's bodily activity, first by
asking for his voluntary cooperation and later by

capitalizing on whatever muscular immobilization
begins to appear as a result of the induction process itself. Finally, still with the intent to impoverish and to deprive, the hypnotist makes it
very difficult for the subject to have much to think
about. The well known hypnotic pattern is precisely
this."[6]

The hypnotist attempts to establish a special
relationship between himself and the subject:
"Usually implied, though sometimes explicitly
stated, is the 'promise' to the subject that if he
will permit the hypnotist to bring about the deprivation and losses of power we have discussed, he
will be rewarded by an unprecedented kind of experience; the precise nature of this experience is
usually left ambiguous. Sometimes the implication
is that new worlds will be open to him, providing
an emotional adventure of a sort he has never
known."[7]

The repetition of Daddy, Daddy, Daddy, by the
subject plus the loud and repetitious music of the
band fulfills the first requirement of this specific
kind of sensory deprivation in which the subject is
surrounded completely by specific stimuli. The interviewed subject remarks that the key to getting
the Holy Ghost is the elimination of other feelings
such as tactile sensory perception which inhibits
the process.

The promise to the subject of a special experience is clear in the doctrine of the Holy Ghost
and the feelings of freedom, euphoria, etc. described by those who have had trance. B. as the
representative of Daddy Grace is able to impose his
personality on the subject. In addition to this he
relies on the suggestive power of those who are
highly vulnerable to trance, using them to stimulate
possession through direct contact with the subject.
When a person who is seeking touches a person in
trance, he is in effect touching the Holy Ghost.

[6]Gill and Brenman, *op. cit.*, p. 6.
[7]*Ibid.*, p. 10.

B. also utilizes shame in subjects to weaken their defences by parading them in front of the congregation. Not to get the Holy Ghost is evidence of sin. What appears to happen both in hypnosis proper and in trance is that the subject enters into a transference relationship with the hypnotist[8] in which he trades self-control for a dependency relationship. In the case of the church this dependency relationship revolves around what the Holy Ghost can do for the seeking individual.

Observation in the church suggests that the occurrence of the all-important first trance experience is maximized by the following conditions and pressures upon the seeking individual which tend to lower ego defences and prepare the subject for the hypnotic transference:

1. Physical conditions

(a) Heat. A hot, stuffy room seems to be the pattern for all seeking sessions. *(b) High percentage of CO_2.* "A mixture (completely non toxic) of seven parts of O_2 and three of CO_2 produces in those who inhale it certain physical and psychological changes. Among these changes the most important, in our present context, is a marked enhancement of the ability to 'see things' when the eyes are closed. In some cases only swirls of patterned color are seen. In others there may be vivid recalls of past experiences. In yet other cases CO_2 transports the subject to the other world at the antipodes of his everyday consciousness, and he enjoys very briefly visionary experiences entirely unconnected with his own personal history or with the problems of the human race in general. In the light of these facts it becomes easy to understand the rationale of yogi breathing exercises. Practiced systematically, these exercises result, after a time, in prolonged suspensions of breath. Long suspensions of breath lead to a high concentration of CO_2 in the lungs and blood, and this increase in the concentration of CO_2

[8]*Ibid.,* pp. 60-100.

lowers the efficiency of the brain as a reducing
valve and permits the entry into consciousness of
experiences, visionary or mystical, from 'out
there'."[9]
    Windows in the House of Prayer are rarely
opened and most seeking sessions are attended by
enough people to create a situation which, in combination with the hot air heating system, is probably
high in CO_2.

2. *Physiological-psychological conditions*

    (a) *Loud, rhythmic music with a simple, repeti-
tious beat.* This type of sensory stimulus tends to
create ideal hypnotic conditions. It leads to the
situation described by Gill and Brenman, cited
above, in which the inflow of sensory stimulus is
impoverished, almost paradoxically in this case, by
the overwhelming power of one stimulus which tends
to exclude all others. This may also relate to a
relationship between sensory deprivation and sensory
overloading that has been investigated by Lindsley,
who feels that these two conditions lead to a similar response in the organism due to the operation of
the reticular formation: "With an excess of stimulation from two or more sense modalities, especially
a sudden, intense barrage from afferent and cortico-
fugal sources, as for example, in startle or fear,
blocking of the reticular formation may occur and
behavioral immobilization and general confusion may
result. In each of these conditions, there is a
circumstance which upsets the balance of the regulating system, namely the ARAS. When this happens
persistently, perception is disrupted, attention
gives way to distraction, and interest to boredom. Behavior performance is either held in abeyance or becomes
highly stereotyped and not adaptive."[10] In the case

[9]Huxley, A., *Heaven and Hell,* New York: Harper
and Brothers, 1955.
    [10]Lindsley, D. B., "Common Factors in Sensory
Deprivation, Sensory Distortion and Sensory Over-
load," *in* Solomon, P. et. al., *Sensory Deprivation,*
Cambridge: Harvard University Press, 1961.

of the seeking subject interest and awareness do not
give way to boredom but fall into the hypnotic pattern of the possessive state, which is made easier
by lowered ego defenses. The suggested result is a
physiological response to a culturally-patterned behavior sequence (the music) which in turn feeds into
the individual's culturally-patterned response (the
trance).

(b) Fasting. Fasting contributes to a general
weakening. *(c) Motivation.* The motivation for
trance is high. It represents salvation for the individual and demonstrates to the group that a particular individual is worthy not only of God's affection but of their respect.

3. *Socio-cultural conditions*

*(a) The presence of strong models for trance in
significant others who set the pattern for behavior
in the church.* Children coming to services night
after night with their parents see them and others
in trance. *(b) Lack of information.* For the phenomenon of trance to impress initiates they must be
ignorant of its possible explanations. It must fit
into what becomes a mystical experience.

(c) Isolation. The activities of the United
House of Prayer tend, as we have pointed out, to
isolate the faithful from the community at large and
cut them off from outside relationships. Members
are expected to give most of their reading time to
the Bible which, they are reminded, must be interpreted to them by the pastors of the church. At
work they are thought of as members of a peculiar
sect, which further isolates them from their fellow
workers. Late converts to the church often come
laden with guilt feelings which can be unburdened
through the obviously cathartic experience of trance.

One informant made an interesting comment in
this respect when he told us that people come to
"tarry" before the mountain to get the Holy Ghost
when they are feeling "heavy." "Tarrying lightens
the soul."

Even when all these conditions are optimum and
operating together, many people find it difficult to

have their first trance experience. Seekers continue
their quest until they have received the Holy Ghost.
Receptivity to the trance is most certainly influenced by personal differences such as: range of experience, needs of the individual, and tolerance for
various physiological stresses. Once the trance is
learned, however, its repetition is assured. Hypnosis becomes auto-hypnosis and after the first experience it becomes less difficult for members to
enter into the trance state. We suggest that certain internal cues (internal sensory states) become
hooked into a system of developed external cues
(associated with appropriate time for trance) which
trigger the behavior pattern. If this is true, then
the gradient hypothesized above for receptivity to
trance should occur. Unfortunately we have no evidence as yet for the existence of such a gradient.
Further research is necessary before this hypothesis
can be tested.

From our field data it is clear that the response is learned. It is probably facilitated by
the learning of internal cues which act as secondary re-inforcers for the behavior pattern. If
these internal cues do function in terms of secondary reinforcement, we would expect that their occurrence outside the initial learning environment
should trigger trance states. Informants tell us
that it is indeed possible for members to have trance
on the outside *once* they have had the experience in
church.

Trance, then, within the context of religious
ceremony, may be defined as a cultural response to
a series of internal and external cues which operate
in a particular kind of motivational state. The
behavior which we have called trance is most likely
a form of hypnosis which later becomes auto-hypnosis
through a continuation of the learning process.

PENTECOSTAL GLOSSOLALIA—
TOWARD A FUNCTIONAL INTERPRETATION

VIRGINIA H. HINE

Editor's introduction. The recent upsurge of
the neo-Pentecostal movement in the unlikely
environment of major universities, recruiting
a wider and better-educated group of adherents,
has drawn attention to the study of glossolalia
("speaking in tongues"), the most common form
of intense religious experience. Hine's article starts with a comprehensive review of the
relevant theoretical and empirical literature.
Approaches that regard glossolalia as an expression of pathology in the individual are
examined and rejected on the basis of empirical
data, and a social-functional theory is proposed. Hine emphasizes the necessary socialization for intense religious activity and offers

[1]The research was directed by Dr. Luther
Gerlach, Department of Anthropology, University of
Minnesota, and supported by grants from the Hill
Family Foundation, the University of Minnesota Grad-
uate School, the McKnight Family Foundation, and the
Ferndale Foundation. The author served as research
assistant.

From the *Journal for the Scientific Study of
Religion*, 1969, 8, 211-226. Reprinted with permission.

the context of the Pentecostal movement as the
most important factor in understanding contemporary glossolalia.

The notion of a relatively uniform religious
orientation is central to the understanding of
individual glossolalics: a religious orientation through which individuals have been socialized to attach themselves to church organizations and to interpret life events in a religious context. Thus, we cannot consider the
appearance of glossolalia a sudden "conversion."
Rather, it is a part of a long process. At the
same time, the first appearance of "speaking in
tongues" is seen as an act of "bridge-burning"
and as an act of commitment to the Pentecostal
movement.

Hine makes it clear that past psychological
theories, which explained glossolalia as indicative of psychopathology, suggestibility,
or hypnosis, and past sociological theories,
which explained it as a result of social disorganization and deprivation, are unable to
explain recent developments in the Pentecostal
movement. The alternative final formulation,
offered by Hine, contains both psychological
and social elements. At the level of individual personality structure, glossolalia is
viewed as learned behavior, or as the occurrence of cognitive changes resulting from an
experience through which the individual's
image of himself is altered, leading to personality reorganization. At the level of
individual/group interaction, glossolalia is
considered as one component in the process of
commitment to a movement. This act of commitment sets the practicing glossolalic apart from
the larger society to some degree, and motivates
him to additional actions in the direction of
group ideals. Being "filled with the Holy
Spirit" can be interpreted as being filled with
the group spirit. This social-psychological
explanation seems indeed more appropriate in
regard to the practice of glossolalia among an
increasing number of religious people. In the
face of growing secularization, such an act of

commitment is needed if one is to "keep the
faith" and remain a member of a "deviant"
group. Hine's explanation is in line with
the one offered by Alland in the previous
article but goes even further in emphasizing
group dynamics as the determinant of intense
religious behavior.

Glossolalia, translated literally from the
Greek, means "tongue speech." It is a form of unintelligible vocalization which has non-semantic
meaning to the speaker, and is interpreted in the
Bible as a divinely inspired spiritual gift. Glossolalia was well-known among the early Christians,
has been associated with almost all of the revivalistic movements that have punctuated the history of
the church, and characterizes the modern Pentecostal
movement. From the beginning it has occasioned
controversy, not only between practitioners and
their critics, but more recently among social scientists attempting to interpret or explain the phenomenon.

The purpose of this article is to review current psychological literature on glossolalia, to
note sociological concepts of pre-disposing conditions, and to suggest a functional explanation of
its role in the spread of the Pentecostal movement.

The research reported here is based on an
anthropological study of the Pentecostal movement
in the United States, Mexico, Haiti, and Colombia.
Data on glossolalia among American Pentecostals were
collected by means of 45 case histories, 239 self-
administered questionnaires, informal interviews
with leaders and members of more than 30 Pentecostal
groups, and participant-observation in seven
churches and prayer groups. Participants who co-
operated with the study included members of traditional Pentecostal sects, as well as so-called
"neo-Pentecostals" in independent churches, and
groups of tongue speakers in non-Pentecostal Protestant and Catholic churches.

DESCRIPTION OF THE PHENOMENON

The phenomenon of glossolalia, it should be
noted, is not limited to a Christian or even a religious context. The term has been used to refer
to a wide range of sounds from animal-like grunts
and "gibberish" to well-patterned articulations
(May, 1956). Glossolalia, as observed among participants in the modern Pentecostal movement, involves utterances of varying lengths, lasting from
a few seconds to an hour or more. Though unintelligible, they are usually patterned sufficiently
so that the tongue speech of one individual may be
distinguished from that of another. Often one tongue
speaker uses two or more different patternings or
"languages." The experience is interpreted by
Pentecostals as control of the speech organs by the
Holy Spirit who is praying through the believer in
"a heavenly language." It is felt to be more often
praise than petition, and is usually accompanied by
sensations of great freedom, tranquility, and joy.
These emotions often continue long after the glossolalic utterance itself. Glossolalics frequently
refer to the experience as one of being "in another
dimension," "beyond oneself," or "truly out of this
world."

Glossolalia in the Pentecostal context is sometimes associated with an altered mental state, with
some degree of dissociation or trance. It occasionally involves involuntary motor activity or, rarely,
complete loss of consciousness. These behaviors
are most common during the initial experience of
glossolalia which usually is associated with the
Baptism of the Holy Spirit, a subjective experience
of being filled with or possessed by the Holy Spirit.
Subsequent use of the "gift of tongues" is most often
independent of any altered mental state or trance
behavior. Speaking with tongues may even occur
without the usual emotional rewards. Particularly
is this likely to be true in a clinical setting
where the Pentecostal is cooperating with a scientific observer.

Linguists who have studied Pentecostal glossolalia stress the fact that the linguistic event

can and should be distinguished from religious behaviors or from particular psychological and emotional states. It has even been suggested that the
word "glossolalia" be reserved for a type of vocalization that can be produced without an altered
mental or emotional state and which can occur in
contexts other than religious ones (Jaquith, 1967;
Samarin, 1968a). For the purposes of linguistic
analysis, this is clearly a useful approach and has
contributed much to our understanding of the whole
phenomenon.

An anthropological analysis, however, requires
contextualization of the linguistic phenomenon, an
attempt to identify possible psychological and sociological correlates, and an interpretation of its
function in the cross-cultural spread of Pentecostalism as a movement.

PSYCHOLOGICAL INTERPRETATIONS

Glossolalia as Pathological

During the nineteenth and early twentieth
century, glossolalia in revivalistic religion was
often associated with an energetic form of religious
enthusiasm which inspired such labels as "Holy
Rollers." Scholarly interpretations of these verbal
and motor "automatisms" tended to assume some form
of psychological pathology. The classic and most
oft-quoted source, even by modern psychologists, is
Speaking With Tongues, written in 1927 by George
Cutten, a Baptist minister and educator. He illustrates his analysis with descriptive accounts of
tongue speaking, and draws very unflattering conclusions as to the psychological and sociological correlates. He makes fairly extravagant statements
about the gift of tongues being received only by
non-verbal individuals of low mental ability in whom
the capacity for rational thought, a comparatively
recent human achievement according to Cutten, was
under-developed.

Members of our research team can only wish that
Dr. Cutten had been able to join us in interviewing
modern Pentecostals. A more verbal group of people

would be difficult to imagine. One of the remarkable
things about tongue speakers is the degree to which
they can communicate both the quality and the effect
of their subjective religious experiences. Were it
not so, they would have been much less disruptive in
their churches of origin. This fact, indeed, is
basic to the ability of Pentecostals to recruit, and
is therefore crucial to the successful spread of the
movement.

As for "low mental ability" and "under developed
rational capacity," even those who began with very
little formal education bring to their study of the
scriptures an intensity of mentation that would stand
any college student in good stead.

Cutten's contentions concerning psychopathology,
quoted and re-quoted through the years, have taken
on an aura of fact among non-Pentecostal churchmen
who are critical of the movement. His assumption
that glossolalia is linked to schizophrenia and
hysteria has not been supported by an empirical evidence. Studies had been made of psychotic individuals in mental institutions who spoke in tongues,
and the temptation to generalize from these cases
to otherwise normal glossolalics was seldom resisted.
More recent studies have clarified the difference
between schizophrenic and non-pathological religious
behavior.

Non-Pathological Glossolalia

Alexander Alland (1961) found that older psychological explanations of glossolalia as schizophrenia
or hysteria are no longer acceptable in view of recent socio-cultural data. Tongue speaking members
of the Negro Pentecostal church he studied were well
adjusted to their social environment and behaved normally except for their glossolalic experiences.
According to Alland, this weakens the interpretation
of glossolalia as indicative of schizophrenia since
schizophrenics are unable to limit their problems
to one segment of behavior.

He also considers hysteria an inadequate explanation of the "religious trance states" which he
found associated with glossolalia among his

informants. This, he contends, is learned behavior,
and not necessarily a result of personality disorder.

Anton Boisen (1939) interviewed and observed
members of a Holy Rollers church and compared them
to certain of his psychiatric patients who displayed
superficially similar behaviors. He noted a conceptual similarity between the Pentecostals' interpretation of tongue speaking as possession by the
Holy Spirit and the psychiatric patients' feeling
that they are controlled by a power external to
themselves. But he could find no evidence of mental
illness in the tongue speakers from the church. A
crucial difference, he believed, were the social influences brought into play when the glossolalic experience occurred within the matrix of church life.

Boisen had previously treated several cases of
mentally disordered individuals who also experienced
the Baptism of the Holy Spirit and tongues within
the church context. He found that for the most part
the experience was therapeutic for them. According
to Boisen, glossolalia within a social matrix in
which it is structured, and in which pressure for
constructive behavioral results is exerted by group
expectations, tends to be a constructive experience
for both mentally disordered and for normal individuals.

Ari Kiev (1964) made a comparative study of ten
West Indian schizophrenics in English mental hospi-
tals and a group of normal West Indian immigrants
who were Pentecostals. He found that:

> unlike nonpsychotic individuals who participate
> in various religious cults and in the revivalist
> sects in which dissociative phenomena and pos-
> session are permitted and encouraged, the schiz-
> ophrenic patients could not maintain sufficient
> control of autistic and regressive behavior to
> fit into the prescribed ritual patterns.

The difference between the glossolalic behavior
of psychotic individuals and that of nonpsychotic individuals was perfectly clear to the normal Pentecostals in Kiev's study.

Our interview data support this observation.
Pentecostals of a wide range of socioeconomic and

educational backgrounds are aware of the different
results of glossolalic experience for normal as
compared with emotionally unstable individuals.
Many Pentecostal leaders have pragmatically developed ways of evaluating potential converts, and do
not encourage the glossolalic experience in persons
they consider to be in questionable mental or emotional health.

Psychological Testing of Modern Glossolalics

Four recent studies, using reliable and widely
accepted psychological tests have been conducted,
three with long-established traditional Pentecostal
groups and one with neo-Pentecostals. In none of
these studies has it been shown that Pentecostal
glossolalics as a group are more psychotic or even
neurotic than the control groups or the societal
norms.

L. M. Van Eetvelt Vivier (1960) used a battery
of tests which included the Cattell Personality
Test, the Willoughby test for general level of
neuroticism, the Rosenzweig Picture Frustration
test, a biographical background questionnaire, and
a religious belief and activity questionnaire. The
experimental group consisted of twenty-four tongue
speaking Pentecostals. The control groups were
twenty non-tongue speaking Pentecostals (or pre-
tongue speakers) and twenty members of a Christian
church who did not approve of or practice glossolalia. The three groups were matched as closely
as possible for age, sex, education, occupation and
religious convictions.

Vivier's findings reveal no significant differences between the test and the control groups
except for two factors on the Cattell inventory.
These are "desurgence" and "shrewdness-naivete."
On desurgence--defined by Vivier as the tendency to
renounce immediate satisfactions for long-range goals
and to accept moral restrictions and goals of higher
achievement--glossolalics, although not far from the
median, appeared to be more "long-circuiting" and
renunciative in their habits than the control groups.
Glossolalics were also found to be significantly

different from the control groups in that they were
"less realistic and practical, more concerned with
feeling than thought or action, and more tolerant
and humane in their interests."

Vivier found no significant difference between
the glossolalics and the control groups (or between
the pre-glossolalics and the anti-glossolalics) on
the Willoughby test for general level of neuroticism.
According to this finding there is no more evidence
of persistent, unadaptive anxiety reactions in tongue
speakers, or in Pentecostals who have not yet spoken
in tongues, than in non-Pentecostals of the same
socio-economic and educational backgrounds. Vivier
also specifically concludes that his findings did
not substantiate theories of dissociation as a result of Freudian repression.

Another of Vivier's findings is interesting in
view of the fact that faith healings, which are
widely associated with Pentecostal glossolalia in
all groups, are sometimes assumed to involve only
psychosomatic illnesses which are symptoms of conversion hysteria (in the clinical sense of psychic tensions "converted" into physical dysfunction).
Vivier found that glossolalics scored low on the
three factors of the Cattell Personality inventory
which are associated with conversion hysteria, and
were not significantly different from the control
groups.

Vivier characterized the glossolalics he studied
as generally more sensitive, less bound by traditional or orthodox thought processes, less depressed,
having less generalized fear, but more need for emotional catharsis.

William Wood (1965) approached the subject with
the hypothesis that personality types participating
in highly emotional religions will vary in some
regular way from types participating in more sedate
religions. He used the Rorschach technique because
he felt it reflected perceptual processes, and that
these were essentially what religious emotion was.
Wood conducted field observations in two Southern
rural communities in an economically marginal area,
and administered the Rorschach test to two socio-
economically similar groups, one Pentecostal and one
non-Pentecostal.

The most significant differences between the Pentecostal and non-Pentecostal Rorschach records were in the area of shading. Unfortunately, according to Wood, this is the chief "area of dispute" among Rorschach authorities concerning the scoring responses. The frequency of shading responses was the same for the test as for the control group, but the groups differed significantly in that Pentecostals were more likely to produce perspective, depth, and distance responses.

A second difference between the groups was in the area of movement responses. Pentecostals tended to use animal or inanimate forms more frequently, and to formulate their human percepts only partially or vaguely.

Wood feels that these findings establish regular differences between Pentecostal and non-Pentecostal Rorschach responses, and that this indicates, if not a difference in personality type, at least a difference in basic habits of perception.

Wood interprets the differences in personality type in the form of fifteen hypotheses rather than conclusions because of the "degree of doubt concerning Rorschach interpretive principles." Several of these hypotheses suggest that Pentecostals have inadequately structured value-attitude systems. Another suggests that Pentecostals have an uncommon degree of uncertainty regarding personal relationships, but are highly motivated to establish close interpersonal involvements. This hypothesis appears to be inconsistent with the following one which states that Pentecostals are able to canalize their emotions normally into interpersonal relationships, and have an emotional organization which makes positive and satisfying interpersonal relationships possible. The next hypothesis suggests that Pentecostalism attracts uncertain, threatened, inadequately organized people who are strongly motivated to reach a state of personal integrity. Several following hypotheses suggest that Pentecostal religious experiences lead to personality integration.

Apparent inconsistencies between hypotheses may be due to Wood's view that Pentecostals are in the process of restructuring attitude systems and social relationships. He makes an important and little-

recognized point that his study provides no information about whether the "Pentecostal type" is attracted to or is developed by participation in the
movement.

Wood's study provides no evidence, nor does he
suggest, that the differences he found indicate ab-
normality or psychological pathology of any kind.

Stanley Plog conducted a study of neo-Pentecostal groups in Los Angeles and Seattle using two
questionnaire forms, one for samples taken at regular meetings of three different groups and the other
for interviews in depth. Over eight hundred group
questionnaires were tabulated and two hundred individual interviews. Plog also used the California
Psychological Inventory. He reported (personal
communication) that individuals who were entering
into the tongues experience were "very responsible
and normally well-controlled individuals." He noted
that the one dimension of the test in which they
tended to fall low was that of interpersonal relationships. Plog considers this significant since
this is the area in which he received "consistent
responses *[during interviews]* as to the benefits
participants have derived from tongues." Most report that they get along better with others after
having received the gift. This supports Wood's
hypothesis concerning changes in interpersonal relationships.

Our own observations, made during interviews
and as participant-observers, are also consistent
with Wood's and Plog's. Pentecostals as a group
appear to be normally adjusted and productive members of society. In observing family interaction
of participants, we noted that when both husband
and wife participate actively in the "tongues movement," family life tends to be more than normally
well-integrated. On our written questionnaire,
responses to a question about specific changes in
behavior patterns, habits, or ways of acting toward
others could be grouped into three general categories, all of which had implications for interpersonal relationships. Forty-four per cent mentioned increased capacity for love toward, sensitivity to, or concern for others. Thirty-seven per
cent mentioned the "fruits of the Spirit," such as

love, patience, kindness, gentleness, etc. The remaining nineteen per cent described an increase in
self-confidence and the "power to witness," an active
attempt to influence others.

   Gerrard. One of the most conclusive studies of
the psychological correlates of glossolalia and related phenomena is that of Nathan Gerrard. Over a
period of several years, he conducted a sociological-
anthropological study of a serpent-handler cult in
West Virginia. Although serpent handling is an independent outgrowth of nineteenth century Holiness
movements, and thus only indirectly related to modern
Pentecostalism, glossolalia is an important part of
the religious behavioral complex.

   Gerrard's field work included a thorough sociological study of the rural area in which the serpent-
handler church is located. He compared the serpent
handlers with other religious groups in the community
with respect to economic, social, and political variables.

   Repeated observation in the snake handlers
church and interviews with members in their homes
led Gerrard to the hypothesis that snake handlers
are not psychologically or emotionally disturbed
people. To test this hypothesis, he administered
the Minnesota Multiphasic Personality Inventory to
the snake handlers group, and to members of a conventional church of a major Protestant denomination
in the same rural area. Both experimental and control groups were similar in age and sex distribution.

   The 96 MMPIs (46 from the snake handlers and 50
from the conventional church) were sent to the Department of Psychology of the University of Minnesota for analysis. The analysis consisted of (1)
an analysis of variance of scores, using church
membership, sex, and age group (old versus young)
as the factorial design; (2) an interpretation of
the MMPI profiles of the two groups by three clinical judges; and (3) a sorting of the individual
profiles by four other clinical judges.

   Results of the analysis of variance revealed
significant differences between the two groups on
three MMPI scales. The conventional church members
scored higher on the K scale and scale 3 (Hysteria)
than the serpent handlers. A significant age/church

group interaction on scale 2 (Depression) indicated
that old members of the conventional denomination
show particularly high Depression scores. Serpent
handlers scored higher on scales 4 (Psychopathic
Deviate) and 9 (Hypomania) but not at a significant
level.

These differences were interpreted by the consultant from the Department of Psychology at the
University of Minnesota as follows:

> The conventional denomination, compared to the
> serpent handlers, are on the average more de-
> fensive, less inclined to admit undesirable
> traits, more ready to use mechanisms of denial
> and repression. The older members of the con-
> ventional denomination, in addition, show indi-
> cations of marked depressive symptomatology.
> The serpent handlers appear less defensive and
> restrained. On the contrary, they seem to be
> more exhibitionistic, excitable, and pleasure-
> oriented...and are less controlled by considera-
> tions of conformity to the general culture, par-
> ticularly middle class culture. There is no
> evidence for systematic differences between
> the two groups on dimensions of thought disorder
> (psychoticism). (Gerrard and Gerrard, 1966:56)

Clinical interpretation of the findings was done
by three psychologists for whom the two church groups
were identified only as church A and church B. They
were provided with a brief description of the sociological background common to the two groups. Gerrard
summarized their findings as follows: The serpent
handlers, like the members of the conventional denomination, are essentially within the "normal limits"
established by wide use of the MMPI. With respect to
neuroticism, the clinicians found a higher incidence
among the conventional denomination than among the
serpent handlers although it was not statistically
significant. Members of the conventional denomination presented a "somewhat more repressive and dys-
phoric picture" and were also found to be "more
likely to present more symptoms of psychological
distress" than were the snake-handling glossolalics.
In general, the comparison of all serpent handlers

with all members of the conventional denomination
showed no marked differences with respect to mental
health. What differences there were, were in the
direction of the serpent handlers being more "normal" than members of the conventional denomination
(Gerrard and Gerrard, 1966: 65-67).

The sorting of the MMPI profiles was done by
four other clinicians who were told that one of the
groups was a snake handlers church and one a conventional church, but were not told which profiles came
from which group. They were asked to categorize the
profiles diagnostically and then to sort out the
profiles they thought belonged to the snake handlers.
The four clinicians assigned most of the profiles
they judged to be "abnormal" to the serpent handlers
and most "normal" profiles to the conventional denomination. The actual distribution showed that the
reverse was true. According to the consultant who
directed the analysis, "analysis of the data makes
it clear that the clinicians did have rather definite
ideas as to how serpent handlers' and conventional
denomination members' profiles ought to look.
These ideas, however, were quite erroneous."

The obvious bias revealed here is not uncommon.
Informal interviews with four psychotherapists about
our Pentecostal data revealed a remarkable readiness
to assume pathology in glossolalics without adequate
knowledge of the groups involved. This tendency to
evaluate unusual religious behavior negatively has
been noted by other students of glossolalia (McDonnell
1968) and religious trance (Bourguignon and Pettay
1964).

*   *   *

Quite clearly, available evidence requires that
an explanation of glossolalia as pathological must
be discarded. Even among those who accept this position, however, there often remains a sort of non-
specific suspicion of emotional immaturity, of sub-
clinical anxiety, or of some form of personal inadequacy. This is particularly true of churchmen in
whose denominations the ranks of Spirit-filled
Christians are swelling (Martin 1960, Lapsley and
Simpson 1964a and b, Hoekema 1966, Protestant

Episcopal Church 1963, American Lutheran Church 1964).
As yet there is no empirical, scientific evidence
for this interpretation of glossolalia. Future
studies of it might usefully include an examination
of possible bias on the part of non-glossolalic observers.

Suggestibility and Hypnosis

Another psychological theory that is commonly
used to explain the occurrence of glossolalia, but
which assumes no pathology, is that of suggestibility
or pre-disposition to hypnosis. One of the problems
with this theory is the definitional difficulty.
According to social psychologist Hans Toch, suggestibility is characteristic of those who join movements, and is created by a strong increase in susceptibility (1956:12). It involves an awareness of
a problem and a readiness to jump at promising solutions.

Hadley Cantril, in his study of social movements
(1941), has defined the conditions of suggestibility
as either (1) lack of adequate mental context, or
frame of reference within which to interpret experience, or (2) a fixed mental context which, in its
simplest form, is conditioned response. Presumably
there is some area between these two states which is
inhabited by individuals who have an adequate but
not fixed mental context, and who would therefore
not be likely to join movements or get caught up in
revivalistic fervor.

Suggestibility is often poised against critical
ability, sometimes with the connotations of the former as a more "primitive" type of mental functioning
(Meares 1963). Several students of Pentecostal glossolalia suggest that it results from "a regression
in the service of the ego" in a form of group hypnosis, and that glossolalics tend to be submissive
as well as suggestible (Alland 1961, Kildahl 1966).

Our data pose a problem with regard to the hypnosis theory, as we have found that tongue speaking
occurs frequently in solitary situations. After the
initial experience of glossolalia, most Pentecostals
speak with tongues as frequently, if not more

frequently, alone in private prayer as in group situations where hypnosis could be practiced. Auto-
suggestion and self-hypnosis are commonly used to
explain this fact. Twenty-three per cent of our
questionnaire respondents, however, experienced the
Baptism of the Holy Spirit and spoke with tongues
for the first time when they were alone.

This would suggest a sophisticated and calculated use of post-hypnotic suggestion during previous
group meetings, and this we did not observe.

Vivier, in the study discussed above, provides
empirical data with respect to the suggestibility
theory. He specifically challenges the notion of
tongue speakers as highly susceptible to suggestion
since his test group scored lower, though not significantly, than the control group on this factor of the
personality inventory.

The problem of viewing suggestibility as a pre-
disposing characteristic for experiencing glossolalia
is complicated by the fact that suggestibility is
also the basis for normal processes of socialization,
education, and successful psychotherapy, and that the
only truly nonsuggestible person is the psychopath
(Frank 1961, Kimball 1966, Sargant 1957). Cantril
argues that suggestibility is a function of the situation in which any individual might find himself
rather than a characteristic of the individual.
Toch also stresses the specificity of susceptibility
in different individuals, and in the same individual
at different points in his life. Until we know more
about the relationship between suggestibility and
type of group interaction, and can measure the degree
of suggestibility more accurately, generalizations
about glossolalics as suggestible individuals do not
seem either very useful or supported by available
data.

SOCIOLOGICAL INTERPRETATIONS

Deprivation and Disorganization Theories

Two sociological theories which have been used
to explain Pentecostal religious behavior should be
mentioned, even if only in passing. One is the view

that Pentecostalism spreads where there is social
disorganization; the other is that it flourishes
primarily among economically or socially deprived
classes.

Disorganization theory. Our cross-cultural
survey of the movement does not support the social
disorganization theory either in this country or in
others. While many Pentecostal congregations are
located in socially disorganized communities, neither Pentecostal churches nor the practice of tongue
speaking are limited to groups suffering from these
conditions. In non-Western societies, the movement
is successful in rural areas where traditional
tribal or village social structures have not been
disrupted or disorganized.

Deprivation theory. The same is true of the
deprivation theory. Not only are members of the
long-established Pentecostal sects, such as the
Assemblies of God, moving up the socio-economic
scale into the middle class, the movement itself
is spreading into Catholic, Episcopalian, Presbyterian, Baptist, Lutheran, and other denominational
groups. Converts are being drawn from a wide range
of socio-economic and educational backgrounds.

The disorganization and deprivation models are
analyzed in more detail in other reports and publications (Gerlach and Hine 1968, Hine 1967).

Conceptual Predispositions

Finding the psychological maladjustment, social
disorganization and deprivation theories inadequate
to explain the spread of glossolalic behavior as we
had observed it, we turn to those characteristics
which were common to the glossolalics in our study
as potentially explanatory. In the analysis of our
data collected by interviews and questionnaires, we
found that in spite of wide differences in socio-
economic, educational, or church backgrounds, our
respondents were strikingly similar in the area of
pre-conversion conceptual orientation.

71% of our respondents considered their religious training to have been conservative or
fundamentalist.
74% were brought up to consider smoking and
drinking wrong.
83% were trained to accept the scriptures as
authoritative.
91% attended church regularly every week
even before conversion to Pentecostalism.
54% were involved as officers or committee
members in the organization of their churches
(non-Pentecostal in three-fourths of the cases)
before receiving the Baptism of the Holy Spirit.
Only 16% reported that they were experiencing
any sort of crisis just prior to their Spirit
Baptism and glossolalic experience, with 84%
describing their pre-conversion situation as
one of gradual spiritual growth.

Although these percentages must not be extra-
polated to the movement as a whole, field observation and available historical accounts of case histories tend to support this general characterization
of Christian glossolalics.
The picture that emerges from these data is one
of individuals trained to orient their lives around
a church organization and to interpret experiences
and events in a religious context. J. M. Yinger
points out that it is a serious mistake to identify
religious interests and "needs" with the more anxious or insecure members of a society. The need
for and interest in religion is largely, though not
entirely, a result of training and variations in the
socialization process (1957:91-94). Thus a possible
pre-disposition to glossolalia would be what Clifford
Geertz (1965) would call the "religious perspective"
--a mode of seeing, a way of construing the world,
a conceptual framework by which experience is ordered into what we know as "meaning." The religious
perspective, according to Geertz, is one of several
equally workable ways of looking at life. The scientific perspective is another, the "common sensical"
a third. As Geertz defines it, the religious perspective differs from the common sensical because

"it moves beyond the realities of everyday life to
wider ones which correct and complement them," and
from the scientific because "it questions the realities of everyday life not out of institutionalized
skepticism which dissolves the world's givenness into
a swirl of probablistic hypotheses, but in terms of
what it takes to be wider, non-hypothetical truths."
Rather than detachment, the religious perspective
demands commitment; rather than analysis, encounter.
Such a perspective is generated out of habitual,
concrete acts of religious observances.

Learned Behavior Theory

Clearly an orientation to which an individual
is socialized does not produce a specific behavior;
otherwise all those who have acquired a religious
perspective would practice glossolalia. Several
students of the phenomenon would go beyond what
might be called the socialization theory and view
glossolalia as learned behavior. E. Mansell Pattison, studying the glossolalia of a group of neo-
Pentecostals from the point of view of speech
pathology, also rejects the theory that glossolalics are socio-economically deprived or emotionally disturbed. His thesis is rather that glossolalia is an experience available to any normal
person who is willing to "adopt a passive attitude
about controlling speech," and who is supplied with
the "appropriate motivation, group setting and examples" (1964). He concludes that glossolalia is
an accompaniment of an intense and meaningful
spiritual experience for normal, devoutly religious
people, but that it must be seen as incidental to
the attainment of spiritual goals and that it can
be achieved as an end in itself. He emphasizes the
fact that glossolalia is produced by natural speech
mechanisms, and defines it as "a stereotyped pattern
of unconsciously controlled vocal behavior."
Recent linguistic studies of glossolalic utterances have been used to support a "learned behavior" theory. James Jaquith (1967) compared the
glossolalic and casual speech of his informants,
and found that the phones, the distribution patterns

of phones, the syllable types, and even the stress
patterns of glossolalia were similar to those either
in the natural speech of the individual or in familiar preaching patterns and intonations. William
Samarin (1968a) also found that glossolalic utterances, analyzed linguistically, were derivative from
casual speech patterns. But he observed in addition
several innovative features, such as simplified syl-
labic structure, repetition of both phones and syl-
lables, and the use of sound units not found in the
native speech. Samarin suggests that further study
of glossolalia might reveal much about the nature
of man's language-creating ability, and about the
unconventional use of speech "as an expression of
the ineffable."

In his attention to the means by which a "tongue"
is acquired, Samarin's observations parallel our own.
The two studies were conducted independently in different cities, and neither principal investigator
was aware of the other's work until later. Samarin
records several instances of individuals for whom
the first experience of glossolalia occurred with
no previous knowledge of the phenomenon and no
acquaintance with another glossolalic (1968b). Our
records also include several such incontestable
cases. There is no question that glossolalic utterances of length and fluency can be generated
quite spontaneously. We have observed, however, as
has Samarin, that the vast majority of Pentecostal
tongue speakers "received the gift" in the context
of a religious group, as part of a larger set of
behavioral patterns and ideological formulations.
One cannot learn to speak with tongues in the same
sense that natural semantic languages are learned.
Each glossolalic utterance is produced *de novo*. In
a very much more general sense, however, glossolalia
may be considered learned behavior.

Most candidates for the Baptism of the Holy
Spirit have heard tongues at one time or another.
Although they may or may not expect glossolalia to
accompany the subjective experience they are seeking, most have received minimal instructions concerning such facilitating mechanics as bodily posture, relaxation, vocalized exhalations, and "turning your tongue over to the Lord." Some are

instructed to praise God in their own language until
another is given to them by the Spirit. Others are
told just to start to speak, but not in English, and
to let the Holy Spirit take over. In a few cases,
a candidate may be instructed to "repeat after me"
and copy the glossolalic utterances of the person
who is helping him "pray through" to the Baptism of
the Holy Spirit. Many candidates, on the other hand,
have received no instructions concerning glossolalic
vocalizations and concentrate only on the subjective
experience of the Baptism. For these, glossolalia
may be considered learned behavior only in that they
are aware of a model. Expectations have been structured through study of New Testament references to
the phenomenon, through discussion, or through witnessing others' glossolalic behavior.

                    *   *   *

    Even if it is true that a certain "cognitive
set" is a predisposing condition and that glossolalia is learned behavior, the phenomenon is still
not explained or even interpreted adequately. Not
all individuals with the same cognitive set become
glossolalics. Furthermore, almost all human behavior may be considered learned behavior. Evidence
of glossolalia as learned behavior or as a result
of variations in the socialization process merely
clears the ground for more questions.

    FUNCTIONAL INTERPRETATION
GLOSSOLALIA AS A FACTOR IN MOVEMENT DYNAMICS

    *Personal Changes Associated with Pentecostal
Glossolalia*

    Conversion. An analysis of variance on our
data revealed several significant correlations between glossolalia and other variables which support
a functional interpretation of glossolalia in terms
of movement dynamics. The sample of 239 were classified according to frequency of glossolalic experience. Those who reported that they speak with
tongues daily or more than once a week were defined

as frequent tongue speakers. All others were classified as non-frequent.

We found that the second generation Pentecostals
in our sample (those who had been socialized to accept glossolalia as a valued experience) spoke with
tongues less frequently than those who had been converted from denominations where the practice was
either ignored or devalued. Furthermore, frequent
tongue speakers were more often those who reported
that their religious education had been "liberal"
rather than "conservative" or "fundamentalist."
(These differences were significant at the .001
level.) It would appear, then, that although the
glossolalics in our study shared the common background of a generally religious orientation, the
most frequent glossolalics were those who had been
least socialized to accept the practice.

Fundamentalist ideology. Another and related
observation concerns the ideology commonly associated with the practice of Pentecostal glossolalia.
Sixty-six per cent of our respondents had always accepted the Bible as authoritative. Seventeen per
cent had been trained as children to accept the
authority of the scriptures, but had come to doubt
it as adults. The Pentecostal experience brought
them back to acceptance of Biblical authority. Of
the remaining seventeen per cent, whose religious
upbringing was liberal and who had not been trained
to accept the scriptures as authoritative, all but
one per cent became "fundamentalist" on this score
before or just after the Baptism of the Holy Spirit
and the initial experiences of glossolalia. Within
the broad category of religiously-oriented individuals, changes in the belief system in a defined
direction appear to be associated with Pentecostal
glossolalia.

Personal attitudes and social behavior. Other
changes, of even more importance to glossolalics,
were reported by all informants. Case histories
invariably include a "before and after" statement
describing changes in attitudes, behavior, and often
social situations. These changes were traced by our
informants not to glossolalia *per se,* but to the

experiential complex of which the linguistic behavior is one component. The perception of themselves as being different after the glossolalic experience was characteristic. Attitudinal changes
were generally described in terms of greater capacity for love toward others, a sense of tranquility
and joy, and more confidence in their beliefs.

Frequent tongue speakers perceived themselves
as better off physically since the Baptism and the
onset of glossolalic experience, as compared with
non-frequent tongue speakers (at the .003 level of
significance).

Frequent tongue speakers also reported changes
in the friends they see socially more often than
non-frequent (.05 level). In the context of Pentecostalism, glossolalia appears to be associated with
changes in both personal attitudes and social behavior.

*Cognitive Reorganization Associated with Pente-
costal Glossolalia*

This interpretation of Pentecostal glossolalia
as functional in processes of personal change is
supported by four psychological analyses of conversion phenomena.

William Sargant (1949, 1957) points to functional
similarities in the processes of religious conversion,
thought reform, and psychotherapy. He notes that all
three of these processes involve extensive cognitive
reorganization, and contends that there are physiological mechanisms which produce such reorganization.
His argument is built on an analysis of the most extreme forms of these phenomena. His examples of religious conversion are drawn from accounts of nineteenth century revival movements involving not only
glossolalia, but various forms of trance behavior,
violent motor "automatisms," and visual and auditory
hallucinations. He quotes from the extended verbal
assaults on the part of evangelists which seemed
calculated to heighten guilt and anxiety, and producing a type of nervous exhaustion. He points to
the similarities between this and the induced physical stress and carefully manipulated disruption of
expectations used in brain washing or thought reform

methods. His data on psychotherapeutic processes
are based on his own treatment of victims of war
neurosis. The functionally similar event here was
drug-induced physical collapse which allowed therapeutic recall of incidents and subsequent cognitive
reorganization eliminating neurotic patterns.

Sargant uses Pavlov's findings concerning
physiological breakdown and the cessation, alteration, and even reversal of normal brain function in
dogs. He suggests that permanent behavioral, as
well as attitudinal, changes can result from a physiological state of the brain during which cognitive
restructuring, even complete reversal of beliefs or
cognitive patterns can occur. In order to explain
this cognitive restructuring, Sargant postulates a
temporary, but dramatic interruption of normal brain
functioning. He suggests that experiences such as
revivalistic conversions, snake handling and glossolalia can produce an effect similar to that of
electro-shock therapy--temporary cortical inhibition
that breaks up previous mental and emotional patterns
and frees the individual to develop new ones.

It is difficult to find evidence for this degree of physiological breakdown in most of the
Baptism or glossolalic experiences we have observed,
even though cognitive changes were reported by participants. However, it is not impossible that this
process involves a greater or lesser degree of interruption of normal functioning, and that there are
physiological correlates of lesser intensity. In
discussing the physiological aspects of the experience with Pentecostals, we found some support for
this theory. Most could describe definite physical
changes during the infilling of the Holy Spirit and
certain experiences of glossolalia. Even those who
experienced no involuntary motor activity reported
release of muscular tension and pricklings or sensations of electric currents coursing through the body.

Jerome Frank (1961), expanding on Sargant's
theory, compared the nature of revivalistic religious experiences with the process of psychotherapy,
and suggested that such experiences serve as a mechanism through which attitudes toward God, the self,
and those in significant relationships can shift in
such a way as to lead to permanent attitude and

behavior changes. These changes stem from a reorganization of the "assumptive system" or worldview
that is possible during such experiences. Similar
results can be obtained through the process of successful psychotherapy.

Both Sargant and Frank stress that the dynamics
of revivalism and conversion are such that pre-disposing personality characteristics, emotional or
sociological maladjustments are not required to explain participation. They offer evidence of successful involvement on the part of normal individuals,
not only in religious conversion including glossolalia, but also in processes of thought reform and
brain washing. They emphasize that, contrary to
popular belief, resistance to such processes if one
is exposed to them can be maintained only by a condition of emotional detachment, by pathological im-
munity to suggestion, or by a countercommitment to
some other belief system or way of life that is as
obsessive. According to Frank and Sargant, the common denominator in the changes wrought by psychotherapy, religious conversion, or brain washing is
not a psychological state, but a physiological state
which can be brought about in any individual.

Abraham Maslow has also noted the relationship
between intense emotional experiences and personality
changes, in his observation of "peak experiences."
Maslow has found that peak experiences may involve
disorientation in time and space, and a type of cognition very different from that of normal states.
Visual and auditory perception may also be different.
The perceptions of his "peakers" are similar to those
reported by Pentecostals during their glossolalic or
Baptism experiences. Maslow considers such experiences contributive to personality growth and self-
actualization, and notes that permanent changes are
sometimes effected:

> To have a clear perception (rather than a
> purely abstract and verbal philosophical ac-
> ceptance) that the universe is all of a piece
> and that one has a place in it...can be so
> profound and shaking an experience that it
> can change the person's character and his
> *Weltanschaung* forever after. (1964 :59)

William Wood (1965) found that his data supported the hypothesis that emotionally intense religious experience is connected in an important way
with the process of perceptual reorientation. He
feels that his Rorschach results indicate that Pentecostals are in the process of personality reorganization, changing value and belief systems, and restructuring of interpersonal relationships. The
Pentecostals in Wood's study were drawn from a low
status group in a community where there was a widespread social disorganization. Assuming a correlation between social disruption and personality disorganization, Wood views the personal changes which
he found correlated with Pentecostal religious practices as necessary because of pre-existing personality
disorganization.

Pentecostal Glossolalia as Commitment Act

Observations in a wider range of types of Pentecostal groups make it clear that not only glossolalia, but attitudinal and behavioral changes associated with it, occur also among well-educated, socially successful, and well-adjusted personality types.
This can be understood only if the phenomenon of
glossolalia and characteristic personal changes are
set in the context of the movement as a whole. As
we have shown in other articles (Gerlach and Hine
1968, 1969) there are five factors crucial to the
growth and success of a movement. One of these is
personal commitment on the part of participants.
We found that glossolalia was significantly related
to commitment in Pentecostalism as a movement.

As an indicator of involvement in the movement,
we used frequency of interaction with other "Spirit-
filled" Christians (tongue speakers in non-Pentecostal
churches, as well as members of Pentecostal sects or
independent groups of glossolalics). Individuals
were assigned a score from one to seven based on
whether they reported meeting with other participants
daily, four times a week, twice a week, once a week,
once or twice a month, a few times a year, or never.
We found that frequent glossolalics were indeed significantly more involved in movement activities (at

the .04 level).

The two components of commitment which we have
been able to identify in Pentecostalism, Black Power,
and other movements are: first, an experience
through which an individual's image of himself is
altered and some degree of cognitive reorganization
in the direction of movement ideology takes place;
and second, the performance of an objectively observable act. This must be what we have called a
"bridge-burning" act which sets the individual apart
from the larger society to some degree, identifies
him with the group in which he experienced it, and
commits him to certain changes in attitudinal or
behavioral patterns.

It has already been suggested that glossolalia
is part of an experiential complex through which
cognitive changes occur. For American Pentecostals,
glossolalia can also constitute a bridge-burning act.
In a society where public display of intense emotion
is reserved for spectator sports, and where the appropriate background for spontaneous and uninhibited
self-expression is the cocktail party, the abandonment
of one's self to a joyous flow of unintelligible vocalizations and possibly some non-consciously controlled physical behavior is considered indecent if
not insane. The enthusiastic "witnessing" or recruitment activities that seem to be an irresistible
after-effect are thought by many outsiders to be
equally unseemly. The type of criticism that tongue-
speakers in non-Pentecostal churches are subject to,
the many instances of removal of ministers who become involved, the economic pressures for "recanting,"
etc., make it quite clear that glossolalia can and
does function to set its practitioners apart from
the rest of church-going America in a significant way.

Functional Alternatives

We found in our survey of the movement in Haiti,
Mexico, and Colombia that there are functional alternatives for the bridge-burning act in other cultural
settings.

In Mexico and other Latin American countries,
particularly in rural areas, the break with the

Catholic church often results in social and sometimes
economic cleavages. In some cases just walking into
an *Evangelico* church constitutes a bridge-burning
act. We noted that those who were converted to Pentecostalism from other Protestant denominations--i.e.
those who were not making the break with Catholicism
and thus for whom attendance at the Pentecostal
church would seem less radical--tended to put more
emphasis on glossolalia as an important part of the
Spirit-filled life.

In Haiti, where spirit possession is characteristic of Voodoo, the majority religion, and where
glossolalia is a socially acceptable form of behavior,
commitment to Pentecostalism was reinforced by a
ritual burning of Voodoo objects. This was an act
which involved risk and separation from the larger
community.

Summary

Cross-cultural studies of religious behavior
support the assumption accepted by most anthropolo-
gists that the capacity for ecstatic experience and
trance, or other associated behaviors is panhuman.
Only the interpretation of it, the techniques designed to facilitate or inhibit it, and the form it
takes differ cross-culturally. When such states and
behaviors are valued in a society (as they are in
many non-Western societies), this capacity can be
systematically encouraged in some or all of its
members. When they are devalued, they can be culturally inhibited, and appear only as deviant behavior. If such "deviant" behavior functions to
set practitioners apart from the larger society
through specific and desired personal changes, these
extra-ordinary experiences may be institutionalized
to make what David Aberle would call "religious
virtuosi of the ordinary worshippers" (1966).

Through a functional approach to the phenomenon,
we have come to assess glossolalia as a non-pathological linguistic behavior which functions in the
context of the Pentecostal movement as one component
in the generation of commitment. As such, it operates
in social change, facilitating the spread of the

Pentecostal movement affecting nearly every denomination within organized Christianity, and in personal change, providing powerful motivation for
attitudinal and behavioral changes in the direction
of group ideals.

REFERENCES

Aberle, David F. 1966. *The Peyote Religion Among
the Navaho.* Wenner-Gren Foundation for Anthropological Research, No. 42. Viking Fund Publ.,
New York.

Alland, Alexander. 1961. Possession in a Revivalist
Negro Church. *Journal for the Scientific Study
of Religion,* 1, 204-213.

American Lutheran Church. 1964. *Report of the Field
Study Committee on Speaking in Tongues.* Commission on Evangelism. Minneapolis, Minnesota.

Boisen, Anton. 1939. Economic Distress and Religious Experience: A Study of the Holy Rollers.
Psychiatry, 2: 185-194.

Bourguignon, E. and L. Pettay. 1964. Spirit Possession, Trance, and Cross-Cultural Research.
Proc. Amer. Ethnological Soc., Spring 1964:
38-49.

Cantril, Hadley. 1941. *The Psychology of Social
Movements.* Chapman and Hall, Ltd. or Science
Editions (1963), N.Y.

Cutten, George B. 1927. *Speaking With Tongues.*
Yale University Press, New Haven.

Frank, Jerome D. 1961. *Persuasion and Healing:
A Comparative Study of Psychotherapy.* Johns
Hopkins Press, Baltimore.

Geertz, Clifford. 1965. Religion as a Cultural
System. In *Anthropological Approaches to the
Study of Religion.* M. Banton, ed. Praeger,
New York.

Gerlach, L. P. and Virginia H. Hine. 1968. Five
    Factors Crucial to the Growth and Spread of a
    Modern Religious Movement. *Journal for the
    Scientific Study of Religion,* 7: 23-40.

    1969. The Social Organization of a Movement of
    Revolutionary Change: Case Study, Black
    Power. In *Afro-American Anthropology.* N.
    Whitten, ed. Free Press.

Gerrard, Nathan L. and Louise B. 1966. *Scrabble
    Creek Folk: Mental Health, Part II.* Unpubl.
    report, Dept. of Sociology, Morris Harvey
    College, Charleston, W. Va.

Hine, Virginia H. 1967. The Deprivation and Dis-
    organization Theories of Social Movements.
    Unpubl. report prepared for Dr. Luther Gerlach,
    Department of Anthropology, University of
    Minnesota.

Hoekema, Anthony A. 1966. *What About Tongue
    Speaking?* Eerdmans. Grand Rapids.

Jaquith, James R. 1967. Toward a Typology of
    Formal Communicative Behaviors: Glossolalia.
    Anthropological Linguistics, 9 (No. 8).

Kiev, Ari. 1964. The study of Folk Psychiatry.
    In *Magic, Faith and Healing: Studies in Prim-
    itive Psychiatry.* Glencoe, Free Press. 3-35.

Kildahl, John. 1966. Unpublished Report to the
    Commission on Evangelism, American Lutheran
    Church.

Kimball, Solon T. 1966. Individualism and the
    Formation of Values. *Journal of Applied Be-
    havioral Sciences,* 2: 465-482.

Lapsley, J. N. and J. M. Simpson. 1964a. Speaking
    in Tongues: Token of Group Acceptance and Di-
    vine Approval. *Pastoral Psychology,* May:
    48-55.

1964b. Speaking in Tongues: Infantile Babble or
Song of the Self? *Pastoral Psychology*, Sept.:
16-24.

Martin, Ira. 1960. *Glossolalia in the Apostolic
Church*. Berea College Press, Berea, Ky.

Maslow, Abraham H. 1964. *Religions, Values, and
Peak Experiences*. Ohio State University Press,
Columbus.

May, L. Carlyle. 1956. A Survey of Glossolalia and
Related Phenomena in Non-Christian Religions.
American Anthropologist, 58: 75-96.

McDonnell, Kilian. 1968. Pentecostalism and Drug
Addiction. *America*, 118: 402-406.

Meares, Ainslee. 1963. Theories of Hypnosis. In
Hypnosis in Modern Medicine. J. Schneck, ed.
Springfield.

Pattison, E. Mansell. 1964. Speaking in Tongues
and About Tongues. *Christian Standard*, Feb. 15.

Protestant Episcopal Church, Diocese of California.
1963. *Study Commission Report on Glossolalia*.
Division of Pastoral Services. San Francisco.

Samarin, William. 1968a. The Linguisticality of
Glossolalia. *Hartford Quarterly*, 8 (No. 4):
49-75.

1968b. Glossolalia as Learned Behavior. Unpubl.
paper presented to the annual meeting of the
Society for the Scientific Study of Religion,
Montreal.

Sargant, William. 1949. Some Cultural Group Abre-
active Techniques and their Relation to Modern
Treatments. *Proc. Royal Soc. of Medicine*,
42: 367.

1957. *Battle for the Mind*. Doubleday, New York.

Toch, Hans.   1965.   *The Social Psychology of Social Movements*.   Sams, New York.

Vivier, Lincoln M.V.E.   1960.   *Glossolalia*.   Unpubl. thesis, University of Witwatersrand, Department of Psychiatry.   Microfilm at University of Chicago and Union Theological Seminary.

Wood, William W.   1965.   *Culture and Personality Aspects of the Pentecostal Holiness Religion*. Mouton, Paris.

Yinger, J. Milton.   1957.   *Religion, Society and the Individual*.   Macmillan, New York.

ADAPTIVE REGRESSION AND INTENSE RELIGIOUS EXPERIENCES[1]

JOEL ALLISON

Editor's introduction. "Conversion is in its
essence a normal adolescent phenomenon, incidental to the passage from the child's small
universe to the wider intellectual and spiritual life of maturity" (James, 1961, p. 167).
Much has changed in the world of normal adolescence since William James made this statement
in 1903. We may speculate that other forms of
"conversion," or drastic changes in adolescent
beliefs, have taken the place of traditional
religious experience. Adolescence is a time
of decision and struggle, and young people
today are showing sudden, and gradual, changes
in non-religious ways, which are reminiscent
of the traditional adolescent conversion. We
may still regard religious conversion, when it

[1]This study was supported by Grant MH 10661-01
from the National Institute of Mental Health, USPHS.
The author wishes to thank Dr. Alan Feirstein for
assistance with the statistical analyses.

occurs, as the model of intense identity crisis
and resolution in adolescence.

Allison's approach to conversion is in line
with that of Alland and Hine. He moves away
from seeing conversion as a pathological experience and analyzes it in the context of adaptation and development. At the same time,
Allison uses the notions of individual dynamics
to explain the conversion experience. The ego-
psychological analysis is highly sophisticated.
The use of the Rorschach test, and the theoretical discussion, may intimidate the uninitiated
reader, but the essential concepts are presented
simply and clearly.

The specific question for study was whether
conversion experiences are disruptive or adaptive for the individual's personality integration. The hypothesis was that if conversion is
indeed an integrative experience, persons who
had experienced it would be better able to integrate primitive ideation on the Rorschach test.
Those who had experienced sudden conversion were
considered more likely to regress and present
primitive, nonlogical material, but they were
also considered likely to deal with it adequately. The hypothesis was supported by
Rorschach scores. This finding does not imply
that the ability to integrate primitive material
was a result of the conversion experiences. It
is probable that the subjects had had this ability before their conversions. The major significance of the finding lies in the indication
that conversion experiences in this population
are related to the presence of adaptive, rather
than pathological, traits.

Allison's discussion points to possible limitations and extensions of the results. While
he may be criticized for overemphasizing individual factors, Allison's article is an out-
standing example of what can be achieved in the
individual psychology of religion with the help
of theoretical sophistication and imaginative
use of instruments. A related article (Allison,
1969) analyzes in detail the experiences of one

of the subjects in the present study and gives
due attention to family dynamics and environmental factors.

REFERENCES

Allison, J. Religious conversion: Regression and
progression in an adolescent experience. *Journal for the Scientific Study of Religion,* 1969,
8, 23-38.

James, W. *The varieties of religious experience.*
New York: Collier, 1961.

Despite a flurry of interest in the study of
religious phenomena around the turn of the century
(9, 26, 48, 49), the study of religious conversion
experiences is still in its infancy. Even efforts
to arrive at an adequate definition of the essential
characteristics of a conversion experience have not
proceeded beyond earlier attempts. Most often, conversion experiences have been classified according
to two types: one "mild and gradual," progressive
in development, the result of conscious volitional
efforts and a "reasoned search"; the other more
"dramatic and sudden," in which there occurs an
abrupt eruption of nonconscious forces which the
person feels to be located outside of himself. Some
writers, however, in an attempt to circumvent any
distinction among types of conversions, have defined
conversion simply as a change in one's way of life
(23). But since conversion experiences have been
said to have different characteristics, depending
on whether they are mild and gradual or sudden and
dramatic, it may make most sense at this point to
treat the two types separately. Whereas there is
general agreement that mild and gradual conversion
experiences tend to be progressive and maturing,
there has been considerable controversy regarding
the nature of the more sudden and dramatic experiences and centering around their progressive or
regressive characteristics. This paper, therefore,

will be concerned with the more intense conversion
experiences, defined here as sudden and dramatic incidents which are subjectively characterized as spiritual awakenings, have a special intensity often involving strong emotional arousal, are at times accompanied by hallucinatory-like phenomena, and lead
to changes in subsequent behavior.

Several lines of recent theoretical investigation suggest that a fuller understanding of such
conversion experiences may aid in clarifying some
salient issues confronting the psychology of human
behavior. On the one hand, certain similarities have
been noted (18, 45) among the diverse processes of
religious healing, religious revivalism (the aim of
which is to produce conversions), thought reform and
psychotherapy--processes which aim to promote changes
in one's "highly structured, complex, interacting
sets of values, expectations and images of oneself
and others..." (18, p. 21). These seemingly disparate processes are similar in that they involve
emotional crises, upheaval and initial disorganization which lead ultimately to personality reorganization. The significance of "crises" in facilitating
personality development has also been given special
consideration in Erikson's (14) work and in Dabrowski's (11) recent theory of "positive disintegration,"
which states that the most accelerated personality
growth takes place during states of apparent disintegration and acute crisis.

Concurrently, there has been an increased concern within psychoanalytic theory with the adaptive,
integrative and maturing facets of behavior (22, 40)
and with the importance of hitherto neglected patterns
of religious, political and ethnic orientation (13).
This development has led to a revision of an earlier
treatment of religious experiences solely along
libidinal and pathological lines that neglected the
progressive, adaptive aspects of the experiences.
One tendency reflecting the earlier approach has been
to emphasize the essentially pathological, destructive and disintegrating features of sudden and dramatic conversion experiences, their close resemblance
to psychosis, and their likelihood of occurrence in
authoritarian, totalistic religious frameworks (43,
44). Increasingly, however, an alternate view has

emphasized that conversion (as one type of mystical or "peak" [32] experience) is generally a "phenomenon functioning to reintegrate the ego" (8, p. 216) that can result in the "loss of a certain kind of anxiety-generated self-consciousness...and thereby serve a creative rather than regressive movement" (17, p. 33). As in creativity (29, 46), empathy (47) and hypnotic states (21), the religious conversion experience may tap more primitive or unconscious modes of thought, affect and action in order to achieve a new and more advanced level of personality integration and organization (6, 35, 38).

A major consequence of the recent psychoanalytic interest in adaptive, maturing facets of behavior and of the shift away from a sole emphasis on disturbance of function has been an increased clarity in the differentiation between pathological regressive states (like most psychotic regression) and states of regression which serve personality integration and adaptation. One of the hallmarks of the difference between creative activity, for example, and pathological regression is the degree to which the ego is overwhelmed and inundated by primitive, nonlogical ideas or the degree to which the ego more flexibly allows itself access to such ideation. In psychosis, of course, the experience is one of inundation. Although mystical experiences and states of religious fervor and exaltation may exist in psychosis, they are more likely to give way rapidly to terror (20). In creativity, however, access to primitive, non-logical content and modes of thought serves the purpose of productive, enriching activity. Furthermore, some writers agree that the duration, reversibility and effects of a seemingly regressive experience are the dominant aspects by which one can differentiate pathological regression (*i.e.*, psychotic states) from the more beneficial regressive experiences like creativity (commonly labeled regression in the service of the ego [3, 19, 21, 46]). Adaptive regressive experiences are more circumscribed in time; they have a definite beginning and end and tend to be transitory. They also are reversible--the usual organization of the psyche is reinstated suddenly and totally, not slowly and gradually, and sober reality and everyday life activities are returned to.

They increase self-esteem and the sense of being a
worthwhile and active individual, and they sometimes
have direct constructive influences on the lives of
others.

When we turn from anecdotal reports and theoretical statements to empirical studies in order to assess the relative destructive or progressive nature
of intense religious conversion experiences, we are
confronted with a paucity of such studies. One study
found that 1st year divinity students who had one
rather dramatic religious experience which markedly
affected the course of their lives (28) had lower intelligence scores (on the ACE) and scored higher on
the Minnesota Multiphasic Personality Inventory (MMPI)
hysteria scale than did a control group. However,
their hysteria scores were within the normal range
and no differences were found in authoritarianism,
repression, humanitarianism or religious conservatism.
In a study of members of the Pentecostal Holiness
religion, for whom conversion is a regular experience,
Wood found some evidence that Pentecostalism can help
people reach a state of satisfactory interpersonal
relatedness (53). Although these two studies seem
to offer some tentative support for viewing conversion
phenomena as a means of promoting personality integration, both are limited in that the authors do not
fully use their test findings, especially by not exploring qualitative aspects of their subjects' thought
processes to determine more closely the type and degree of any regressive modes of thought.

The purpose of this study is, by its focus on the
thought processes of people who have had conversion
experiences, to explore the degree to which intense
conversion experiences are either destructive and
disintegrating or constructive and integrating. If
conversion experiences tend to be destructive and
pathological, we might expect people who have had intense conversions to show a less adaptive use of
primitive, nonlogical ideation and be more inundated
by it than would people with weak or no conversion
experience. On the other hand, if conversion experiences serve as integrative, adaptive experiences,
people who have such experiences should demonstrate

a significant adaptive use of nonlogical ideation.[2]
     Recent work with the Rorschach test reflects
the conceptual differentiation made by psychoanalytic
ego psychologists between pathological regression
and adaptive regressive experience. A system recently derived for scoring the Rorschach in terms of
the capacity for adaptive regressive experiences (24,
25) can help clarify the extent to which people vary
in their capacity to employ more primitive or unconscious modes of thinking in the service of the ego
and adaptation. This socring system could tell us
something about the relative intactness of the ego
functioning of people who have religious conversion
experiences, particularly the degree of their adaptive and maladaptive thought processes.

     METHOD

     Subjects

     The subjects were 20 male students working to-
ward a Bachelor of Divinity degree in a northern university who were selected on the basis of an autobiographical statement made when applying to divinity
school and also in terms of whether they had indicated
"unusual or mystical" experiences on a routinely administered paper and pencil questionnaire of their
religious motivations. Ten were selected who had

     [2]The assumption underlying this focus on the
characteristics of thought processes is, of course,
basic to all clinical psychological testing, namely
that patterns of cognition are an important index of
an individual's more general thought processes, affective experience and behavior. Moreover, there has
been increasing interest in basic thought processes
in conceptualizing psychopathology rather than in
overt symptomatology alone. Witness the significant
recent research on schizophrenia which concentrates
on patterns of verbal communication among families
which have a schizophrenic child and demonstrates
similar, illogical modes of thinking and communicating
in family members who show no overt schizophrenic
symptomatology (31, 51, 52).

reported sudden identifiable religious experiences.
Ten control subjects were selected who were matched
in age, religious denomination, geographical background and marital status, but who did not report
religious conversion or religious mystical experiences; therefore, their religious development was
probably more gradual and less eventful. The selection criteria did not differentiate between subjects
whom the conversion experience had led to the decision
to enter the ministry and those for whom it was an
important experience which facilitated religious
growth but had not directly resulted in a decision
for the ministry. Subjects were selected by two
assistants so that the experimenter would not know
whether the student was a "conversion" or "nonconversion" subject until after testing. When the subjects were contacted by phone and asked to participate
in a study of the psychological characteristics of
divinity students, no mention was made of an interest
in conversion. All but two subjects (1 conversion;
1 nonconversion) volunteered to participate, and these
were replaced. All were seen for a total of 7 hours
in three separate sessions. The first two sessions
were taken up with a battery of psychological tests--
the Wechsler Adult Intelligence Scale, the Thematic
Apperception Test and the Rorschach--and the final
session consisted entirely of a loosely structured
interview. Only the Rorschach and adaptive regression
findings are presented here.

Rorschach Test

Rorschachs were administered and scored according to the procedure described by Rapaport *et al.*
(41). In addition, scoring also followed Holt's
criteria (24, 25) for assessing Rorschach responses
in terms of how much, if any, primitive drive content or nonlogical thinking they involve (*i.e.*, their
primary process aspects) and what degree of adaptive
control the subject has over such thinking.
Drive content: Responses are scored according
to whether they contain content with libidinal or
aggressive characteristics. More specifically, responses are classified in terms of whether the drive

content is oral, anal, sexual, exhibitionistic and
voyeuristic, homosexual or aggressive.

Formal aspects: The formal characteristics of
responses include the "perceptual organization of
the response," "the thought process that underlies
responding" and "the language in which the response
is verbalized" (24, p. 5). In large part, the scoring for formal aspects includes indications on the
Rorschach of syncretic thought mechanisms, such as
condensations, displacement, substitution and sym-
bolization, as well as on the relative absence of
"conjunctions and causal, temporal and other relationships" (39, p. 229).

Defense demand ($\sum DD/R$): This is what Holt refers to as the "shock value" of the response. This
score essentially indicates the strength, directness,
primitiveness and deviance from conventional logical
considerations both of the drive content and of the
formal aspects. Defense demand is scored on a five-
point scale (1 to 5), ranging from more "socialized"
communications (*e.g.*, food, an angry look, a man with
wings--Icarus) to more blatant expressions of drive
content (*e.g.*, mutilative and cannibalistic imagery)
and of formal features (*e.g.*, the unrealistic combination of a crab with bat's wings; the contaminatory
response of a lion egg because it is the shape of an
egg and is the color of a lion). Several scores for
defense demand are derived: one is based on the combined content and formal features (defense demand
total); one is based solely on the content features
(defense demand content); and the third is based on
the formal features (defense demand formal). An additional way of scoring defense demand, other than
by the five-point scale, is to consider only extreme
and mild instances of primitive, nonlogical thinking.
Level 1 makes up the more extreme examples and level
2 the milder, more socialized ones.

*Defense effectiveness ($\sum DE/No.$ of primitive re-
sponses):* The success of control over drive-infused,
nonlogical ideation. Adequate control over the expression of drive and formal aspects consists of
supplying a relatively good match between the response and the properties of the card (good form
level), of supplying an appropriate intellectual,
esthetic or cultural context for the images, and

also of demonstrating affective pleasure in the responses. This latter characteristic--the attitude
of the subject toward his responses--is crucial. A
way out idea accompanied by a playful relaxation of
ego controls will be sharply distinct from a similar
idea blandly expressed or accompanied by signs of
discomfort and disturbance, such as fear, terror or
forced gaiety.

   Adaptive regression ($\sum DD \times DE/R$): A measure of
the degree of meaningful integration both of drive
content and of nonlogical thinking; it is obtained
by multiplying the defense demand of each response
containing drive content and/or nonrealistic thinking
by its defense effectiveness, summing the products,
and dividing them by the total number of Rorschach
responses. This procedure places subjects with great
amounts of primitive, unrealistic thinking coupled
with poor control at the maladaptive end of a continuum and subjects with great amounts of primitive,
unrealistic thinking accompanied by good control at
the adaptive end.

   RESULTS

   Although at the outset this study was intended
to analyze the results in terms of the two groups of
10 subjects each (conversion and nonconversion), it
was discovered during the interviews conducted after
the testing that the two groups were not as distinct
as was thought. Four subjects selected as controls
who did not report conversion experiences in their
autobiographical statements in their application to
divinity school or the presence of religious mystical
experience in an inventory of religious motivations,
turned out to have had some sort of very mild conversion experience, the religious significance of
which they were now unsure or else rejected as of
minor importance. Therefore, an alternate procedure
was devised for analyzing the findings. All 20 subjects were divided into three separate groups varying
in intensity of conversion experiences (none, $N = 6$;
weak, $N = 7$; or strong, $N = 7$) and these groups were
compared on the relevant dimensions. Both the author
and another psychologist independently placed the

subjects into the groups; the two raters agreed on
the placement of 19 of the 20 subjects (95 per cent)
according to the intensity of the emotional arousal
and degree of hallucinatory-like phenomena involved
in the conversion experience. Since the variation
in intensity of experience merely extended the initial classification of two groups with and without
conversion experiences, the original matching procedure still ensured little relationship of intensity
of experience with marital status, religious denomination or geographical location.

Some details about the entire sample show that
their mean IQ is 124, and their mean age 23; 13 are
Methodists, 2 are Presbyterian, 1 is Congregational,
1 is Southern Baptist, 1 is of the United Church of
Christ, and 2 others are from small revivalistic denominations. Nine are from the South, 6 from the
Midwest, 4 from the Northeast and 1 from the South-
west.

All Rorschachs were scored by the experimenter
and then independently by another psychologist. Reliability for defense demand scores ($\sum DD/R$) was .99;
for defense effectiveness scores ($\sum DE$/No. of primitive
respones) .81; and for the combined adaptive regression score ($\sum DD \times DE/R$) .67. In instances in which
a disagreement in scoring existed, a composite score
based on the average of the two raters' scores was
used.

Table 1 presents mean scores for each group on
three measures of primitive, nonlogical thinking:
defense demand ($\sum DD/R$), defense effectiveness ($\sum DE$/No.
of primitive responses) and adaptive regression ($\sum DD
\times DE/R$). Table 1 also presents the means for drive
content and formal scores separately. Statistical
analysis consisted of analyses of variance among the
three groups. Moreover, in order to assess the
source of variation among the groups, separate tests
of the trend of the data were carried out to determine whether results with the F tests reflected a
difference among the groups based on a step-wise
linear increase in intensity of conversion or whether
some other type of relationship existed.

Table 1 shows significant F test results and
significant linear trends for defense demand total
and adaptive regression total scores. Therefore, an

increase in intensity of conversion experience from none to weak to strong is related to corresponding increases both in the extent of primitive nonlogical thinking and in the degree of successful integration of this more primitive thinking. Thus, subjects with increasingly intense conversion experiences also show a correspondingly increasing capacity for adaptively controlled regressive thinking. Table 1 also shows that defense effectiveness total scores by themselves do not discriminate the groups. Inasmuch as the accuracy of form of Rorschach responses is one important facet of what constitutes effective control over primitive content and modes of thought, a supplemental assessment was also made of the degree to which the form level of the response by itself (determined by the Mayman [34] scoring system) is a sufficient indication of control. Scores similar to the defense effectiveness and adaptive regression scores were computed, using only form level as the index of control. Although Cohen (10) and Feirstein (15) found that form level by itself can be significantly discriminative as an indication of control over primitive, nonlogical thinking, this study found no significant relationships (F tests or trend analyses) between intensity of the conversion experience and either defense effectiveness or adaptive regression when determined by form level alone.

TABLE 1

Mean Rorschach Scores of Primitive Ideation and Its Integration for Religious Conversion Groups

	Total			Content			Formal		
	Defense Demand $\Sigma DD/R$	Defense Effectiveness $\Sigma DE/$ No. of Primitive Responses	Adaptive Regression $\Sigma DD \times DE/R$	$\Sigma DD/R$	$\Sigma DE/$ No. of Primitive Responses	$\Sigma DD \times DE/R$	$\Sigma DD/R$	$\Sigma DE/$ No. of Primitive Responses	$\Sigma DD \times DE/R$
None $N = 6$	1.08	.58	.51	.83	.58	.41	.38	.51	.18
Weak $N = 7$	1.13	.60	.63	.85	.58	.46	.51	.48	.26
Strong, $N = 7$	1.56	.65	.95	1.09	.66	.69	.95	.60	.53
F	5.11*	0.33	3.66*	2.00	0.33	3.00	8.43†	0.50	4.02*
Linear trend	8.22*	0.33	6.40*	3.14	0.67	5.20*	14.71†	0.50	6.96*
Residual trend	2.11	0.33	0.93	0.86	0.00	1.00	2.28	0.50	1.07

* $p < .05$.
† $p < .01$.

When we consider differences in defense demand for content and formal variables separately (Table 1), we see that it is primarily the defense demand of the

formal variables which contributes to the overall
difference between the groups, although significant
linear trends appear in adaptive regression for content as well as for formal variables. Furthermore,
when the content and formal variables are broken
down in terms of their amount of level 1 (direct and
blatant manifestations) and level 2 (more socialized
manifestations) (Table 2), it appears that both level
1 and level 2 formal responses show significant linear
trends. This means that the overall difference among
the groups in formal defense demand is not solely due
to an abundance of more socialized primary process
ideation which often has a defensive component built
into it (level 2), but also that the increase in defense demand reflects an increase in both more and
less primitive ideation.

TABLE 2

*Mean Rorschach Scores of Extreme (Level 1)
and Mild (Level 2) Primitive Ideation for
Religious Conversion Groups*

	Level 1		Level 2	
	Drive Content/ R	Formal/R	Drive Content/ R	Formal/R
None	.04	.07	.55	.12
Weak	.03	.08	.58	.19
Strong	.08	.18	.73	.27
F	1.00	3.12	1.25	3.50
Linear trend	1.00	5.06*	2.02	6.00*
Residual trend	1.00	1.17	.048	1.00

* $p < .05$.

DISCUSSION

    The major findings presented here indicate that
stronger, more intense conversion experiences of the
sudden and dramatic type are associated with greater
amounts of primitive, nonlogical thought manifestations and, particularly significant, that they are
also associated with better integration of such
ideation. Thus, persons with more intense experiences appear to demonstrate a more pronounced capacity for regressive experiences of an adaptive nature.

If we also consider that several studies have demonstrated that the capacity for adaptive regression is
positively related to greater tolerance for ambiguity
(10, 15) and to better quality of imaginative produc-
tiveness (37) and is inversely related to dogmatism
(10), it appears even more likely that intense conversion experiences do not of necessity occur within
authoritarian, rigid or pathological contexts. These
findings are at variance with the notion that abrupt,
sudden conversion experiences are essentially pathological, destructive, and closely akin to psychosis.
    From the point of view of recent efforts to
differentiate pathological regression from more beneficial regressive experiences (regression in the
service of the ego) in terms of the duration, reversibility and effects of seemingly regressive phenomena,
the conversions of these subjects also appear to possess some characteristics of adaptive regressive experiences, since their experiences are transitory and
appear to lead to increased self-esteem (at least
temporarily). What is less clear, however, is whether
the mental organization of the subjects is reinstated
suddenly and totally, whether it is the "usual" organization which is reinstated or whether some sort
of mental reorganization has resulted, possibly at
an even higher level than previously.
    Thus, although the findings of this study reveal
that at present subjects who have had conversion experiences are clearly able to employ more primitive
or unconscious modes of thinking in the service of
the ego and adaptation, they do not indicate the degree of intactness of ego functioning prior to the
conversion experience. Various possibilities exist:
the conversion experience helped to integrate subjects during a crisis and enabled them to reach a
mental organization on a higher level than previously,
or the capacity to employ regressive modes of thought
adaptively reflects a predispositional, charactero-
logical openness to experiences of an unrealistic
nature. In other words, are we confronted with a
phenomenon that strengthens a weak ego or one that
reflects a strong ego that could tolerate such experiences in the first place? On the one hand,
Maslow's work (33) on "peak" experiences demonstrates
that persons characterized by self-actualizing efforts

and more advanced and richer states of psychological
organization have a particular capacity to experience
states of mystical union and ecstasy--states which
reflect for his subjects an expansion of ego boundaries temporarily for the purpose of personality
gain and enrichment. Research in attitude formation,
in interpersonal communication and impression formation (16, 30, 42, 54) and in subthreshold stimulation
(2, 12) also suggests that cognitive attitudes and
beliefs which are organized into more flexible, open
and complex systems are better able to assimilate
new and disparate information than is a rigid, in-
flexible, simple and closed system. Accordingly,
one would surmise that systems which are initially
more flexible and open should tend to make one more
receptive to disparate and undifferentiated information from inner urges as well as from external reality.

However, we must also consider the equally
strong likelihood that conversion experiences serve
to a greater extent to help reorganize a weakened
ego rather than to reflect a preexisting strength
and capacity for unusual experiences. In fact, it
is this likelihood which has been most prominently
emphasized in the conversion literature. It has
been noted, for example, that conversion experiences
tend to occur during adolescence, that is, during a
period of life marked by an upsurge of instinctual
urges, by a weakened and sometimes fluid state of
personality organization and by changeability and
seeming disorder. Christensen, among others, has
discussed the role of the conversion experience in
reintegrating the weakened ego of the adolescent to
solve "an acute confusional state" (8, p. 208). The
body of research on attitude and personality change,
however, although it has been concerned with initial
states of cognitive organization, has tended to focus on flexible *vs*. rigid, complex *vs*. simple, or
open *vs*. closed systems. This body of research has
been less concerned with very unstructured initial
personality organization like that emphasized in
preconversion feelings of unsureness and inability
to solve problems. Perhaps, however, the less structured initial personality organization of the pre-
convert suggests a state of organization which is

more open and receptive to new attitudes that can
serve to supply a sense of integration and unity to
the personality. The appeal of ideologies to the
alienated has been well documented (14), as has the
greater persuasibility of persons with low self-
esteem and general passivity (27); both reports high-
light the search for structure, order and integration in those who feel themselves to be diffuse,
deficient and unintegrated.

The degree to which unrealistic experiences,
like conversion phenomena, are encouraged and have
meaning within a particular cultural context supplies
another crucial factor in assessing the adaptiveness
of an experience for any particular individual.
Cultures which place a considerable premium on highly
logical, realistic, conventional behavior will inevitably have a reduced tolerance for seemingly deviant forms of behavior. Some communities, however,
provide a high valuation of conversion experiences by
making church membership contingent on "conversion
signalled by a vision." Several studies (1, 50, 53)
have shown how glossolalia, trance and visions can
be requisites for church membership and even how the
content of the religious experience can reflect the
culture's goal. Recent studies of shamans also
tentatively suggest that shamans may, relative to
other members of their societies, possess a more
developed capacity to regress in the service of the
ego (7). That most subjects in this study are Methodists indicates an identification with a tradition
in which conversion experiences have long been emphasized. Nevertheless, there is a marked inconsistency
in the emphasis placed on the importance of conversion
experiences nowadays by their churches. Only two
subjects were brought up in denominations that required a conversion experience for church membership.
Most other subjects were familiar with conversions,
but conversion was not expected or encouraged in
their churches, especially in those of larger cities.
Neither was the conversion experience necessarily
linked with a specific decision ("call") to enter the
ministry, although in most cases it supplied a sense
of commitment and religious conviction that other
subjects felt they lacked and, to some extent, wist-
fully yearned for. Nonetheless, conversion was not

an unexpected or rare phenomenon in the life experience of these subjects; it had important historical
and cultural roots, even though it may not have been
highly valued within their particular church group.

In order for us to look further into the differences obtained among subjects in amount of primitive, unconscious modes of thinking, separate analyses of formal and drive content ideation were conducted. Interestingly, it appears that greater
amounts of primitive thinking of the formal type,
both of levels 1 and 2, characterize subjects with
intense conversion experiences. In order for us to
understand this finding, it may be helpful to consider recent efforts to clarify different kinds of
adaptive regressive experiences and also to examine
the nature of the conversion experience itself.
Schafer, for example, has suggested that in problem
solving in the sciences and in mathematics, the
capacity to regress in the service of the ego may
involve primarily a capacity for primitivization of
formal aspects of thought, that is, an ability to
recombine elements in new, unusual ways "without
obvious drive representation" (46, p. 132), whereas
other creative activities may require more access
to drive components of primary process thinking.
Arlow and Brenner (3), also discussing the different
senses in which the concept of regression is used,
suggest a distinction between instinctual regression
(to specific psychosexual phases of development and
the content associated with each) and other forms of
regression, including a regression of ego functions.
Few studies, however, have attempted to assess differential effects for formal and drive content aspects of thinking. Feirstein (15) found that subjects
who showed more tolerance for unrealistic experiences
also demonstrated greater adaptive regression (total
adaptive regression and also content and formal adaptive regression separately). However, the amount
(defense demand) of neither content nor formal primitive, nonlogical ideation related to the tolerance
for unrealistic experiences, demonstrating in his
study the greater importance of control variables
over indices of amount of primitive thinking. A
study of the relationship of primitive thinking to
problem solving of a highly logical nature (5) also

demonstrated that adaptive regression scores for
both formal and drive content ideation significantly
relate to efficient performance but that the amount
(defense demand) of neither formal nor drive content
thinking is related to problem-solving efficiency.
In another study of the capacity for adaptive regression (36), however, overall measures of the amount
of primitive thinking were found to be important in
a sample of unemployed actors, but control (adaptive
regression) variables were not found to be significant, and no effort was made to treat formal and
drive content variables separately. The difference
between the present study of conversion experiences
and adaptive regression and other studies of adaptive
regression, then, is the demonstration that the amount
(defense demand) of primitive ideation in particular
--is a significant factor in addition to the control
(adaptive regression) scores.

In order to try to understand the importance of
the amount of formal primitive thinking in subjects
in this study, we should consider the nature of conversion experiences. We find that conversion typically involves a loss generally of usual ego intactness, including a loss of temporal boundaries, a
fusion between self and God, and an inability to
distinguish percept from wish. These characteristics
tap essentially formal aspects of primitive (primary
process) thinking. When one approaches conversion
experiences in terms of their degree of drive content
(oral, anal, sexual, exhibitionistic, homosexual and
aggressive), the picture is somewhat changed. Although mystical experiences have often contained
striking manifestations of drive content--witness
the obvious sexual imagery of certain female mystics
--conversion experiences have not been explored systematically from this point of view. Subjects in
this study report content that is mostly gratifying
and positive in tone and relatively tame in terms of
psychosexual content. Dominant themes include feelings of loss of a heavy burden, of sorrow, sin and
desire, and an increase in feelings of joy, salvation,
mystical knowledge, perfection, and a new life. One
subject reported feeling heartwarmed, reunited and
close to God; one saw through God's eyes and experienced a pattern of eternal beauty in which the

generations of man merged in a procession before God;
another experienced a hallucinatory-like, agonizing
image of Christ on a crucifix, who seemed to call
out "why are you running?"; still another student
felt a chill up his spine as if a hand had removed
all opposition to his becoming a minister. Therefore, despite many formal alterations of states of
consciousness via mystical union, states of dedif-
ferentiation and hallucinatory-like imagery in these
subjects, drive content representations are relatively inconspicuous in conversion experiences.
Similarly, in a content analysis of the religious
visions of members of a Gulf State Negro community
in which church membership is contingent on "conversion signalled by a vision" (50, p. 330), the content of the visions largely stresses the positive
characteristics of attainment, aspiration, rebirth
and purity. This content was relatively undramatic
from a drive viewpoint; yet it occurred in the context of a dramatic formal alteration of usual experience via a vision. In sharp contrast to the
visions of the members of this Negro community and
of subjects in this study is Freud's discussion (20)
of the Schreber case. Among other mystically toned
psychotic manifestations, we find in Schreber's
thinking a pervasive primitivization by drive content as well as by formal primitive components; *e.g.*,
"rays of God not infrequently thought themselves entitled to mock at me by calling me 'Miss Schreber'"
(20, p. 399). Thus, it may be that primitivization
by drives, particularly when accompanied by a disturbed affect, occurs in mystically toned religious
contexts which more clearly approach psychotic proportions, whereas many conversion experiences may
entail primarily a formal primitivization in the absence of a conspicuous alteration of drive content
elements. Moreover, the greater importance of the
amount of formal primitive thinking in subjects in
this study, as compared with the studies of Feirstein
(15) and Blatt and Allison (5), may stem from the
greater degree of formal primitivization inherent in
a conversion experience than in performance in a variety of perceptual tasks (such as the phi phenomenon,
reversible figures, aniseikonic lenses and stimulus
incongruity) or in problem solving of a highly

logical, abstractive and synthetic nature.

The subjects of this study, although divergent in their background and religious training, make up a fairly homogeneous group--rather bright male divinity students in a university divinity school in which students are confronted with many liberal theological viewpoints. In such a school, unlike many denominational schools, less emphasis is often placed on the more enthusiastic forms of religious experience such as religious conversions. Contrary to the revivalistic preaching of Billy Sunday that "in a dispute between enthusiasm and scholarship, scholarship can go to hell" (4, p. 355) scholarship is instead rigorously emphasized. Thus, it may be that people with religious experiences which were seemingly more pathological were rejected by the school in the first place or did not choose to apply. Whereas a more inclusive study of the phenomenon of religious conversion and its potentially adaptive, integrative function would have to include other such subjects, this study nonetheless does demonstrate that conversion *can* occur in a setting of adaptive potential and realization.

REFERENCES

1. Alland, A. "Possession" in a revivalistic Negro church. J. Sci. Stud. Religion, 1: 204-213, 1962.

2. Allison, J. Cognitive structure and receptivity to low intensity stimulation. J. Abnorm. Soc. Psychol., 67: 132-138, 1963.

3. Arlow, J. A. and Brenner, C. *Psychoanalytic Concepts and the Structural Theory.* Int. Universities Press, New York, 1964.

4. Bell, D. Social sciences and law. In Hutchins, R. M. and Adler, M. S., eds. *The Great Ideas Today, 1964, pp.* 314-366. Encyclopedia Britannica, Atheneum, New York, 1964.

5. Blatt, S. J. and Allison, J. Non-intellectual
   factors in cognitive efficiency [Final Report
   on Project 1931]. Office of Education, U.S.
   Department of Health, Education and Welfare,
   1967.

6. Boisen, A. T. *The Exploration of the Inner
   World*. Harper & Row, New York, 1936.

7. Boyer, L. B. Comparisons of the shamans and
   pseudo-shamans of the Apaches of the Mescalero
   Indian reservation: A Rorschach study. J.
   Project Tech., 28: 173-180, 1964.

8. Christensen, C. W. Religious conversion. Arch.
   Gen. Psychiat. (Chicago), 9: 207-216, 1963.

9. Coe, G. A. *The Spiritual Life*. Abingdon, New
   York, 1900.

10. Cohen, I. H. Adaptive regression, dogmatism and
    creativity. Doctoral dissertation, Michigan
    State University, East Lansing, 1960.

11. Dabrowski, K. *Positive Disintegration*. Little,
    Brown, Boston, 1964.

12. Dember, W. N. *Psychology of Perception*. Holt,
    New York, 1960.

13. Erikson, E. H. *Childhood and Society*. Norton,
    New York, 1950.

14. Erikson, E. H. *Young Man Luther*. Norton, New
    York, 1958.

15. Freirstein, A. Personality correlates of toler-
    ance for unrealistic experiences. J. Consult.
    Psychol., 31: 387-395, 1967.

16. Festinger, L. *A Theory of Cognitive Dissonance*.
    Row, Peterson, Evanston, Illinois, 1957.

17. Fingarette, H. The ego and mystic selflessness.
    Psychoanal. Rev., 45: 5-40, 1958.

18. Frank, J. D. *Persuasion and Healing.* The Johns
    Hopkins Press, Baltimore, 1961.

19. Freud, A. Regression as a principle in mental
    development. Paper presented to the Topeka
    Psychoanalytic Society and Topeka Institute
    of Psychoanalysis, Topeka, 1962.

20. Freud, S. Psychoanalytic notes upon an autobio-
    graphical account of a case of paranoia. In
    Collected Papers, vol. 3, pp. 390-467. Hogarth
    Press, London, 1953.

21. Gill, M. M. and Brenman, M. *Hypnosis and Related
    States*, International Universities Press, New
    York, 1961.

22. Hartmann, H. *Ego Psychology and the Problem of
    Adaptation (1939)*. International Universities
    Press, New York, 1958.

23. Hill, W. S. The psychology of conversion. Pas-
    toral Psychol., 6(58): 43-46, 1955.

24. Holt, R. R. Manual for the scoring of primary
    process manifestations in Rorschach responses
    [Reproduced in mimeographed form at the Research
    Center for Mental Health], New York, 1962.

25. Holt, R. R. and Havel, J. A method for assessing
    primary and secondary process in the Rorschach.
    In Rickers-Ovsiankina, M. A., ed. *Rorschach
    Psychology*, pp. 263-315, Wiley, New York, 1960.

26. James, W. *The Varieties of Religious Experience.*
    Random House, New York, 1902.

27. Janis, I. L., Hovland, C. I., Field, P. B.,
    Linton, H., Graham, E., Cohen, A. R., Rife, D.,
    Abelson, R. P., Lesser, G. S. and King, B. T.
    Personality and Persuasability. Yale University
    Press, New York, 1959.

28. Kildahl, J. P. The personalities of sudden re-
    ligious converts. Pastoral Psychol., 16(156):
    37-45, 1965.

29. Kris, E. *Psychoanalytic Explorations in Art.*
    International Universities Press, New York,
    1952.

30. Leventhal, H. The effects of set and discrepancy
    on impression change. J. Personality, 30: 1-15,
    1962.

31. Lidz, T., Fleck, S., and Cornelison, A. *Schizo-
    phrenia and the Family.* International Univer-
    sities Press, New York, 1965.

32. Maslow, A. H. Cognition of being in the peak ex-
    perience. J. Genet. Psychol., 94: 43-67, 1959.

33. Maslow, A. H. *Toward a Psychology of Being.*
    Van Nostrand, Princeton, New Jersey, 1962.

34. Mayman, M. Rorschach form level manual. Repro-
    duced in mimeographed form at the Menninger
    Foundation, 1960.

35. Peterson, G. Regression in healing and salva-
    tion. Chicago Theological Seminary Register,
    55: 16-21, 1965.

36. Pine, F. Creativity and primary process: Sample
    variations. J. Nerv. Ment. Dis., 134: 506-511,
    1962.

37. Pine, F. and Holt, R. R. Creativity and primary
    process: A study of adaptive regression. J.
    Abnorm. Soc. Psychol., 61: 370-379, 1960.

38. Prince, R. H. and Savage, C. Mystical states
    and the concept of regression. In *Proceedings
    of the First Annual Conference of the R. M.
    Bucke Memorial Society.* Montreal, 1965.

39. Rapaport, D. The conceptual model of psycho-
    analysis. In Knight, R. P. and Friedman, C. R.,
    eds. *Psychoanalytic Psychiatry and Psychology.*
    International Universities Press, New York,
    1954.

40. Rapaport, D.   The structure of psychoanalytic theory: A systematizing attempt.   Psychol. Issues, 2: 1-158, 1960.

41. Rapaport, D., Gill, M. M. and Schafer, R.   *Diagnostic Psychological Testing,* vol. 2.   Yearbook, Chicago, 1946.

42. Rokeach, M.   *The Open and Closed Mind.*   Basic Books, New York, 1960.

43. Salzman, L.   The psychology of religious and ideological conversion.   Psychiatry, 16: 177-187, 1953.

44. Salzman, L.   Types of religious conversion. Pastoral Psychol., 17(166): 8-21, 1966.

45. Sargant, W.   *Battle for the Mind: A Physiology of Conversion and Brainwashing.*   Heinemann, London, 1957.

46. Schafer, R.   Regression in the service of the ego: The relevance of a psychoanalytic concept for personality assessment.   In Lindzey, G., ed.   *Assessment of Human Motives,* pp. 119-148. Grove Press, New York, 1960.

47. Schafer, R.   Generative empathy in the treatment situation.   Psychoanal. Quart., 28: 342-373, 1959.

48. Starbuck, E.   A study of conversion.   Amer. J. Psychol., 8: 268-308, 1897.

49. Starbuck, E.   *The Psychology of Religion.* Scribner, New York, 1912.

50. Stone, O. M.   Cultural uses of religious visions: A case study.   Ethnology, 1: 329-348, 1962.

51. Wild, C.   Disturbed styles of thinking.   Arch. Gen. Psychiat. (Chicago), 13: 464-470, 1965.

52. Wild, C., Singer, M., Rosman, B., Ricci, J. and
    Lidz, T. Measuring disordered styles of think-
    ing. Arch. Gen. Psychiat. (Chicago), 13: 471-
    476, 1965.

53. Wood, W. W. Culture and personality aspects of
    the Pentecostal Holiness religion. Doctoral
    dissertation. University of North Carolina,
    Chapel Hill, 1961.

54. Zajonc, R. The process of cognitive tuning in
    communication. J. Abnorm. Soc. Psychol., 61:
    159-168, 1960.

SELECTED ADDITIONAL READINGS ON INTENSE RELIGIOUS EXPERIENCE

Allison, J. Religious conversion: Regression and progression in an adolescent experience. *Journal for the Scientific Study of Religion*, 1969, 8, 23-38.

Dewhurst, K., & Beard, A. W. Sudden religious conversions in temporal lobe epilepsy. *British Journal of Psychiatry*, 1970, 117, 497-507.

Glenn, M. L. Religious conversion and the mystical experience. *Psychiatric Quarterly*, 1970, 44, 636-651.

Goodman, F. D. Phonetic analysis of glossolalia in four cultural settings. *Journal for the Scientific Study of Religion*, 1969, 8, 227-239.

Hood, R. W., Jr. Religious orientation and the report of religious experience. *Journal for the Scientific Study of Religion*, 1970, 9, 285-291.

Leary, T. The religious experience: Its production and interpretation. *Journal of Psychedelic Drugs*, 1970, 3, 76-86.

Pahnke, W. N., & Richards, W. A. Implications of LSD and experimental mysticism. *Journal of Religion and Health*, 1966, 5, 175-208.

Scoggs, J., & Douglas, W.   Issues in the psychology
    of religious conversion. *Journal of Religion
    and Health,* 1967, 6, 204-216.

Spellman, C. M., Baskett, G. D., & Byrne, D.   Mani-
    fest anxiety as a contributing factor in reli-
    gious conversion. *Journal of Consulting and
    Clinical Psychology,* 1971, 26, 245-247.

PART FIVE

RELIGION AND POLITICAL BEHAVIOR

RELIGIOUS COMMUNALITY
AND PARTY PREFERENCE

CHARLES H. ANDERSON

Editor's introduction. The continuing tradition
of religious group-voting in the United States
has lessened the taboo on the discussion of the
combination of religion and politics. Despite
the formal separation of church and state, the
use of religious symbols by political leaders
in this century, from Woodrow Wilson to Richard
Nixon, is so common as to go unnoticed. Religious affiliation of political candidates is generally known and openly discussed in connection
with the presumed effects of religious voting.
   Anderson suggests that since it is "highly
improbable" that religious voting is an extension of doctrinal differences among the laity,
and since major class differences among religious groups have been reduced or eliminated,
there must be other possible sources for the
relationship between religion and party preference. Both of these suggestions may still be
challenged by others, and the first one is
challenged by Benton Johnson (whose article is
also included in this volume). Anderson's explanation for religious voting hinges on the
concept of religious communality and the religious subsociety. The religious subsociety

From *Sociological Analysis,* 1969, 30, 32-41.
Reprinted with permission.

consists of a set of interlocking families and
formal and informal groups in one local community, and the subsociety serves as the context for interaction, identification, and the
interpretation of reality. The degree of religious communality is defined as the degree
of involvement in the religious subsociety.

The hypothesis in this study was that a
person's degree of involvement in his religious community is positively related to the
chance that he will prefer the traditional majority political party within his religious
group. This relationship must also be independent of social-class position and political
socialization per se. The hypothesis was supported in samples of white Protestants and
Mormons but not in a sample of white Catholics.
Among Catholics, those with medium and low communality voted more heavily Democratic than the
other respondents, and the conclusion has to be
that the Catholic tendency to vote Democratic
is strong regardless of communality. It is
important to note that Anderson separates Mormons and Protestants in his analysis and accepts the Mormon doctrinal position, which sees
Mormons as neither Catholics nor Protestants
but as followers of the "true church." The
fact that this is a theological separation and
not a sociological one is borne out by the data,
which show Mormons as identical to the Protestant Anglo-Saxon majority. Both Protestants
and Mormons showed the same trends in communality and party support, and we may see this as
another indication of the "return" of Mormonism
to the fold of the Protestant majority.

Religious voting has a long and tumultuous history in American politics. (For the historical background to Protestant-Catholic tensions in the political arena, see Farnham, 1961; Odgard, 1960; Lipset,
1964; Billington, 1964; and Higham, 1963.) As Lipset
has noted, the first era of party politics witnessed
a division between the Established and non-Established

Protestant churches, the former aligning themselves
with the conservative Federalists and the latter
with the more liberal Democratic-Republicans (Lipset,
1964). With the demise of the Federalists, Congregationalists and Episcopalians shifted their loyalties to the conservative heirs, the Whigs, and
finally, the Republicans. At the same time, a large
segment of the burgeoning and upwardly mobile ranks
of Presbyterians, Methodists, and Baptists were ac-
complishing the transition from Jacksonian Democrat
to Republican, many by way of native American parties
(Billington, 1964). There were other than class in-
centives moving native Protestants to the Republican
party by the 1850's, one of the most compelling being
that Catholic immigrants--accumulating rapidly since
the 1830's--linked themselves to the Democrats. The
same organization could not accommodate both Celt
and Saxon.

Later Protestant immigrants from Germany and
Scandinavia usually, though not always, entered the
Republican fold despite its covert and sometimes
overt nativism. Catholic and Jewish immigrant
minorities, by contrast, were attracted to Democratic
politics.

Thus, the conditions were present for future
links between religion and political preference. A
number of empirical surveys have disclosed a relationship between religion and voting behavior (cf.
Lazarsfeld, 1948; Berelson, 1954; Campbell, 1960;
Lenski, 1963). It is possible, however, that religion is spuriously related to political preference
through such confounding variables as income and education. Social class position has, of course, tra-
ditionally been associated with voting tendencies.
Religion and social class have apparently been mutually reinforcing phenomena in party preference
until recently when Catholics entered the middle
classes on a large scale (see Glenn and Hyland,
1967). Research on the relative weight of social
class and religion in voting behavior since 1936
indicate that both have been nearly equally powerful
determinants (Lipset, 1964; Alford, 1963). However,
in 1960, with a Catholic heading the Democratic
ticket, religious differences in party preference
between Protestants and Catholics were much greater

than differences between social classes within religious groups. In brief, the tie between religion
and party preference has continued past mid-twentieth
century--long after national origin conflicts have
subsided and after major social class differences
between Protestants and Catholics have been largely
eliminated. What, then, serves to sustain the tie?
        It is, of course, much too facile to argue that
Protestants contribute disproportionately to the
Republican party because they perceive an affinity
between the Protestant religious dictum "The priest-
hood of all believers" (often misconstrued to mean
that each individual is his own religious inter-
preter) and the Republican political aphorism "rugged
individualism," while Catholic ecclesiastical organization predisposes Catholics toward collectivism and
the Democratic party.
        This is not to argue that there are not connec-
tions between theological position and party preference. Johnson (1966) has argued empirically that
there is considerable overlap between theological
and political liberals in the clergy. Johnson (1962)
has also hypothesized and presented inferential evidence that religiously liberal ministers tend to
stimulate Democratic voting among active laity while
religious conservatives evoke a Republican vote.
While Johnson's research suggests that the theological stance of Protestant ministers has implications
for their own party preference and for certain of
their parishioners (though he has not raised the possibility of political self-selection by laymen), it
has not shed direct light on the connection between
religious and political liberalism among the laity
as such. It is doubtful that frequency of participation in the religiously liberal churches (Methodist,
Congregational, Episcopalian, and Presbyterian)[1] is
related to Democratic voting in congregations that
do not have a vocal and politically liberal minister
--the large majority outside of university towns and
large metropolitan areas.

[1]These four denominations constituted the left
half of the religious continuum in research reported
in *Religion and Society in Tension* by Charles Y. Glock
and Rodney Stark (1965: Chapters 5 and 8).

Related data of my own failed to reveal a positive relationship between frequency of participation
in a religiously liberal denomination and Democratic
preference,[2] nor did a study by D. Anderson (1966).
Rather both sets of data indicated that Democratic
voting was inversely proportional to frequency of attendance in both liberal and conservative churches.
Presumably, if Johnson's hypothesis is correct, most
of these congregations were not served by liberal
pastors.

To account for voting differences between Protestants and Catholics, and probably for religiously
related (as opposed to economically related) differences in voting among the bulk of white Protestants
themselves, one must look beyond organizational and
doctrinal phenomena.

RELIGIOUS COMMUNALITY

One possible source of the perpetuation of
religious voting is the religious subsociety. The
religious subsociety consists of a set of more or
less interlocking families and informal and formal
groups, and serves as a context for primary interaction, psychological identification, and cultural
interpretation (for a discussion of the notion of
subsociety, see Gordon, 1964: especially chapters 2
and 7).

If the religious subsociety is in fact a pivotal
variable in voting behavior, then the greater a
person's involvement in that subsociety the greater
should be his tendency to vote in the appropriate
or traditional direction. Specifically, since
Protestantism and Mormonism (though Joseph Smith
was himself a Democrat) have historically been linked

[2]In 1960, 63 percent of weekly attenders in
conservative denominations voted Republican compared
to 47 percent of those less regular, figures which
would concur with Johnson's; however, 66 percent of
the regular attenders in the liberal churches voted
Republican compared to 48 percent of those less regular. The same relationships obtained for 1964.

with the Republican party, then the higher the involvement of an individual within the Protestant or
Mormon group the greater the chance that he will
vote Republican. Conversely, the likelihood of a
Democratic vote should vary directly with the extent
of participation within the Catholic or Jewish community. The general relationship should hold at all
social class levels.

POLITICAL SOCIALIZATION

     A second possible source of the perpetuation of
religious voting may be found in the process of political socialization within the family, closely related to but quite separate from religious variables
per se. Parents may transmit their political attitudes and beliefs to their children just as they
transmit a plethora of others concerning education,
work, religion, out-groups, and so on. Thus, Republican parents might be expected to produce Republican
children and Democratic parents Democratic children.
     A question of some import concerns the degree
to which, if any, religious communality affects party
preference apart from political socialization. In
methodological terms, if a relationship is discovered
between strength of religious communality and party
preference, could it withstand, for example, a control for father's party choice?
     The objectives before us, then, are to explore
the possible relationships between religious communality, political socialization, and party preference.

PROCEDURES

     Samples. The data for the study were compiled
from questionnaires sent to random samples of male
heads of households in three different communities.
The communities were selected on the basis of prior
information regarding their religious composition.
Each contained a different religious majority. Out
of 500 sent to "Protestant City," a North Central
urban center of over 70,000 people, 212 were returned

completed--166 (78 percent) from Protestants and 43
(20 percent) from Catholics. A second set of 500
was sent to "Catholic City," another North Central
urban place with a population of nearly 40,000, of
which 207 were returned--126 (61 percent) from
Catholics and 75 (36 percent) from Protestants.
Finally, of 500 sent to "Mormon City," an Inter-
mountain community of 190,000, 225 were returned--
164 (73 percent) from Mormons and the remainder from
Protestants and Catholics but too few to analyze
here.

All respondents were white males above the age
of twenty-one, but nearly all were over twenty-five.
More than half of each sample were over forty, figures which compared closely to those in the respec-
tive universes as enumerated in the 1960 census.
Age was, however, unrelated to party preference.
Overall, about two-thirds of respondents were white
collar and about one-half had some college, larger
proportions of these categories than in the universes
according to the 1960 census. Denominationally,
Lutherans were the most prevalent group in both North
Central samples with Methodists being the second most
numerous. The vast majority of all respondents reporting a religious preference claimed church membership. Only specific sets of Protestant, Catholic,
and Mormon respondents and fathers were included in
the analysis.

Measures. Strength of religious communality
was assessed with four items derived mainly from
Gordon's (1964: Chapter 3) assimilation-communality
paradigm: religious preference of three closest
friends, strength of identification with the religious group, frequency of church attendance, and attitude toward religious intermarriage. If a person's
three closest friends are co-religionists, if he
strongly identifies himself with his religious group,
if he attends religious services regularly, and if he
is strongly opposed to inter-religious marriage, then
it is argued that this person is highly communal in
ethnic posture. Conversely, if his close friendships are religiously mixed, if his religious self-
identification is weak or absent, if he rarely or
never attends religious functions, and if he has
no objections to mixed marriages, then it is reasoned

that this person is dissociated from the religious community. The four items were categorized and scored to an eight-point index as follows:[3]

Friends: 3 of 3 of own religion = 2; 2 of 3 = 1; 1 or 0 of 3 = 0.

Religious Identification: Very strong or strong = 2; moderate = 1; weak or none = 0.

Church Attendance: At least twice a month = 2; once a month = 1; a few times a year or less = 0.

Intermarriage: Strongly opposed = 2; mildly opposed = 1; no objections = 0.

For analytical purposes, respondents with scores of seven or eight were considered high in communality, those below as medium or low.

As an indirect measure of political socialization, respondents were requested to state the usual party preference of their father. Father's religiosity, a control variable in one of the tables presented below, was defined in terms of respondent's evaluation of their father's strength of identification with his religious group. Party preference of respondents was defined according to their vote or preference in the 1960 and 1964 presidential elections.

RESULTS

Religious voting. Table 1 indicates that religious voting was strong in both Protestant and Catholic Cities, especially in Catholic City in 1960. Differences between Protestants and Catholics persisted at both white- and blue-collar levels, though the disparity was much less in the case of the blue-collarites (Table 1). Democrats were a minority in the Mormon sample as a whole, but a rather large percentage of Mormon blue-collar workers voted Democratic (Table 2).

[3]These four items were related with one another beyond the .05 level of significance in every case. Each was given equal weight in the index on the basis of approximately equal prominence in the communality-assimilation process.

TABLE 1
PERCENTAGE OF PROTESTANTS AND CATHOLICS IN TWO CITIES WHO VOTED
FOR OR PREFERRED THE DEMOCRATIC CANDIDATE IN THE 1960 AND 1964
PRESIDENTIAL ELECTIONS: OCCUPATIONAL GROUPS

City, Occupation and Election	Protestants	Catholics	x^2 (d.f. $= 1$)	P	Q
Protestant City					
Total					
1960	48 (N-161)	84 (N-43)	17.90	.01	.69
1964	43 (N-160)	74 (N-43)	13.19	.01	.58
White Collar					
1960	38 (N-96)	85 (N-27)	19.19	.01	.81
1964	29 (N-96)	74 (N-27)	17.80	.01	.74
Blue Collar					
1960	67 (N-63)	81 (N-16)	1.38	N.S.	.36
1964	66 (N-62)	75 (N-16)	.45	N.S.	.21
Catholic City					
Total					
1960	36 (N-70)	80 (N-122)	38.33	.01	.76
1964	44 (N-72)	64 (N-121)	6.61	.01	.37
White Collar					
1960	31 (N-58)	75 (N-77)	26.75	.01	.74
1964	42 (N-60)	60 (N-78)	4.15	.01	.35
Blue Collar					
1960	80 (N-10)	88 (N-43)	.49	N.S.	.31
1964	60 (N-10)	70 (N-43)	.35	N.S.	.21

TABLE 2
PERCENTAGE OF MORMONS WHO VOTED FOR OR PREFERRED THE DEMOCRATIC
CANDIDATE IN THE 1960 AND 1964 PRESIDENTIAL ELECTIONS
BY OCCUPATIONAL GROUP

Election	Total	White Collar	Blue Collar	x^2 (d.f. $= 1$)	P	Q
1960	45 (N $=$ 157)	34 (N $=$ 99)	70 (N $=$ 44)	16.47	.01	.64
1964	41 (N $=$ 157)	28 (N $=$ 98)	62 (N $=$ 45)	14.14	.01	.60

Religious communality and voting. Protestant
respondents who rated high in communality were de-
cidedly more Republican than their less communally
oriented co-religionists (Table 3). The influence
of a Catholic candidate on high communal Protestants
was not definitive, although in Catholic City it did
seem to encourage a higher Republican vote. Of
greater interest was the finding that a majority of

Protestant blue-collar workers with high religious communality voted Republican in Protestant City, whereas their less communal counterparts voted Democratic in the more customary working-class manner (Table 3). Highly communal Protestants were strongly Republican.

TABLE 3

PERCENTAGE OF PROTESTANTS IN TWO CITIES WHO VOTED FOR OR PREFERRED
THE REPUBLICAN CANDIDATE IN THE 1960 AND 1964 PRESIDENTIAL ELECTIONS
BY STRENGTH OF RELIGIOUS COMMUNALITY; OCCUPATIONAL GROUPS IN
PROTESTANT CITY[*]

City, Occupation, and Election	High Communality	Medium and Low Communality	x^2 (d.f. = 1)	P	Q
Protestant City					
Total					
1960	65 (N-60)	43 (N-100)	7.10	.01	.42
1964	73 (N-60)	46 (N-99)	10.36	.01	.52
White Collar					
1960	69 (N-39)	57 (N-56)	5.94	.01	.25
1964	85 (N-39)	61 (N-56)	6.13	.01	.56
Blue Collar					
1960	57 (N-21)	21 (N-42)	8.28	.01	.66
1964	52 (N-21)	24 (N-41)	4.63	.01	.54
Catholic City					
1960	81 (N-27)	51 (N-41)	6.49	.01	.61
1964	65 (N-26)	50 (N-46)	1.91	.10	.30

[*] Too few Protestant blue-collar persons in Catholic City sample to control for occupation.

By contrast, religious communality was unrelated to Democratic preference among Catholic City Catholics (Table 4). Among Mormons, however, we observed that those with strong communal orientations were much more likely to have supported the Republican candidates than those Mormons less involved in the religious community (Table 5). Blue-collar Mormons who

TABLE 4

PERCENTAGE OF CATHOLICS IN CATHOLIC CITY WHO VOTED FOR OR PREFERRED
THE DEMOCRATIC CANDIDATE IN THE 1960 AND 1964 PRESIDENTIAL ELECTIONS
BY STRENGTH OF RELIGIOUS COMMUNALITY

Election	High Communality	Medium and Low Communality	x^2 (d.f. = 1)	P	Q
1960	79 (N = 34)	81 (N = 83)	.02	N.S.	−.04
1964	63 (N = 35)	69 (N = 83)	.37	N.S.	−.13

reported high communality, like their Protestant
counterparts, went for Republicans significantly
more often than Mormon workers more peripheral to
the Mormon subsociety (Table 5). The influence of
communal involvement on Mormon voting could also be
observed among white-collar persons.

TABLE 5

PERCENTAGE OF MORMONS WHO VOTED FOR OR PREFERRED THE REPUBLICAN
CANDIDATE IN THE 1960 AND 1964 PRESIDENTIAL ELECTIONS BY STRENGTH
OF RELIGIOUS COMMUNALITY: OCCUPATIONAL GROUPS

Occupation and Election	High Communality	Medium and Low Communality	x^2 (d.f. $= 1$)	P	Q
Total					
1960	68 (N-88)	40 (N-69)	12.62	.01	.51
1964	71 (N-88)	47 (N-69)	9.12	.01	.46
White Collar					
1960	74 (N-64)	52 (N-35)	4.43	.01	.44
1964	77 (N-64)	62 (N-34)	2.16	.05	.33
Blue Collar					
1960	43 (N-16)	22 (N-28)	2.79	.01	.48
1964	57 (N-16)	28 (N-29)	3.13	.01	.54

*Political Socialization versus Religious Com-
munality.* Thus, among Protestants and Mormons, a
person's depth of participation in his religious
subsociety seemingly has important implications for
his political behavior. But as Table 6 reveals, so
did political socialization. In all three religious
groups, father's influence on respondent's party
preferences was plainly visible. Yet, religious influences may also be observed at work in Table 6

TABLE 6

PROTESTANT, CATHOLIC, AND MORMON RESPONDENT'S PARTY PREFERENCE
(1964) BY FATHER'S PARTY PREFERENCE: PERCENT

Respondent's Preference	Protestant Fathers Protestant City		Catholic Fathers Catholic City		Mormon Fathers	
	Rep. (N $= 96$)	Dem. (N $= 42$)	Rep. (N $= 35$)	Dem. (N $= 55$)	Rep. (N $= 66$)	Dem. (N $= 52$)
Republican	73	36	66	19	72	47
Democrat	27	64	34	81	28	53
	$x^2 = 17.17$		$x^2 = 20.29$		$x^2 = 7.71$	
	P $= .01$		P $= .01$		P $= .01$	
	Q $= .65$		Q $= .79$		Q $= .48$	

inasmuch as Protestant and Mormon Democrat fathers and Catholic Republican fathers--or the minority party within the religion--were less successful in transmitting the party line to their sons than were fathers of the majority party.[4] On the other hand, respondent's party preference revealed no relationship--regardless of religious group--to the degree of their father's religiosity (Table 7).

TABLE 7

PROTESTANT, CATHOLIC, AND MORMON RESPONDENT'S PARTY PREFERENCE
(1964) BY FATHER'S PARTY PREFERENCE AND RELIGIOSITY: PERCENT

Respondent's Preference	Republican Protestant Fathers Protestant City		Democrat Catholic Fathers Catholic City		Republican Mormon Fathers	
	High Rel. $(N = 57)$	Low Rel. $(N = 39)$	High Rel. $(N = 36)$	Low Rel. $(N = 20)$	High Rel. $(N = 46)$	Low Rel. $(N = 20)$
Republican	74	72	20	15	72	70
Democrat	26	28	80	85	28	30
	$x^2 = .03$ N.S. $Q = .04$		$x^2 = .17$ N.S. $Q = .15$		$x^2 = .02$ N.S. $Q = .04$	

The importance of political socialization to party preference, and the absence of any link between father's religiosity and respondent's party preference, suggests that political socialization may be much more of a key variable in voting behavior than religious communality, and that a control for the former might obviate the latter's role in producing voting variance. This, however, was not the case. Given similar political backgrounds, Protestants and Mormons with strong commitments to their religious communities were stronger Republicans than their communally weaker co-religionists (Table 8).

[4]Lenski (1963: 140-42) discovered a similar type of relationship among Detroit Protestants and Catholics and on that basis argued that religion is a cause rather than a correlate of party preference. Although I would agree with Lenski's conclusions, and would argue similarly on the basis of Table 6, the success ratio of political inheritance is a less direct ground for inference that religion is a cause than variation by strength of religious communality.

TABLE 8
PROTESTANT AND MORMON RESPONDENT'S POLITICAL PREFERENCE (1964) BY
FATHER'S PARTY PREFERENCE AND RESPONDENT'S STRENGTH OF RELIGIOUS
COMMUNALITY: PERCENT

| | Protestant Father's Preference Protestant City | | | |
| | Republican | | Democrat | |
Resp. Preference	Resp. High Comm. (N = 41)	Resp. Low Comm. (N = 55)	Resp. High Comm. (N = 14)	Resp. Low Comm. (N = 28)
Republican	88	64	72	22
Democrat	12	36	28	78
	$x^2 = 7.50$		$x^2 = 9.15$	
	P = .01		P = .01	
	Q = .60		Q = .80	

| | Mormon Father's Preference | | | |
| | Republican | | Democrat | |
	Resp. High Comm. (N = 43)	Resp. Low Comm. (N = 21)	Resp. High Comm. (N = 30)	Resp. Low Comm. (N = 22)
Republican	77	67	60	28
Democrat	23	33	40	72
	$x^2 = .72$		$x^2 = 5.21$	
	N.S.		P = .01	
	Q = .24		Q = .60	

DISCUSSION

    The findings tend to confirm the hypothesis that
a person's degree of involvement in his religious
community is positively related to the tendency to
vote in the religion's traditional political direction for Protestants and Mormons, but not for Catholics. The Catholic voters in the study displayed
considerably stronger religious voting than either
Protestants or Mormons. Not only did the analysis
fail to turn up differences in party preference
among Catholics of stronger and weaker religious
communality, but white-collar/blue-collar differences
were also insignificant. Although in the 1960 election Catholics were so strongly Democrat that there
was slight margin for in-group differences to emerge,

there were sufficient numbers of Republican Catholics
in 1964 to allow for variation along communality and
class lines, but none were manifest. An explanation
does not at once seem evident, and there is nothing
in this data to suggest any. The customary reasoning
for lack of differences within a minority group is
that as an "out-group" the minority, i.e., Catholics,
are likely to respond politically in terms of their
ethnic-religious group identification alone more so
than Protestants, and thus override other possible
internal differences (Lipset, 1964: 95). The mere
fact of Catholic identity, it might be argued, is
sufficient to stimulate a Democratic vote, whereas
among Protestants involvement in the religious community in the more general sense is necessary to
stimulate a Republican vote. However, it is also
conceivable that another type of measure of communality could differentiate among Catholics, if there
were a large enough Republican margin to work with.

   However, the Mormons, much more of a solidary
religious subsociety and religious minority than
Catholics, were internally divided along communal
and class lines in party preference as much as were
Protestants. Actually, Mormons are in broader ethnic
terms part of the Anglo-Saxon majority, and hence
seemingly react, at least politically, in a way similar to Protestants rather than according to the
"out-group" thesis.

   The importance of political inheritance cannot
be challenged. Nevertheless, religion does seem to
exert a tangible and independent effect on party
preference as well. The autonomy of religious communality was very much in evidence for Protestants
and Mormons. Even among Catholics, almost twice as
many sons of Republican fathers defected to the Democratic party as did sons of Democratic fathers to
the Republican.

   A comparison of percentage point differences in
voting produced by political socialization (Table 6)
and religious communality (for example, Tables 3, 5,
and 8) will indicate that religious communality is
an explanatory variable of a roughly similar magnitude
of importance as that of political socialization,
and for that matter, social class, among Protestants
and Mormons.

Since a related analysis revealed that the younger Protestants and Mormons were as strong in communality as the older, and higher status persons were somewhat stronger (much stronger among Mormons) than lower status persons (C. Anderson, 1968: 501-508), no decline in the role of communality in these two groups in perpetuating religious voting seems imminent.

If religious communality intensifies religious voting (Is strong Jewish communality responsible, in part, for a heavy Democratic vote?), then structural assimilation--the large scale mixture of ethnic persons in cliques, clubs, organizations, and families--should reduce religious voting. However, assimilation seems indefinitely far off. Paradoxically, Democratic and Republican politics seem to be converging (rhetoric aside) in the face of religious voting. Do Protestants and Catholics actually have different political interests which they feel are met in the Republican and Democratic parties, respectively? If this is true, and if political practices of the two parties are converging, the two parties might be expected to lose their special appeal to Protestants and Catholics and religious voting should thus decline. On the other hand (and this seems to be the case), if religious voting is carried on mainly by the momentum of ethnic loyalties and opposition, then religious voting should continue despite convergence in party politics. It would be remarkable indeed if inter-party lines softened and blurred before religious voting declined through religious group assimilation.

REFERENCES

Alford, Robert. 1963. Party and Society. Chicago: Rand McNally.

Anderson, Charles H. 1968. "Religious Communality Among White Protestants, Catholics, and Mormons." Social Forces 46 (June): 501-508.

Anderson, Donald C. 1966. "Ascetic Protestantism and Political Preference." Review of Religious Research 7 (Spring): 167-71.

Berelson, Bernard, et. al. 1954. Voting. Chicago: University of Chicago.

Billington, Ray Allen. 1964. The Protestant Crusade: 1800-1860. Chicago: Quadrangle.

Campbell, Angus, et. al. 1960. The American Voter. New York: John Wiley and Sons.

Farnham, Wallace D. 1961. "The 'Religious Issue' in American Politics: An Historical Commentary." Queens Quarterly 68 (Spring): 47-65.

Glenn, Noval D. and Ruth Hyland. 1967. "Religious Preference and Worldly Success: Some Evidence from National Surveys." American Sociological Review 32 (February): 73-85.

Glock, Charles Y., and Rodney Stark. 1965. Religion and Society in Tension. Chicago: Rand McNally.

Gordon, Milton M. 1964. Assimilation in American Life. New York: Oxford University.

Higham, John. 1963. Strangers in the Land: Patterns of American Nativism 1860-1925. New York: Atheneum.

Johnson, Benton. 1962. "Ascetic Protestantism and Political Preference." Public Opinion Quarterly 26 (Spring): 35-46.

   1964. "Ascetic Protestantism and Political Preference in the Deep South." American Journal of Sociology 69 (January): 359-66.

   1966. "Theology and Party Preference Among Protestant Clergymen." American Sociological Review 31 (April): 200-208.

Lazarsfeld, Paul, et. al. 1948. The People's Choice. New York: Columbia University.

Lenski, Gerhard. 1963. The Religious Factor. New York: Doubleday.

Lipset, Seymour M.   1964.   "Religion and Politics in
     the American Past and Present."   Pp. 69-126 in
     Robert Lee and Martin E. Marty (eds.), Religion
     and Social Conflict.   New York: Oxford University.

Odgard, Peter H. (ed.).   1960.   Religion and Politics.
     Englewood, New Jersey: Oceana Publications.

ASCETIC PROTESTANTISM AND POLITICAL PREFERENCE*

BENTON JOHNSON

Editor's introduction. The main contention of
Johnson's article is that religious influences
in the form of politically relevant values emanating from religious training are responsible
for political party preferences. Johnson takes
issue with most of the previous literature dealing with this subject, and with C. H. Anderson's
findings presented in the previous article,
when he claims that specifically religious factors and not merely denominational identification
are responsible for variations in political behavior. The thesis that religious teachings
have specific political implications in American
society has far-reaching results, going beyond
the safe boundaries set by both sociologists and
politicians. However, as Johnson himself pointed
out in a later article (1966), this relationship
exists only among the "ascetic" branches of
Protestantism in the United States.

The data reported here are from a larger survey
supported by the Office of Scientific and Scholarly
Research of the University of Oregon. The author is
indebted to Robert A. Ellis and James L. Price of the
University of Oregon for suggestions and criticisms
during the preparation of this paper.

From *Public Opinion Quarterly*, 1962, 26, 35-46.
Reprinted with permission.

The sometimes paradoxical relationship of class position, religious preference, and political party preference is the focus of the empirical investigation. Johnson describes the paradox that fundamentalism, with its social conservatism, prevails among the working class, while liberalism, in the Social Gospel tradition, prevails among the upper classes. This is the opposite of what could be expected on the basis of rational choice and class interest. The data show that the groups with the highest percentage of Republicans are the white-collar fundamentalists who are frequent church attenders and white-collar members of liberal churches who attend church only seldom. In general, fundamentalist Protestants tend to be Republican, regardless of social class.

The tendency of working-class Protestants to adopt fundamentalist positions has had a stabilizing effect on the political system. According to Johnson, religious influences operate to reduce class-based political differences, and religious values have contributed to the prevention of polarization in American political life. The liberalizing influences of the Social Gospel on the upper classes make them more moderate, while the working class accepts the hard-work ethic without complaints. This analysis comes close to the Marxian view of religion as a "false ideology," but the benign terms used by Johnson make it clear that he is far from hardnosed Marxism.

Johnson's original study, done in Eugene, Oregon, was replicated in Tallahassee, Florida (Johnson, 1964), with essentially identical findings. The only difference stemmed from the relative rarity of liberal churches in the South. The moderating influence of fundamentalism on the working class was still at work in the Southern sample. D. Anderson (1966) challenged the Johnson thesis directly by replicating the Eugene, Oregon, study in Bureau County, a rural county in northern Illinois. His conclusion was that attendance in any church, and not just a fundamentalist church, increased Republican

voting. Anderson stated that "...the frequent
church attender consistently inclines toward
the Republican party," but "The 'Liberal-
Fundamentalist' split does not exist in Bureau
County" (p. 170). However, Anderson's replication was not complete. He defined a church as
liberal not on the basis of its theology but on
the fact that it belonged to the National Council
of Churches. In the original Johnson study the
Baptist church was classified as fundamentalist,
while Anderson classified it as liberal. This
difference and the rural-urban differences,
which tend to favor fundamentalist majorities
in rural areas, may account for the contradictions in findings (see also Johnson & White,
1967). Summers et al. (1970) criticized both
Johnson and Anderson for their methodology and
the lack of statistical significance in their
findings.

REFERENCES

Anderson, D. Ascetic Protestantism and political
     preference. *Review of Religious Research*, 1966,
     7, 167-171.

Johnson, B. Ascetic Protestantism and political
     preference in the deep South. *American Journal
     of Sociology*, 1964, 69, 359-366.

Johnson, B. Theology and party preference among
     Protestant clergymen. *American Sociological
     Review*, 1966, 31, 200-208.

Johnson, B., & White, R. H. Protestantism, political
     preference and the nature of religious influence:
     Comment on Anderson's paper. *Review of Religious
     Research*, 1967, 9, 28-35.

Summers, G. F., Hough, R. L., Johnson, D. P., & Veath,
     K. A. Ascetic Protestantism and political pref-
     erence: A re-examination. *Review of Religious
     Research*, 1970, 12, 17-25.

Public attention has recently been focused on
the relationship of religion to political behavior
in the United States. Religious factors have long
been thought to play at least some part in shaping
the voting behavior of many people in certain elections. The campaign of 1960 accentuated the importance of these factors and brought their existence
into the forum of public discussion for the first
time since 1928.

A number of facts regarding the relationship of
religion to political behavior have been established
by social scientists. It is well documented that
Catholics tend to prefer the Democratic Party to the
Republican Party. It is also well established that
outside the South white Protestants are more inclined
toward the Republican Party than are nonwhites or
non-Protestants. More importantly, both these relationships have been found to be partly independent
of economic class factors.[1]

Still, despite these demonstrated relationships,
the effect of specifically religious factors, as opposed to factors associated with religion, is not
well understood. Lazarsfeld and Berelson, for example, are of the opinion that factors associated
with minority-group status rather than religion per
se underlie the Catholic inclination toward the Democratic party.[2] Furthermore, a number of investigators

[1]See Paul Lazarsfeld, Bernard Berelson, and
Hazel Gaudet, *The People's Choice,* New York, Columbia
University Press, 1948, p. 22; also Seymour M. Lipset
et al., "The Psychology of Voting: An Analysis of
Political Behavior," in Gardner Lindzey, editor,
Handbook of Social Psychology, Boston, Addison-
Wesley, 1954, p. 1140; also, Oscar Glantz, "Prote-
stant and Catholic Voting Behavior in a Metropolitan
Area," *Public Opinion Quarterly,* Vol. 23, 1959, pp.
73-82; also Luke Ebersole, "Religion and Politics,"
*The Annals of the American Academy of Political and
Social Science,* Vol. 332, 1960, pp. 101-111; etc.

[2]Lazarsfeld, Berelson, and Gaudet, *op. cit.,*
p. 23; Ebersole, *op. cit.,* p. 108; etc.

doubt whether religion in itself has much, if any,
influence on political beliefs and behavior in
America.[3]
  We will argue in this paper that religious
factors by themselves significantly account for an
important part of the political propensities of individuals who are involved in denominations that are
part of the tradition that Max Weber has called
"Ascetic Protestantism."[4] We will also argue that
the political implications of the religious teachings of this tradition are not uniformly Republican,
though it is likely that this party has been the
major historical beneficiary of their influence.
The reason for this statement is that a basic split
exists within Ascetic Protestantism that is in some
ways analogous to the two-party political division
in the nation as a whole. As the data below will
show, religious involvement and the branch of Ascetic
Protestantism that is adhered to are associated with
political behavior. We will suggest that this phenomenon, in conjunction with the peculiar relationship of the two factions of Ascetic Protestantism to

[3]See especially Robert E. Lane, *Political Life,*
Glencoe, Ill., Free Press, 1959, p. 247. The basis
for this view is the success of the "minority group"
hypothesis in explaining the Democratic tendencies
not only of Catholics but of Negroes and Jews as well.
Although less attention has been given to the political tendencies of Protestants, the findings of the
Allinsmiths have strongly supported the view that
economic and not religious factors account for political differences within Protestantism. See Wesley
and Beverly Allinsmith, "Religious Affiliation and
Politico-Economic Attitude," *Public Opinion Quarterly,*
Vol. 12, 1948, pp. 377-389. See also Seymour M.
Lipset, *Political Man,* New York, Doubleday, 1959,
p. 289; and Ebersole, *op. cit.,* p. 107. It should
be pointed out that many authorities agree that specifically religious factors probably do play a significant part in shaping the political opinions of Jews.
  [4]Weber used the term "Ascetic Protestantism" to
refer to denominations within the Calvinist, Pietist,
and Revivalist traditions. See Max Weber, *The Protestant Ethic and the Spirit of Capitalism,* New York,
Scribner, 1930, pp. 95ff.

the stratification system, may contribute positively
to the stability of the American political system.

Max Weber has called attention to the similarity
between the orientation to the world that was historically promoted by Ascetic Protestant groups and
the orientation which is conducive to successful
operation of a modern rationalized business enterprise.[5] The Ascetic Protestant ideal of the *calling*
emphasized methodical and consistent striving toward
the accomplishment of long-range goals. It stressed
output of effort from the individual toward the physical and social environment and markedly deemphasized
the input of gratifications from the environment to
the individual. In short, the idea of the calling
constrained the believer to adopt an instrumental,
manipulative posture, to produce and to achieve, and
to curtail his interest in immediate consumption.
At the same time it strengthened his determination
to be self-reliant and to reap only rewards of his
own making.

Weber has placed chief emphasis on the moral
impetus which Ascetic Protestantism gave to modern
capitalism in producing a corps of disciplined, pro-
duction-minded actors. But the success of capitalism
did not depend on a moral climate alone. It depended
fully as much on the development of an institutional
structure favorable to privately managed economic
development. The attainment and maintenance of a
favorable institutional structure ordinarily requires
political action. If we accept Weber's thesis and
if we accept the necessity for the forces of capitalism to resort to political as well as other means
to secure their interests, then it is reasonable to
conclude that Ascetic Protestantism may have contributed to economic development by functioning as an
agency of support of political movements favorable
to business. To be sure, the motivation for this
support among churchmen may be primarily moral or

[5]*Ibid.* It should be noted that the Weber thesis is still subject to controversy. For a recent
survey of the principal contending viewpoints, see
Robert W. Green, editor, *Protestantism and Capitalism:
The Weber Thesis and Its Critics*, Boston, Heath, 1959.

even theological, but the effect of these sentiments
in the case of Ascetic Protestantism should be to
recruit a large segment of the Protestant population
for the political forces of capitalism.

An affinity between the values and norms of
Ascetic Protestantism and the ideals and interests
of the business community has been noted by many
observers. Cole, for one, in his study of the social ideas of evangelists in the northern states
prior to the Civil War, found "a strong impulse toward the protection of property, the defense of the
capitalistic system, and the appeasing of the moneyed
classes."[6] Cole also asserts that, in addition to
encouraging such Ascetic Protestant traits as "thrift,
frugality and industriousness," most of the prominent
evangelists also opposed poor relief, labor unions,
and laws regulating hours in industrial plants. In
their view, wealth, while not free from moral dangers,
"should be a recompense for doing something useful."[7]
Henry F. May and others have documented similar ideas
in Ascetic Protestant circles from a later era.[8]

The Ascetic Protestant tradition is not a uni-
tary one, however. In addition to its long-standing
fragmentation into scores of independent denominations,
a bifurcation into two prominent branches has also
occurred. This is the division into what is often
called the "liberal" and the "fundamentalist" factions.
Although the controversies which ostensibly gave rise
to these factions were primarily theological, divergent social and economic views were also involved.
A large sector of Protestant thinking, especially
that in close touch with the intellectual developments disseminated through the major universities,
has retreated from many of the traditional Christian

[6]Charles C. Cole, Jr., *The Social Ideas of the
Northern Evangelists,* New York, Columbia University
Press, 1954, p. 166.

[7]*Ibid.,* pp. 181, 186-189.

[8]Henry F. May, *Protestant Churches and Industrial
America,* New York, Harper, 1949, pp. 4, 7, 91; Eric
F. Goldman, *Rendezvous with Destiny,* New York, Knopf,
1952, pp. 89-90.

"fundamentals" in the realm of theology. A humanitarian, this-worldly point of view has increasingly
prevailed. One of the most influential outgrowths
of the liberal movement within Protestantism was the
Social Gospel. Viewing the burgeoning industrial
order with humanitarian disdain, many Protestant
leaders became sharply critical of economic arrange-
ments which made for gross inequalities of rewards
and opportunities. They called instead for concrete
improvements in the security and physical well-being
of the working class. The Social Gospel movement
gained momentum in the 1890's and attracted wide attention and support in the years between 1900 and
1915. In these latter years it appears to have been
in close sympathy with the forces and ideals of political liberalism or progressivism in the United
States.[9] For example, Walter Rauschenbusch, perhaps
the single most influential spokesman of the Social
Gospel movement, wrote bitingly of "the power of the
conservative interests" and the "icy indifference of
class selfishness."[10] He urged political action by
Christians to set matters right. Although recent
theological developments in liberal church circles
have dampened the optimistic ardor for reform, especially among the younger seminarians, it is probably
safe to say that the general social outlook of many
Protestant leaders today is more "liberal" in the
political sense than it is "conservative."[11]

From all these developments a very large sector
of Protestantism stood aloof. Robin Williams is essentially correct in describing fundamentalism as
representing "past Protestant orthodoxy."[12] In the

[9]May, *op. cit.*, pp. 204-234.

[10]Walter Rauschenbusch, *Christianizing the Social
Order*, New York, Macmillan, 1912, p. 31.

[11]See J. Milton Yinger, *Religion in the Struggle
for Power*, Durham, N.C., Duke University Press, 1946,
p. 157.

[12]Robin M. Williams, Jr., *American Society*, rev.
ed., New York, Knopf, 1960, p. 359.

area of social doctrine it has remained true to the
historic business-oriented conservatism of the older
Ascetic Protestantism. For example, *Christianity
Today,* a new publication of intellectual fundamentalism, espouses a thoroughly conservative social policy. Its editorial pages have expressed concern
over "the loss of such biblical ideals as industry
and thrift."[13] Its editor has attacked the Social
Gospel on religious and political grounds, declaring
that the "detachment of social principles from a
supernatural source and sanction has indirectly
aided the socialistic and totalitarian assault on
free enterprise, private property and the profit motive."[14] Recently the liberal-supported National
Council of Churches, always boycotted by fundamentalists, has come under renewed attack by the two
major interdenominational associations of fundamentalists. Often this attack is based on the supposed
sympathy of the National Council for left-wing ideas.[15]

The social doctrinal controversies involved in
the liberal-fundamentalist split within Protestantism
parallel to a striking extent the controversies involved in the political division obtaining in the
nation as a whole. It is paradoxical, however, that
the relationship of these two Protestant factions to
the social stratification system is almost exactly
the reverse of what might be predicted on grounds of

[13]"Where Are We Drifting?" editorial in *Christianity Today,* Vol. 3, Dec. 22, 1958, p. 21.

[14]Carl F. H. Henry, "Perspectives for Social
Action," *Christianity Today,* Vol. 3, Jan. 19, 1959,
p. 15.

[15]See "Why Is NCC Prestige Slipping?" *Christianity
Today,* Vol. 3, Feb. 2, 1959, pp. 5-7. The affinity
between some branches of fundamentalism and radical
right-wing movements is well documented. See Ralph
L. Roy, *Apostles of Discord: A Study of Organized
Bigotry and Disruption on the Fringes of Protestant-
ism,* Boston, Beacon Press, 1953; also George Younger,
"Protestant Piety and the Right Wing," *Social Action,*
May 15, 1951, pp. 5-35.

economic interest.   It might be expected that the
fundamentalist denominations would appeal chiefly
to the middle and upper classes and that the liberal
denominations would appeal chiefly to the working
class.   Actually, the denominations which have come
under liberal influence are relatively middle and
upper class in the composition of their membership,
whereas the denominations where fundamentalism holds
sway are relatively working class in composition.[16]
   The reasons for this peculiar relationship of
the two major branches of Ascetic Protestantism to
the stratification system are apparently that middle-
and upper-class congregations have chosen for their
ministers men who have received their training from
the more influential and prestigeful seminaries.
These seminaries, many of which are close to large
universities, have participated in the trend toward
liberal humanitarianism that has been going on in
intellectual circles for many years.[17]   Fundamentalism, having a relatively uneducated constituency
and ministry, has for a number of reasons resisted
this trend, and continues to represent the older
Ascetic Protestant orthodoxy.
   The concentration of liberalism in middle- and
upper-class denominations and the concentration of
fundamentalism in working-class denominations offers
researchers a unique opportunity to investigate the
extent to which religious involvement may independently influence political opinion and behavior.
Economic or occupational influences are ordinarily
thought to be the single most important determinants
of political behavior.   If our proposition concerning
the effect of religious involvement is correct, however, religious involvement should be directly related to preference for the Republican Party among
fundamentalists and inversely related to Republican
preference among liberals, regardless of economic
class.   Moreover, when religiously involved persons

[16]Paul A. Carter, *The Decline and Revival of
the Social Gospel,* Ithaca, N.Y., Cornell University
Press, 1954, p. 52; also May, *op. cit.,* pp. 202, 224,
235.
[17]Carter, *op. cit.,* p. 54.

of the same economic class are compared, fundamentalists should be more inclined to be Republicans
than liberals. The sources so far drawn on do not
yield the kind of data that would allow for a direct
test of these hypotheses. Therefore it is necessary
to turn to survey data in order to press the inquiry
further.

PROCEDURES

The evidence for these propositions was obtained
by means of face-to-face interviews with an area probability sample of 365 male members of the labor force
in Eugene, Oregon, an ethnically and racially homogeneous community of 50,000. The interviews were administered by trained graduate students and advanced
undergraduates during the winter and early spring of
1960.
The independent variables were measured in the
following manner. First, each denomination was classified as liberal or fundamentalist. This classification was based on interviews that the author's
students conducted with a sample of Protestant pastors
in Eugene a year before the present research began.
The denominations were classified in the following
way:

Liberal	*Fundamentalist*
Congregational	Baptist
Methodist	Disciples of Christ
Presbyterian	Churches of Christ
Unitarian	Nazarene
	Free Methodist
	Assemblies of God
	Church of God
	Lighthouse Temple
	Foursquare
	Reformed
	Latter Day Saints
	Seventh Day Adventist

In line with Weber's restriction of the term
"Ascetic Protestant" to denominations stemming from
the Calvinist, Pietist, and Revivalist traditions, a

number of denominations were excluded from analysis.
The most important groups so excluded were the Episcopalians and Lutherans.

Second, church attendance was used as the major
index of religious involvement.[18] The category "attends frequently" includes those who reported that
they had attended church more than once a month during the preceding year. The category "attends seldom"
includes all others who reported that they had attended church at least once during that time.

Two measures were used for the dependent variable, political preference. The first measure,
called "party identification," was based on the
respondents' stated party affiliation.[19] The second
measure, called "voting behavior," was based on the
respondents' reported voting in the 1952 and 1956
presidential elections, the 1956 senatorial election,
and the 1958 gubernatorial election. It was deemed
advisable to use these two independent measures of
political preference for a number of reasons. First,
in view of many nonrandom discrepancies between respondents' stated party affiliations and their voting record, there was no basis for deciding which
indicator better measured political preference. For
example, blue-collar respondents reported far more
frequently than did white-collar respondents that they
had not voted in any of the four elections. In addition, for almost every classification of respondents,

[18]The superiority of church attendance over
church membership as an index of religious involvement is discussed in Michael Argyle, *Religious Behavior*, Glencoe, Ill., Free Press, 1959, p. 9. It
should be noted that what Argyle refers to as "religious activity" is essentially what we mean by the term
"religious involvement."

[19]The actual question posed to respondents was
identical to that used in the recent voting studies
sponsored by the Survey Research Center, University
of Michigan. See Angus Campbell, Philip E. Converse,
Warren E. Miller, and Donald E. Stokes, *The American
Voter*, New York, Wiley, 1960, p. 122.

the proportion Republican as measured by party identification is less than the proportion Republican as
measured by voting behavior. Second, a presentation
of findings utilizing both measures will facilitate
comparison with other results where a single index
has been used. Third, the fact that the direction
of the relationships obtained does not vary with the
measure used is an indication of the reliability of
the results. In each of the tables to follow, both
measures are presented. The percentages in each cell
of the tables represent the proportion of respondents
classified as Republicans. The proportion classified
as Democrats can be obtained by subtracting each percentage from 100.[20]

Occupational class was measured by means of the
census occupational categories. These categories
were collapsed so as to yield a twofold classification.

A simple analysis of the data reveals a number
of relationships among our major variables that have
been established in previous research. The fact that
the present data are in accord with other findings
enhances the likelihood that our data are representative and that our major findings may hold true beyond
the community surveyed.

Table 1 shows that white-collar respondents are
more likely to be Republican than blue-collar respondents. As in all subsequent tables, the relationship
obtains regardless of the measure of political preference. Table 2 presents the proportion of respondents
who are Republican for each of five religious categories. In accord with other findings, Protestants

[20]The party identification measure of political
preference includes only those who reported any degree of identification with either of the two major
parties. Those who reported no party identification
or who identified with a third party were excluded
from analysis. The voting behavior measure excludes
those who reported that they did not vote in any of
the four elections or whose reported voting history
showed that they had evenly split their votes between the two parties.

TABLE 1

REPUBLICAN PREFERENCE, BY
OCCUPATIONAL CLASS
(in per cent)

Occupational Class	Party Identification	Voting Behavior
White collar	50 (169)	66 (157)
Blue collar	28 (154)	46 (108)

TABLE 2

REPUBLICAN PREFERENCE, BY RELIGION
(in per cent)

Religion	Party Identification	Voting Behavior
Catholic	22 (41)	52 (29)
Ascetic Protestant	50 (135)	61 (109)
Other Protestant	53 (36)	78 (27)
Nonattenders	27 (108)	44 (79)

are more likely to be Republicans than Catholics are.
Table 3 presents the proportion of blue-collar and
white-collar respondents who are Republicans within
the liberal and fundamentalist categories. Again,
it will be seen that within each religious category
the white-collar respondents are more inclined to
be Republicans than are the blue-collar respondents.

TABLE 3

REPUBLICAN PREFERENCE OF LIBERALS AND
FUNDAMENTALISTS, BY OCCUPATIONAL CLASS
(in per cent)

Occupational Class	Party Identification	Voting Behavior
Liberal:		
White collar	57 (44)	73 (40)
Blue collar	50 (18)	50 (16)
Fundamentalist:		
White collar	55 (33)	64 (28)
Blue collar	42 (38)	48 (23)

Moreover, there is a tendency for white-collar liberals to be more heavily Republican than white-collar
fundamentalists and for blue-collar liberals to be
more heavily Republican than blue-collar fundamentalists. This finding is in line with the finding
reported by Lipset that white-collar members of low-
status churches are more likely to be Democrats than
white-collar members of high-status churches and that
working-class members of high-status churches are
more likely to be Republicans than working-class members of low-status churches.[21]

FINDINGS

When degree of religious involvement, as measured by frequency of church attendance, is taken into
account for both liberals and fundamentalists, the
results are in the direction predicted by our hypotheses. Table 4 shows that liberals who attend
church frequently are less inclined to be Republicans
than liberals who attend seldom. Fundamentalists who
attend frequently are more inclined to be Republicans
than fundamentalists who attend seldom. Moreover,
when frequent attenders are compared, fundamentalists
are more heavily Republican than are liberals.

TABLE 4

REPUBLICAN PREFERENCE OF LIBERALS AND
FUNDAMENTALISTS, BY FREQUENCY OF ATTENDANCE
(*in per cent*)

Frequency of Attendance	Party Identification	Voting Behavior
Liberal:		
Attend frequently	51 (37)	56 (34)
Attend seldom	60 (25)	82 (22)
Fundamentalist:		
Attend frequently	55 (44)	62 (34)
Attend seldom	37 (27)	47 (17)

21 Lipset, *Political Man*, as cited, p. 289.

21 Lipset, *Political Man,* as cited, p. 289.

Table 5 demonstrates that these results are not
a simple consequence of the operation of occupational
class factors. When occupational class is controlled,
the relationships obtained in Table 4 continue to
hold. For liberals, Republicanism is inversely related to frequency of attendance among both white-
collar and blue-collar respondents. For fundamentalists, Republicanism is directly related to frequency of attendance among both white-collar and blue-
collar respondents. Again, when liberal white-collar
and blue-collar frequent attenders are compared with
their fundamentalist counterparts, fundamentalists
are more inclined to be Republicans than are liberals.
In short, although occupational-class factors operate
in the expected direction, the data show that religious factors are also strongly effective.

TABLE 5

REPUBLICAN PREFERENCE OF LIBERALS AND FUNDAMENTALISTS, BY
FREQUENCY OF ATTENDANCE AND OCCUPATIONAL CLASS

(in per cent)

Occupational Class and Frequency of Attendance	Party Identification	Voting Behavior
Liberal:		
White collar:		
A. Attend frequently	54 (28)	62 (26)
B. Attend seldom	63 (16)	93 (14)
Blue collar:		
C. Attend frequently	44 (9)	38 (8)
D. Attend seldom	56 (9)	63 (8)
Fundamentalist:		
White collar:		
E. Attend frequently	65 (17)	71 (17)
F. Attend seldom	44 (16)	55 (11)
Blue collar:		
G. Attend frequently	48 (27)	53 (17)
H. Attend seldom	27 (11)	33 (6)

HYPOTHESES: A is less than B; C is less than D; E is greater than F; G is
greater than H. A is less than E; C is less than G.

Although our hypotheses concerning the relationship between Ascetic Protestantism and political
preference are strongly supported, the data cannot
be made to reveal the actual processes which have
produced the results obtained. It is our contention
that socializing influences in the form of politically

relevant values emanating from the two major factions
of Ascetic Protestantism are largely responsible for
the findings summarized in Tables 4 and 5. On the
other hand, it is likely that the doctrines espoused
by the churches have attracted some individuals whose
political views were already cast in the appropriate
mold. Moreover, these doctrines may have repelled
those with strongly opposed views. This latter effect may well be responsible for the heavy concentration of Republicans in the "seldom" category of
liberal church attendance and for the heavy concentration of Democrats in the "seldom" category of
fundamentalist church attendance. Further investigation is clearly necessary to clarify the specific
processes that produce the effects we have documented.

IMPLICATIONS: RELIGION AND THE REDUCTION OF
CLASS-BASED POLITICAL DIFFERENCES

Table 5 demonstrates that both occupational-
class factors and religious factors have an effect
on political preference. Since the direction of the
effect of each of these influences is known, it should
be possible to make statements regarding their combined effect. Considering frequently attending respondents only, it is possible to distinguish two
categories of respondents on the basis of the kinds
of political influence to which they are subjected.
One of these categories is politically cross-pressured, or subjected to political influences that
contradict each other. The other category is not
cross-pressured but is instead subjected to political
influences that reinforce each other. The cross-
pressured category consists of blue-collar fundamentalists and white-collar liberals. The non-cross-
pressured category consists of white-collar fundamentalists and blue-collar liberals. It is reasonable to hypothesize that class-based political differences should be relatively sharper among those
subjected to mutually reinforcing political influences than among those subjected to contradictory
political influences. Referring again to Table 5,
it will be seen that the difference in Republican
preference between white-collar fundamentalists and

blue-collar liberals is 21 per cent when political
preference is measured by party identification and
33 per cent when it is measured by voting behavior.
By contrast, the difference between white-collar
liberals and blue-collar fundamentalists is 6 per
cent when measured by party identification and 9 per
cent when measured by voting behavior. In other
words, where religious influences are in accord with
class-based political influences, class differences
in political preference are considerably greater than
where religious influences run counter to class-based
political influences.

Because of the relationship of the factions of
Ascetic Protestantism to the class system, it is
likely that religious influences operate far more
frequently to *reduce* or narrow class-based political
differences than to accentuate them. This likelihood
is suggested in the present data. Of frequent attenders (N = 81), 68 per cent are "cross-pressured"
and 32 per cent are not.

In view of these considerations, it is possible
that one of the major effects of Ascetic Protestantism
in the United States is to counteract to some extent
class-based political influences. This is clearly a
proposition which should open up new areas of investigation to the sociological student of political processes. The isolation of those factors[22] which operate systematically against the interest-based or

[22]These forces should not be thought of as exclusively, or even mainly, religious. Rather, Ascetic
Protestantism should be regarded as one of a number
of such forces. For example, the secular educational
system in the United States may function in a manner
similar to that of Ascetic Protestantism. There is
evidence that primary and secondary education attempt
to inculcate middle-class traits of self-reliance and
achievement. A large proportion of school attenders,
particularly at the younger age levels, are children
of working-class background. There is also some evidence that, through university training and other contacts with the intellectual community in America, the
middle and upper classes may regularly be exposed to
liberalizing values.

received values of various sectors of the population
may enable the sociologist to gain a more adequate
understanding of the mechanisms through which political, and perhaps also societal, stability are
attained in the United States. If all the media
through which ideas are transmitted to a group were
perfectly consistent with tradition or with a pursuit
of established interests, it is conceivable that, in
situations of tension and conflict between groups, a
radical polarization of ideologies of limited appeal
might occur that would make reconciliation difficult
except by force and in all-or-nothing terms. Yet we
know, for example, that in American political history
such a polarization has seldom occurred. The appeal
of movements of the radical right and the radical
left has ordinarily been limited and transitory.
Perhaps the privileged classes in the United States,
partly owing to exposure to liberalizing influences,
have been less intransigent in the face of pressure
for economic reform than they would have been under
other circumstances. And perhaps the working class,
through exposure to indoctrination in habits of
"frugality and industry," have accepted the demands
of a rationally organized economy with less complaint
than might otherwise have been the case. The two
factions of Ascetic Protestantism, with their peculiar relationship to the stratification system, may
have played an important, though unintended, part in
producing this situation.

RELIGION: OPIATE OR INSPIRATION OF CIVIL RIGHTS MILITANCY AMONG NEGROES?*

GARY T. MARX

Editor's introduction. Karl Marx's dictum about religion as the opium of the people is well-known and often quoted. The problem with this familiar quotation, as with many others, is that it is normally used out of context, in a brief and truncated form. As a result, its full significance is rarely considered, and only a few stop to think about what the function and meaning of "opium" are. Marx said much more than that about the function of religion among the oppressed, as is clear in the following, fuller quotation:

> *Religious* suffering is at the same time an *expression* of real suffering and a *protest* against real suffering. Religion is the

This paper may be identified as publication A-72 of the Survey Research Center, University of California, Berkeley. I am grateful to Gertrude J. Selznick and Stephen Steinberg for their work on the early phase of this project, and to the Anti-Defamation League for support.

From *American Sociological Review*, 1967, 32, 64-72. Reprinted with permission.

sigh of the oppressed creature, the heart
of a heartless world, and the soul of soul-
less conditions. It is the *opium* of the
people (Marx, 1964, pp. 43-44; original
date 1844).

No other episode in human history seems better
designed to illustrate Marx's assertions than
the story of black people in the United States.
The suffering, the protest, the heart, and the
soul were all there. We have heard the sigh
in black spirituals, yearning for salvation
from the evils and suffering of this world.
We have seen the struggle to overcome the ravages of slavery and post-slavery oppression
in a world that was mostly heartless and soul-
less. Religion gave black people a way of expressing their suffering and also a method of
channeling it away from the real world. Biblical suffering became the model for identification and acceptance. The Hebrew slaves in
Egypt who were eventually delivered to the
promised land became the models of black suffering. Waiting for their Moses was for most
blacks a most intense process, which contributed to an unusual richness and importance of
religious activities. Black impatience with
Christianity has become more pronounced over
the last twenty years, but the church is still
one of the most powerful forces in the black
community. The existence of the civil rights
movement in the 1960s created a new opportunity
for testing the effects of religiosity in an
oppressed group.
    The following study by Gary Marx is a compre-
hensive attitude survey conducted in 1964 among
blacks. A national sample of blacks was assessed on militancy and on several dimensions
of religiosity. The results are quite clear:
religiosity, on the whole, tends to inhibit
protest and encourage acceptance of the status
quo. However, as Gary Marx points out, when we
distinguish between an otherworldly religious

commitment and a temporal religious commitment, the latter tends to lead to greater militancy. Still, for the majority of blacks, religion is a reactionary force, tied to an acceptance of things as they are.

Eckhardt (1970) carried out a faithful replication of Marx's study with a random sample of white students in nine private Midwestern colleges. Eckhardt used the same measures used by Marx and obtained almost identical results. His conclusion was that "... while the net effect of religion is to inhibit attitudes of militancy, it is also true that there are significant exceptions" (p. 201). The same difference in the effect of otherworldly versus temporal orientation was found among whites.

McConahay (1970) studied attitudes of blacks toward the church in the Watts area of Los Angeles following the 1965 riots there. His survey showed that blacks expressed strong approval of the church and ranked it third among their allies, behind the Democratic party and the U.S. Congress. Black clergymen were also highly regarded as representatives of the black community. Those less favorable to the church were males, the better-educated, the urban-socialized, and those identifying themselves as working class. These results indicate that most blacks have not read or have not subscribed to either Karl Marx or Gary Marx and that the traditional position of the church in the black community has remained strong.

REFERENCES

Eckhardt, K. W. Religiosity and civil rights militancy. *Review of Religious Research*, 1970, 11, 197-203.

Marx, K. *Early Writings*. New York: McGraw Hill, 1964.

McConahay, J. B. Attitudes of Negroes toward the church following the Los Angeles riot. *Sociological Analysis,* 1970, 31, 12-22.

The relationship between religion and political radicalism is a confusing one. On the one hand, established religious institutions have generally had a stake in the status quo and hence have supported conservatism. Furthermore, with the masses having an otherworldly orientation, religious zeal, particularly as expressed in the more fundamentalist branches of Christianity, has been seen as an alternative to the development of political radicalism. On the other hand, as the source of universal humanistic values and the strength that can come from believing one is carrying out God's will in political matters, religion has occasionally played a strong positive role in movements for radical social change.

This dual role of religion is clearly indicated in the case of the American Negro and race protest. Slaves are said to have been first brought to this country on the "good ship Jesus Christ."[1] While there was occasional controversy over the effect that religion had on them it appears that most slaveowners eventually came to view supervised religion as an effective means of social control. Stampp, in commenting on the effect of religion, notes:

> ... through religious instruction the bondsmen learned that slavery had divine sanction, that insolence was as much an offense against God as against the temporal master. They received the Biblical command that servants should obey their masters, and they heard of the punishments awaiting the disobedient slave in the hereafter. They heard, too, that eternal salvation would be their reward for faithful service...[2]

In discussing the period after the Civil War, Myrdal states that "... under the pressure of political reaction, the Negro church in the South came

---

[1]Louis Lomax, *When the Word is Given*, New York: New American Library, 1964, p. 34.

[2]Kenneth Stampp, *The Peculiar Institution*, New York: Alfred A. Knopf, 1956, p. 158.

to have much the same role as it did before the Civil
War. Negro frustration was sublimated into emotion-
alism, and Negro hopes were fixed on the after
world."[3] Many other analysts, in considering the
consequences of Negro religion from the end of slavery until the early 1950's reached similar conclusions about the conservatizing effect of religion
on race protest.[4]

However, the effect of religion on race protest
throughout American history has by no means been exclusively in one direction. While many Negroes were
no doubt seriously singing about chariots in the sky,

[3]Gunnar Myrdal et al., *An American Dilemma*,
New York: Harper, 1944, pp. 851-853. About the
North he notes that the church remained far more
independent "but on the whole even the Northern
Negro church has remained a conservative institution
with its interests directly upon other-worldly matters and has largely ignored the practical problems
of the Negro's fate in this world."

[4]For example Dollard reports that "religion
can be seen as a mechanism for the social control
of Negroes" and that planters have always welcomed
the building of a Negro church on the plantation
but looked with less favor upon the building of a
school. John Dollard, *Caste and Class in a Southern
Town*, Garden City: Doubleday Anchor, 1957, p. 248.
A few of the many others reaching similar conclusions
are, Benjamin E. Mays and J. W. Nicholson, *The Negro's
Church*, New York: Institute of Social and Religious
Research, 1933; Hortense Powdermaker, *After Freedom*,
New York: Viking Press, 1939, p. 285; Charles John-
son, *Growing Up in the Black Belt*, Washington, D.C.:
American Council of Education, 1941, pp. 135-136;
Horace Drake and St. Clair Cayton, *Black Metropolis*,
New York: Harper and Row, 1962, pp. 424-429; George
Simpson and Milton Yinger, *Racial and Cultural Minor-
ities*, New York: Harper, rev. ed., 1958, pp. 582-587.
In a more general context this social control conse-
quence of religion has of course been noted through-
out history from Plato to Montesquieu to Marx to
Nietzsche to Freud to contemporary social theorists.

Negro preachers such as Denmark Vesey and Nat Turner and the religiously inspired abolitionists were actively fighting slavery in their own way. All Negro churches first came into being as protest organizations and later some served as meeting places where protest strategy was planned, or as stations on the underground railroad. The richness of protest symbolism in Negro spirituals and sermons has often been noted. Beyond this symbolic role, as a totally Negro institution, the church brought together in privacy people with a shared problem. It was from the church experience that many leaders were exposed to a broad range of ideas legitimizing protest and obtained the savoir faire, self-confidence, and organizational experience needed to challenge an oppressive system. A recent commentator states that the slave churches were "the nucleus of the Negro protest" and another that "in religion Negro leaders had begun to find sanction and support for their movements of protest more than 150 years ago."[5]

Differing perceptions of the varied consequences religion may have on protest have continued to the present time. While there has been very little in the way of empirical research on the effect of the Negro church on protest,[6] the literature of race relations

[5] Daniel Thompson, "The Rise of Negro Protest," *Annals of the American Academy of Political and Social Science,* 357 (January, 1965).

[6] The empirical evidence is quite limited. The few studies that have been done have focused on the Negro minister. Thompson notes that in New Orleans Negro ministers constitute the largest segment of the Negro leadership class (a grouping which is not necessarily the same as "protest leaders") but that "The vast majority of ministers are primarily interested in their pastoral role...their sermons are essentially biblical, dealing only tangentially with social issues." Daniel Thompson, *The Negro Leadership Class,* Englewood Cliffs, New Jersey: Prentice-Hall, 1963, pp. 34-35. Studies of the Negro ministry in Detroit and Richmond, Calif. also stress that only a small fraction of Negro clergymen show any active concern with the civil rights struggle. R. L. Johnstone, *Militant and Conservative Community Leadership Among Negro Clergymen,* Ph.D. dissertation, U. Michigan, Ann Arbor, 1963, and J. Bloom, *The Negro Church and the Movement for Equality,* M.A. thesis, U. California, Berkeley, Dept. Sociology, 1966.

is rich with impressionistic statements which generally contradict each other about how the church either encourages and is the source of race protest or
inhibits and retards its development. For example,
two observers note, "as primitive evangelism gave
way to a more sophisticated social consciousness,
the church became the spearhead of Negro protest in
the deep South,"[7] while another indicates "the Negro
church is a sleeping giant. In civil rights participation its feet are hardly wet."[8] A civil rights
activist, himself a clergyman, states: "... the
church today is central to the movement... if there
had been no Negro church, there would have been no
civil rights movement today."[9] On the other hand,
a sociologist, commenting on the more involved higher
status ministers, notes: "... middle class Negro
clergymen in the cities of the South generally advo-
cated cautious gradualism in race activities until
the mid-1950's when there was an upsurge of protest
sentiment among urban Negroes... but most of them
[ministers] did not embrace the more vigorous techniques of protest until other leaders took the initiative and gained widespread support."[10] Another
sociologist states, "Whatever their previous conservative stance has been, the churches have now become 'spearheads of reform.'"[11] Still another indicates: "... the Negro church is particularly culpable

[7]Jane Record and Wilson Record, "Ideological
Forces and the Negro Protest," *Annals, op. cit.*, p.
92.

[8]G. Booker, *Black Man's America*, Englewood
Cliffs, N.J.: Prentice-Hall, 1964, p. 111.

[9]Rev. W. T. Walker, as quoted in William Brink
and Louis Harris, *The Negro Revolution in America*,
New York: Simon and Schuster, 1964, p. 103.

[10]N. Glenn, "Negro Religion in the U.S." in
L. Schneider, *Religion, Culture and Society*, New York:
John Wiley, 1964.

[11]Joseph Fichter, "American Religion and the
Negro," *Daedalus* (Fall, 1965), p. 1087.

for its general lack of concern for the moral and social problems of the community...it has been accommodating. Fostering indulgence in religious sentimentality, and riveting the attention of the masses on the bounties of a hereafter, the Negro church remains a refuge, and escape from the cruel realities of the here and now."[12]

Thus one faces opposing views, or at best ambiguity, in contemplating the current effect of religion. The opiating consequences of religion are all too well-known as is the fact that the segregated church is durable and offers some advantages to clergy and members that might be denied them in a more integrated society. On the other hand, the prominent role of the Negro church in supplying much of the ideology of the movement, many of its foremost leaders, and an institution around which struggle might be organized--particularly in the South-- can hardly be denied. It would appear from the bombings of churches and the writings of Martin Luther King and other religiously inspired activists that for many, religion and protest are closely linked.

Part of this dilemma may lie in the distinction between the church as an institution in its totality and particular individual churches within it, and the further distinctions among different types of individual religious concern. This paper is concerned with the latter subject; it is an inquiry into the relationship between religiosity and response to the civil rights struggle. It first considers how religious denomination affects militancy, and then how

---

[12]E. U. Essien-Udom, *Black Nationalism*, New York: Dell Publishing Co., 1962, p. 358.
Many other examples of contradictory statements could be offered, sometimes even in the same volume. For example, Carleton Lee stresses the importance of religion for protest while Rayford Logan sees the Negro pastor as an instrument of the white power structure (in a book published to commemorate 100 years of emancipation). Carleton Lee, "Religious Roots of Negro Protest," and Rayford Logan, "Educational Changes Affecting American Negroes," both in Arnold Rose, *Assuring Freedom to the Free*, Detroit: Wayne University Press, 1964.

various measures of religiosity, taken separately
and together, are related to civil rights concern.
The question is then asked of those classified as
"very religious" and "quite religious," how an
"otherworldly orientation"--as opposed to a "temporal" one--affects militancy.

In a nationwide study of Negroes living in
metropolitan areas of the United States, a number
of questions were asked about religious behavior
and beliefs as well as about the civil rights
struggle.[13] Seven of the questions dealing with
civil rights protest have been combined into an index of conventional militancy.[14] Built into this
index are a number of dimensions of racial protest
such as impatience over the speed of integration,
opposition to discrimination in public facilities
and the sale of property, perception of barriers to
Negro advancement, support of civil rights demonstrations, and expressed willingness to take part
in a demonstration. Those giving the militant response to five or more of the questions are considered

[13]This survey was carried out in 1964 by the
Survey Research Center, University of California,
Berkeley. A non-Southern metropolitan area probability sample was drawn as well as special area
samples of Negroes living in New York City, Chicago,
Atlanta and Birmingham. Since the results reported
here are essentially the same for each of these
areas, they are treated together. More than 90%
of the interviews were done with Negro interviewers.
Additional methodological details may be found in
Gary Marx, *Protest and Prejudice: A Study of Belief
in the Black Community,* New York: Harper & Row, 1967.

[14]Attention is directed to conventional militancy rather than to that of the Black Nationalist
variety because a very small percentage of the sample
offered strong and consistent support for Black Nationalism. As in studying support for the KKK, the
Birch Society or the Communist Party, a representative sample of normal size is inadequate.

militant, those giving such a response to three or
four of the questions, moderate, and fewer than
three, conservative.[15]

DENOMINATION

It has long been known that the more fundamentalist sects such as the Holiness groups and the
Jehovah's Witnesses are relatively uninterested in
movements for secular political change.[16] Such
transvaluational movements with their otherworldly
orientation and their promise that the last shall be
first in the great beyond, are said to solace the
individual for his lowly status in this world and
to divert concern away from efforts at collective
social change which might be brought about by man.
While only a minority of Negroes actually belong to
such groups, the proportion is higher than among
whites. Negro literature is rich in descriptions of
these churches and their position on race protest.

[15]Each of the items in the index was positively
related to every other and the index showed a high
degree of internal validity. The index also received external validation from a number of additional questions. For example, the percentage belonging to a civil rights organization went from
zero among those lowest in militancy to 38 percent
for those who were highest, and the percentage thinking that civil rights demonstrations had helped a
great deal increased from 23 percent to 58 percent.
Those thinking that the police treated Negroes very
well decreased from 35 percent to only 2 percent
among those highest in militancy.

[16]Liston Pope, *Millhands and Preachers*, New
Haven: Yale University Press, 1942, p. 137. J.
Milton Yinger, *Religion, Society, and the Individual*, New York: The Macmillan Company, 1957, pp.
170-173.

In Table 1 it can be seen that those belonging
to sects are the least likely to be militant; they
are followed by those in predominantly Negro denominations. Ironically those individuals in largely
white denominations (Episcopalian, Presbyterian,
United Church of Christ, and Roman Catholic) are
those most likely to be militant, in spite of the
perhaps greater civil rights activism of the Negro
denominations. This pattern emerged even when social class was held constant.

TABLE 1. PROPORTION MILITANT (%) BY DENOMINATION*

Denomination	% Militant
Episcopalian	46 (24)
United Church of Christ	42 (12)
Presbyterian	40 (25)
Catholic	40 (109)
Methodist	34 (142)
Baptist	32 (658)
Sects and Cults	20 (106)

* 25 respondents are not shown in this table
because they did not specify a denomination, or belonged to a non-Christian religious group, or other
small Christian group.

In their comments members of the less conventional religious groups clearly expressed the classical attitude of their sects toward participation
in the politics of the secular world. For example,
an Evangelist in the Midwest said, "I don't believe
in participating in politics. My church don't vote
--they just depends on the plans of God." And an
automobile serviceman in Philadelphia stated, "I,
as a Jehovah's Witness, cannot express things involving the race issue." A housewife in the Far
West ventured, "In my religion we do not approve of
anything except living like it says in the Bible:
demonstrations mean calling attention to you and
it's sinful."
The finding that persons who belong to sects
are less likely to be militant than the non-sect
members is to be expected; clearly this type of
religious involvement seems an alternative for most
people to the development of radicalism. But what

of the religious style of those in the more conventional churches which may put relatively less stress
on the after-life and encourage various forms of
secular participation? Are the more religiously
inclined within these groups also less likely to be
militant?

RELIGIOSITY

The present study measured several dimensions
of religious involvement. Those interviewed were
asked how important religion was to them, several
questions about orthodoxy of belief, and how frequently they attended worship service.[17] Even with
the sects excluded, irrespective of the dimension of
religiosity considered, the greater the religiosity
the lower the percentage militant. (See Tables 2,
3 and 4.) For example, militancy increases consistently from a low of only 29 percent among those who
said religion was "extremely important" to a high of
62 percent for those who indicated that religion was
"not at all important" to them. For those very high
in orthodoxy (having no doubt about the existence

TABLE 2. MILITANCY BY SUBJECTIVE IMPORTANCE ASSIGNED TO RELIGION*

Importance	% Militant
Extremely important	29 (668)
Somewhat important	39 (195)
Fairly important	48 (96)
Not too important	56 (18)
Not at all important	62 (13)

* Sects are excluded here and in all subsequent
tables.

[17]These dimensions and several others are suggested by Charles Y. Glock in "On the Study of Religious Commitment," *Religious Education Research
Supplement*, 57 (July-August, 1962), pp. 98-100.
For another measure of religious involvement, the
number of church organizations belonged to, the
same inverse relationship was noted.

TABLE 3. MILITANCY BY ORTHODOXY

Orthodoxy	% Militant
Very high	27 (414)
High	34 (333)
Medium	39 (144)
Low	47 (68)
Very low	54 (35)

TABLE 4. MILITANCY BY FREQUENCY OF ATTENDANCE AT WORSHIP SERVICES

Frequency	% Militant
More than once a week	27 (81)
Once a week	32 (311)
Once a month or more but less than once a week	34 (354)
Less than once a month	38 (240)

of God or the devil) 27 percent were militant while
for those totally rejecting these ideas 54 percent
indicated great concern over civil rights. Militancy also varies inversely with frequency of attendance at worship service.[18]

[18]There is a popular stereotype that Negroes are
a "religious people." Social science research has
shown that they are "over-churched" relative to whites,
i.e., the ratio of Negro churches to the size of the
Negro population is greater than the same ratio for
whites. Using data from a nation-wide survey of
whites, by Gertrude Selznick and Stephen Steinberg,
some comparison of the religiosity of Negroes and
whites was possible. When these various dimensions
of religiosity were examined, with the effect of education and region held constant, Negroes appeared as
significantly more religious *only* with respect to the
subjective importance assigned to religion. In the
North, whites were more likely to attend church at
least once a week than were Negroes; while in the South
rates of attendance were the same. About the same percentage of both groups had no doubts about the existence
of God. While Negroes were more likely to be sure about
the existence of a devil, whites, surprisingly, were
more likely to be sure about a life beyond death.
Clearly, then, any assertions about the greater religiosity of Negroes relative to whites are unwarranted unless one specifies the dimension of religiosity.

Each of these items was strongly related to every other; when taken together they help us to better characterize religiosity. Accordingly they have been combined into an overall measure of religiosity. Those scored as "very religious" in terms of this index attended church at least once a week, felt that religion was extremely important to them, and had no doubts about the existence of God and the devil. For progressively lower values of the index, frequency of church attendance, the importance of religion, and acceptance of the belief items decline consistently until, for those scored "not at all religious," church is rarely if ever attended, religion is not considered personally important and the belief items are rejected.

Using this measure for non-sect members, civil rights militancy increases from a low of 26 percent for those labeled "very religious" to 30 percent for the "somewhat religious" to 45 percent for those "not very religious" and up to a high of 70 percent for those "not at all religious."[19] (Table 5.)

TABLE 5. MILITANCY BY RELIGIOSITY

Religiosity	Very Religious	Somewhat Religious	Not Very Religious	Not at All Religious
% Militant	26	30	45	70
N	(230)	(523)	(195)	(36)

Religiosity and militancy are also related to age, sex, education, religious denomination and region of the country. The older, the less educated, women, Southerners and those in Negro denominations are more likely to be religious and to have lower

[19]When the sects are included in these tables the results are the same. The sects have been excluded because they offer almost no variation to be analyzed with respect to the independent variable. Since virtually all of the sect members scored as either "very religious" or "somewhat religious," it is hardly possible to measure the effect of their religious involvement on protest attitudes. In addition the import of the relationships shown in these tables is considerably strengthened when it is demonstrated that religious involvement inhibits militancy even when the most religious and least militant group, the sects, are excluded.

percentages scoring as militant. Thus it is possible
that the relationship observed is simply a consequence
of the fact that both religiosity and militancy are
related to some third factor. In Table 6 it can be
seen however, that, even when these variables are controlled the relationship is maintained. That is,
even among those in the North, the younger, male,
more educated and those affiliated with predominantly
white denominations, the greater the religiosity the
less the militancy.

The incompatibility between piety and protest
shown in these data becomes even more evident when
considered in light of comments offered by the respondents. Many religious people hold beliefs which
clearly inhibit race protest. For a few there was
the notion that segregation and a lowly status for
Negroes was somehow God's will and not for man to
question. Thus a housewife in South Bend, Indiana,
in saying that civil rights demonstrations had hurt
Negroes, added: "God is the Creator of everything.

TABLE 6. PROPORTION MILITANT (%) BY RELIGIOSITY, FOR EDUCATION, AGE, REGION, SEX, AND DENOMINATION

	Very Religious	Somewhat Religious	Not Very Religious	Not at All Religious
Education				
Grammar school	17 (108)	22 (201)	31 (42)	50 (2)
High school	34 (96)	32 (270)	45 (119)	58 (19)
College	38 (26)	48 (61)	59 (34)	87 (15)
Age				
18–29	33 (30)	37 (126)	44 (62)	62 (13)
30–44	30 (53)	34 (180)	48 (83)	74 (19)
45–59	25 (71)	27 (131)	45 (33)	50 (2)
60+	22 (76)	18 (95)	33 (15)	100 (2)
Region				
Non-South	30 (123)	34 (331)	47 (159)	70 (33)
South	22 (107)	23 (202)	33 (36)	66 (3)
Sex				
Men	28 (83)	33 (220)	44 (123)	72 (29)
Women	26 (147)	28 (313)	46 (72)	57 (7)
Denomination				
Episcopalian, Pres-byterian, United Church of Christ	20 (15)	27 (26)	33 (15)	60 (5)
Catholic	13 (15)	39 (56)	36 (25)	77 (13)
Methodist	46 (24)	22 (83)	50 (32)	100 (2)
Baptist	25 (172)	29 (354)	45 (117)	53 (15)

We don't know why we all dark-skinned. We should
try to put forth the effort to do what God wants
and not question."[20]

A Negro spiritual contains the lines "I'm gonna
wait upon the Lord till my change comes." For our
respondents a more frequently stated belief stressed
that God as the absolute controller of the universe
would bring about change in his own way and at his
own time, rather than expressing segregation as God's
will. In indicating her unwillingness to take part
in a civil rights demonstration, a Detroit housewife
said, "I don't go for demonstrations. I believe that
God created all men equal and at His appointed time
He will give every man his portion, no one can hinder
it." And in response to a question about whether or
not the government in Washington was pushing integration too slowly, a retired clerk in Atlanta said:
"You can't hurry God. He has a certain time for this
to take place. I don't know about Washington."

Others who desired integration more strongly
and wanted immediate social change felt that (as Bob
Dylan sings) God was on their side. Hence man need
do nothing to help bring about change. Thus a
worker in Cleveland, who was against having more
civil rights demonstrations, said: "With God helping to fight our battle, I believe we can do with
fewer demonstrations." And in response to a question
about whether Negroes should spend more time praying

[20]Albert Cardinal Meyer notes that the Catholic
Bishops of the U.S. said in their statement of 1958:
"The heart of the race question is moral and religious." "Interracial Justice and Love," in M. Ahmann,
ed., *Race Challenge to Religion,* Chicago: H. Regnery,
1963, p. 126. These data, viewed from the perspective of the activist seeking to motivate Negroes
on behalf of the civil rights struggle, suggest
that this statement has a meaning which Their Ex-
cellencies no doubt did not intend.

and less time demonstrating, an Atlanta clergyman,
who said "more time praying," added "praying is
demonstrating."[21]

RELIGION AMONG THE MILITANTS

Although the net effect of religion is clearly
to inhibit attitudes of protest it is interesting to
consider this relationship in the opposite direction,
i.e., observe religiosity among those characterized
as militant, moderate, and conservative with respect
to the civil rights struggle. As civil rights concern increases, religiosity decreases. (Table 7.)
Militants were twice as likely to be scored "not
very religious" or "not at all religious" as were
conservatives. This table is also of interest because it shows that, even for the militants, a majority were scored either "very religious" or "somewhat religious." Clearly, for many, a religious orientation and a concern with racial protest are not
mutually exclusive.

TABLE 7. RELIGIOSITY BY CIVIL RIGHTS MILITANCY

	Mili-tants	Mod-erates	Conser-vatives
Very religious	18%	24%	28%
Somewhat religious	48	57	55
Not very religious	26	17	16
Not at all religious	8	2	1
Total	100	100	100
N	332	419	242

[21]A study of ministers in Richmond, California
notes that, although almost all questioned were opposed to discrimination, very few had taken concrete
action, in part because of their belief that God would
take care of them. One minister noted, "I believe
that if we all was as pure...as we ought to be, there
would be no struggle. God will answer my prayer. If
we just stay with God and have faith. *When Peter was
up, did the people march to free him? No. He prayed,
and God did something about it.*" (Bloom, *op. cit.,*
italics added.)

Given the active involvement of some churches,
the singing of protest spirituals, and the ideology
of the movement as it relates to Christian principles
of love, equality, passive suffering,[22] and the appeal to a higher moral law, it would be surprising
if there were only a few religious people among the
militants.

A relevant question accordingly is: Among the
religious, what are the intervening links which determine whether religion is related to an active concern with racial matters or has an opiating effect?[23]
From the comments reported above it seemed that, for
some, belief in a highly deterministic God inhibited
race protest. Unfortunately the study did not measure beliefs about the role of God as against the role
of men in the structuring of human affairs. However,
a related variable was measured which would seem to
have much relevance--the extent to which these religious people were concerned with the here and now
as opposed to the after-life.

The classical indictment of religion from the
Marxist perspective is that by focusing concern on
a glorious after-life the evils of this life are ignored. Of course there are important differences
among religious institutions and among individuals
with respect to the importance given to the otherworldly concerns. Christianity, as with most ideologies, contains within it, if not out-and-out
contradictory themes, then certainly themes which
are likely to be in tension with one another.

[22]Non-violent resistance as it relates to
Christianity's emphasis on suffering, sacrifice,
and privation, is discussed by James W. Vander
Zanden, "The Non-Violent Resistance Movement Against
Segregation." *American Journal of Sociology,* 68
(March, 1963), pp. 544-550.

[23]Of course, a most relevant factor here is
the position of the particular church that an individual is involved in. Unfortunately, it was
difficult to obtain such information in a nation-
wide survey.

In this fact, no doubt, lies part of the explanation
of religion's varied consequences for protest. One
important strand of Christianity stresses acceptance
of one's lot and glorifies the after-life;[24] another
is more concerned with the realization of Judeo-
Christian values in the current life. King and his
followers clearly represent this latter "social
gospel" tradition.[25] Those with the type of temporal

[24]The Muslims have also made much of this theme
within Christianity, and their militancy is certainly
tied to a rejection of otherworldly religiosity. The
Bible is referred to as a "poison book" and the leader
of the Muslims states, "No one after death has ever
gone any place but where they were carried. There is
no heaven or hell other than on earth for you and me,
and Jesus was no exception. His body is still...in
Palestine and will remain there." (As quoted in C.
Eric Lincoln, *The Black Muslims in America*, Boston:
Beacon Press, 1961, p. 123).

However, while they reject the otherworldly theme,
they nevertheless rely heavily on a deterministic Allah; according to E. U. Essien-Udom, this fact leads
to political inactivity. He notes, "The attainment
of black power is relegated to the intervention of
"Almighty Allah" sometime in the future... Not unlike
other religionists, the Muslims too may wait for all
eternity for the coming of the Messiah, the predicted
apocalypse in 1970 notwithstanding." E. U. Essien-
Udom, *Black Nationalism, op. cit.,* pp. 313-314.

[25]He states: "Any religion that professes to be
concerned with the souls of men and is not concerned
with the slums that damn them, the economic conditions
that strangle them, and the social conditions that
cripple them is a dry-as-dust religion." He further
adds, perhaps in a concession, that "such a religion
is the kind the Marxists like to see--an opiate of the
people." Martin Luther King, *Stride Toward Freedom*,
New York: Ballantine Books, 1958, pp. 28-29.

John Lewis, a former SNCC leader and once a Baptist
Divinity student, is said to have peered through the
bars of a Southern jail and said, "Think not that I
am come to send peace on earth. I came not to send
peace, but a sword." (Matthew 10:34.)

concern that King represents would be expected to
be higher in militancy. A measure of temporal vs.
otherworldly concern has been constructed. On the
basis of two questions, those interviewed have been
classified as having either an otherworldly or a
temporal orientation.[26] The evidence is that religiosity and otherworldly concern increase together.
For example, almost 100 percent of the "not at all
religious" groups were considered to have a temporal
orientation, but only 42 percent of the "very religious." (Table 8.) Those in predominantly white denominations were more likely to have a temporal orientation than those in all-black denominations.

TABLE 8. PROPORTION (%) WITH TEMPORAL (AS AGAINST OTHERWORLDLY) CONCERN, BY RELIGIOSITY

Religiosity	% with Temporal Concern
Very religious	42 (225)
Somewhat religious	61 (531)
Not very religious	82 (193)
Not at all religious	98 (34)

Among the religious groups, if concern with the
here and now is a relevant factor in overcoming the
opiating effect of religion then it is to be anticipated that those considered to have a temporal religious orientation would be much higher in militancy
than those scored as otherworldly. This is in fact

[26]The two items used in this index were: "How
sure are you that there is a life beyond death?";
and "Negroes should spend more time praying and less
time demonstrating." The latter item may seem somewhat circular when observed in relation to civil
rights concern. However, this is precisely what militancy is all about. Still it would have been better
to measure otherworldly vs. temporal concern in a less
direct fashion; unfortunately, no other items were
available. Because of this the data shown here must
be interpreted with caution. However it does seem
almost self-evident that civil rights protest which
is religiously inspired is related to a temporal religious outlook.

the case. Among the otherworldly religious, only 16
percent were militant; this proportion increases to
almost 40 percent among those considered "very religious" and "somewhat religious" who have a temporal
religious outlook (Table 9). Thus it would seem
that an important factor in determining the effect
of religion on protest attitudes is the nature of an
individual's religious commitment. It is quite possible, for those with a temporal religious orientation, that--rather than the effect of religion being
somehow neutralized (as in the case of militancy
among the "not religious" groups)--their religious
concern serves to inspire and sustain race protest.
This religious inspiration can, of course, be clearly
noted among some active civil rights participants.

**TABLE 9. PROPORTION MILITANT (%) BY RELIGIOSITY AND
TEMPORAL OR OTHERWORLDLY CONCERN**

Concern	Very Religious	Somewhat Religious
Temporal	39 (95)	38 (325)
Otherworldly	15 (130)	17 (206)

CONCLUSION

The effect of religiosity on race protest depends
on the type of religiosity involved. Past literature
is rich in suggestions that the religiosity of the
fundamentalist sects is an alternative to the development of political radicalism. This seems true in the
case of race protest as well. However, in an overall
sense even for those who belong to the more conventional churches, the greater the religious involvement,
whether measured in terms of ritual activity, orthodoxy of religious belief, subjective importance of
religion, or the three taken together, the lower the
degree of militancy.

Among sect members and religious people with an
otherworldly orientation, religion and race protest
appear to be, if not mutually exclusive, then certainly what one observer has referred to as "mutually

corrosive kinds of commitments."[27] Until such time
as religion loosens its hold over these people or
comes to embody to a greater extent the belief that
man as well as God can bring about secular change,
and focuses more on the here and now, religious involvement may be seen as an important factor working
against the widespread radicalization of the Negro
public.

However, it has also been noted that many militant people are nevertheless religious. When a distinction is made among the religious between the
"otherworldly" and the "temporal," for many of the
latter group, religion seems to facilitate or at
least not to inhibit protest. For these people religion and race protest may be mutually supportive.

Thirty years ago Donald Young wrote: "One function which a minority religion may serve is that of
reconciliation with inferior status and its discriminatory consequences... on the other hand, religious
institutions may also develop in such a way as to be
an incitement and support of revolt against inferior
status."[28] The current civil rights struggle and the
data observed here certainly suggest that this is the
case. These contradictory consequences of religion
are somewhat reconciled when one distinguishes among
different segments of the Negro church and types of
religious concern among individuals.

[27]Rodney Stark, "Class, Radicalism, and Religious Involvement," *American Sociological Review*, 29
(October, 1964), p. 703.

[28]Donald Young, *American Minority Peoples*, New
York: Harper, 1937, p. 204.
These data are also consistent with Merton's statement that it is premature to conclude that "all religion everywhere has only the one consequence of making
for mass apathy" and his insistence on recognizing
the "multiple consequences" and "net balance of ag-
gregate consequences" of a given institution such as
religion. Robert Merton, *Social Theory and Social
Structure*, Glencoe: Free Press, 1957, revised edition,
p. 44.

SELECTED ADDITIONAL READINGS ON
RELIGION AND POLITICAL BEHAVIOR

Connors, J., Leonard, R., & Burnham, K.   Religion
     and opposition to war among college students.
     Sociological Analysis, 1968, 29, 211-219.

Eckhardt, K. W.   Religiosity and civil rights mili-
     tancy. *Review of Religious Research*, 1970, II,
     197-203.

Grier, W. H., & Cobbs, P. M.   *The Jesus Bag*. New
     York: McGraw-Hill, 1971.

Hadden, J. K. (Ed.)   *Religion in Radical Transition*.
     Brunswick, N.J.: Transaction, 1971.

Lenski, G.   *The Religious Factor*. Garden City, N.Y.:
     Doubleday, 1963.

Lewy, G.   *The Catholic Church and Nazi Germany*. New
     York: McGraw-Hill, 1964.

Marx, G. T.   *Protest and Prejudice: A Study of Belief
     in the Black Community*. New York: Harper & Row,
     1967.

McConahay, J. B.   Attitudes of Negroes toward the
     church following the Los Angeles riot. *Socio-
     logical Analysis*, 1970, 31, 12-22.

Stedman, M. S.   *Religion and Politics in America*.
     New York: Harcourt, Brace Jovanovich, 1964.

Tygart, C. E.   Religiosity and university student
     anti-Vietnam War attitudes: A negative or
     curvilinear relationship?   *Sociological Analy-
     sis*, 1971, 32, 120-129.